NEGIMA! 38

Ken Akamatsu

TRANSLATED AND ADAPTED BY
Alethea Nibley and Athena Nibley

LETTERING AND RETOUCH BY
Scott O. Brown

KC
KODANSHA
COMICS

A word from the author

THANK YOU EVERYONE, FOR SUPPORTING THIS SERIES
FOR SO LONG. AFTER NINE YEARS, VOLUME 38 OF
MAGISTER NEGI MAGI WILL BRING THE SERIES TO A
TEMPORARY END.

...BY "TEMPORARY END," I MEAN THE SERIES WILL LIKELY
START AGAIN SOMEDAY.

AS CHAO WOULD SAY, THE ENDING PRESENTED IN THIS
VOLUME REPRESENTS ONLY ONE OF MANY PARALLEL
WORLDS. *NEGIMA!* IS STILL CHOCK-FULL OF UNSOLVED
MYSTERIES, AND IT COULD EASILY TAKE MORE THAN A
HUNDRED VOLUMES TO COVER THEM ALL. (LAUGH)

BUT ALL OF THE DIFFERENT MEDIA FORMS OF *NEGIMA!*
ARE PRETTY MUCH DONE, AND I GOT TO SEE THE
"VERSION B ENDING" IN THE MOVIE, SO I THOUGHT I'D
BRING THE MANGA TO A CONCLUSION FOR NOW, TOO.

IF YOU HAPPEN TO SEE ANOTHER EPISODE OF *NEGIMA!*
SOMEWHERE IN THE FUTURE, THEN I HOPE YOU'LL PICK
IT UP AND TAKE A LOOK. IT MIGHT ANSWER ONE OF YOUR
QUESTIONS.

Ken Akamatsu's home page address*
http://www.ailove.net/

*Please note Akamatsu's website
is in Japanese.

Honorifics Explained

Throughout the Kodansha Comics books, you will find Japanese honorifics left intact in the translations. For those not familiar with how the Japanese use honorifics and, more important, how they differ from American honorifics, we present this brief overview.

Politeness has always been a critical facet of Japanese culture. Ever since the feudal era, when Japan was a highly stratified society, use of honorifics—which can be defined as polite speech that indicates relationship or status—has played an essential role in the Japanese language. When addressing someone in Japanese, an honorific usually takes the form of a suffix attached to one's name (example: "Asuna-san"), is used as a title at the end of one's name, or appears in place of the name itself (example: "Negi-sensei," or simply "Sensei!").

Honorifics can be expressions of respect or endearment. In the context of manga and anime, honorifics give insight into the nature of the relationship between characters. Many English translations leave out these important honorifics and therefore distort the feel of the original Japanese. Because Japanese honorifics contain nuances that English honorifics lack, it is our policy at Kodansha Comics not to translate them. Here, instead, is a guide to some of the honorifics you may encounter in Kodansha Comics.

-san: This is the most common honorific and is equivalent to Mr., Miss, Ms., or Mrs. It is the all-purpose honorific and can be used in any situation where politeness is required.

-sama: This is one level higher than "-san" and is used to confer great respect.

-dono: This comes from the word "tono," which means "lord." It is an even higher level than "-sama" and confers utmost respect.

-kun: This suffix is used at the end of boys' names to express familiarity or endearment. It is also sometimes used by men among friends, or when addressing someone younger or of a lower station.

-chan: This is used to express endearment, mostly toward girls. It is also used for little boys, pets, and even among lovers. It gives a sense of childish cuteness.

Bozu: This is an informal way to refer to a boy, similar to the English terms "kid" and "squirt."

Sempai/Senpai: This title suggests that the addressee is one's senior in a group or organization. It is most often used in a school setting, where underclassmen refer to their upperclassmen as "sempai." It can also be used in the workplace, such as when a newer employee addresses an employee who has seniority in the company.

Kohai: This is the opposite of "sempai" and is used toward underclassmen in school or newcomers in the workplace. It connotes that the addressee is of a lower station.

Sensei: Literally meaning "one who has come before," this title is used for teachers, doctors, or masters of any profession or art.

-[blank]: This is usually forgotten in these lists, but it is perhaps the most significant difference between Japanese and English. The lack of honorific means that the speaker has permission to address the person in a very intimate way. Usually, only family, spouses, or very close friends have this kind of permission. Known as *yobisute*, it can be gratifying when someone who has earned the intimacy starts to call one by one's name without an honorific. But when that intimacy hasn't been earned, it can be very insulting.

NEGIMA!

MAGISTER NEGI MAGI

38

Ken Akamatsu

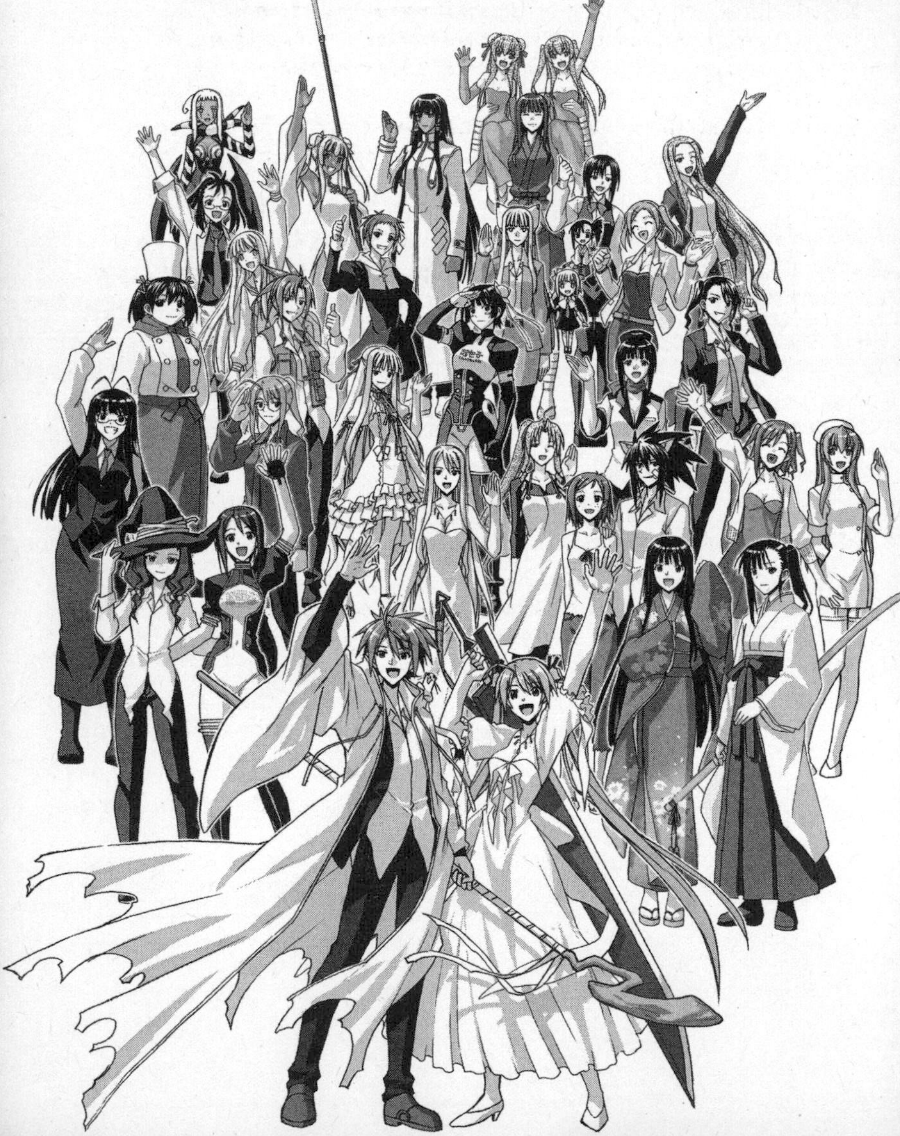

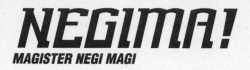

DIPLOMA

Asuna Kagurazaka
Born April 21, 1988

I HEREBY CERTIFY THAT THE PERSON HERE
NAMED HAS COMPLETED OUR ACADEMY'S JUNIOR
HIGH SCHOOL CURRICULUM.

March 3, 2004

MAHORA ACADEMY HEADMASTER
MAHORA JUNIOR HIGH PRINCIPAL

Konoemon Konoe

CONTENTS

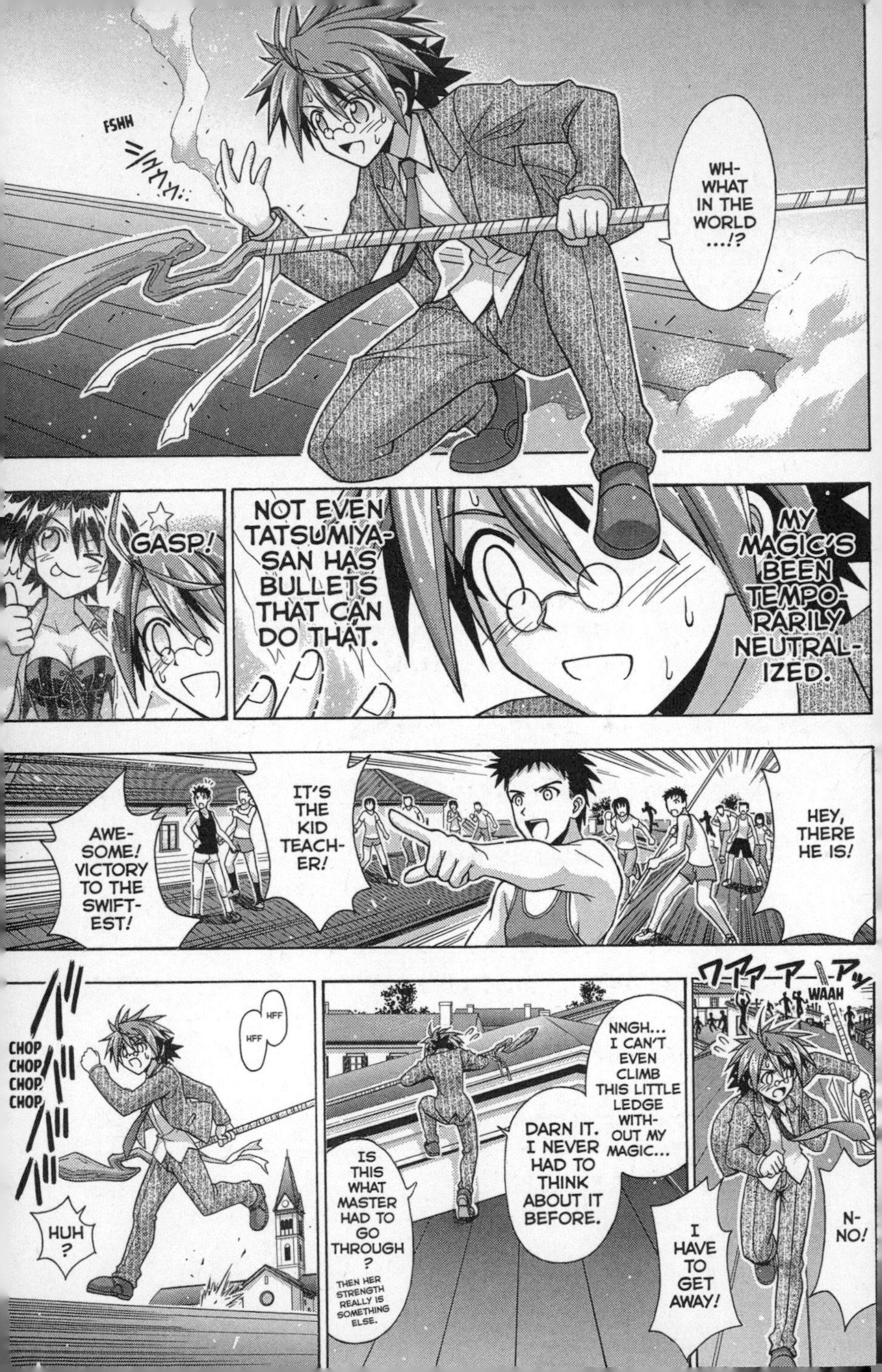
FSHH
WH- WHAT IN THE WORLD ...!?
MY MAGIC'S BEEN TEMPORARILY NEUTRALIZED.
NOT EVEN TATSUMIYA-SAN HAS BULLETS THAT CAN DO THAT.
GASP!
HEY, THERE HE IS!
IT'S THE KID TEACHER!
AWESOME! VICTORY TO THE SWIFTEST!
WAAH
N-NO!
I HAVE TO GET AWAY!
NNGH... I CAN'T EVEN CLIMB THIS LITTLE LEDGE WITHOUT MY MAGIC...
DARN IT. I NEVER HAD TO THINK ABOUT IT BEFORE.
IS THIS WHAT MASTER HAD TO GO THROUGH?
THEN HER STRENGTH REALLY IS SOMETHING ELSE.
HFF HFF
CHOP CHOP CHOP CHOP
HUH?

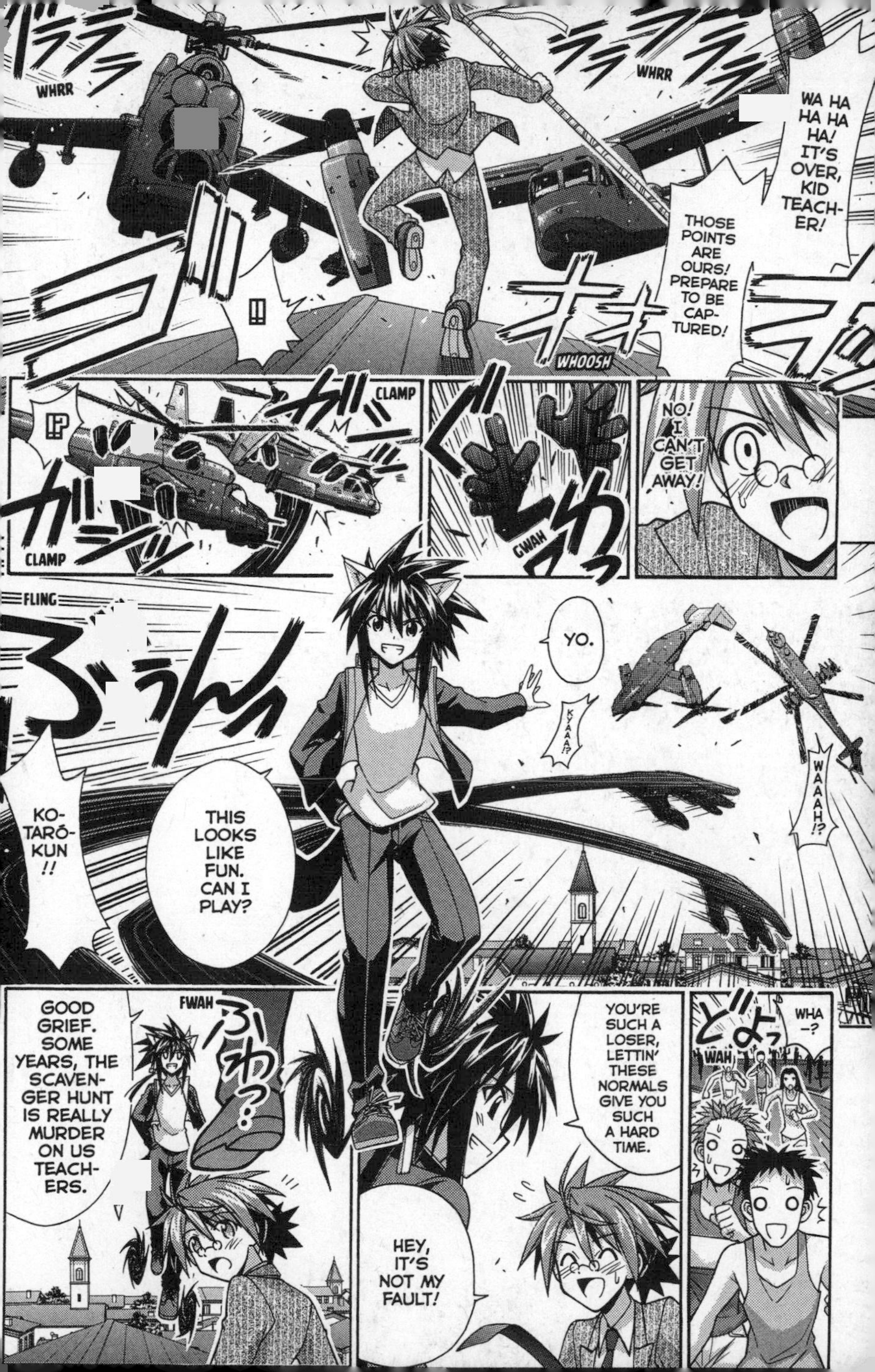
WHRR
WHRR
WA HA HA HA HA! IT'S OVER, KID TEACHER!
THOSE POINTS ARE OURS! PREPARE TO BE CAPTURED!
!!
WHOOSH
NO! I CAN'T GET AWAY!
GWAH
CLAMP
!?
CLAMP
FLING
WAAAAH!?
KYAAA!?
YO.
THIS LOOKS LIKE FUN. CAN I PLAY?
KO-TARŌ-KUN!!
WHA-?
WAH
YOU'RE SUCH A LOSER, LETTIN' THESE NORMALS GIVE YOU SUCH A HARD TIME.
HEY, IT'S NOT MY FAULT!
FWAH
GOOD GRIEF. SOME YEARS, THE SCAVENGER HUNT IS REALLY MURDER ON US TEACHERS.

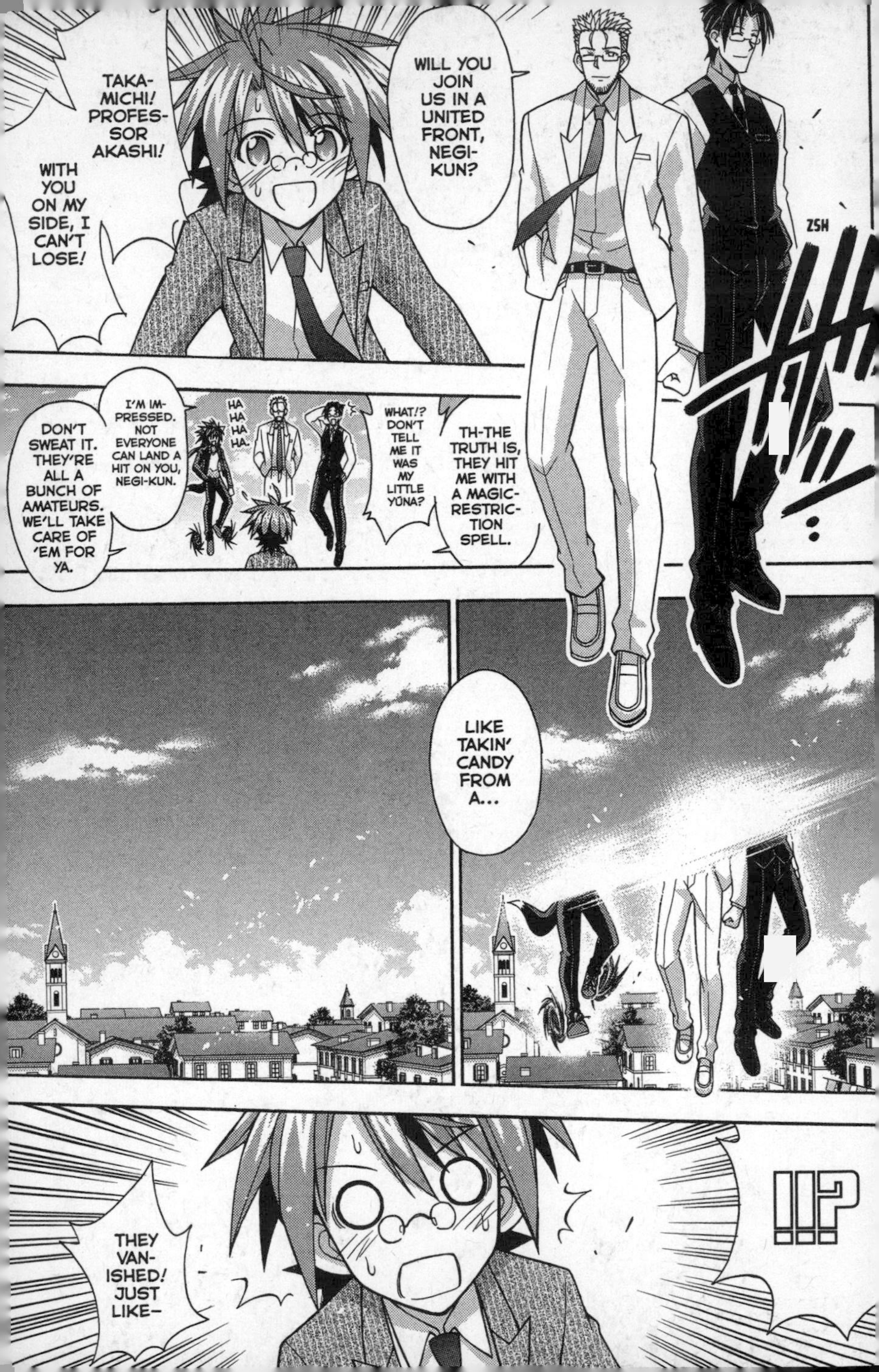
WILL YOU JOIN US IN A UNITED FRONT, NEGI-KUN?
ZSH
TAKA-MICHI! PROFES-SOR AKASHI!
WITH YOU ON MY SIDE, I CAN'T LOSE!
TH-THE TRUTH IS, THEY HIT ME WITH A MAGIC-RESTRIC-TION SPELL.
WHAT!? DON'T TELL ME IT WAS MY LITTLE YŪNA?
HA HA HA HA.
I'M IM-PRESSED. NOT EVERYONE CAN LAND A HIT ON YOU, NEGI-KUN.
DON'T SWEAT IT. THEY'RE ALL A BUNCH OF AMATEURS. WE'LL TAKE CARE OF 'EM FOR YA.
LIKE TAKIN' CANDY FROM A...
!!?
THEY VAN-ISHED! JUST LIKE-

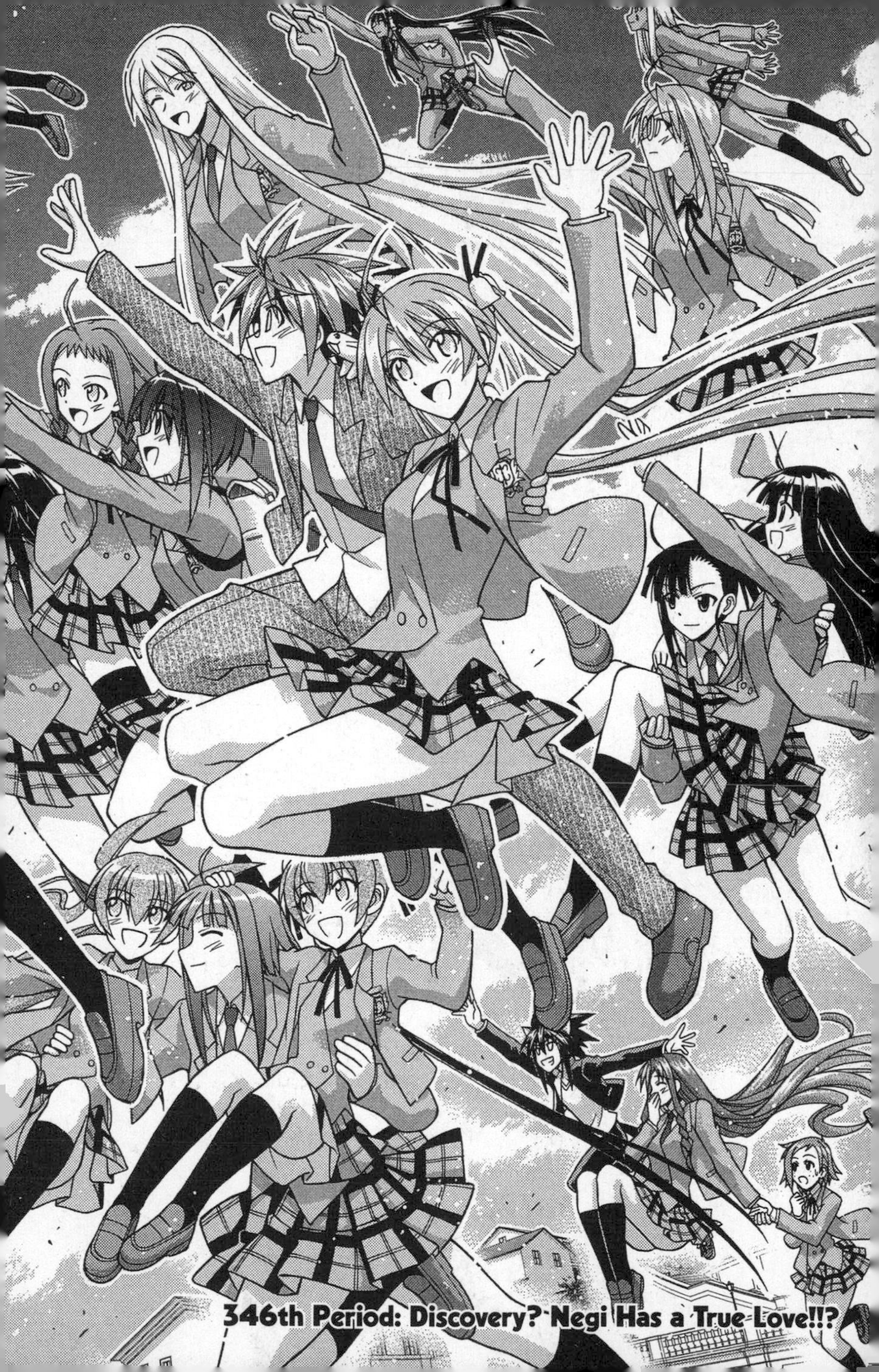
346th Period: Discovery? Negi Has a True Love!!?

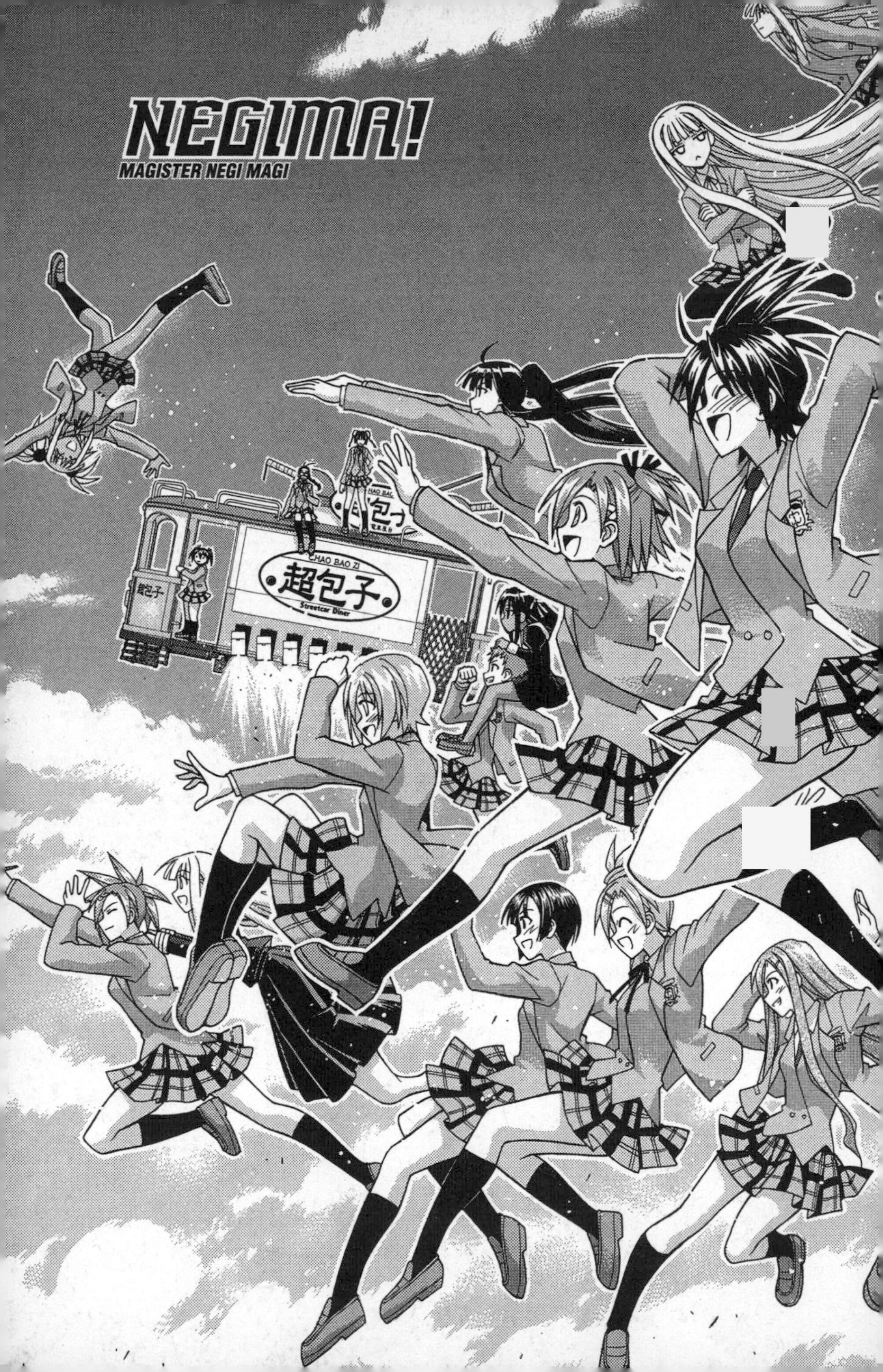
NEGIMA!
MAGISTER NEGI MAGI
CHAO BAO ZI
超包子
Streetcar Diner
超包子

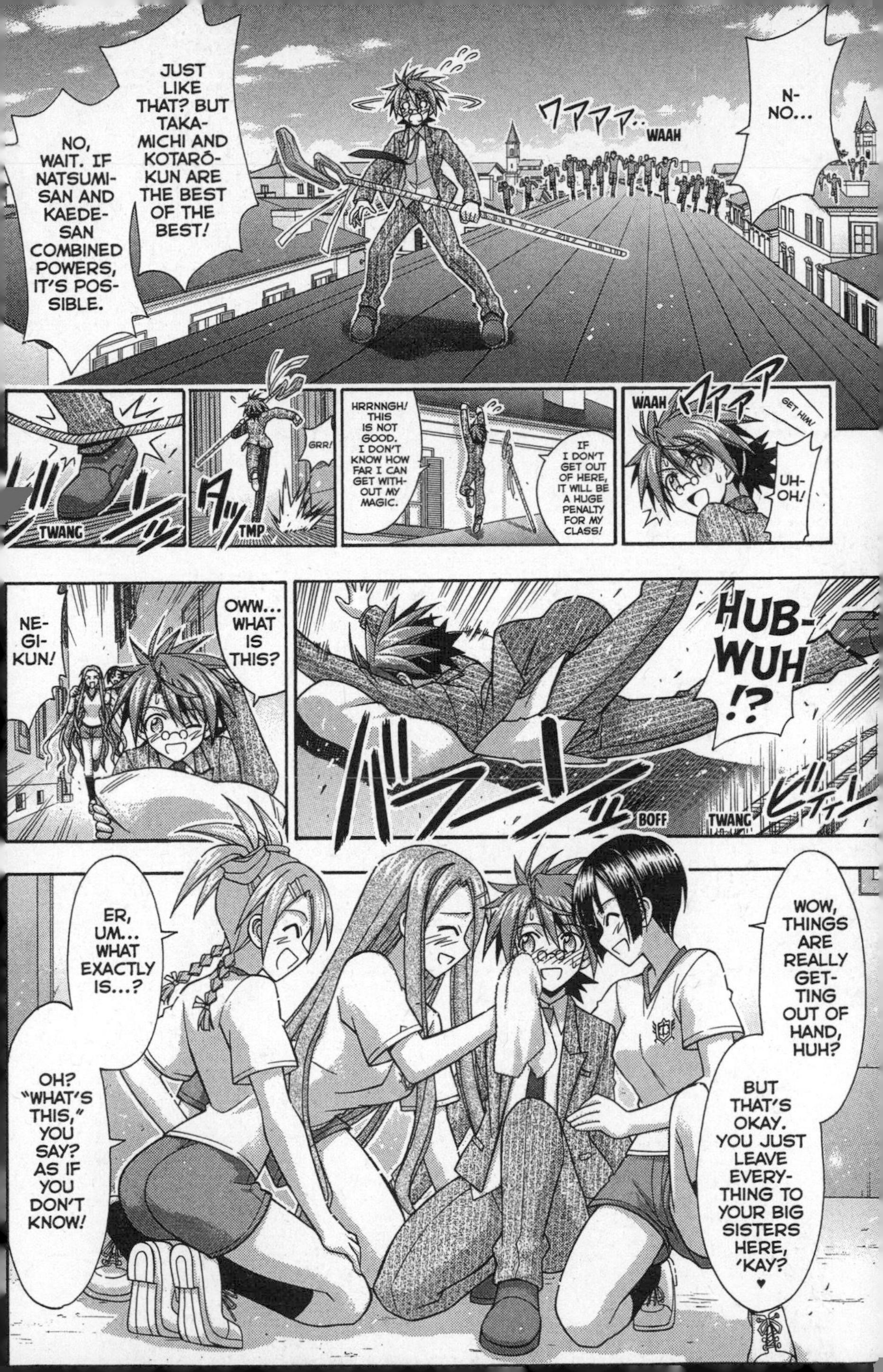
N-
NO...
ワアアア..
WAAH
JUST LIKE THAT? BUT TAKA-MICHI AND KOTARŌ-KUN ARE THE BEST OF THE BEST!
NO, WAIT. IF NATSUMI-SAN AND KAEDE-SAN COMBINED POWERS, IT'S POS-SIBLE.
ワァァァ
WAAH
GET HIM!
UH-OH!
HRRNNGH! THIS IS NOT GOOD. I DON'T KNOW HOW FAR I CAN GET WITH-OUT MY MAGIC.
IF I DON'T GET OUT OF HERE, IT WILL BE A HUGE PENALTY FOR MY CLASS!
GRR!
TMP
TWANG
HUB-WUH!?
TWANG
BOFF
OWW... WHAT IS THIS?
NE-GI-KUN!
WOW, THINGS ARE REALLY GET-TING OUT OF HAND, HUH?
BUT THAT'S OKAY. YOU JUST LEAVE EVERY-THING TO YOUR BIG SISTERS HERE, 'KAY? ♥
ER, UM... WHAT EXACTLY IS...?
OH? "WHAT'S THIS," YOU SAY? AS IF YOU DON'T KNOW!

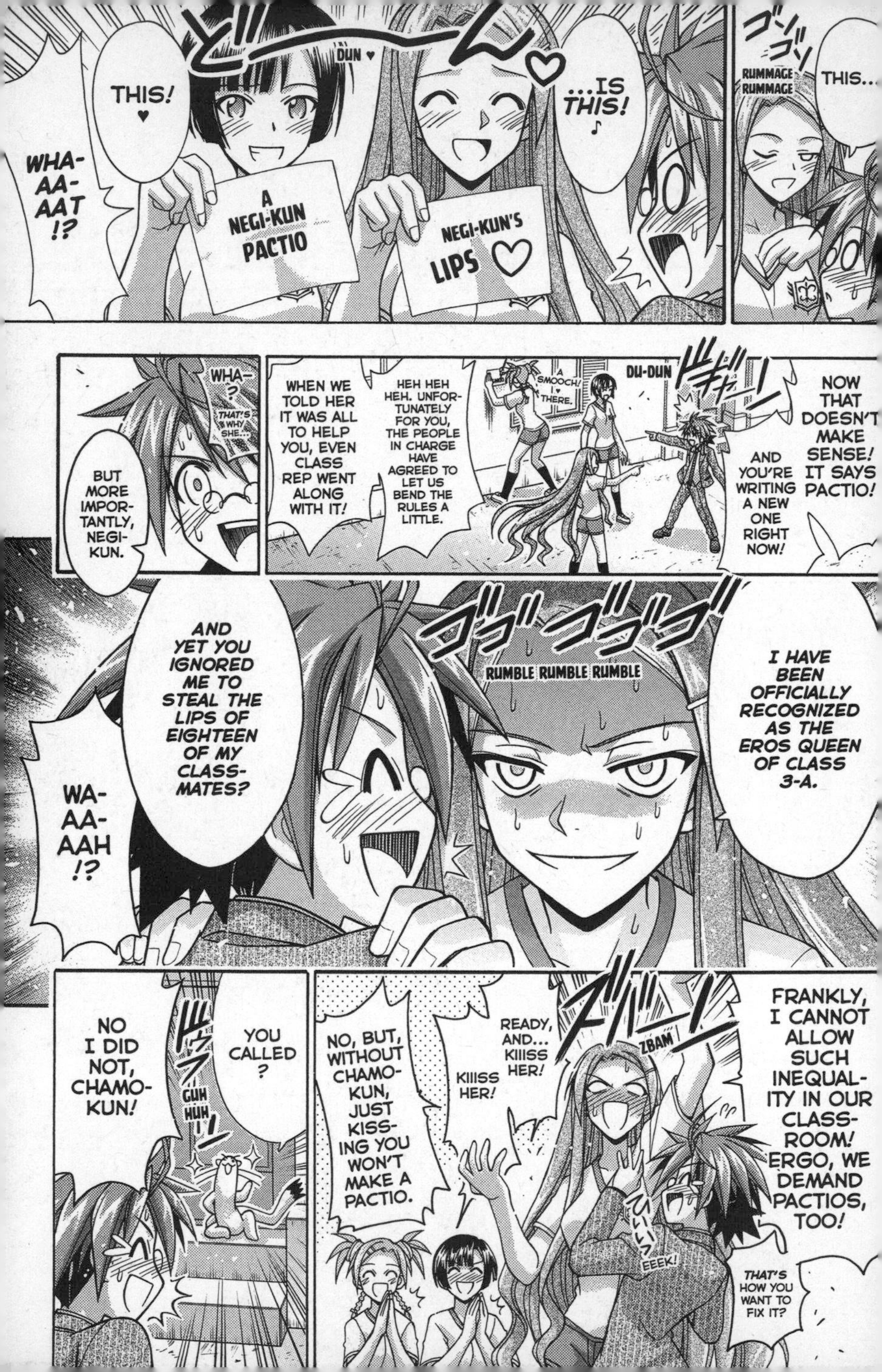
RUMMAGE RUMMAGE
THIS...
...IS THIS! ♪
DUN ♥
THIS! ♥
NEGI-KUN'S LIPS ♡
A NEGI-KUN PACTIO
WHA-AA-AAT !?
NOW THAT DOESN'T MAKE SENSE! IT SAYS PACTIO!
DU-DUN
AND YOU'RE WRITING A NEW ONE RIGHT NOW!
A SMOOCH! I ♥ THERE.
HEH HEH HEH. UNFORTUNATELY FOR YOU, THE PEOPLE IN CHARGE HAVE AGREED TO LET US BEND THE RULES A LITTLE.
WHEN WE TOLD HER IT WAS ALL TO HELP YOU, EVEN CLASS REP WENT ALONG WITH IT!
WHA-?
THAT'S WHY SHE...
BUT MORE IMPORTANTLY, NEGI-KUN.
I HAVE BEEN OFFICIALLY RECOGNIZED AS THE EROS QUEEN OF CLASS 3-A.
RUMBLE RUMBLE RUMBLE
AND YET YOU IGNORED ME TO STEAL THE LIPS OF EIGHTEEN OF MY CLASSMATES?
WA-AA-AAH !?
FRANKLY, I CANNOT ALLOW SUCH INEQUALITY IN OUR CLASSROOM! ERGO, WE DEMAND PACTIOS, TOO!
ZBAM
READY, AND... KIIISS HER!
KIIISS HER!
NO, BUT, WITHOUT CHAMO-KUN, JUST KISSING YOU WON'T MAKE A PACTIO.
EEEK!
THAT'S HOW YOU WANT TO FIX IT?
YOU CALLED?
GUH HUH
NO I DID NOT, CHAMO-KUN!

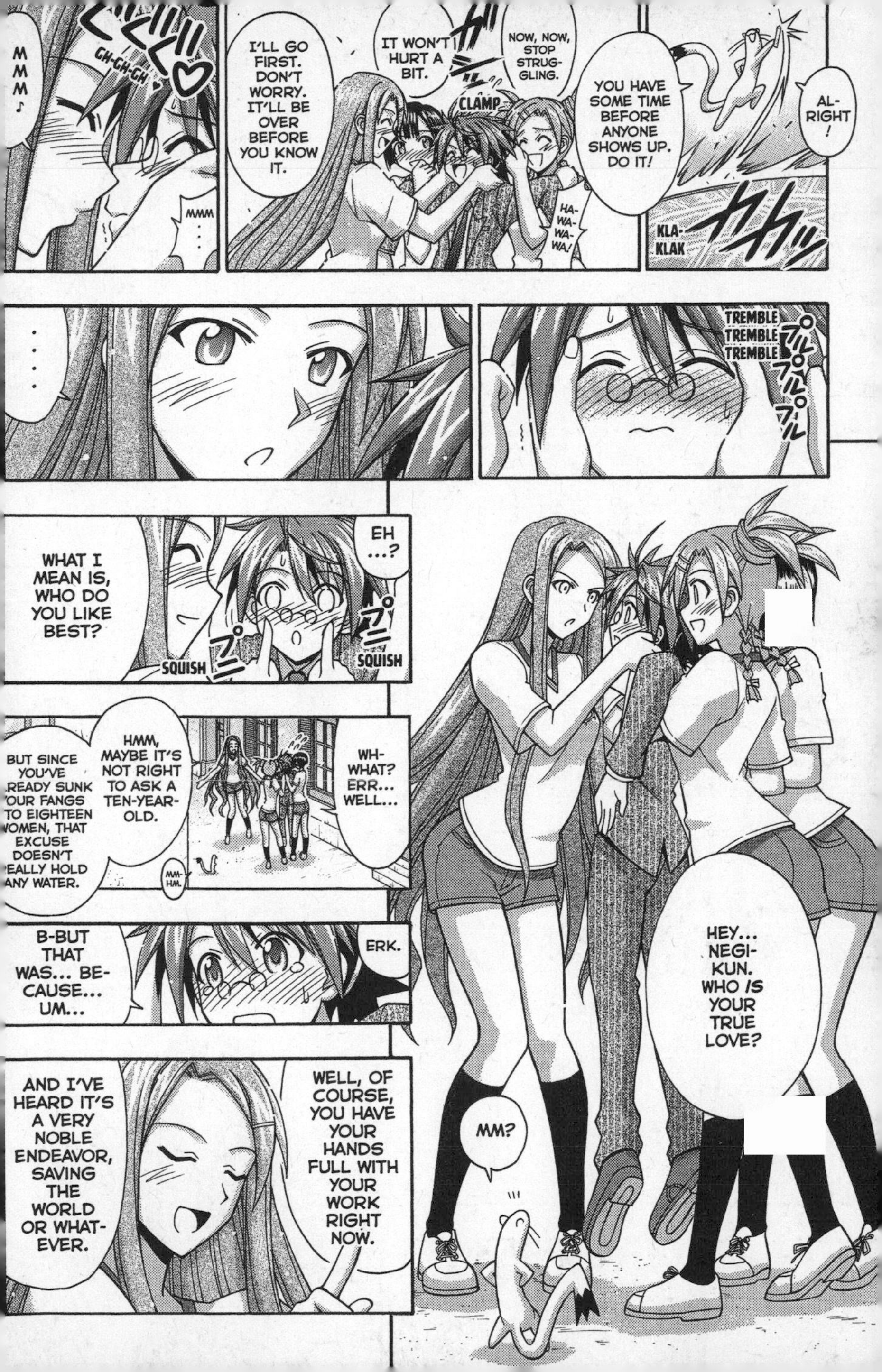
AL-RIGHT!
KLA-KLAK
YOU HAVE SOME TIME BEFORE ANYONE SHOWS UP. DO IT!
NOW, NOW, STOP STRUG-GLING.
CLAMP
IT WON'T HURT A BIT.
I'LL GO FIRST. DON'T WORRY. IT'LL BE OVER BEFORE YOU KNOW IT.
HA-WA-WA-WA!
GH-GH-GH
MMM♪
MMM...
TREMBLE
TREMBLE
TREMBLE
.....
HEY... NEGI-KUN. WHO IS YOUR TRUE LOVE?
MM?
EH...?
SQUISH
SQUISH
WHAT I MEAN IS, WHO DO YOU LIKE BEST?
WH-WHAT? ERR... WELL...
HMM, MAYBE IT'S NOT RIGHT TO ASK A TEN-YEAR-OLD.
MM-HM.
BUT SINCE YOU'VE READY SUNK OUR FANGS TO EIGHTEEN OMEN, THAT EXCUSE DOESN'T EALLY HOLD ANY WATER.
ERK.
B-BUT THAT WAS... BE-CAUSE... UM...
WELL, OF COURSE, YOU HAVE YOUR HANDS FULL WITH YOUR WORK RIGHT NOW.
AND I'VE HEARD IT'S A VERY NOBLE ENDEAVOR, SAVING THE WORLD OR WHAT-EVER.

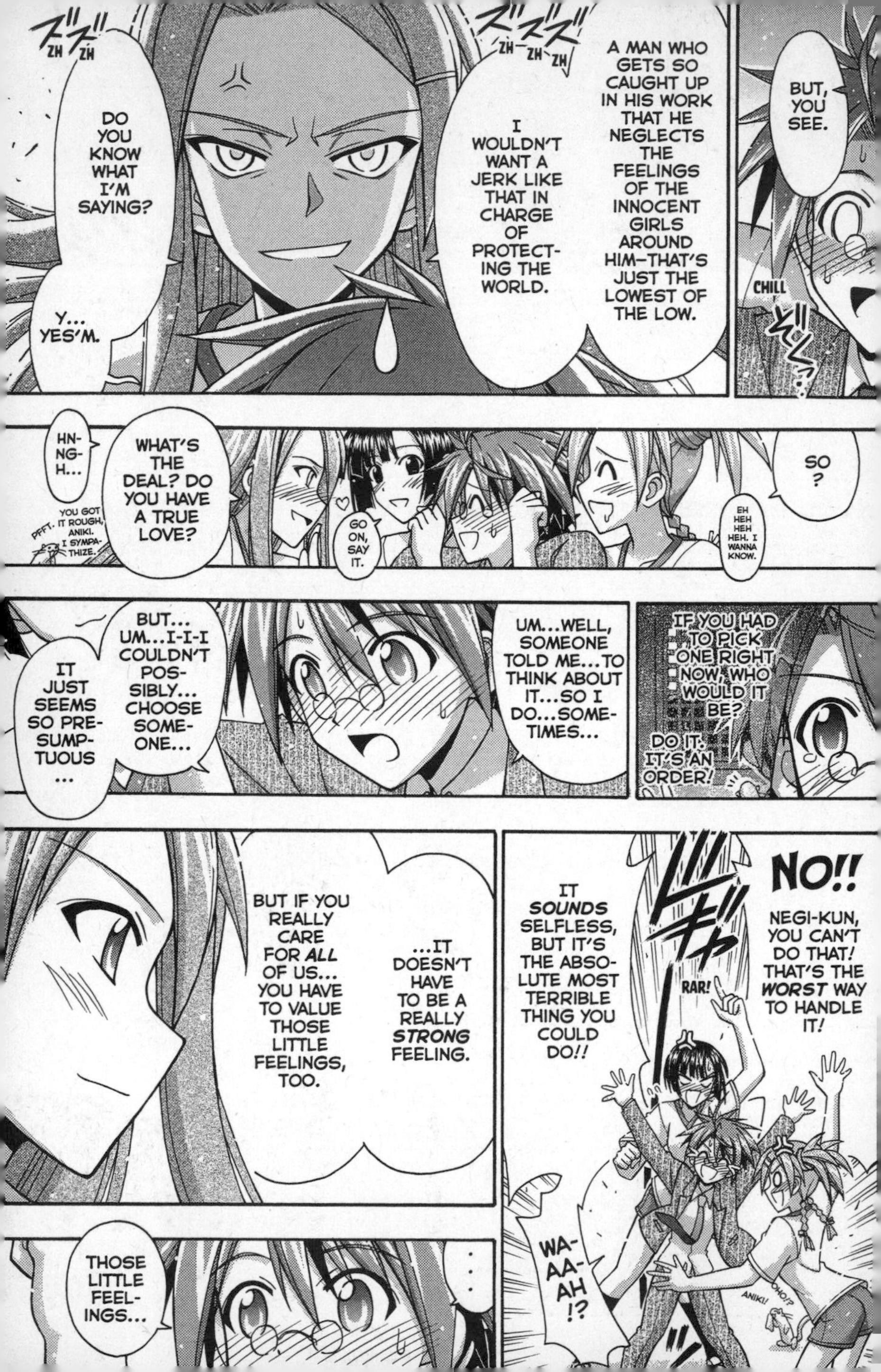
BUT, YOU SEE.
CHILL
ZH ZH ZH
A MAN WHO GETS SO CAUGHT UP IN HIS WORK THAT HE NEGLECTS THE FEELINGS OF THE INNOCENT GIRLS AROUND HIM—THAT'S JUST THE LOWEST OF THE LOW.
I WOULDN'T WANT A JERK LIKE THAT IN CHARGE OF PROTECTING THE WORLD.
ZH ZH
DO YOU KNOW WHAT I'M SAYING?
Y... YES'M.
SO?
EH HEH HEH HEH. I WANNA KNOW.
GO ON, SAY IT.
WHAT'S THE DEAL? DO YOU HAVE A TRUE LOVE?
HN-NG-H...
PFFT. YOU GOT IT ROUGH, ANIKI. I SYMPATHIZE.
IF YOU HAD TO PICK ONE RIGHT NOW, WHO WOULD IT BE?
DO IT. IT'S AN ORDER!
UM...WELL, SOMEONE TOLD ME...TO THINK ABOUT IT...SO I DO...SOMETIMES...
BUT... UM...I-I-I COULDN'T POSSIBLY...CHOOSE SOMEONE...
IT JUST SEEMS SO PRESUMPTUOUS...
NO!!
NEGI-KUN, YOU CAN'T DO THAT! THAT'S THE WORST WAY TO HANDLE IT!
RAR!
IT SOUNDS SELFLESS, BUT IT'S THE ABSOLUTE MOST TERRIBLE THING YOU COULD DO!!
WA-AA-AH!?
OHO!?
ANIKI!
BUT IF YOU REALLY CARE FOR ALL OF US... YOU HAVE TO VALUE THOSE LITTLE FEELINGS, TOO.
...IT DOESN'T HAVE TO BE A REALLY STRONG FEELING.
...
THOSE LITTLE FEELINGS...

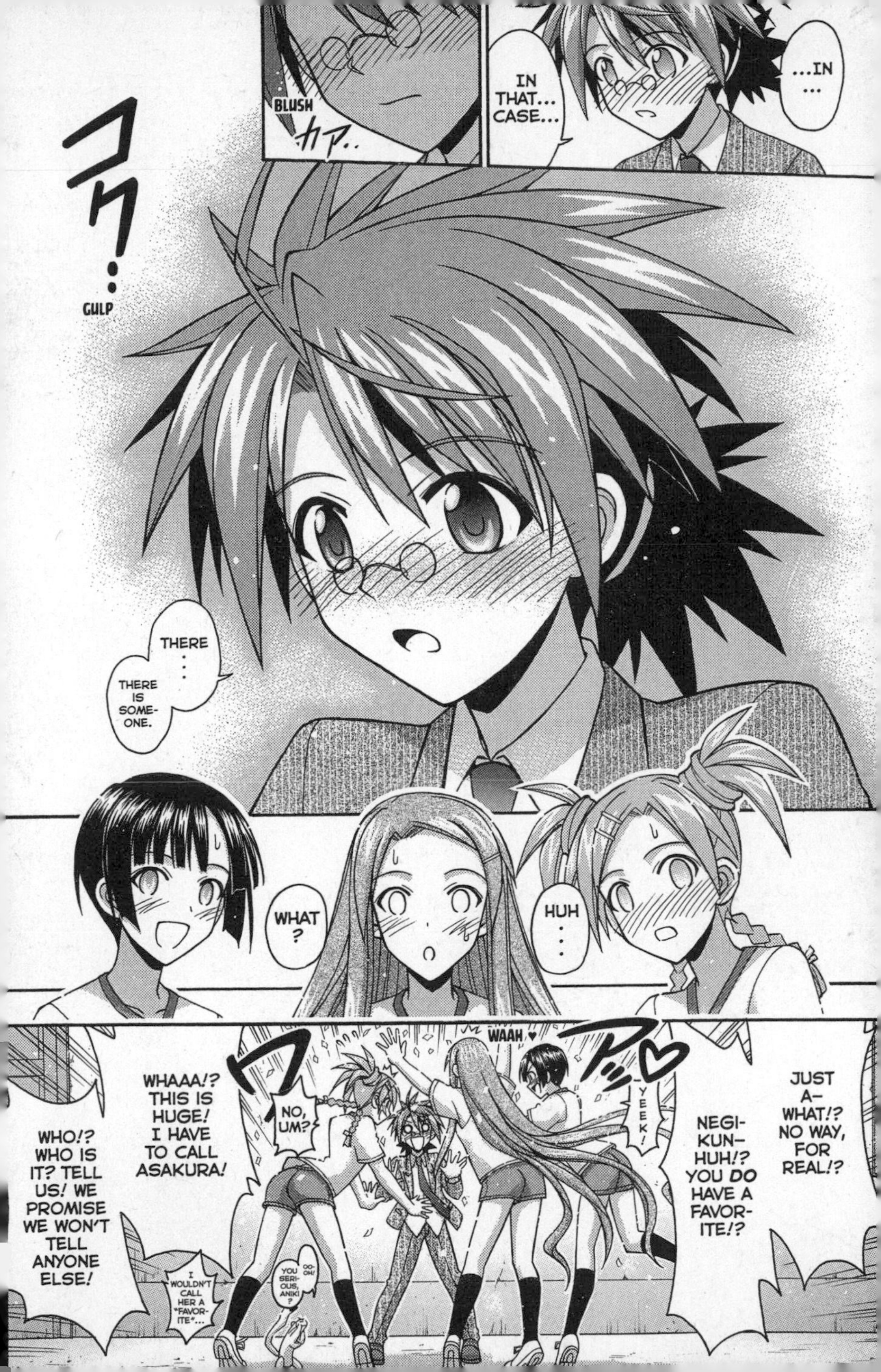
...IN ...
IN THAT... CASE...
BLUSH
カァ..
コク
GULP
THERE... THERE IS SOMEONE.
HUH...
WHAT?
JUST A— WHAT!? NO WAY, FOR REAL!?
NEGI-KUN—HUH!? YOU DO HAVE A FAVOR-ITE!?
WAAH♥
YEEK!
NO, UM?
WHAAA!? THIS IS HUGE! I HAVE TO CALL ASAKURA!
WHO!? WHO IS IT? TELL US! WE PROMISE WE WON'T TELL ANYONE ELSE!
OO-OH! YOU SERI-OUS, ANIKI!
I WOULDN'T CALL HER A "FAVOR-ITE"...

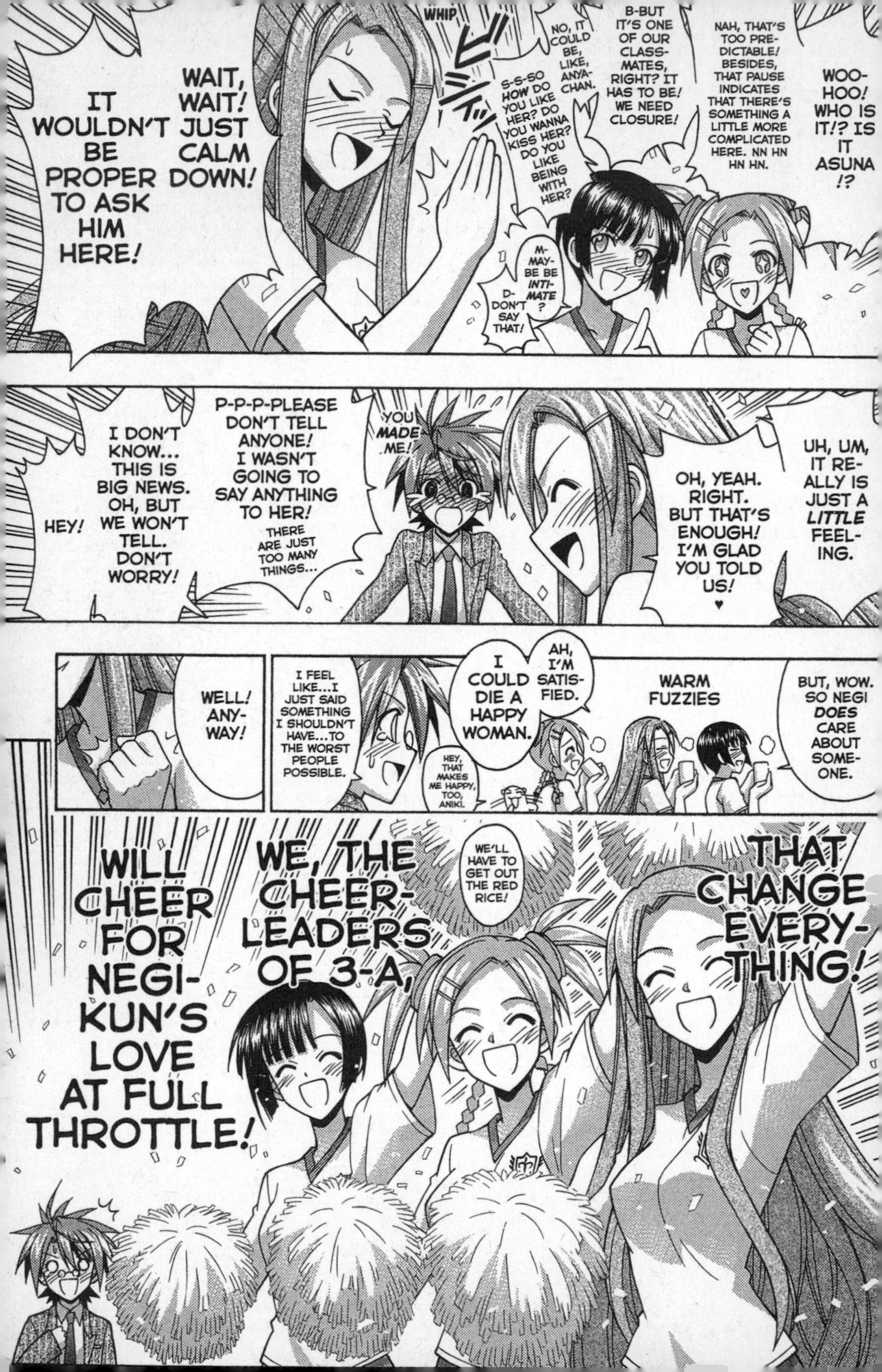

WOO-HOO! WHO IS IT!? IS IT ASUNA!?
NAH, THAT'S TOO PREDICTABLE! BESIDES, THAT PAUSE INDICATES THAT THERE'S SOMETHING A LITTLE MORE COMPLICATED HERE. NN HN HN HN.
B-BUT IT'S ONE OF OUR CLASSMATES, RIGHT? IT HAS TO BE! WE NEED CLOSURE!
NO, IT COULD BE, LIKE, ANYA-CHAN.
WHIP
S-S-SO HOW DO YOU LIKE HER? DO YOU WANNA KISS HER? DO YOU LIKE BEING WITH HER?
M-MAYBE BE INTIMATE?
D-DON'T SAY THAT!
WAIT, WAIT! JUST CALM DOWN!
IT WOULDN'T BE PROPER TO ASK HIM HERE!
UH, UM, IT REALLY IS JUST A LITTLE FEELING.
OH, YEAH. RIGHT. BUT THAT'S ENOUGH! I'M GLAD YOU TOLD US! ♥
YOU MADE ME!
P-P-P-PLEASE DON'T TELL ANYONE! I WASN'T GOING TO SAY ANYTHING TO HER!
THERE ARE JUST TOO MANY THINGS...
I DON'T KNOW... THIS IS BIG NEWS. OH, BUT WE WON'T TELL. DON'T WORRY!
HEY!
BUT, WOW. SO NEGI DOES CARE ABOUT SOMEONE.
WARM FUZZIES
AH, I'M SATISFIED.
I COULD DIE A HAPPY WOMAN.
HEY, THAT MAKES ME HAPPY, TOO, ANIKI.
I FEEL LIKE...I JUST SAID SOMETHING I SHOULDN'T HAVE...TO THE WORST PEOPLE POSSIBLE.
WELL! ANYWAY!
THAT CHANGE EVERYTHING!
WE'LL HAVE TO GET OUT THE RED RICE!
WE, THE CHEERLEADERS OF 3-A,
WILL CHEER FOR NEGI-KUN'S LOVE AT FULL THROTTLE!

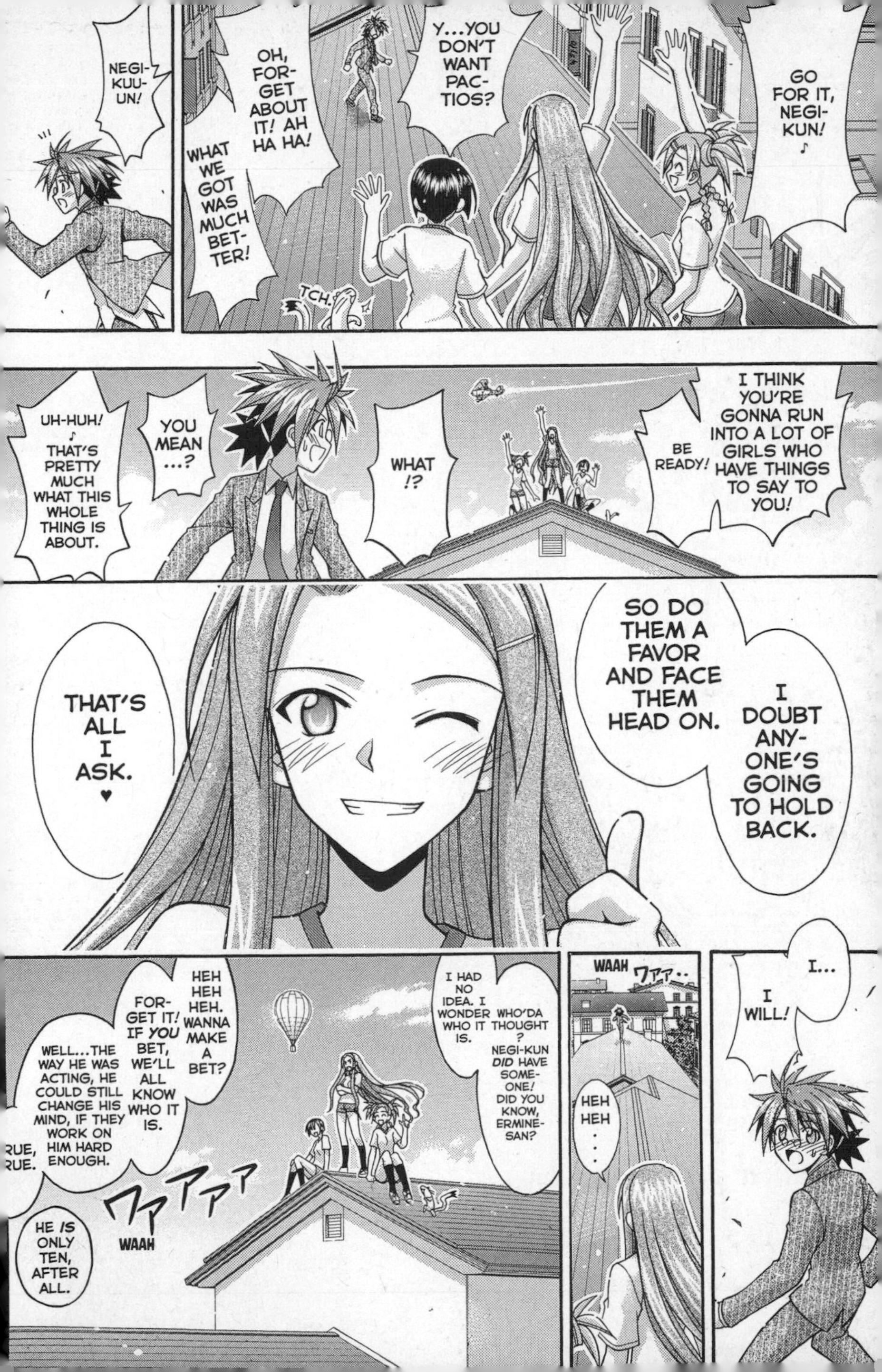
GO FOR IT, NEGI-KUN! ♪
Y...YOU DON'T WANT PACTIOS?
OH, FORGET ABOUT IT! AH HA HA!
WHAT WE GOT WAS MUCH BETTER!
TCH.
NEGI-KUU-UN!
I THINK YOU'RE GONNA RUN INTO A LOT OF GIRLS WHO HAVE THINGS TO SAY TO YOU!
BE READY!
WHAT!?
YOU MEAN ...?
UH-HUH! ♪ THAT'S PRETTY MUCH WHAT THIS WHOLE THING IS ABOUT.
I DOUBT ANYONE'S GOING TO HOLD BACK.
SO DO THEM A FAVOR AND FACE THEM HEAD ON.
THAT'S ALL I ASK. ♥
I...
I WILL!
WAAH ワァア‥
HEH HEH . . .
I HAD NO IDEA. I WONDER WHO IT IS.
WHO'DA THOUGHT? NEGI-KUN DID HAVE SOMEONE! DID YOU KNOW, ERMINE-SAN?
HEH HEH HEH. WANNA MAKE A BET?
FORGET IT! IF YOU BET, WE'LL ALL KNOW WHO IT IS.
WELL...THE WAY HE WAS ACTING, HE COULD STILL CHANGE HIS MIND, IF THEY WORK ON HIM HARD ENOUGH.
RUE, RUE.
ワァアア WAAH
HE IS ONLY TEN, AFTER ALL.

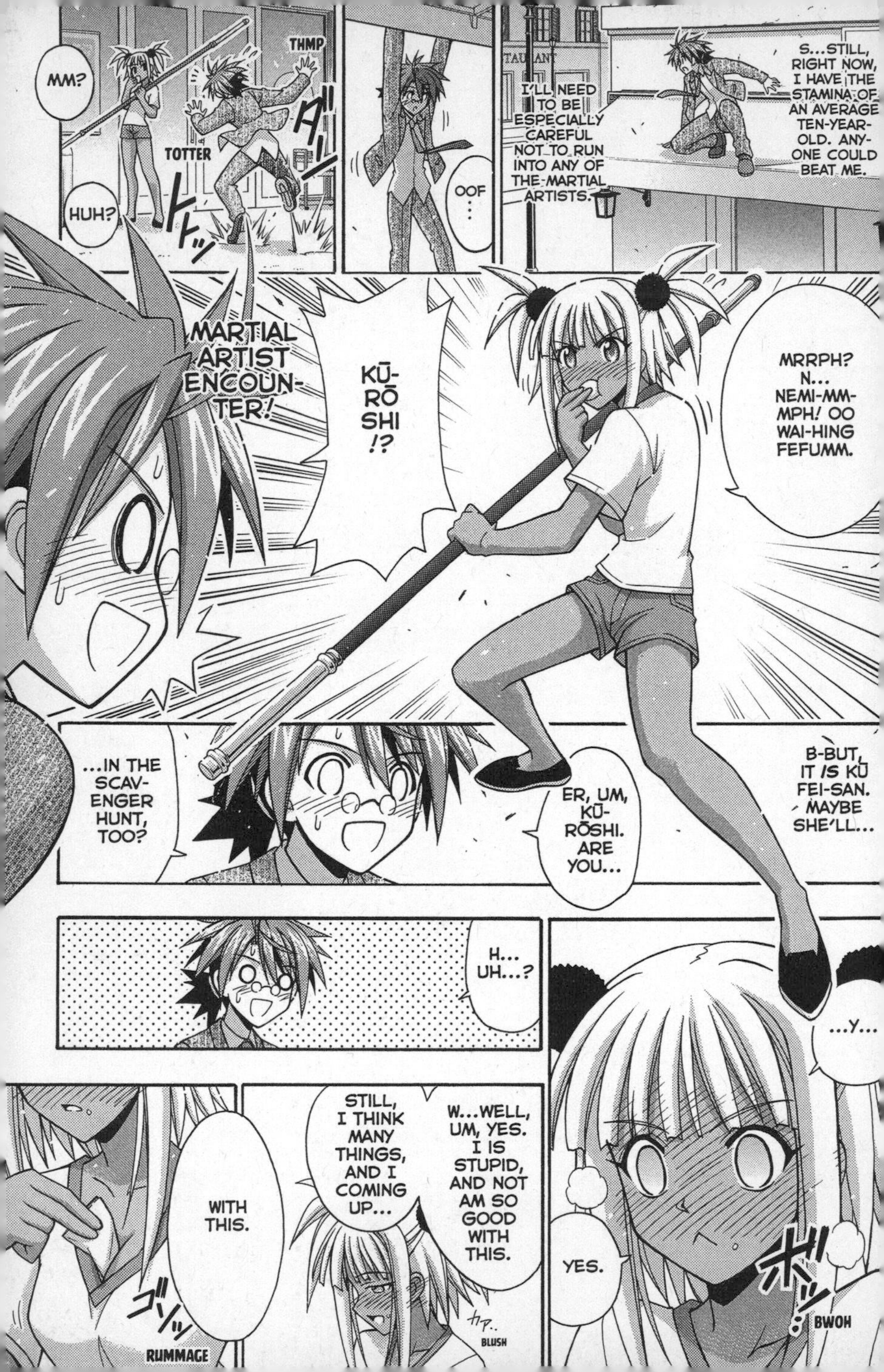
S...STILL, RIGHT NOW, I HAVE THE STAMINA OF AN AVERAGE TEN-YEAR-OLD. ANY-ONE COULD BEAT ME.
I'LL NEED TO BE ESPECIALLY CAREFUL NOT TO RUN INTO ANY OF THE MARTIAL ARTISTS.
OOF...
THMP
MM?
TOTTER
HUH?
MRRPH? N... NEMI-MMMPH! OO WAI-HING FEFUMM.
KŪ-RŌSHI!?
MARTIAL ARTIST ENCOUN-TER!
B-BUT, IT IS KŪ FEI-SAN. MAYBE SHE'LL...
ER, UM, KŪ-RŌSHI. ARE YOU...
...IN THE SCAV-ENGER HUNT, TOO?
...Y...
YES.
BWOH
H... UH...?
W...WELL, UM, YES. I IS STUPID, AND NOT AM SO GOOD WITH THIS.
STILL, I THINK MANY THINGS, AND I COMING UP...
BLUSH
WITH THIS.
RUMMAGE

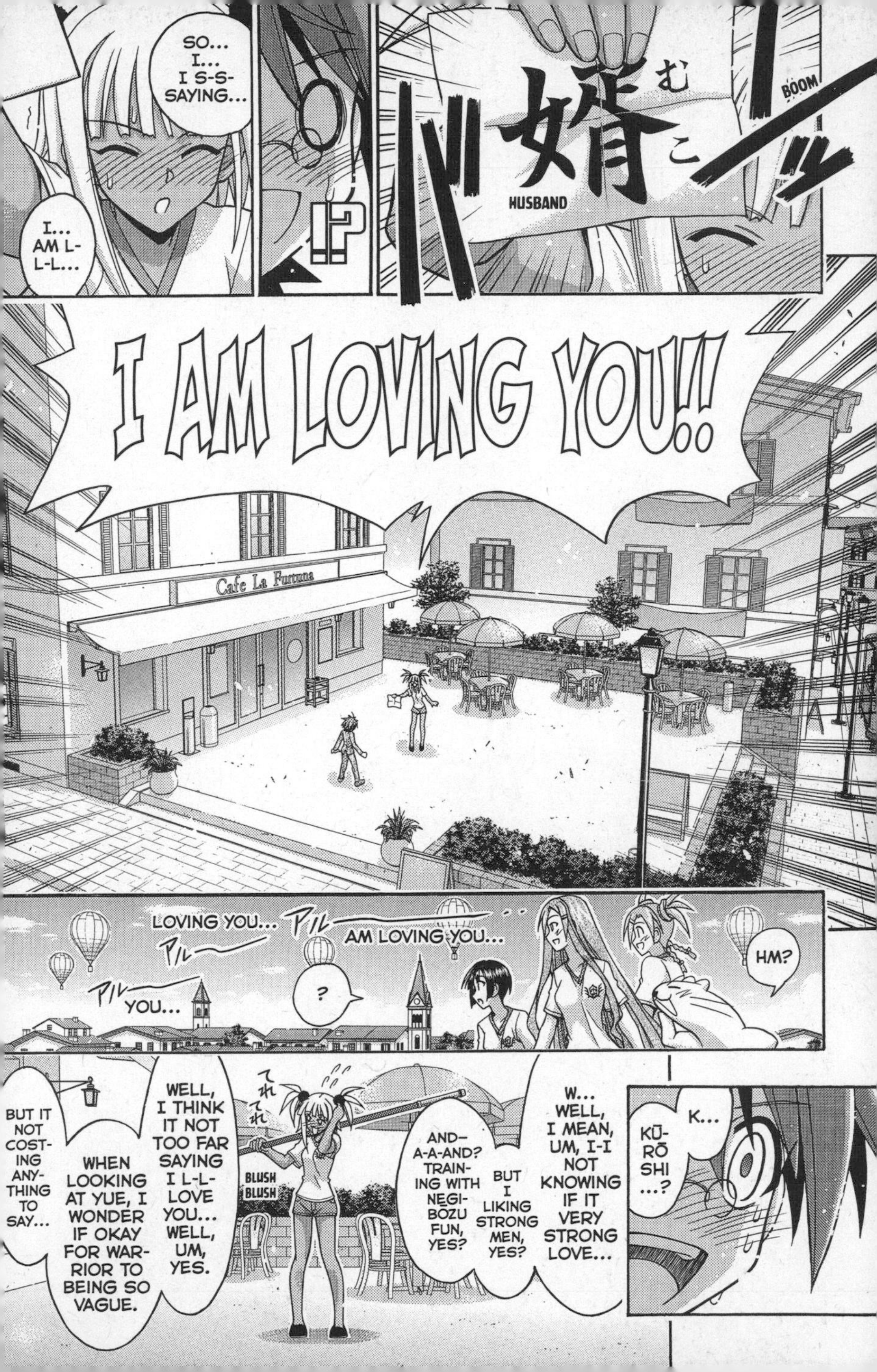

婿
む
こ
HUSBAND
BOOM
!?
SO... I... I S-S-SAYING...
I... AM L-L-L...
I AM LOVING YOU!!
Cafe La Furtuna
HM?
?
AM LOVING YOU...
LOVING YOU... アル
アル
アル
YOU...
K... KŪRŌSHI...?
W... WELL, I MEAN, UM, I-I NOT KNOWING IF IT VERY STRONG LOVE...
BUT I LIKING STRONG MEN, YES?
AND— A-A-AND? TRAINING WITH NEGI-BŌZU FUN, YES?
てれ てれ
BLUSH BLUSH
WELL, I THINK IT NOT TOO FAR SAYING I L-L-LOVE YOU... WELL, UM, YES.
WHEN LOOKING AT YUE, I WONDER IF OKAY FOR WARRIOR TO BEING SO VAGUE.
BUT IT NOT COSTING ANYTHING TO SAY...

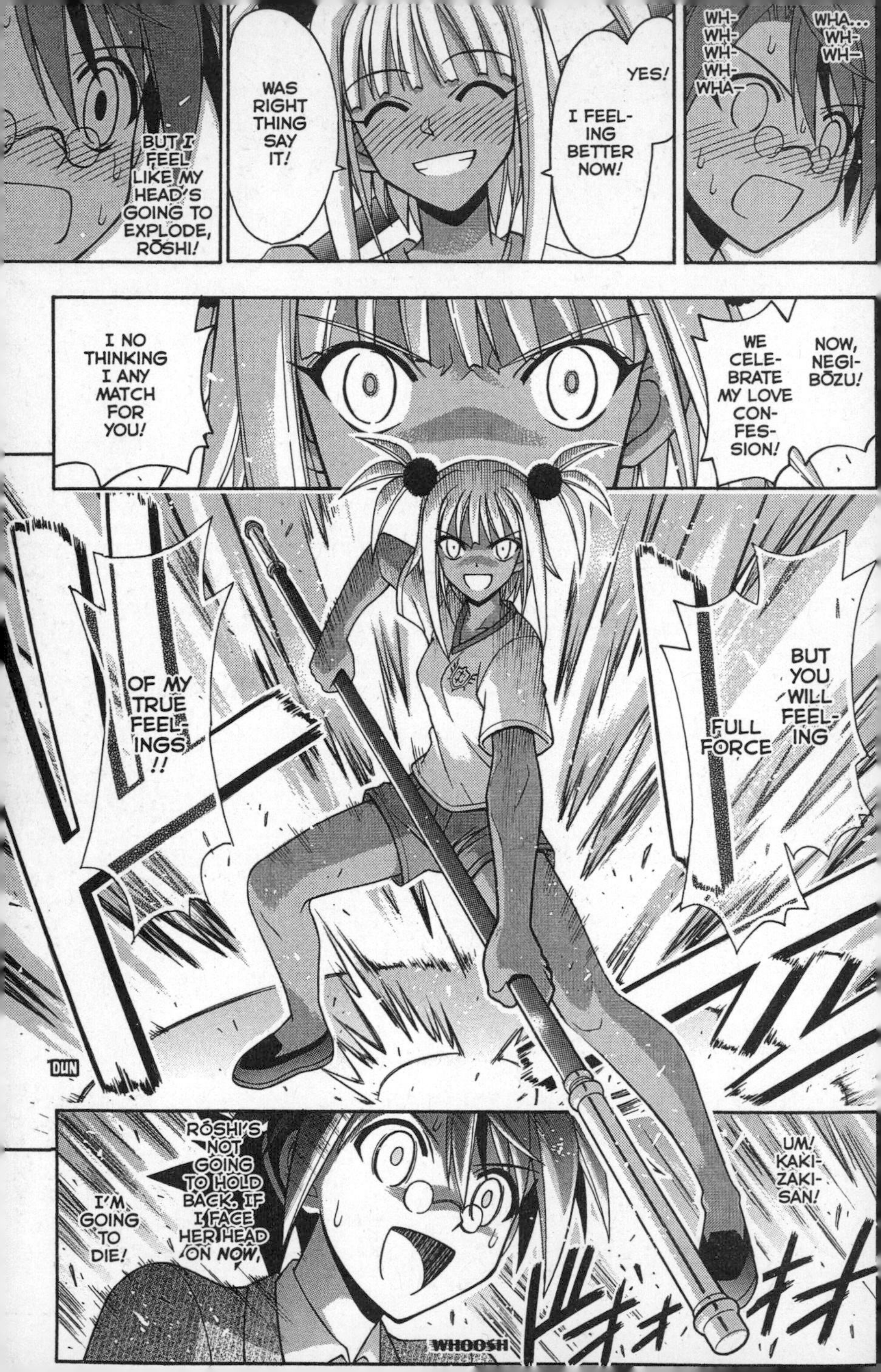
WHA... WH- WH-
WH- WH- WH- WH- WHA-
YES!
I FEEL-ING BETTER NOW!
WAS RIGHT THING SAY IT!
BUT I FEEL LIKE MY HEAD'S GOING TO EXPLODE, RŌSHI!
NOW, NEGI-BŌZU!
WE CELE-BRATE MY LOVE CON-FES-SION!
I NO THINKING I ANY MATCH FOR YOU!
BUT YOU WILL FEEL-ING
FULL FORCE
OF MY TRUE FEEL-INGS!!
DUN
UM! KAKI-ZAKI-SAN!
RŌSHI'S NOT GOING TO HOLD BACK, IF I FACE HER HEAD ON NOW,
I'M GOING TO DIE!
WHOOSH

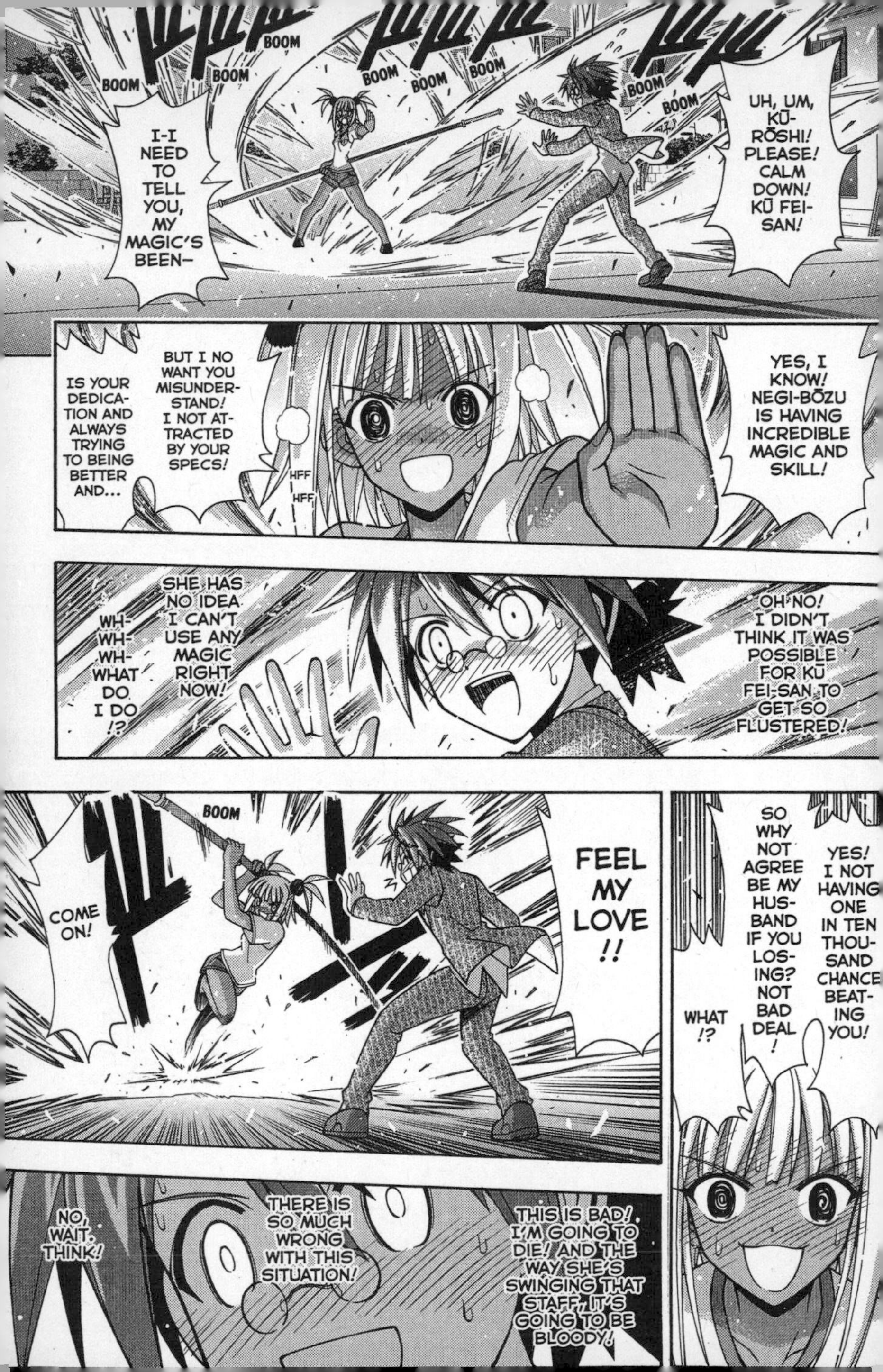
BOOM
BOOM
BOOM
BOOM
BOOM
BOOM
BOOM
BOOM
UH, UM, KŪ-RŌSHI! PLEASE! CALM DOWN! KŪ FEI-SAN!
I-I NEED TO TELL YOU, MY MAGIC'S BEEN—
YES, I KNOW! NEGI-BŌZU IS HAVING INCREDIBLE MAGIC AND SKILL!
BUT I NO WANT YOU MISUNDERSTAND! I NOT ATTRACTED BY YOUR SPECS!
HFF
HFF
IS YOUR DEDICATION AND ALWAYS TRYING TO BEING BETTER AND...
OH NO! I DIDN'T THINK IT WAS POSSIBLE FOR KŪ FEI-SAN TO GET SO FLUSTERED!
SHE HAS NO IDEA I CAN'T USE ANY MAGIC RIGHT NOW!
WH-WH-WH-WHAT DO I DO!?
YES! I NOT HAVING ONE IN TEN THOUSAND CHANCE BEATING YOU!
SO WHY NOT AGREE BE MY HUSBAND IF YOU LOSING? NOT BAD DEAL!
WHAT!?
FEEL MY LOVE!!
BOOM
COME ON!
THIS IS BAD! I'M GOING TO DIE! AND THE WAY SHE'S SWINGING THAT STAFF, IT'S GOING TO BE BLOODY!
THERE IS SO MUCH WRONG WITH THIS SITUATION!
NO, WAIT. THINK!

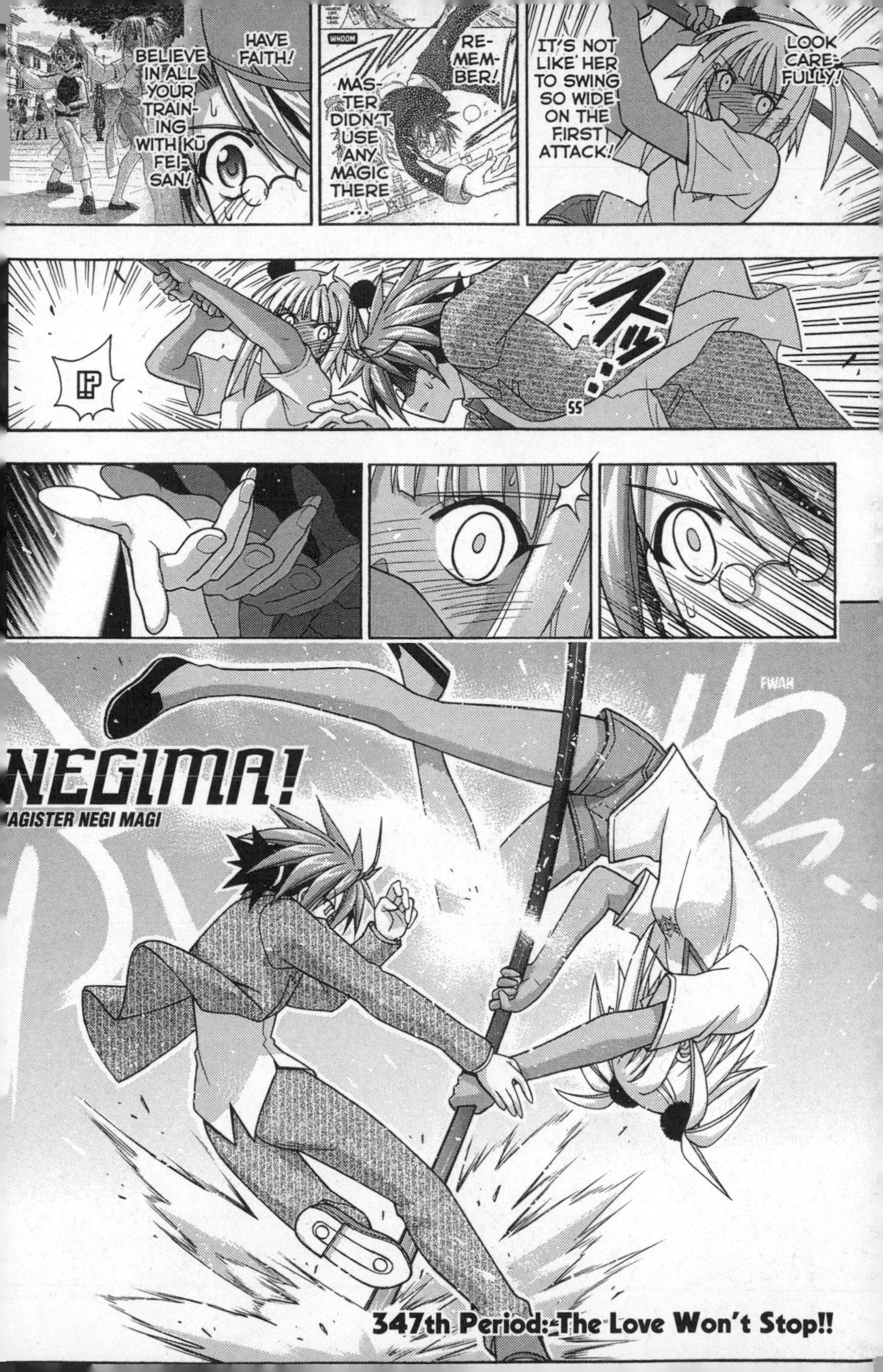
LOOK CAREFULLY!
IT'S NOT LIKE HER TO SWING SO WIDE ON THE FIRST ATTACK!
HANDS OFF, WEAKLING.
WHOOM
REMEMBER!
MASTER DIDN'T USE ANY MAGIC THERE...
HAVE FAITH!
BELIEVE IN ALL YOUR TRAINING WITH KŪ FEI-SAN!
SS
!?
FWAH
NEGIMA!
AGISTER NEGI MAGI
347th Period: The Love Won't Stop!!

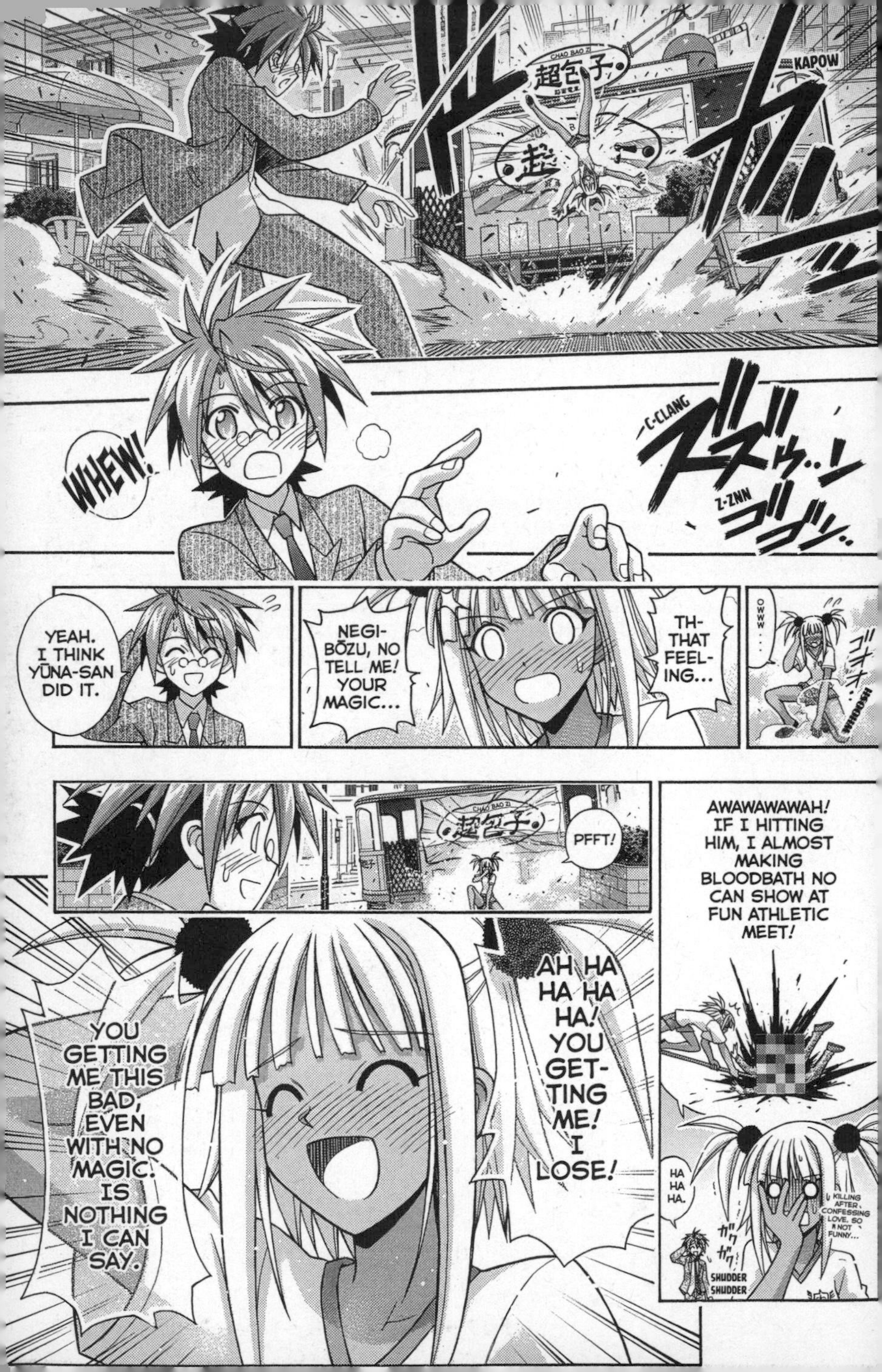
KAPOW
CHAO BAO ZI
超包子
C-CLANG
Z-ZNN
WHEW!
OWW...
TH-THAT FEELING...
NEGI-BŌZU, NO TELL ME! YOUR MAGIC...
YEAH. I THINK YŪNA-SAN DID IT.
AWAWAWAWAH! IF I HITTING HIM, I ALMOST MAKING BLOODBATH NO CAN SHOW AT FUN ATHLETIC MEET!
HA HA HA.
KILLING AFTER CONFESSING LOVE, SO NOT FUNNY...
SHUDDER SHUDDER
CHAO BAO ZI
超包子
PFFT!
AH HA HA HA HA! YOU GETTING ME! I LOSE!
YOU GETTING ME THIS BAD, EVEN WITH NO MAGIC. IS NOTHING I CAN SAY.

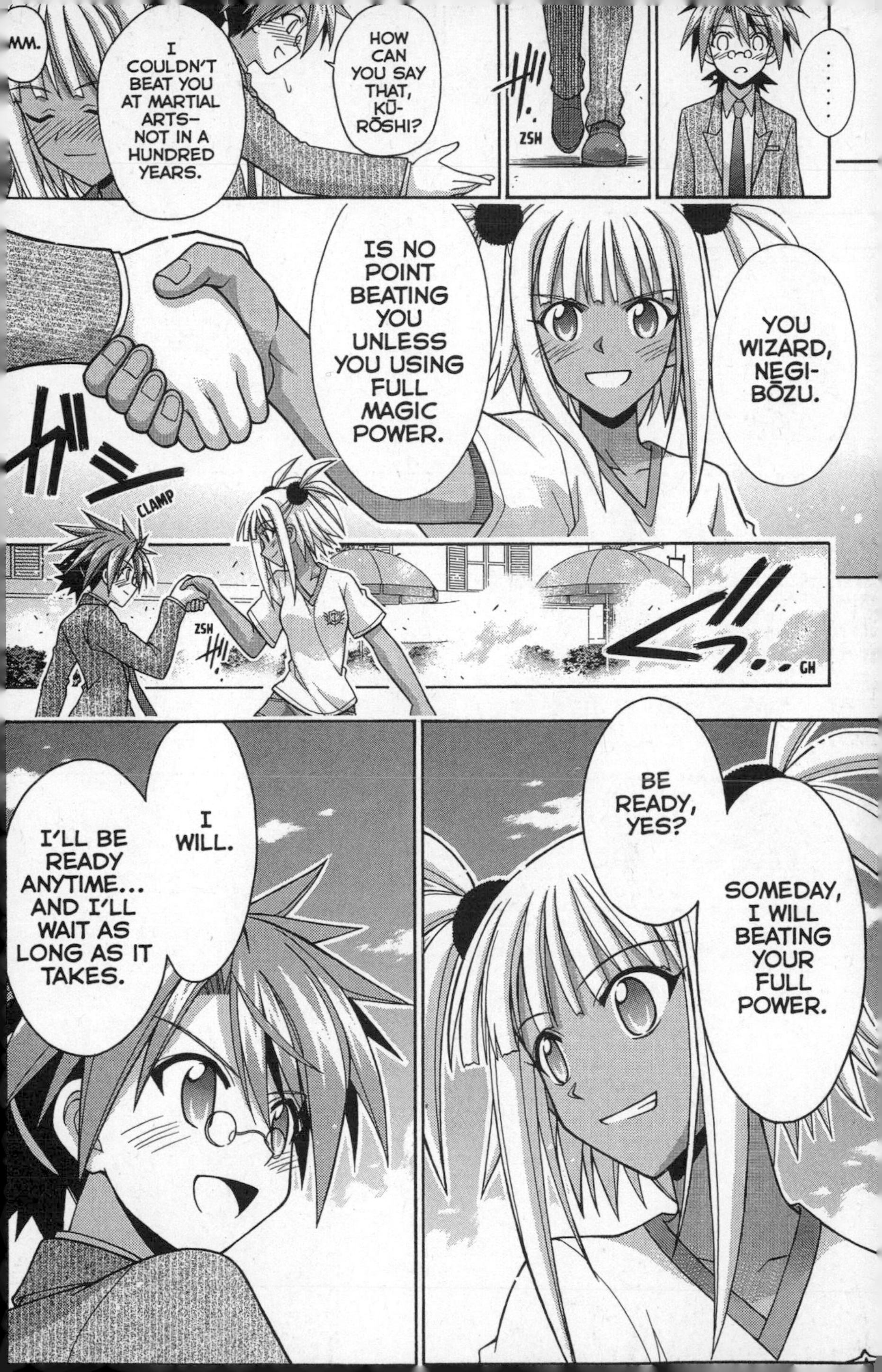
......
ZSH
HOW CAN YOU SAY THAT, KŪ-RŌSHI?
I COULDN'T BEAT YOU AT MARTIAL ARTS— NOT IN A HUNDRED YEARS.
MM.
YOU WIZARD, NEGI-BŌZU.
IS NO POINT BEATING YOU UNLESS YOU USING FULL MAGIC POWER.
CLAMP
GH
ZSH
SOMEDAY, I WILL BEATING YOUR FULL POWER.
BE READY, YES?
I WILL.
I'LL BE READY ANYTIME... AND I'LL WAIT AS LONG AS IT TAKES.

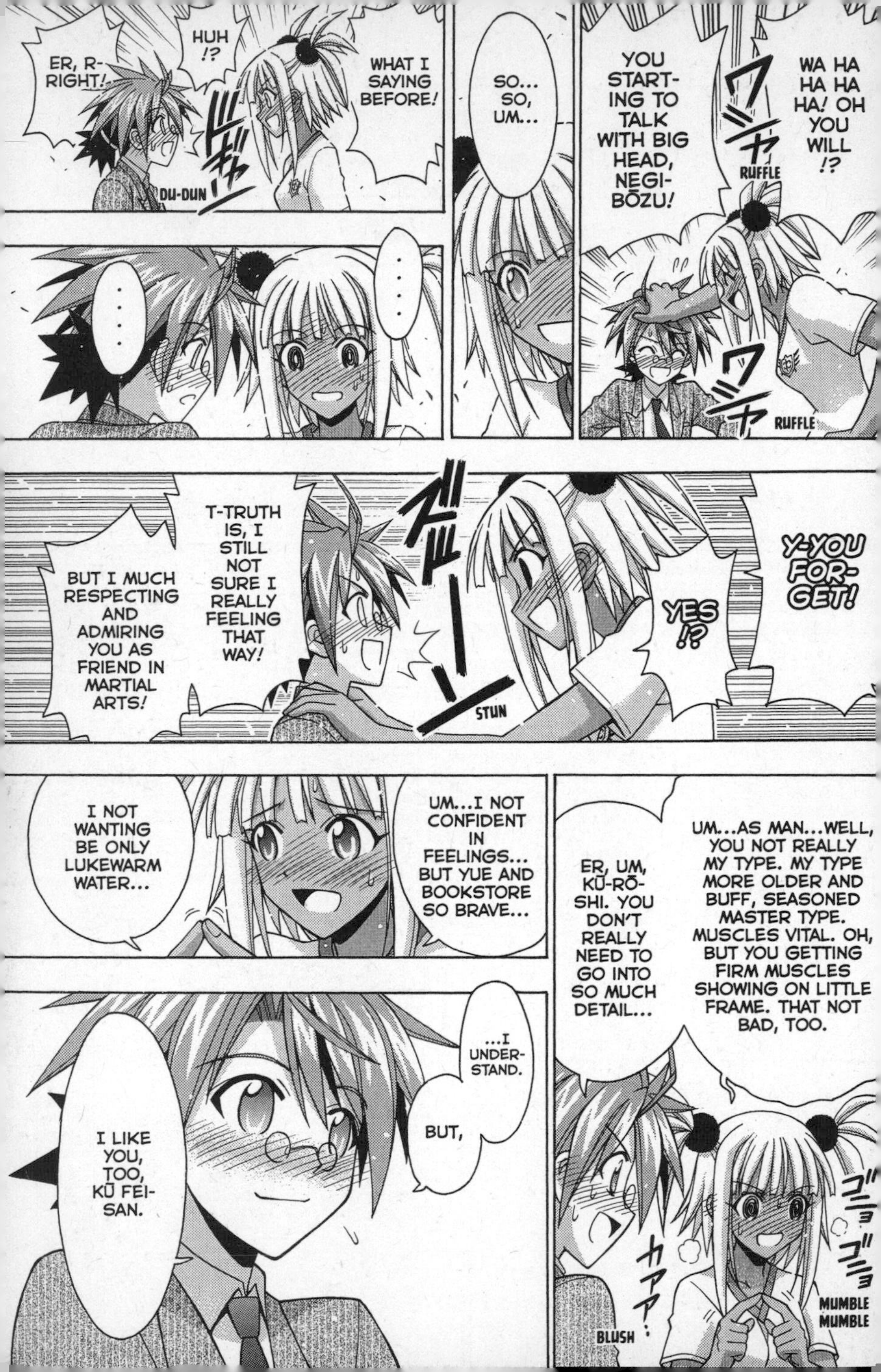
WA HA HA HA! OH YOU WILL !?
YOU STARTING TO TALK WITH BIG HEAD, NEGI-BŌZU!
RUFFLE
RUFFLE
SO... SO, UM...
WHAT I SAYING BEFORE!
HUH !?
DU-DUN
ER, R-RIGHT!
.....
.....
Y-YOU FOR-GET!
YES !?
STUN
T-TRUTH IS, I STILL NOT SURE I REALLY FEELING THAT WAY!
BUT I MUCH RESPECTING AND ADMIRING YOU AS FRIEND IN MARTIAL ARTS!
UM...AS MAN...WELL, YOU NOT REALLY MY TYPE. MY TYPE MORE OLDER AND BUFF, SEASONED MASTER TYPE. MUSCLES VITAL. OH, BUT YOU GETTING FIRM MUSCLES SHOWING ON LITTLE FRAME. THAT NOT BAD, TOO.
ER, UM, KŪ-RŌ-SHI. YOU DON'T REALLY NEED TO GO INTO SO MUCH DETAIL...
MUMBLE MUMBLE
BLUSH
UM...I NOT CONFIDENT IN FEELINGS... BUT YUE AND BOOKSTORE SO BRAVE...
I NOT WANTING BE ONLY LUKEWARM WATER...
...I UNDER-STAND.
BUT,
I LIKE YOU, TOO, KŪ FEI-SAN.

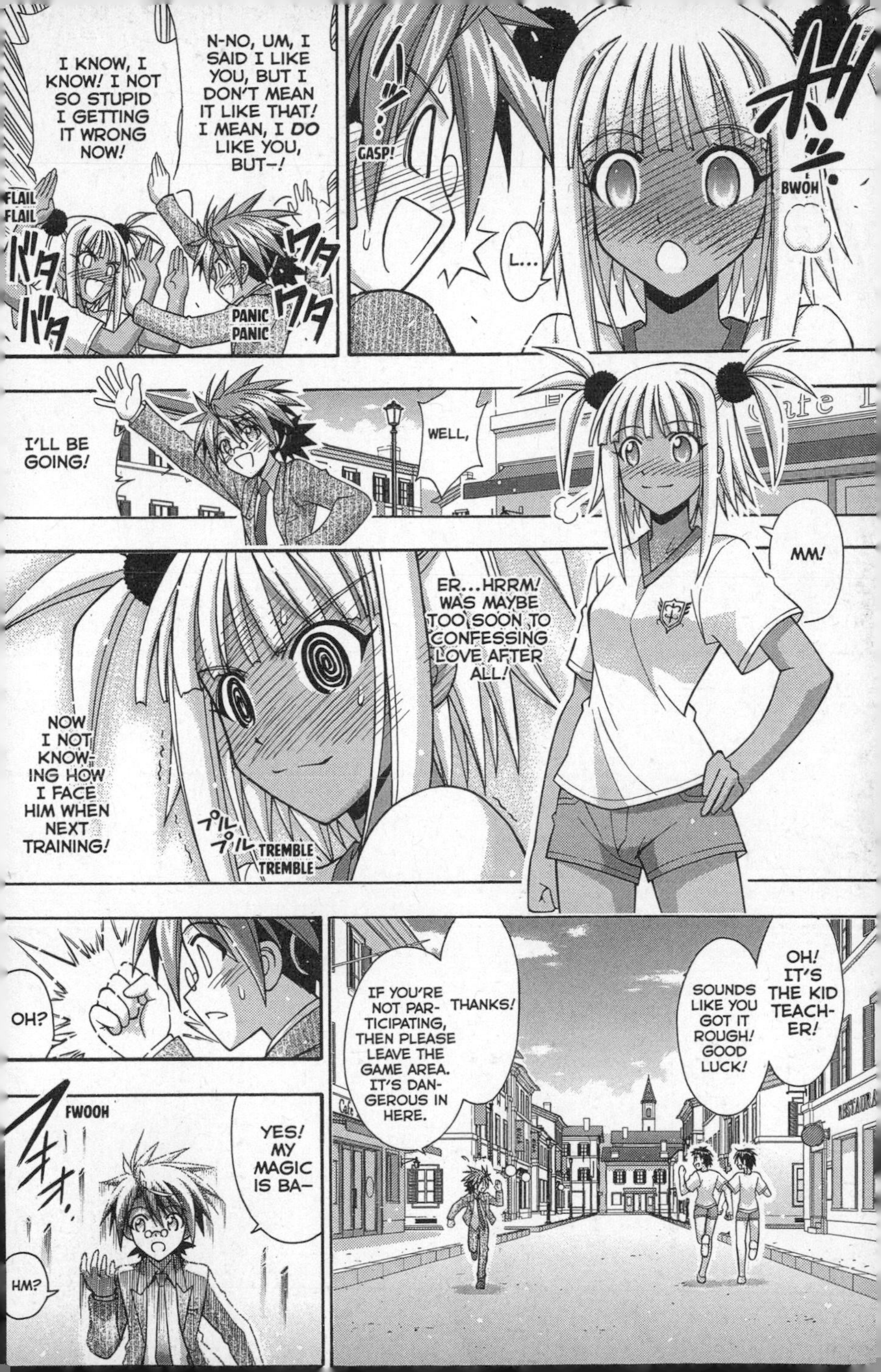
BWOH
L...
GASP!
N-NO, UM, I SAID I LIKE YOU, BUT I DON'T MEAN IT LIKE THAT! I MEAN, I *DO* LIKE YOU, BUT–!
I KNOW, I KNOW! I NOT SO STUPID I GETTING IT WRONG NOW!
FLAIL FLAIL
PANIC PANIC
WELL,
I'LL BE GOING!
MM!
ER...HRRM! WAS MAYBE TOO SOON TO CONFESSING LOVE AFTER ALL!
NOW I NOT KNOW-ING HOW I FACE HIM WHEN NEXT TRAINING!
TREMBLE TREMBLE
OH! IT'S THE KID TEACH-ER!
SOUNDS LIKE YOU GOT IT ROUGH! GOOD LUCK!
THANKS!
IF YOU'RE NOT PAR-TICIPATING, THEN PLEASE LEAVE THE GAME AREA. IT'S DAN-GEROUS IN HERE.
OH?
YES! MY MAGIC IS BA–
FWOOH
HM?

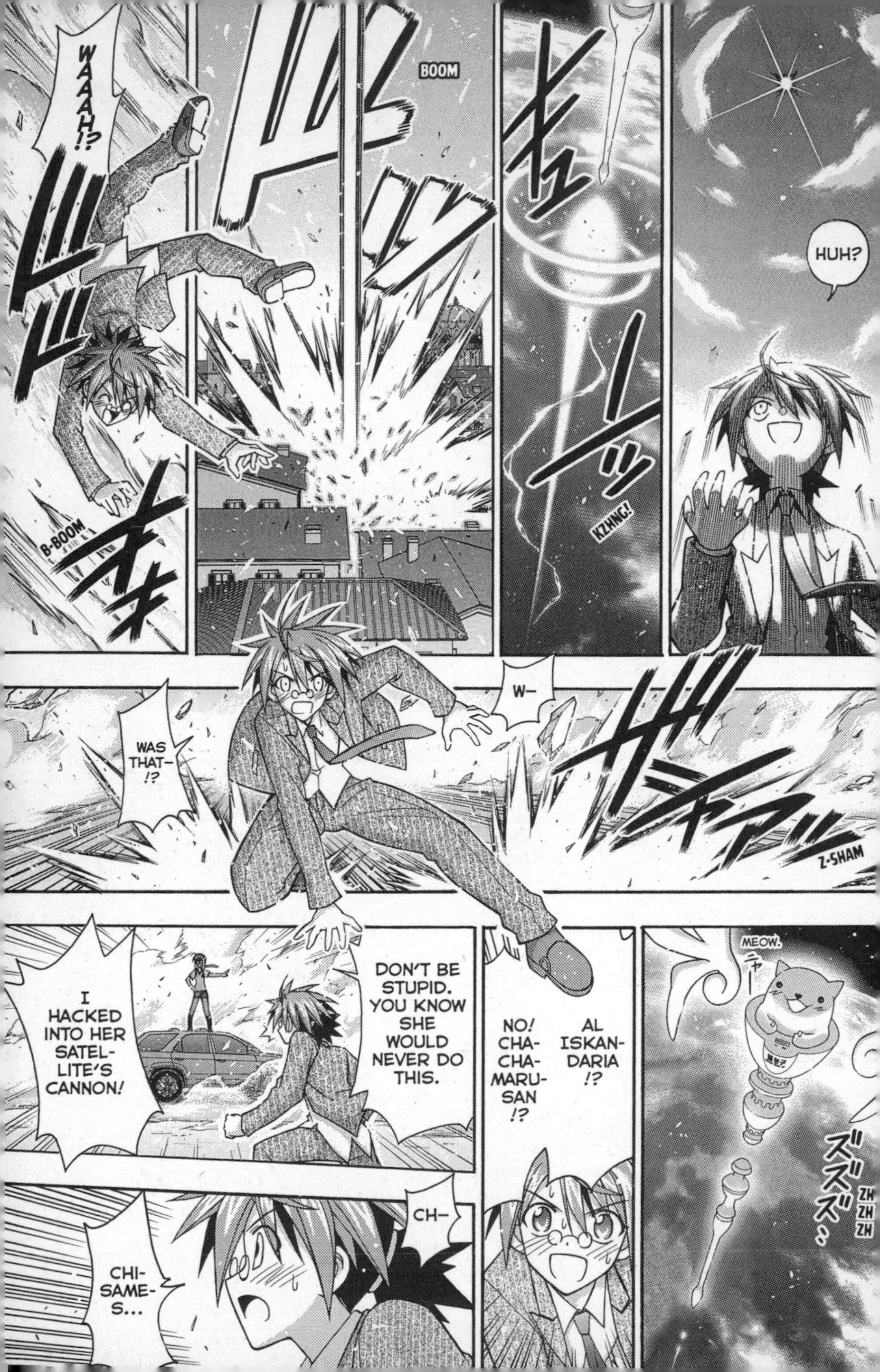
HUH?
KZHNG!
BOOM
WAAAAH!?
B-BOOM
Z-SHAM
W—
WAS THAT—!?
MEOW.
ZH ZH ZH
AL ISKANDARIA!?
NO! CHACHAMARU-SAN!?
DON'T BE STUPID. YOU KNOW SHE WOULD NEVER DO THIS.
I HACKED INTO HER SATELLITE'S CANNON!
CH—
CHISAMES...

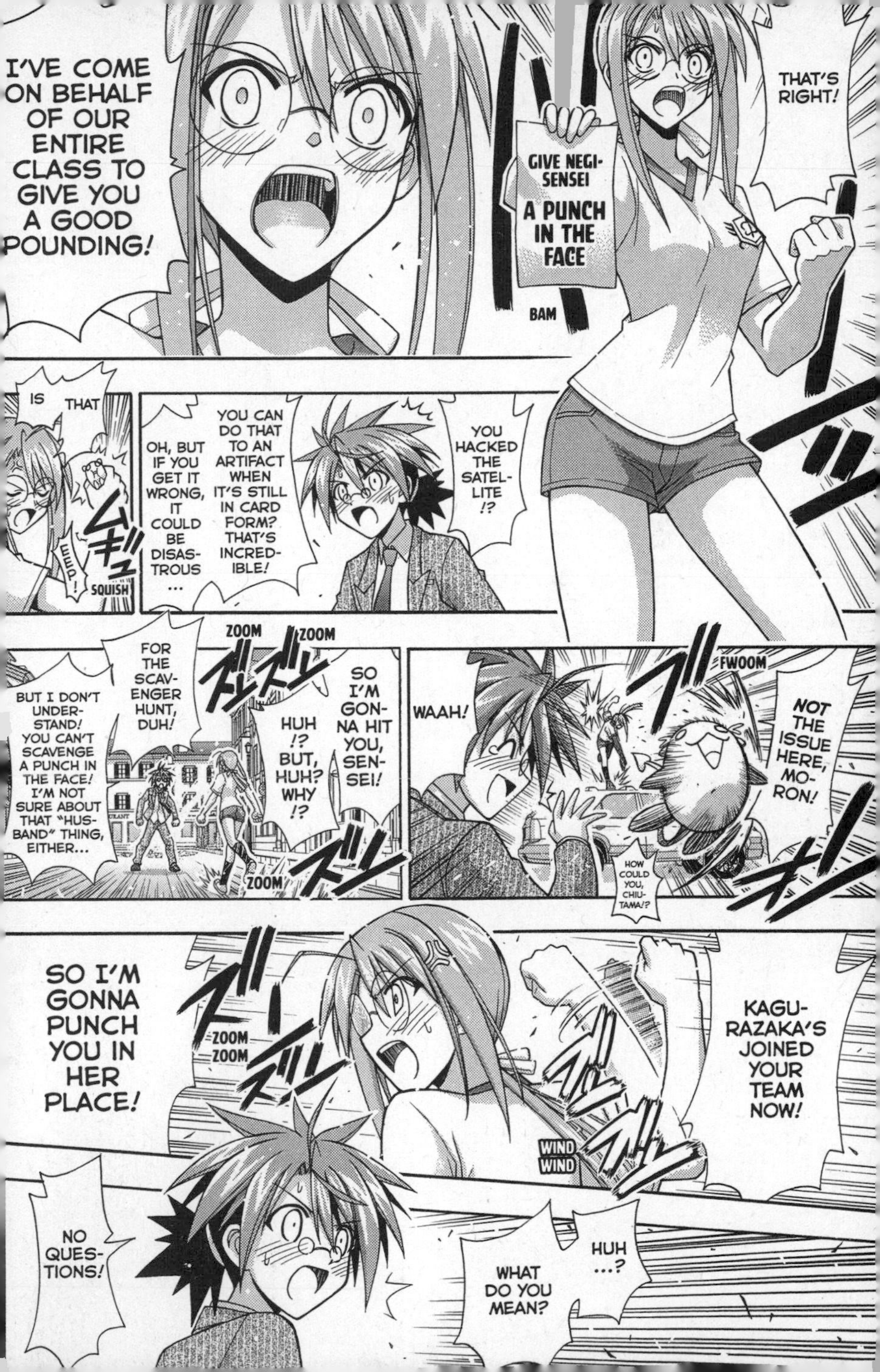
THAT'S RIGHT!
GIVE NEGI-SENSEI A PUNCH IN THE FACE
BAM
I'VE COME ON BEHALF OF OUR ENTIRE CLASS TO GIVE YOU A GOOD POUNDING!
YOU HACKED THE SATELLITE!?
YOU CAN DO THAT TO AN ARTIFACT WHEN IT'S STILL IN CARD FORM? THAT'S INCREDIBLE!
OH, BUT IF YOU GET IT WRONG, IT COULD BE DISASTROUS...
IS THAT
EEP!
SQUISH
NOT THE ISSUE HERE, MORON!
FWOOM
WAAH!
HOW COULD YOU, CHIUTAMA!?
SO I'M GONNA HIT YOU, SENSEI!
ZOOM
ZOOM
HUH!? BUT, HUH? WHY!?
FOR THE SCAVENGER HUNT, DUH!
BUT I DON'T UNDERSTAND! YOU CAN'T SCAVENGE A PUNCH IN THE FACE! I'M NOT SURE ABOUT THAT "HUSBAND" THING, EITHER...
ZOOM
KAGURAZAKA'S JOINED YOUR TEAM NOW!
WIND WIND
ZOOM ZOOM
SO I'M GONNA PUNCH YOU IN HER PLACE!
HUH...?
WHAT DO YOU MEAN?
NO QUESTIONS!

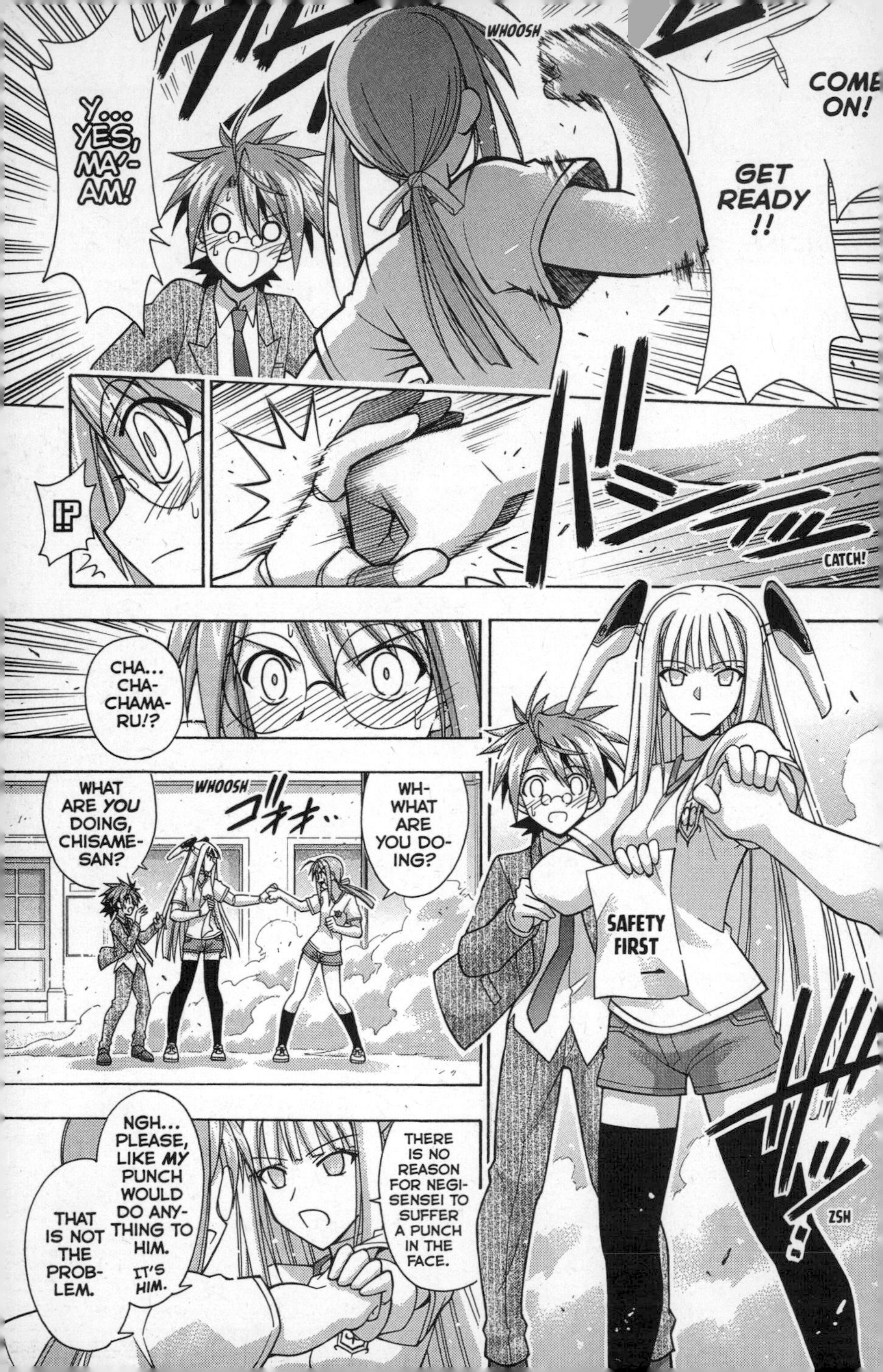
COME ON!
GET READY!!
WHOOSH
Y... YES, MA'-AM!
CATCH!
!?
SAFETY FIRST
ZSH
CHA... CHA-CHAMA-RU!?
WH-WHAT ARE YOU DO-ING?
WHOOSH
WHAT ARE YOU DOING, CHISAME-SAN?
THERE IS NO REASON FOR NEGI-SENSEI TO SUFFER A PUNCH IN THE FACE.
NGH... PLEASE, LIKE MY PUNCH WOULD DO ANYTHING TO HIM.
IT'S HIM.
THAT IS NOT THE PROBLEM.

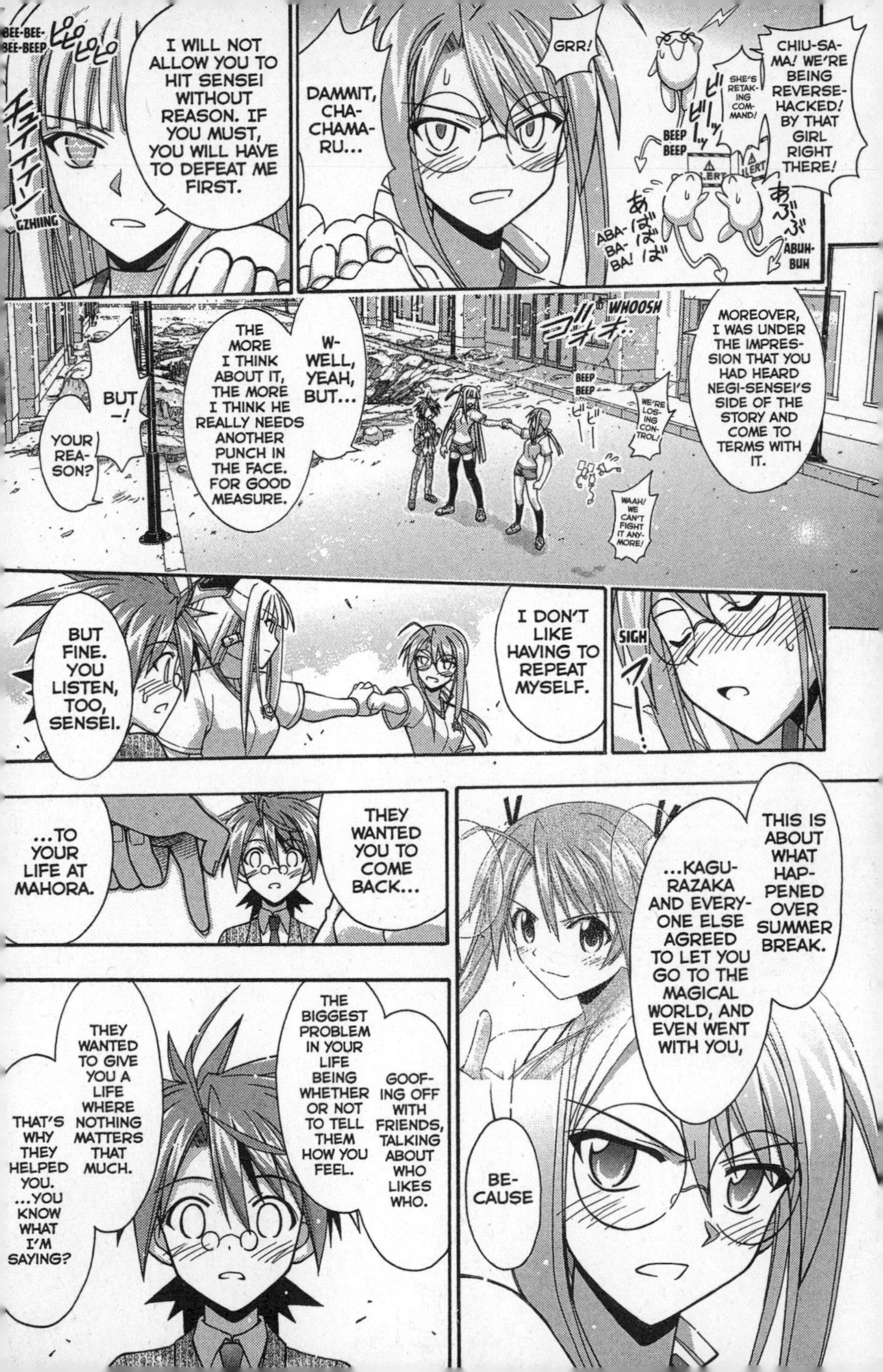

CHIU-SAMA! WE'RE BEING REVERSE-HACKED! BY THAT GIRL RIGHT THERE!
SHE'S RETAKING COMMAND!
BEEP BEEP
ALERT
ABA-BA-BA!
ABUH-BUH
GRR!
DAMMIT, CHA-CHAMA-RU...
I WILL NOT ALLOW YOU TO HIT SENSEI WITHOUT REASON. IF YOU MUST, YOU WILL HAVE TO DEFEAT ME FIRST.
BEE-BEE-BEE-BEEP
GZHIING
MOREOVER, I WAS UNDER THE IMPRESSION THAT YOU HAD HEARD NEGI-SENSEI'S SIDE OF THE STORY AND COME TO TERMS WITH IT.
WHOOSH
BEEP BEEP
WE'RE LOSING CONTROL!
WAAH! WE CAN'T FIGHT IT ANYMORE!
W-WELL, YEAH, BUT...
THE MORE I THINK ABOUT IT, THE MORE I THINK HE REALLY NEEDS ANOTHER PUNCH IN THE FACE. FOR GOOD MEASURE.
BUT—!
YOUR REASON?
SIGH
I DON'T LIKE HAVING TO REPEAT MYSELF.
BUT FINE. YOU LISTEN, TOO, SENSEI.
THIS IS ABOUT WHAT HAPPENED OVER SUMMER BREAK.
...KAGURAZAKA AND EVERYONE ELSE AGREED TO LET YOU GO TO THE MAGICAL WORLD, AND EVEN WENT WITH YOU,
BECAUSE
THEY WANTED YOU TO COME BACK...
...TO YOUR LIFE AT MAHORA.
GOOFING OFF WITH FRIENDS, TALKING ABOUT WHO LIKES WHO.
THE BIGGEST PROBLEM IN YOUR LIFE BEING WHETHER OR NOT TO TELL THEM HOW YOU FEEL.
THEY WANTED TO GIVE YOU A LIFE WHERE NOTHING MATTERS THAT MUCH.
THAT'S WHY THEY HELPED YOU. ...YOU KNOW WHAT I'M SAYING?

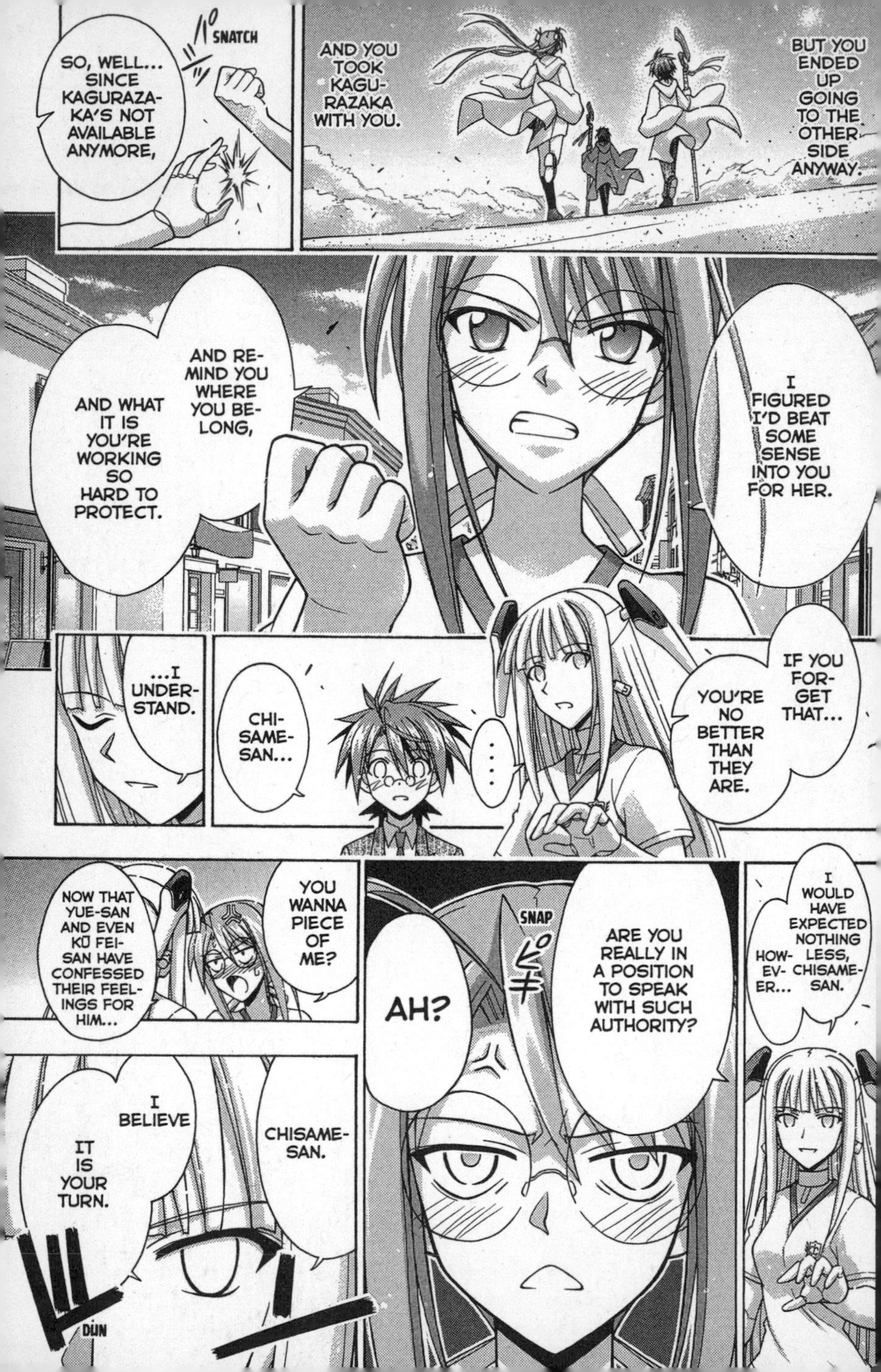
BUT YOU ENDED UP GOING TO THE OTHER SIDE ANYWAY.
AND YOU TOOK KAGURAZAKA WITH YOU.
SNATCH
SO, WELL... SINCE KAGURAZAKA'S NOT AVAILABLE ANYMORE,
SNATCH
I FIGURED I'D BEAT SOME SENSE INTO YOU FOR HER.
AND REMIND YOU WHERE YOU BELONG,
AND WHAT IT IS YOU'RE WORKING SO HARD TO PROTECT.
IF YOU FORGET THAT...
YOU'RE NO BETTER THAN THEY ARE.
.....
CHISAME-SAN...
...I UNDERSTAND.
I WOULD HAVE EXPECTED NOTHING LESS, CHISAME-SAN.
HOWEVER...
ARE YOU REALLY IN A POSITION TO SPEAK WITH SUCH AUTHORITY?
SNAP
AH?
YOU WANNA PIECE OF ME?
NOW THAT YUE-SAN AND EVEN KŪ FEI-SAN HAVE CONFESSED THEIR FEELINGS FOR HIM...
CHISAME-SAN.
I BELIEVE IT IS YOUR TURN.
DUN

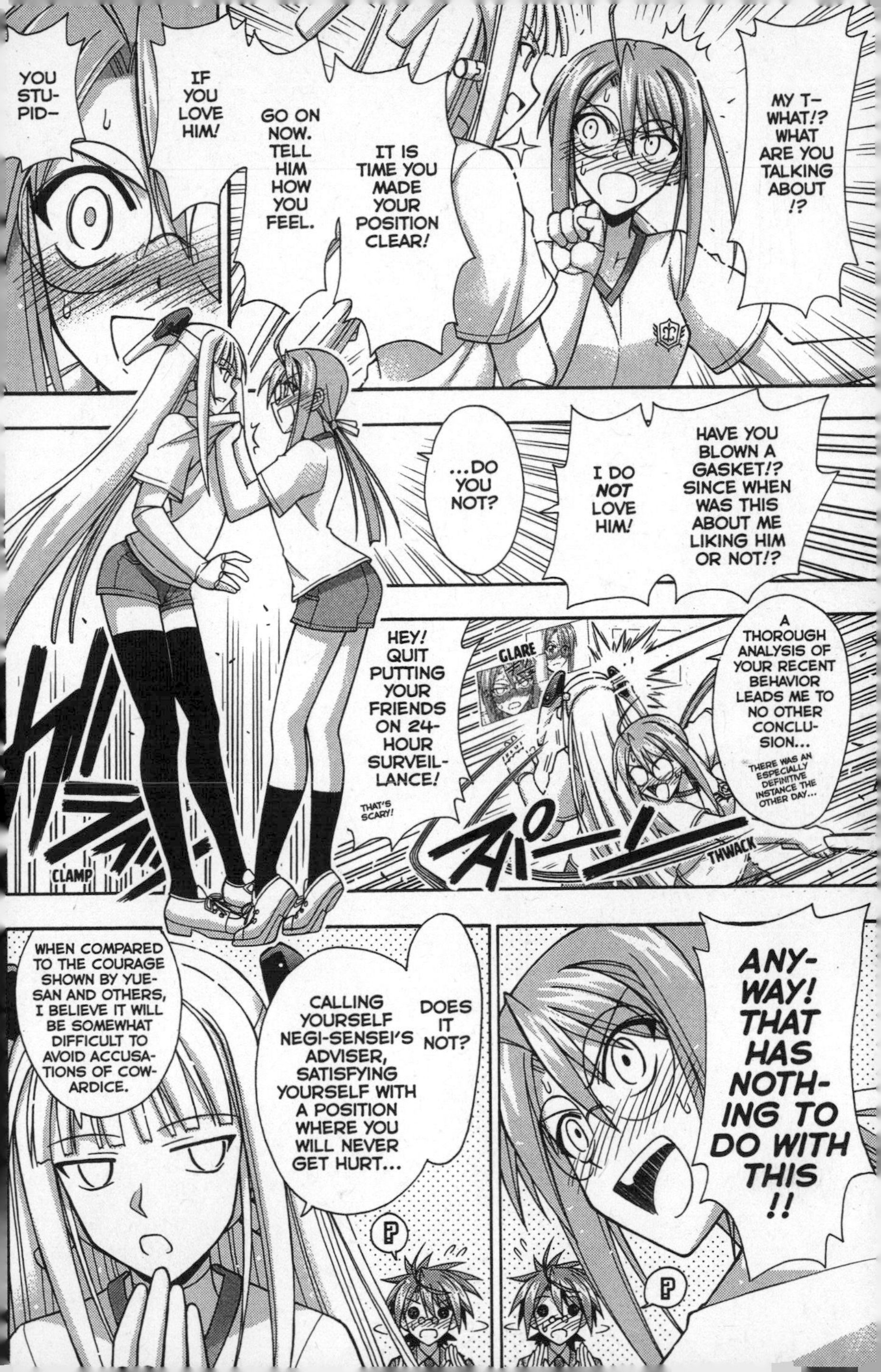
MY T–WHAT!? WHAT ARE YOU TALKING ABOUT !?
IT IS TIME YOU MADE YOUR POSITION CLEAR!
GO ON NOW. TELL HIM HOW YOU FEEL.
IF YOU LOVE HIM!
YOU STUPID–
HAVE YOU BLOWN A GASKET!? SINCE WHEN WAS THIS ABOUT ME LIKING HIM OR NOT!?
I DO NOT LOVE HIM!
...DO YOU NOT?
A THOROUGH ANALYSIS OF YOUR RECENT BEHAVIOR LEADS ME TO NO OTHER CONCLUSION...
THERE WAS AN ESPECIALLY DEFINITIVE INSTANCE THE OTHER DAY...
GLARE
HEY! QUIT PUTTING YOUR FRIENDS ON 24-HOUR SURVEILLANCE!
THAT'S SCARY!
THWACK
CLAMP
ANY-WAY! THAT HAS NOTHING TO DO WITH THIS!!
DOES IT NOT?
CALLING YOURSELF NEGI-SENSEI'S ADVISER, SATISFYING YOURSELF WITH A POSITION WHERE YOU WILL NEVER GET HURT...
WHEN COMPARED TO THE COURAGE SHOWN BY YUE-SAN AND OTHERS, I BELIEVE IT WILL BE SOMEWHAT DIFFICULT TO AVOID ACCUSATIONS OF COWARDICE.

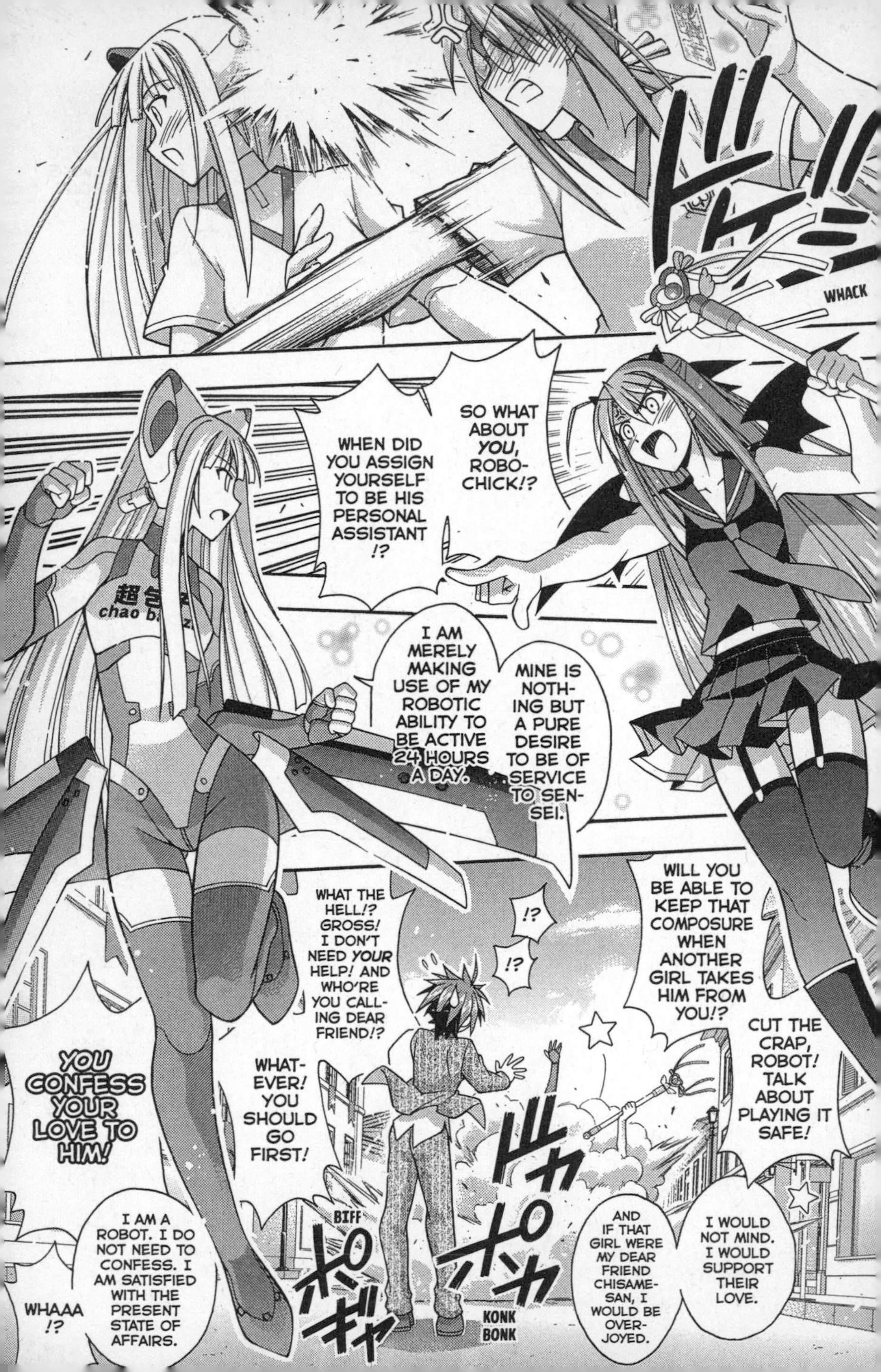
WHACK
SO WHAT ABOUT YOU, ROBO-CHICK!?
WHEN DID YOU ASSIGN YOURSELF TO BE HIS PERSONAL ASSISTANT!?
MINE IS NOTHING BUT A PURE DESIRE TO BE OF SERVICE TO SEN-SEI.
I AM MERELY MAKING USE OF MY ROBOTIC ABILITY TO BE ACTIVE 24 HOURS A DAY.
WILL YOU BE ABLE TO KEEP THAT COMPOSURE WHEN ANOTHER GIRL TAKES HIM FROM YOU!?
CUT THE CRAP, ROBOT! TALK ABOUT PLAYING IT SAFE!
!?
!?
WHAT THE HELL!? GROSS! I DON'T NEED YOUR HELP! AND WHO'RE YOU CALLING DEAR FRIEND!?
I WOULD NOT MIND. I WOULD SUPPORT THEIR LOVE.
AND IF THAT GIRL WERE MY DEAR FRIEND CHISAME-SAN, I WOULD BE OVER-JOYED.
WHAT-EVER! YOU SHOULD GO FIRST!
KONK BONK
BIFF
YOU CONFESS YOUR LOVE TO HIM!
I AM A ROBOT. I DO NOT NEED TO CONFESS. I AM SATISFIED WITH THE PRESENT STATE OF AFFAIRS.
WHAAA!?

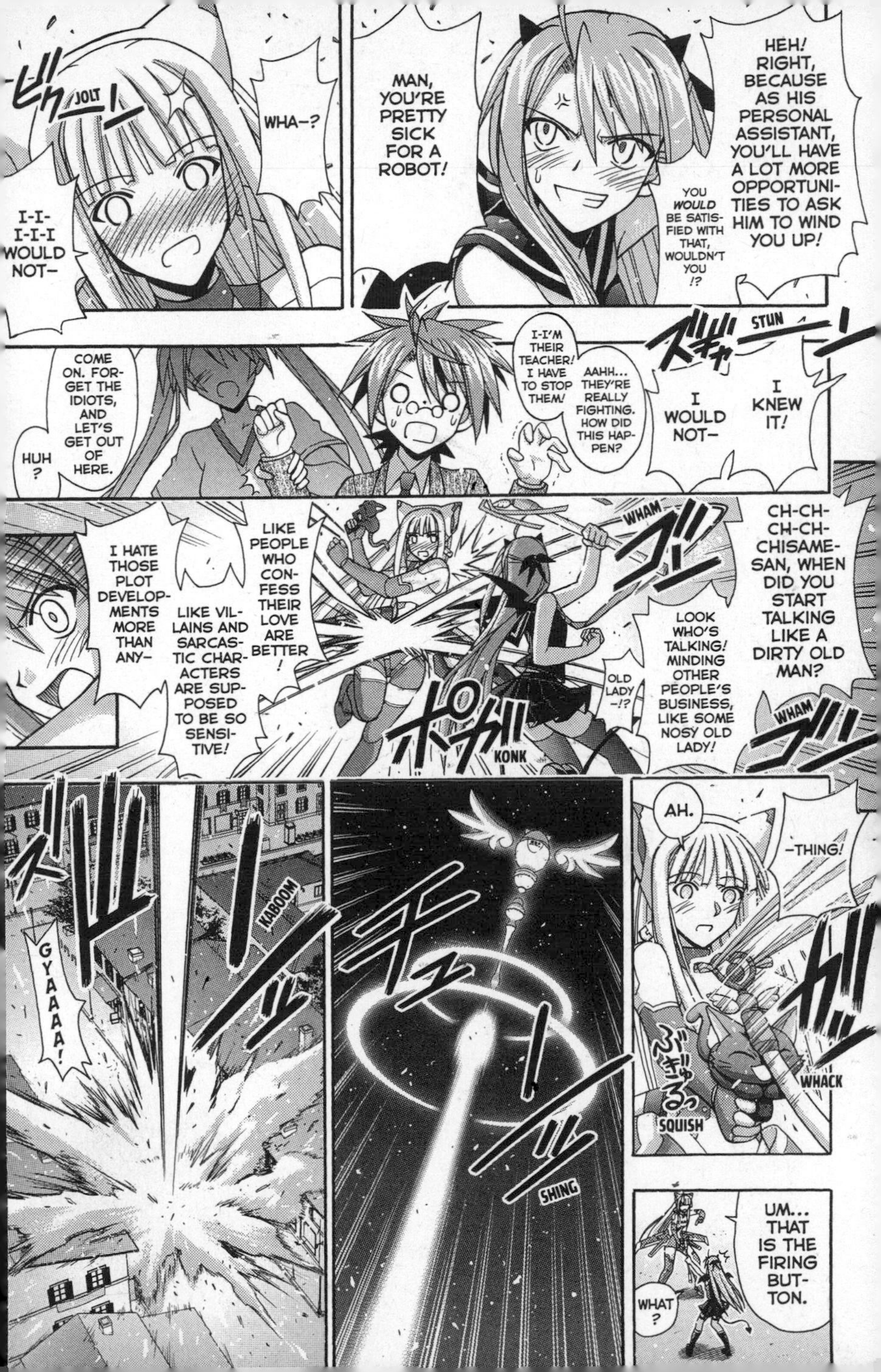
HEH! RIGHT, BECAUSE AS HIS PERSONAL ASSISTANT, YOU'LL HAVE A LOT MORE OPPORTUNITIES TO ASK HIM TO WIND YOU UP!
YOU *WOULD* BE SATISFIED WITH THAT, WOULDN'T YOU!?
MAN, YOU'RE PRETTY SICK FOR A ROBOT!
JOLT
WHA-?
I-I-I-I-I WOULD NOT-
STUN
I KNEW IT!
I WOULD NOT-
AAHH... THEY'RE REALLY FIGHTING. HOW DID THIS HAPPEN?
I-I'M THEIR TEACHER! I HAVE TO STOP THEM!
COME ON. FORGET THE IDIOTS, AND LET'S GET OUT OF HERE.
HUH?
CH-CH-CH-CH-CHISAME-SAN, WHEN DID YOU START TALKING LIKE A DIRTY OLD MAN?
WHAM
WHAM
LOOK WHO'S TALKING! MINDING OTHER PEOPLE'S BUSINESS, LIKE SOME NOSY OLD LADY!
OLD LADY-!?
KONK
LIKE PEOPLE WHO CONFESS THEIR LOVE ARE BETTER!
LIKE VILLAINS AND SARCASTIC CHARACTERS ARE SUPPOSED TO BE SO SENSITIVE!
I HATE THOSE PLOT DEVELOPMENTS MORE THAN ANY-
AH.
-THING!
WHACK
SQUISH
UM... THAT IS THE FIRING BUTTON.
WHAT?
SHING
KABOOM
GYAAAA!

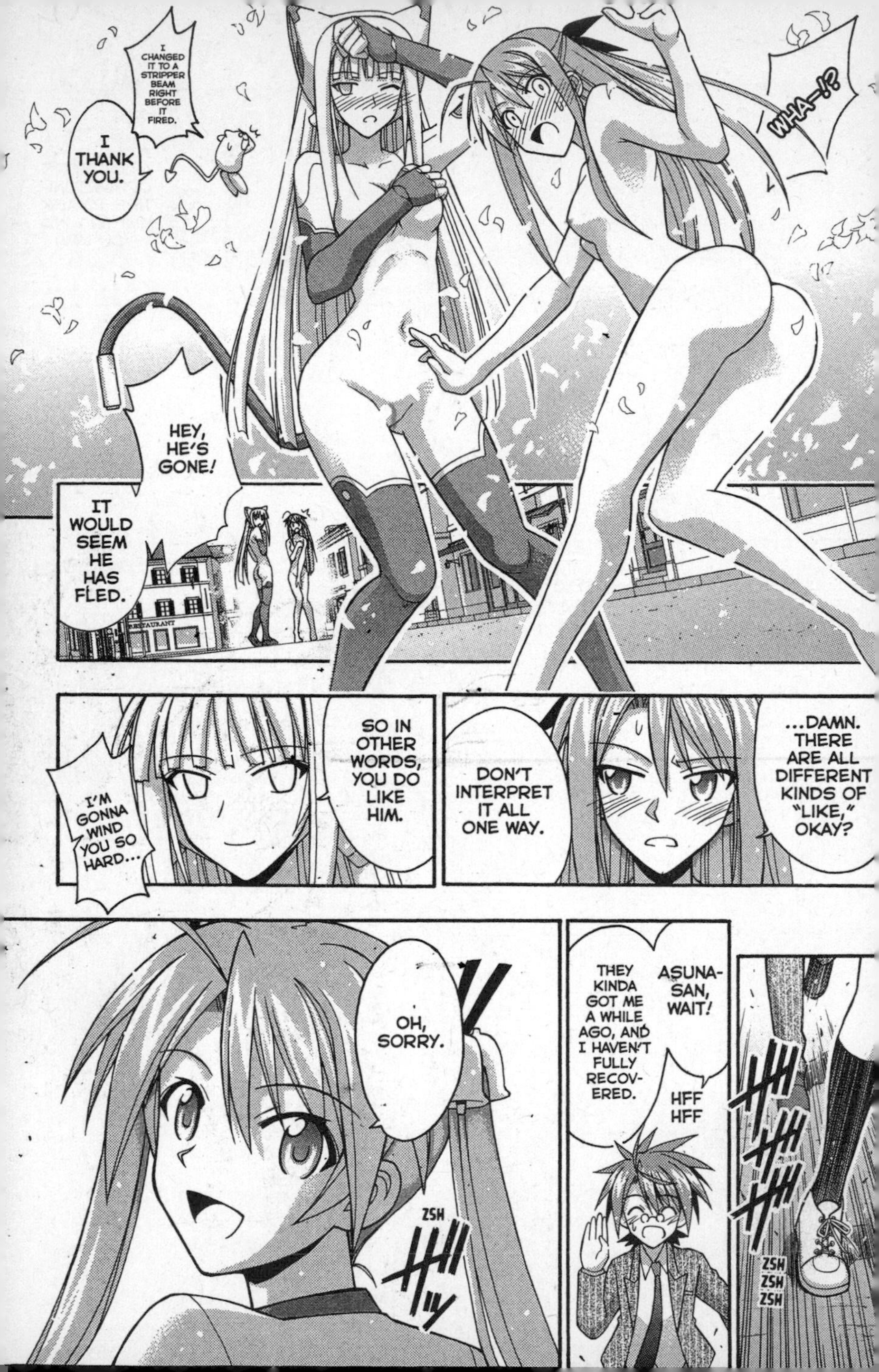
WHA—!?
I CHANGED IT TO A STRIPPER BEAM RIGHT BEFORE IT FIRED.
I THANK YOU.
HEY, HE'S GONE!
IT WOULD SEEM HE HAS FLED.
RESTAURANT
...DAMN. THERE ARE ALL DIFFERENT KINDS OF "LIKE," OKAY?
DON'T INTERPRET IT ALL ONE WAY.
SO IN OTHER WORDS, YOU DO LIKE HIM.
I'M GONNA WIND YOU SO HARD...
ZSH
ZSH
ZSH
ASUNA-SAN, WAIT!
HFF HFF
THEY KINDA GOT ME A WHILE AGO, AND I HAVEN'T FULLY RECOVERED.
OH, SORRY.
ZSH

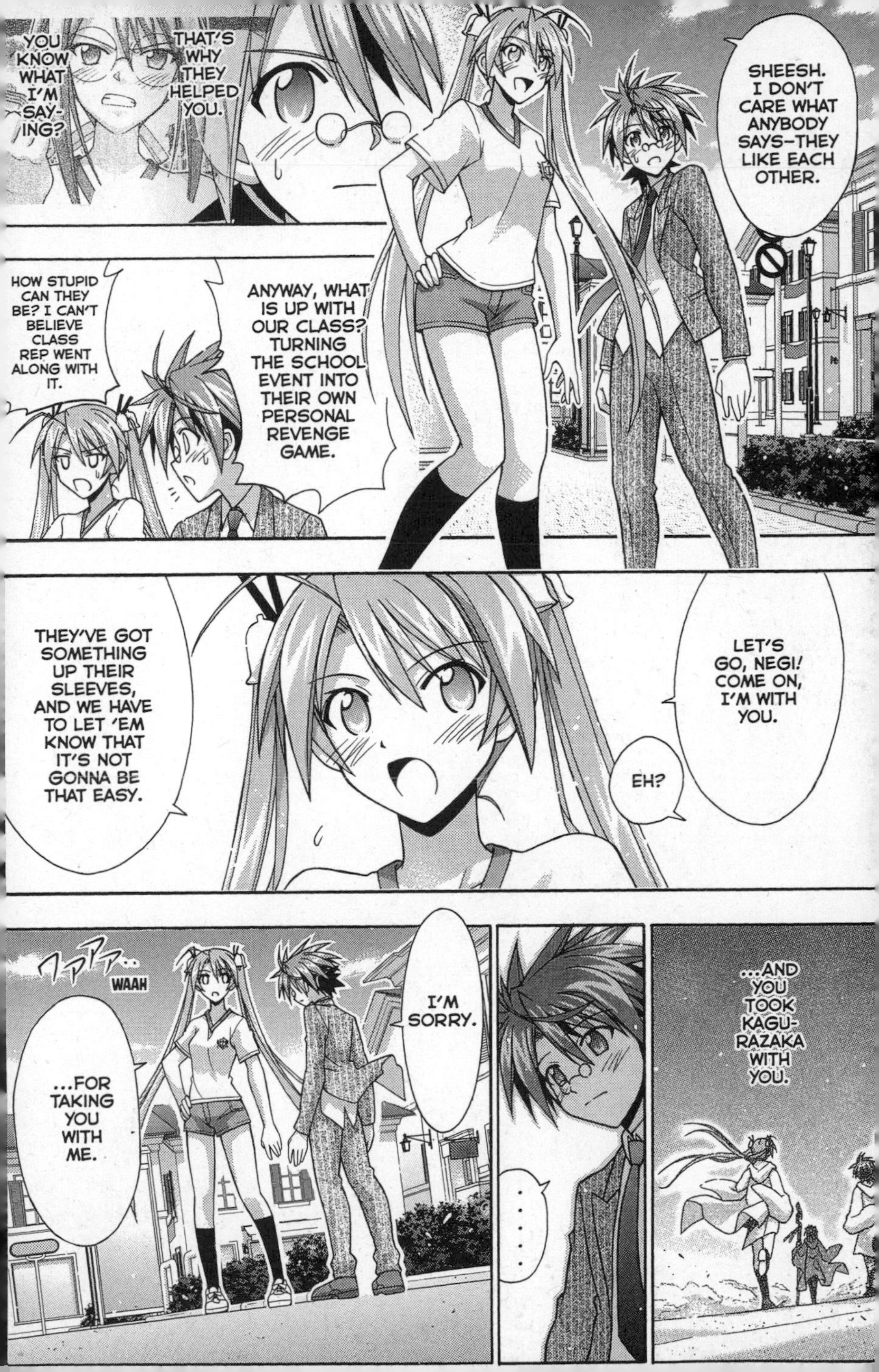
SHEESH. I DON'T CARE WHAT ANYBODY SAYS—THEY LIKE EACH OTHER.
THAT'S WHY THEY HELPED YOU.
YOU KNOW WHAT I'M SAY-ING?
ANYWAY, WHAT IS UP WITH OUR CLASS? TURNING THE SCHOOL EVENT INTO THEIR OWN PERSONAL REVENGE GAME.
HOW STUPID CAN THEY BE? I CAN'T BELIEVE CLASS REP WENT ALONG WITH IT.
LET'S GO, NEGI! COME ON, I'M WITH YOU.
EH?
THEY'VE GOT SOMETHING UP THEIR SLEEVES, AND WE HAVE TO LET 'EM KNOW THAT IT'S NOT GONNA BE THAT EASY.
...AND YOU TOOK KAGU-RAZAKA WITH YOU.
......
I'M SORRY.
ワァァ...
WAAH
...FOR TAKING YOU WITH ME.

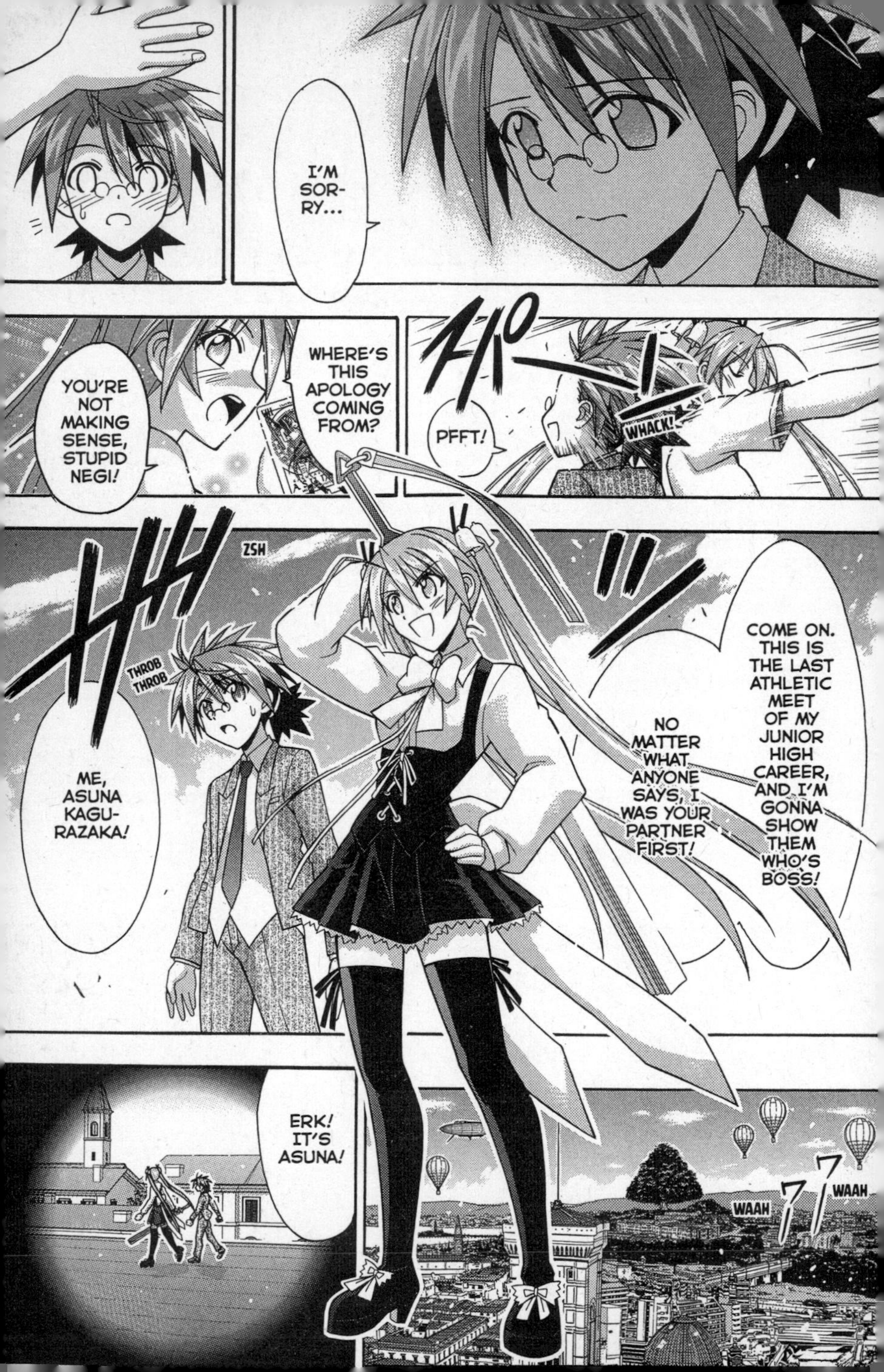
I'M SORRY...
PFFT!
WHACK!
WHERE'S THIS APOLOGY COMING FROM?
YOU'RE NOT MAKING SENSE, STUPID NEGI!
COME ON. THIS IS THE LAST ATHLETIC MEET OF MY JUNIOR HIGH CAREER, AND I'M GONNA SHOW THEM WHO'S BOSS!
NO MATTER WHAT ANYONE SAYS, I WAS YOUR PARTNER FIRST!
ZSH
THROB THROB
ME, ASUNA KAGURAZAKA!
WAAH
WAAH
ERK! IT'S ASUNA!

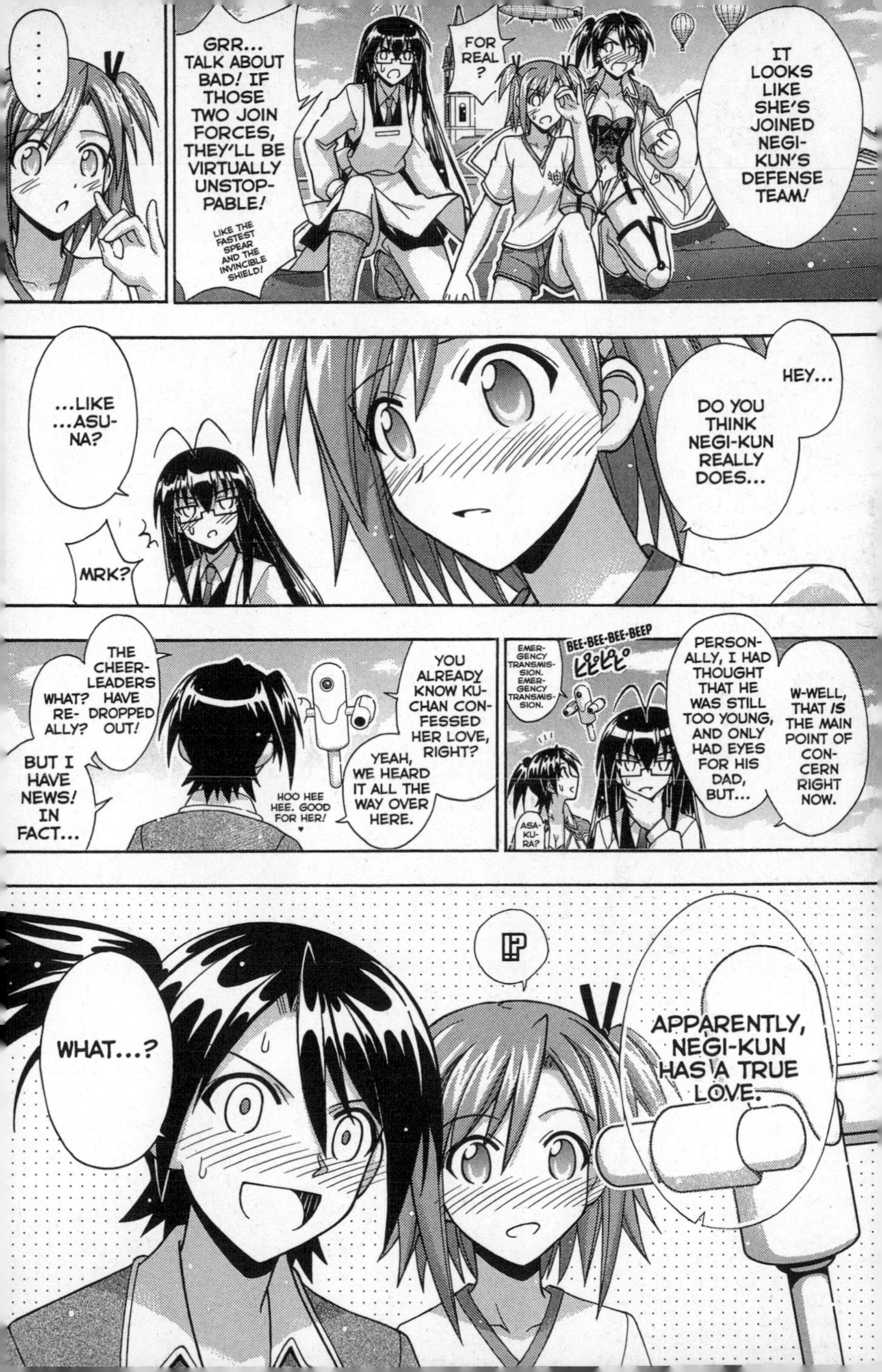

IT LOOKS LIKE SHE'S JOINED NEGI-KUN'S DEFENSE TEAM!
FOR REAL?
GRR... TALK ABOUT BAD! IF THOSE TWO JOIN FORCES, THEY'LL BE VIRTUALLY UNSTOP-PABLE!
LIKE THE FASTEST SPEAR AND THE INVINCIBLE SHIELD!
......
HEY...
DO YOU THINK NEGI-KUN REALLY DOES...
MRK?
...LIKE ...ASU-NA?
PERSON-ALLY, I HAD THOUGHT THAT HE WAS STILL TOO YOUNG, AND ONLY HAD EYES FOR HIS DAD, BUT...
W-WELL, THAT *IS* THE MAIN POINT OF CON-CERN RIGHT NOW.
BEE-BEE-BEE-BEEP
ピピピピ
EMER-GENCY TRANSMIS-SION. EMER-GENCY TRANSMIS-SION.
ASA-KU-RA?
YOU ALREADY KNOW KU-CHAN CON-FESSED HER LOVE, RIGHT?
YEAH, WE HEARD IT ALL THE WAY OVER HERE.
HOO HEE HEE. GOOD FOR HER! ♥
THE CHEER-LEADERS HAVE DROPPED OUT!
WHAT? RE-ALLY?
BUT I HAVE NEWS! IN FACT...
APPARENTLY, NEGI-KUN HAS A TRUE LOVE.
!?
WHAT...?

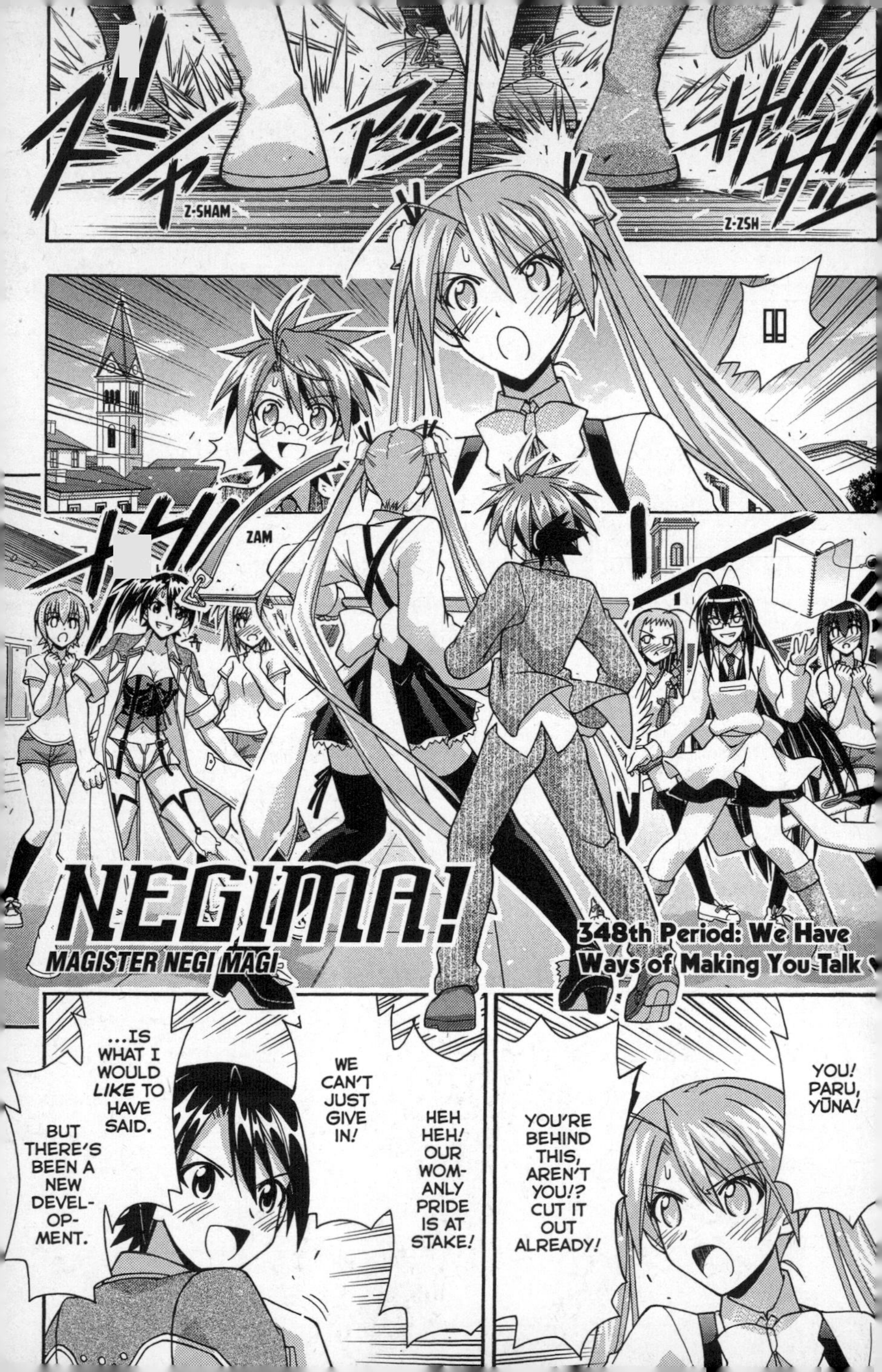
Z-ZSH
Z-SHAM
!!
ZAM
NEGIMA!
MAGISTER NEGI MAGI
348th Period: We Have Ways of Making You Talk
YOU! PARU, YŪNA!
YOU'RE BEHIND THIS, AREN'T YOU!? CUT IT OUT ALREADY!
HEH HEH! OUR WOMANLY PRIDE IS AT STAKE!
WE CAN'T JUST GIVE IN!
...IS WHAT I WOULD *LIKE* TO HAVE SAID.
BUT THERE'S BEEN A NEW DEVELOPMENT.

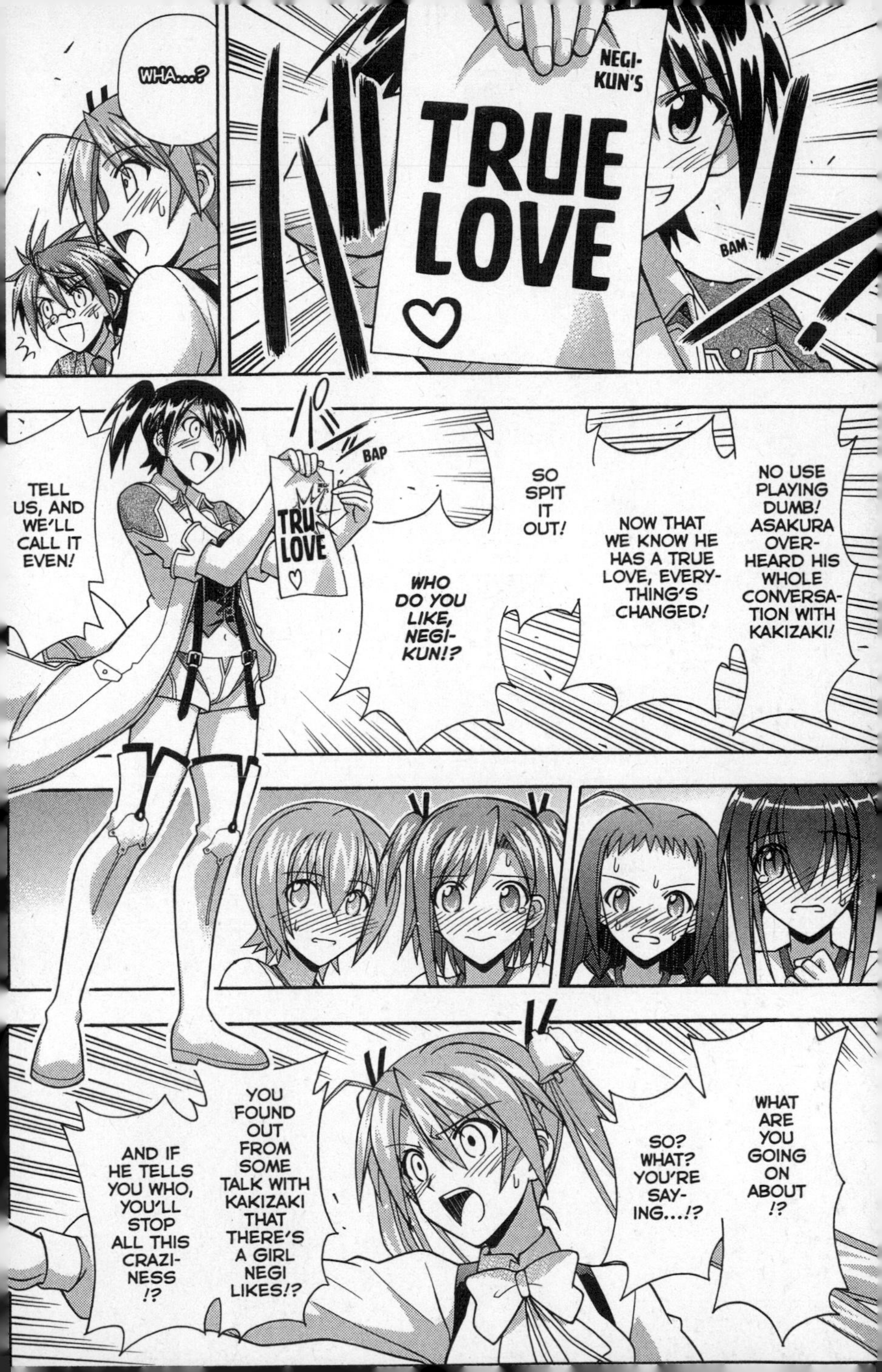
NEGI-KUN'S
TRUE LOVE
BAM
WHA...?
NO USE PLAYING DUMB! ASAKURA OVERHEARD HIS WHOLE CONVERSATION WITH KAKIZAKI!
NOW THAT WE KNOW HE HAS A TRUE LOVE, EVERYTHING'S CHANGED!
SO SPIT IT OUT!
WHO DO YOU LIKE, NEGI-KUN!?
BAP
TRU LOVE
TELL US, AND WE'LL CALL IT EVEN!
WHAT ARE YOU GOING ON ABOUT!?
SO? WHAT? YOU'RE SAYING...!?
YOU FOUND OUT FROM SOME TALK WITH KAKIZAKI THAT THERE'S A GIRL NEGI LIKES!?
AND IF HE TELLS YOU WHO, YOU'LL STOP ALL THIS CRAZINESS!?

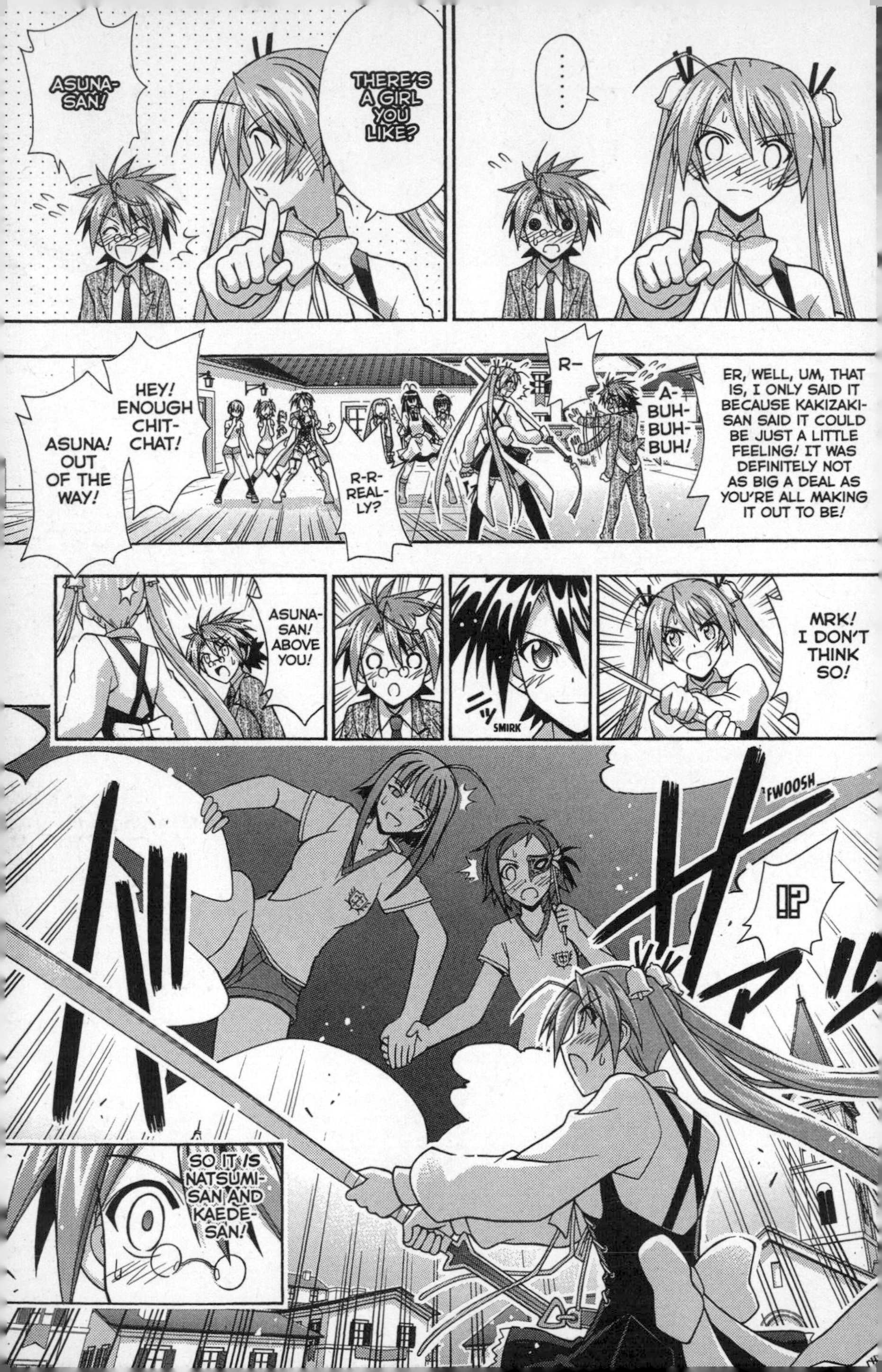
……
THERE'S A GIRL YOU LIKE?
ASUNA-SAN!
ER, WELL, UM, THAT IS, I ONLY SAID IT BECAUSE KAKIZAKI-SAN SAID IT COULD BE JUST A LITTLE FEELING! IT WAS DEFINITELY NOT AS BIG A DEAL AS YOU'RE ALL MAKING IT OUT TO BE!
A-BUH-BUH-BUH!
R–
R-R-REALLY?
HEY! ENOUGH CHIT-CHAT!
ASUNA! OUT OF THE WAY!
MRK! I DON'T THINK SO!
SMIRK
ASUNA-SAN! ABOVE YOU!
FWOOSH
!?
SO IT IS NATSUMI-SAN AND KAEDE-SAN!

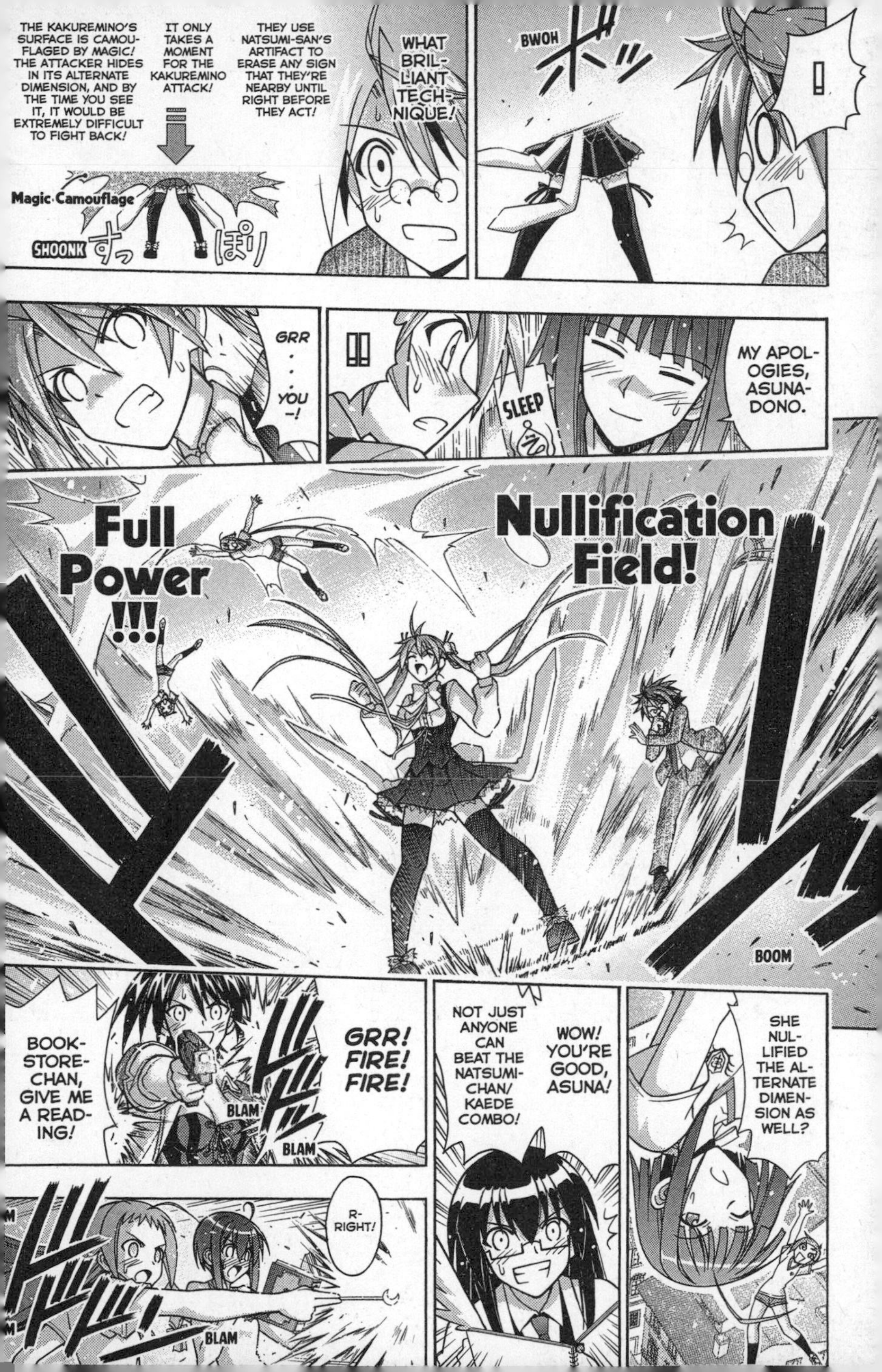
!
BWOH
WHAT BRILLIANT TECHNIQUE!
THEY USE NATSUMI-SAN'S ARTIFACT TO ERASE ANY SIGN THAT THEY'RE NEARBY UNTIL RIGHT BEFORE THEY ACT!
IT ONLY TAKES A MOMENT FOR THE KAKUREMINO ATTACK!
THE KAKUREMINO'S SURFACE IS CAMOUFLAGED BY MAGIC! THE ATTACKER HIDES IN ITS ALTERNATE DIMENSION, AND BY THE TIME YOU SEE IT, IT WOULD BE EXTREMELY DIFFICULT TO FIGHT BACK!
Magic Camouflage
SHOONK
MY APOLOGIES, ASUNA-DONO.
SLEEP
!!
GRR... YOU—!
Nullification Field!
Full Power!!!
BOOM
SHE NULLIFIED THE ALTERNATE DIMENSION AS WELL?
WOW! YOU'RE GOOD, ASUNA!
NOT JUST ANYONE CAN BEAT THE NATSUMI-CHAN/KAEDE COMBO!
GRR! FIRE! FIRE!
BOOKSTORE-CHAN, GIVE ME A READING!
BLAM
BLAM
R-RIGHT!
BLAM

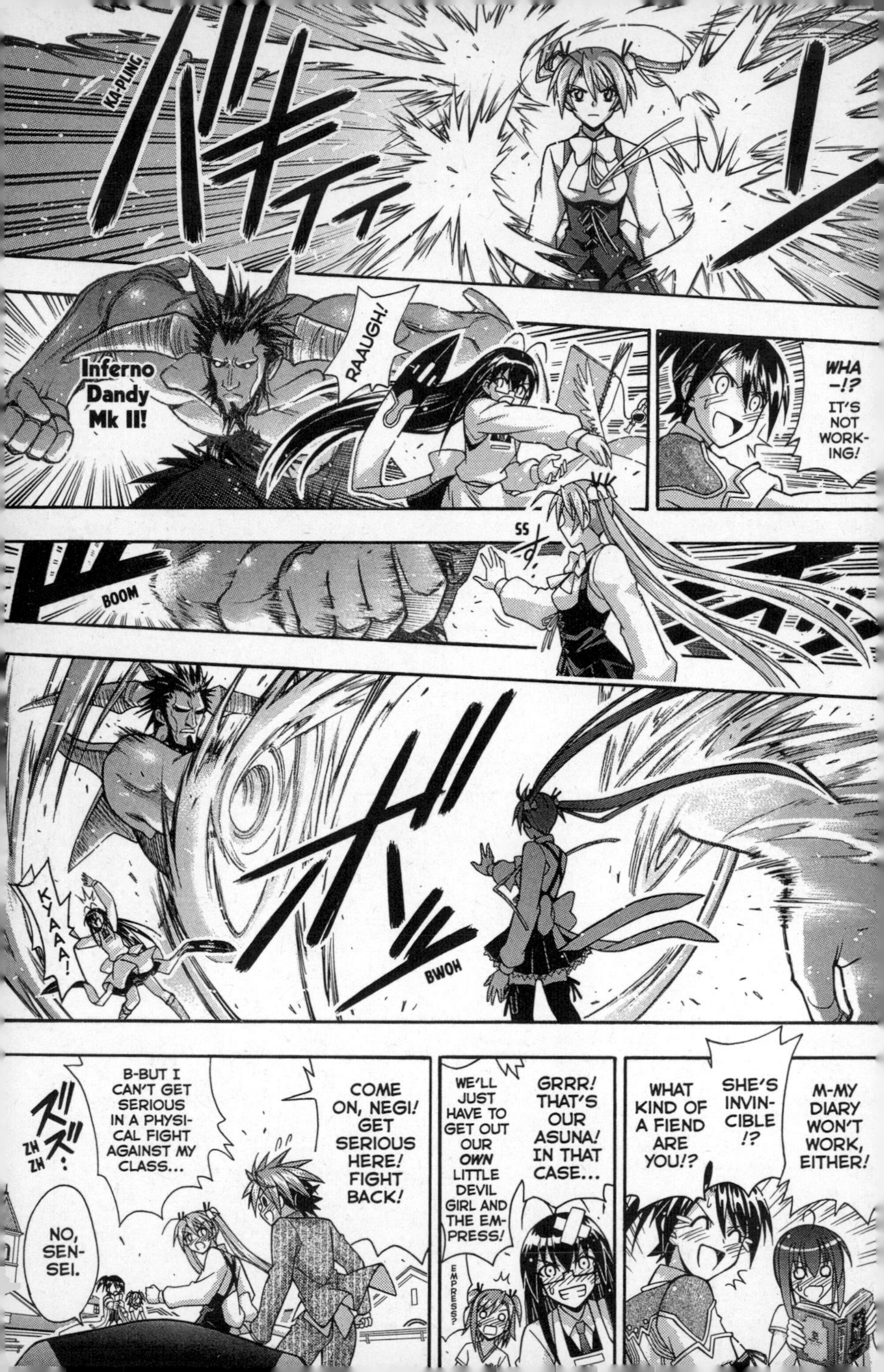
KA-PLING
WHA—!? IT'S NOT WORKING!
RAAUGH!
Inferno Dandy Mk II!
SS
BOOM
BWOH
KYAAA!
M-MY DIARY WON'T WORK, EITHER!
SHE'S INVINCIBLE!?
WHAT KIND OF A FIEND ARE YOU!?
GRRR! THAT'S OUR ASUNA! IN THAT CASE...
WE'LL JUST HAVE TO GET OUT OUR OWN LITTLE DEVIL GIRL AND THE EMPRESS!
EMPRESS?
COME ON, NEGI! GET SERIOUS HERE! FIGHT BACK!
B-BUT I CAN'T GET SERIOUS IN A PHYSICAL FIGHT AGAINST MY CLASS...
ZH ZH
NO, SENSEI.

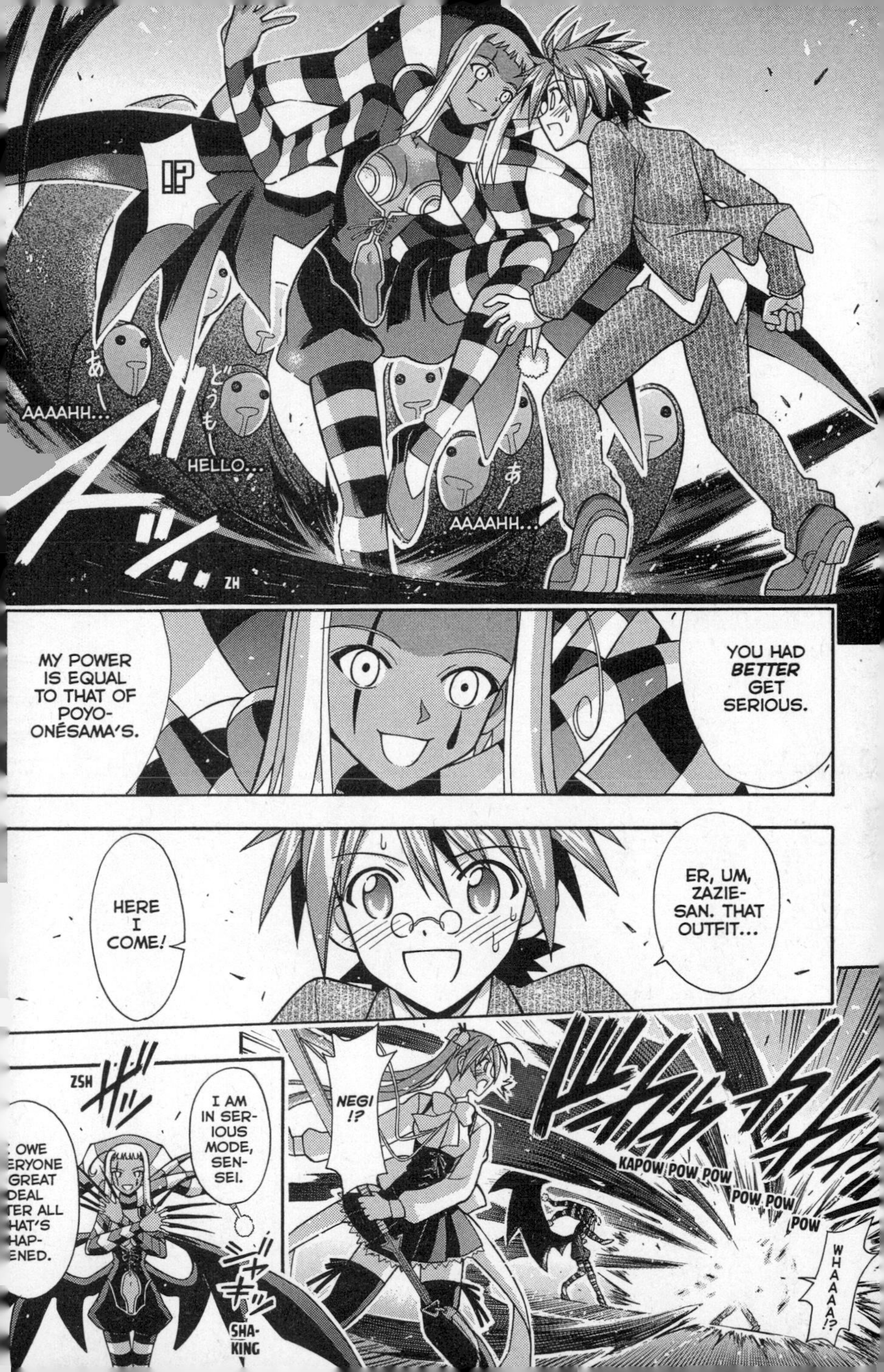
!?
あー
AAAAHH...
どうもー
HELLO...
あー
AAAAHH...
ZH
YOU HAD BETTER GET SERIOUS.
MY POWER IS EQUAL TO THAT OF POYO-ONÉSAMA'S.
ER, UM, ZAZIE-SAN. THAT OUTFIT...
HERE I COME!
KAPOW POW POW POW POW POW
WHAAAAA!?
NEGI!?
SHA-KING
I AM IN SERIOUS MODE, SENSEI.
OWE ERYONE GREAT DEAL TER ALL HAT'S HAP- ENED.
ZSH

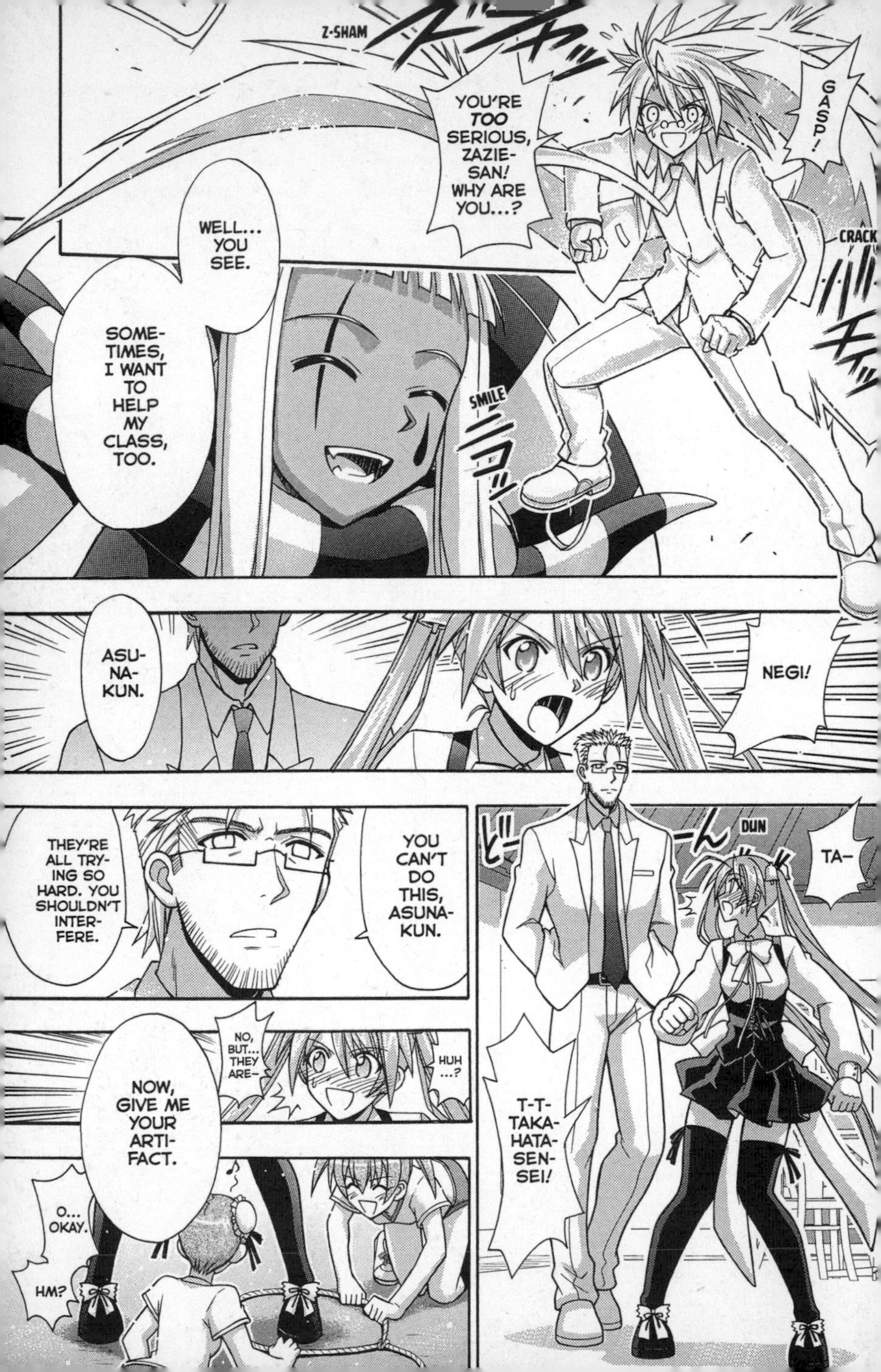
Z-SHAM
GASP!
YOU'RE *TOO* SERIOUS, ZAZIE-SAN! WHY ARE YOU...?
CRACK
WELL... YOU SEE.
SOME-TIMES, I WANT TO HELP MY CLASS, TOO.
SMILE
NEGI!
ASUNA-KUN.
TA-
DUN
T-T-TAKA-HATA-SEN-SEI!
YOU CAN'T DO THIS, ASUNA-KUN.
THEY'RE ALL TRY-ING SO HARD. YOU SHOULDN'T INTER-FERE.
HUH ...?
NO, BUT... THEY ARE—
NOW, GIVE ME YOUR ARTI-FACT.
O... OKAY.
HM?

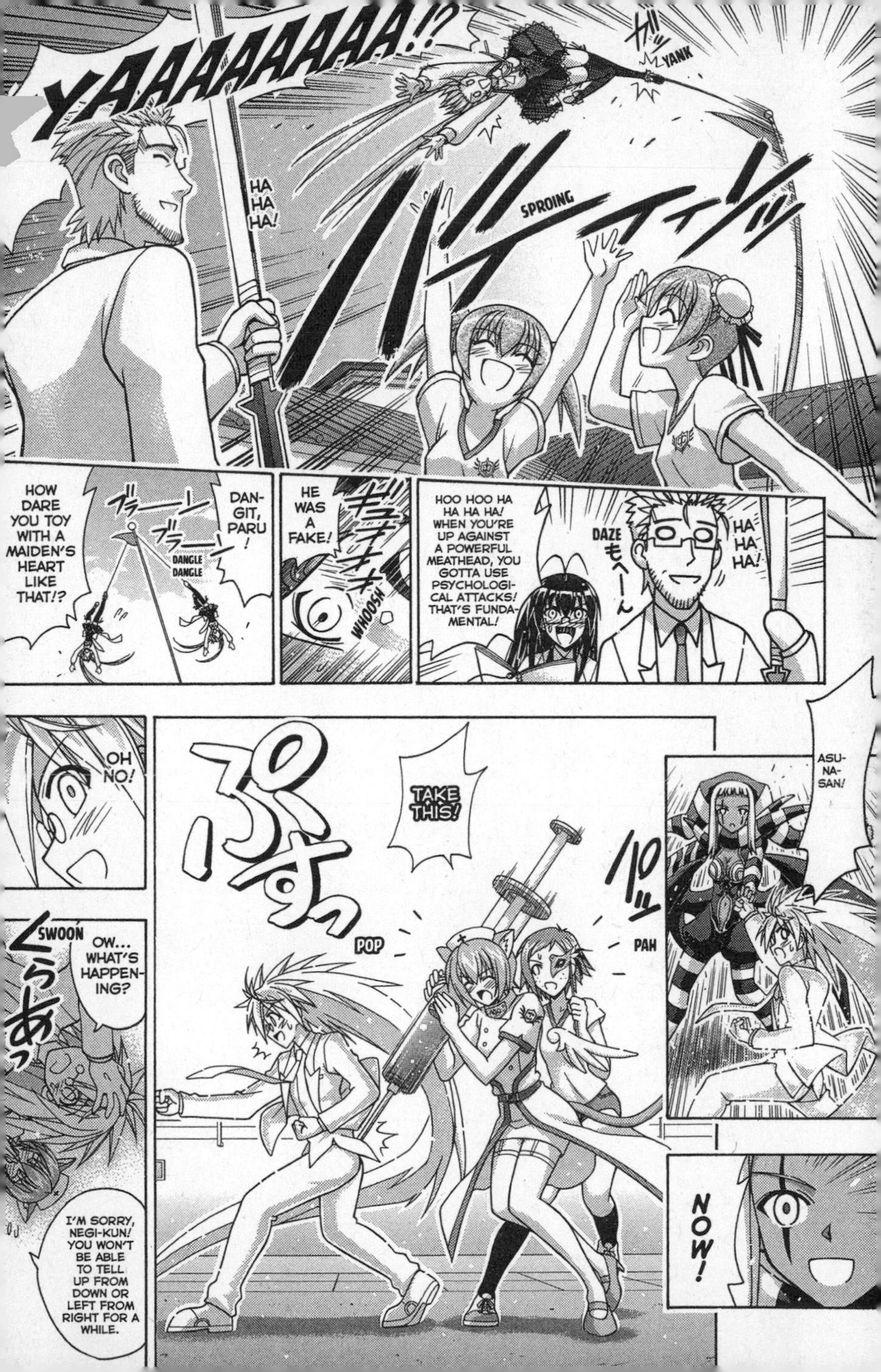
YAAAAAAAAA!?
YANK
HA HA HA!
SPROING
HOO HOO HA HA HA HA! WHEN YOU'RE UP AGAINST A POWERFUL MEATHEAD, YOU GOTTA USE PSYCHOLOGICAL ATTACKS! THAT'S FUNDAMENTAL!
HA HA HA!
DAZE
HE WAS A FAKE!
WHOOSH
DAN-GIT, PARU!
HOW DARE YOU TOY WITH A MAIDEN'S HEART LIKE THAT!?
DANGLE DANGLE
ASU-NA-SAN!
NOW!
TAKE THIS!
ぷすっ
POP
PAH
OH NO!
SWOON
OW... WHAT'S HAPPENING?
I'M SORRY, NEGI-KUN! YOU WON'T BE ABLE TO TELL UP FROM DOWN OR LEFT FROM RIGHT FOR A WHILE.

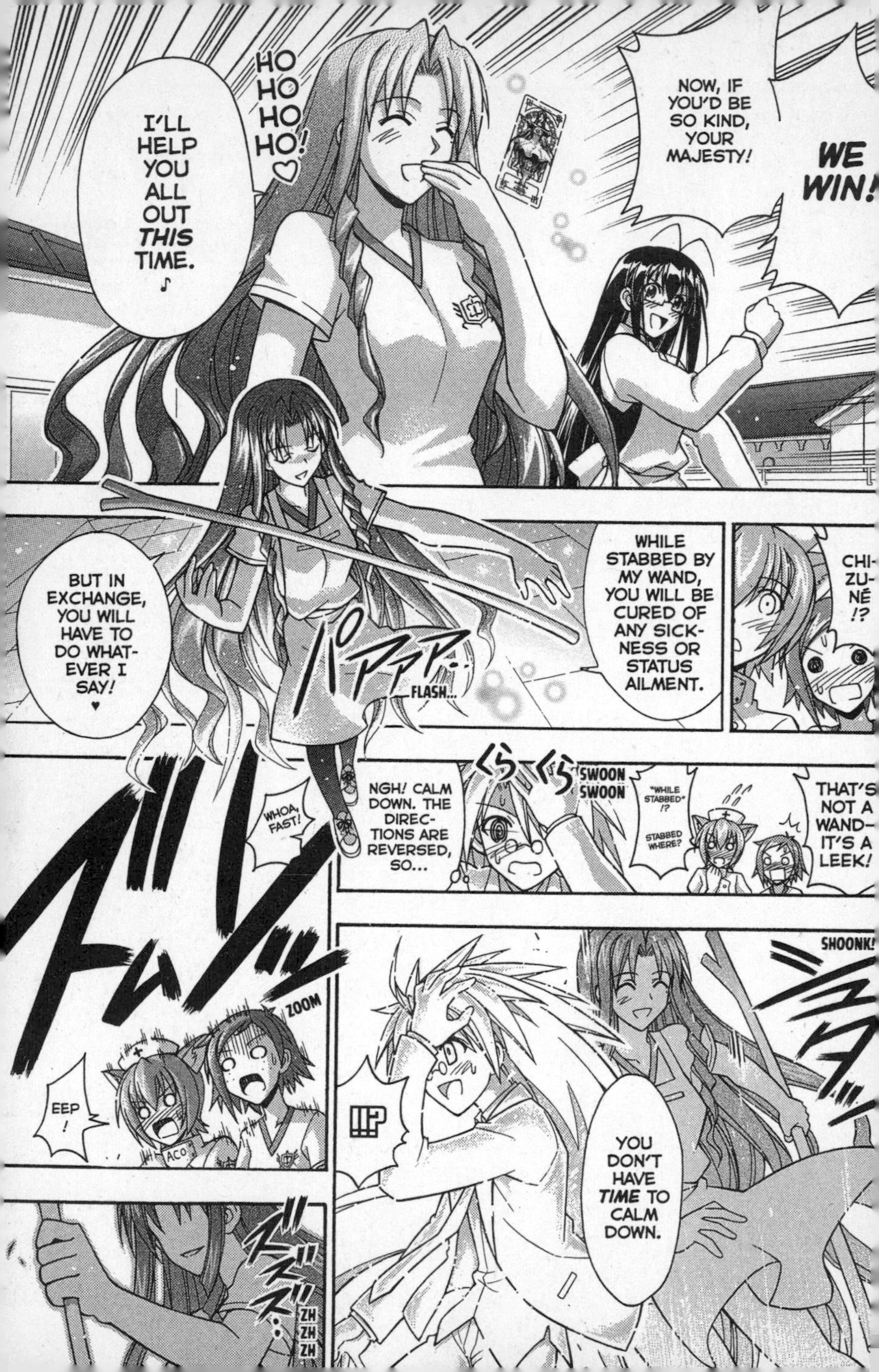
WE WIN!
NOW, IF YOU'D BE SO KIND, YOUR MAJESTY!
HO HO HO HO! ♡
I'LL HELP YOU ALL OUT *THIS* TIME. ♪
CHI-ZU-NÉ!?
WHILE STABBED BY MY WAND, YOU WILL BE CURED OF ANY SICKNESS OR STATUS AILMENT.
FLASH...
BUT IN EXCHANGE, YOU WILL HAVE TO DO WHATEVER I SAY! ♥
THAT'S NOT A WAND—IT'S A LEEK!
"WHILE STABBED"!?
STABBED WHERE?
SWOON SWOON
NGH! CALM DOWN. THE DIRECTIONS ARE REVERSED, SO...
WHOA, FAST!
ZOOM
EEP!
SHOONK!
YOU DON'T HAVE *TIME* TO CALM DOWN.
!!?
ZH ZH ZH

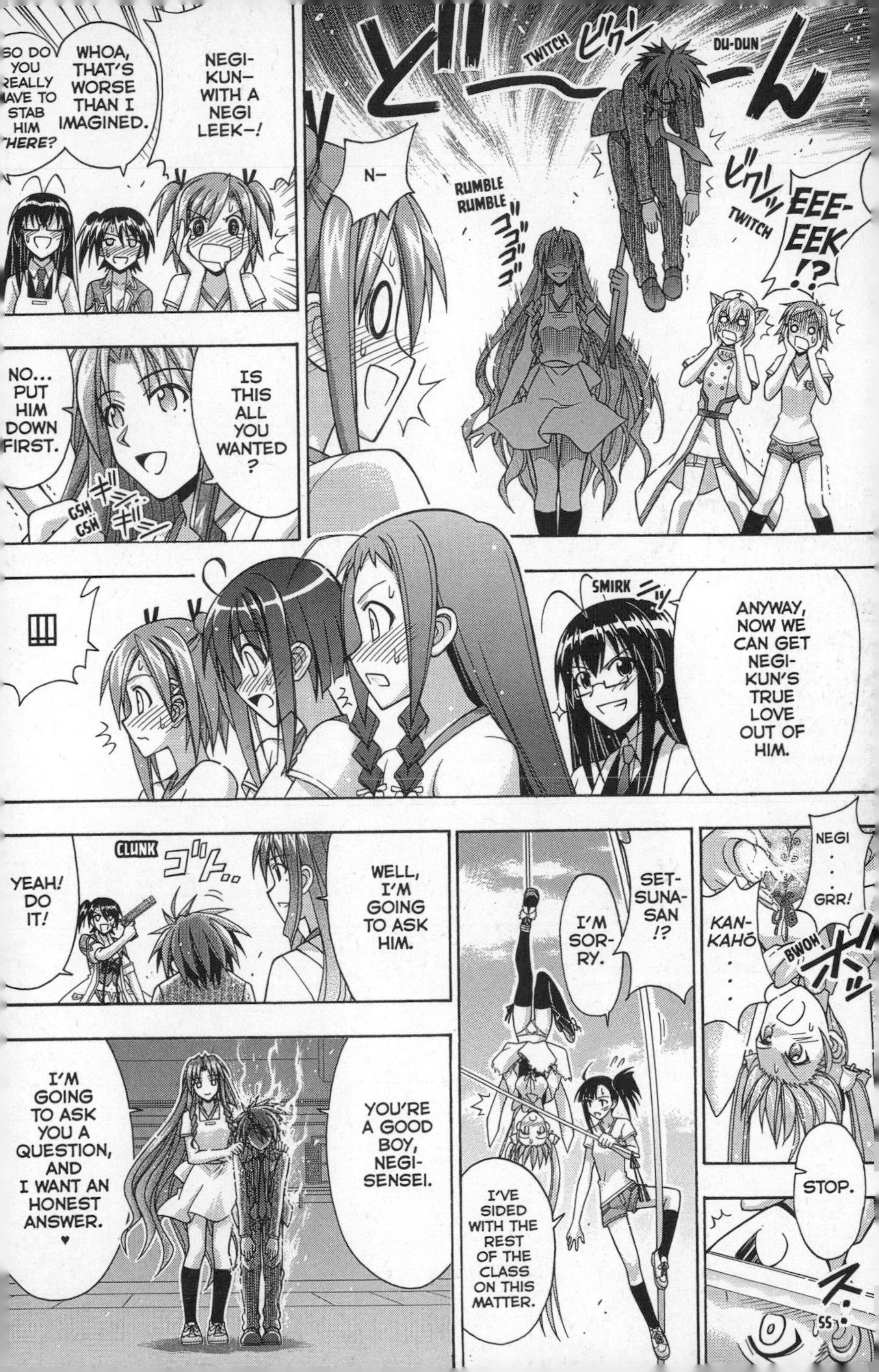
DU-DUN
TWITCH
EEE-EEK!?
TWITCH
RUMBLE RUMBLE
N–
NEGI-KUN–WITH A NEGI LEEK–!
WHOA, THAT'S WORSE THAN I IMAGINED.
SO DO YOU REALLY HAVE TO STAB HIM THERE?
IS THIS ALL YOU WANTED?
NO... PUT HIM DOWN FIRST.
GSH GSH
SMIRK
ANYWAY, NOW WE CAN GET NEGI-KUN'S TRUE LOVE OUT OF HIM.
!!!
NEGI... GRR!
KAN-KAHŌ...
BWOH
STOP.
SS
SET-SUNA-SAN!?
I'M SORRY.
I'VE SIDED WITH THE REST OF THE CLASS ON THIS MATTER.
WELL, I'M GOING TO ASK HIM.
CLUNK
YEAH! DO IT!
YOU'RE A GOOD BOY, NEGI-SENSEI.
I'M GOING TO ASK YOU A QUESTION, AND I WANT AN HONEST ANSWER. ♥

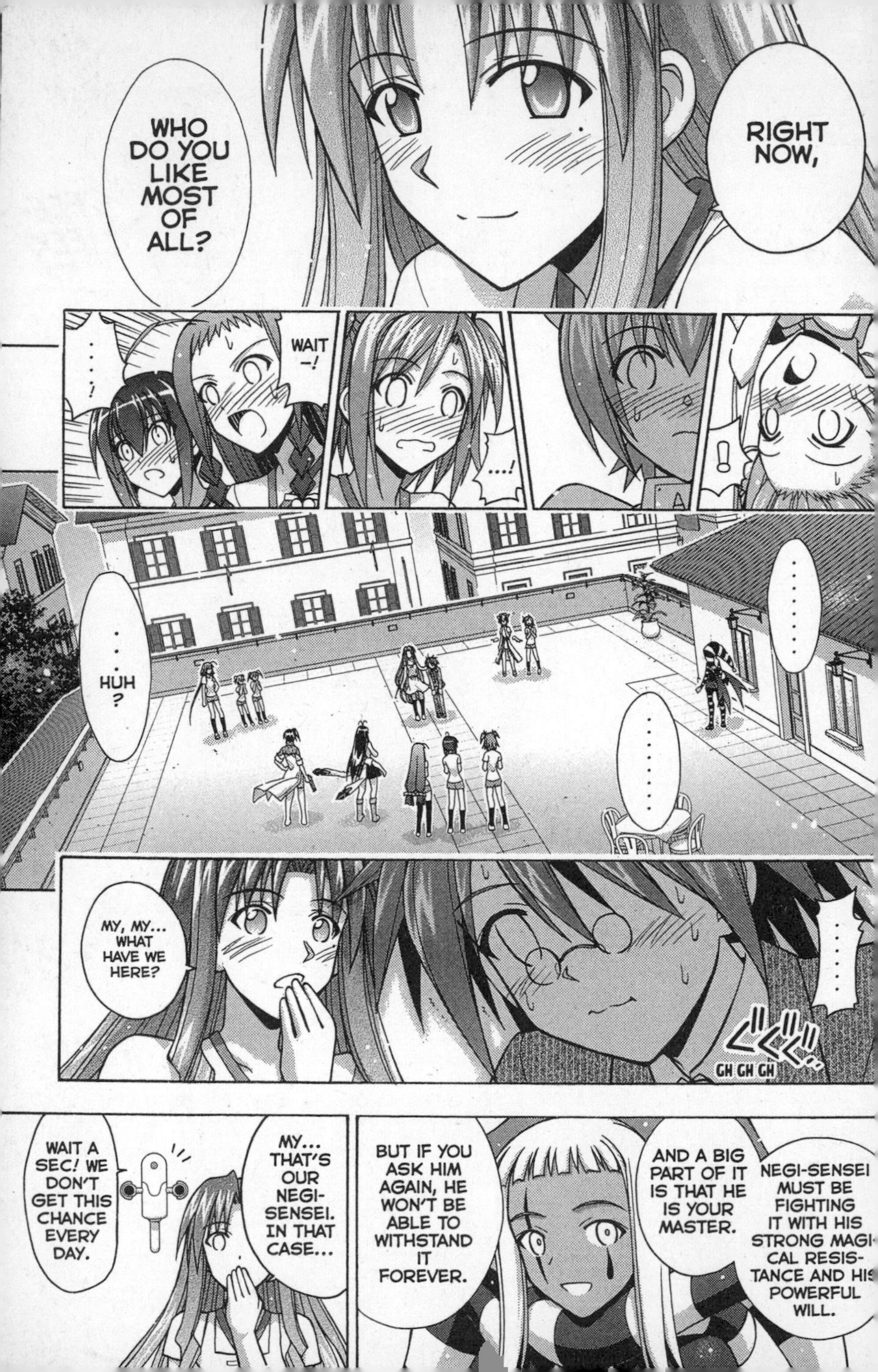
RIGHT NOW,
WHO DO YOU LIKE MOST OF ALL?
!
...!
WAIT —!
...?
......
......
... HUH?
......
GH GH GH
MY, MY... WHAT HAVE WE HERE?
NEGI-SENSEI MUST BE FIGHTING IT WITH HIS STRONG MAGICAL RESISTANCE AND HIS POWERFUL WILL.
AND A BIG PART OF IT IS THAT HE IS YOUR MASTER.
BUT IF YOU ASK HIM AGAIN, HE WON'T BE ABLE TO WITHSTAND IT FOREVER.
MY... THAT'S OUR NEGI-SENSEI. IN THAT CASE...
WAIT A SEC! WE DON'T GET THIS CHANCE EVERY DAY.

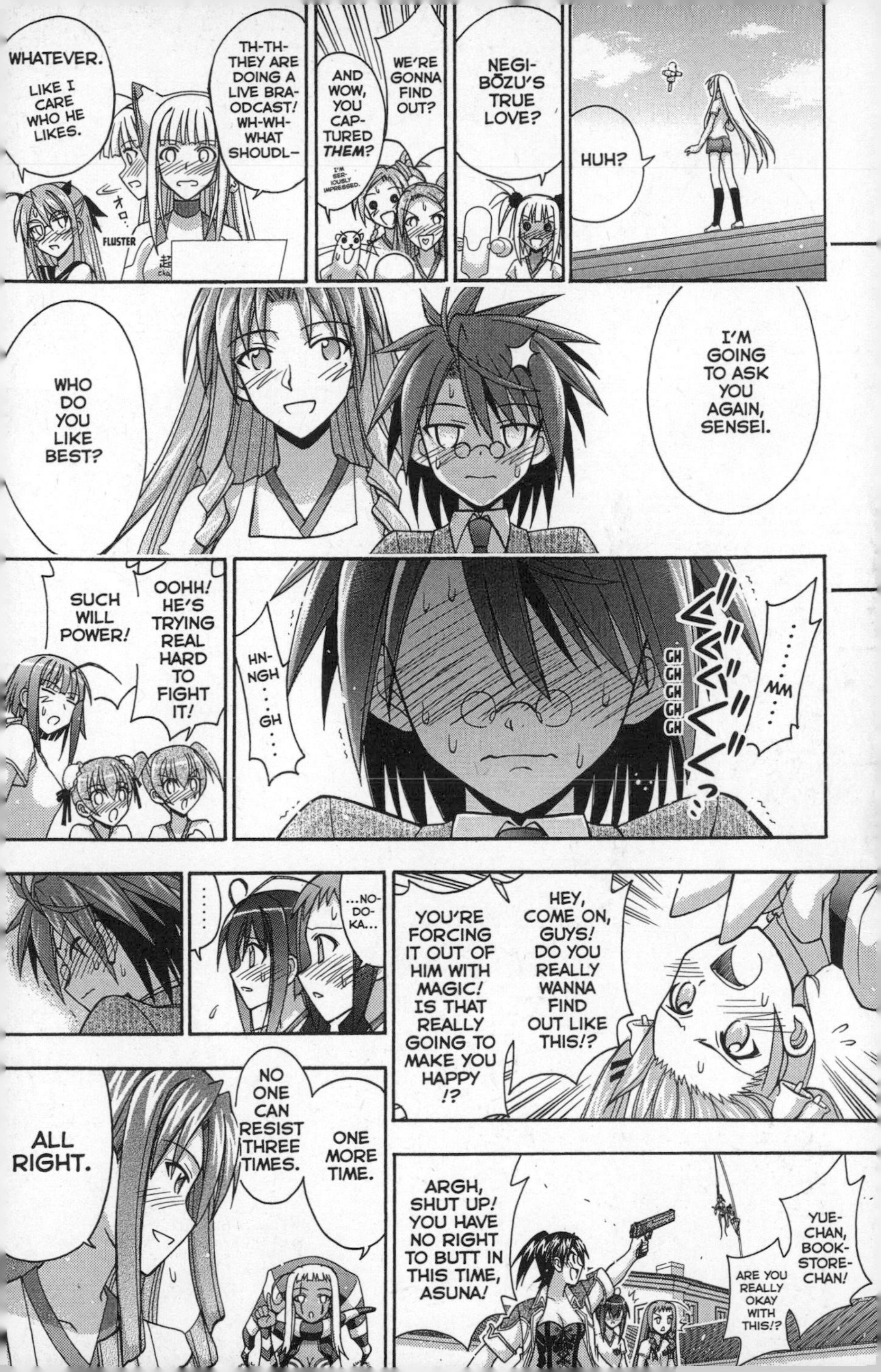
HUH?
NEGI-BŌZU'S TRUE LOVE?
WE'RE GONNA FIND OUT?
AND WOW, YOU CAPTURED THEM?
I'M SERIOUSLY IMPRESSED.
TH-TH-THEY ARE DOING A LIVE BRA-ODCAST! WH-WH-WHAT SHOUDL–
WHATEVER.
LIKE I CARE WHO HE LIKES.
オロ…
FLUSTER
I'M GOING TO ASK YOU AGAIN, SENSEI.
WHO DO YOU LIKE BEST?
......MM......
GH GH GH GH GH
HN-NGH......GH......
OOHH! HE'S TRYING REAL HARD TO FIGHT IT!
SUCH WILL POWER!
HEY, COME ON, GUYS! DO YOU REALLY WANNA FIND OUT LIKE THIS!?
YOU'RE FORCING IT OUT OF HIM WITH MAGIC! IS THAT REALLY GOING TO MAKE YOU HAPPY !?
...NO-DO-KA...
......
YUE-CHAN, BOOKSTORE-CHAN!
ARE YOU REALLY OKAY WITH THIS!?
ARGH, SHUT UP! YOU HAVE NO RIGHT TO BUTT IN THIS TIME, ASUNA!
ONE MORE TIME.
NO ONE CAN RESIST THREE TIMES.
ALL RIGHT.

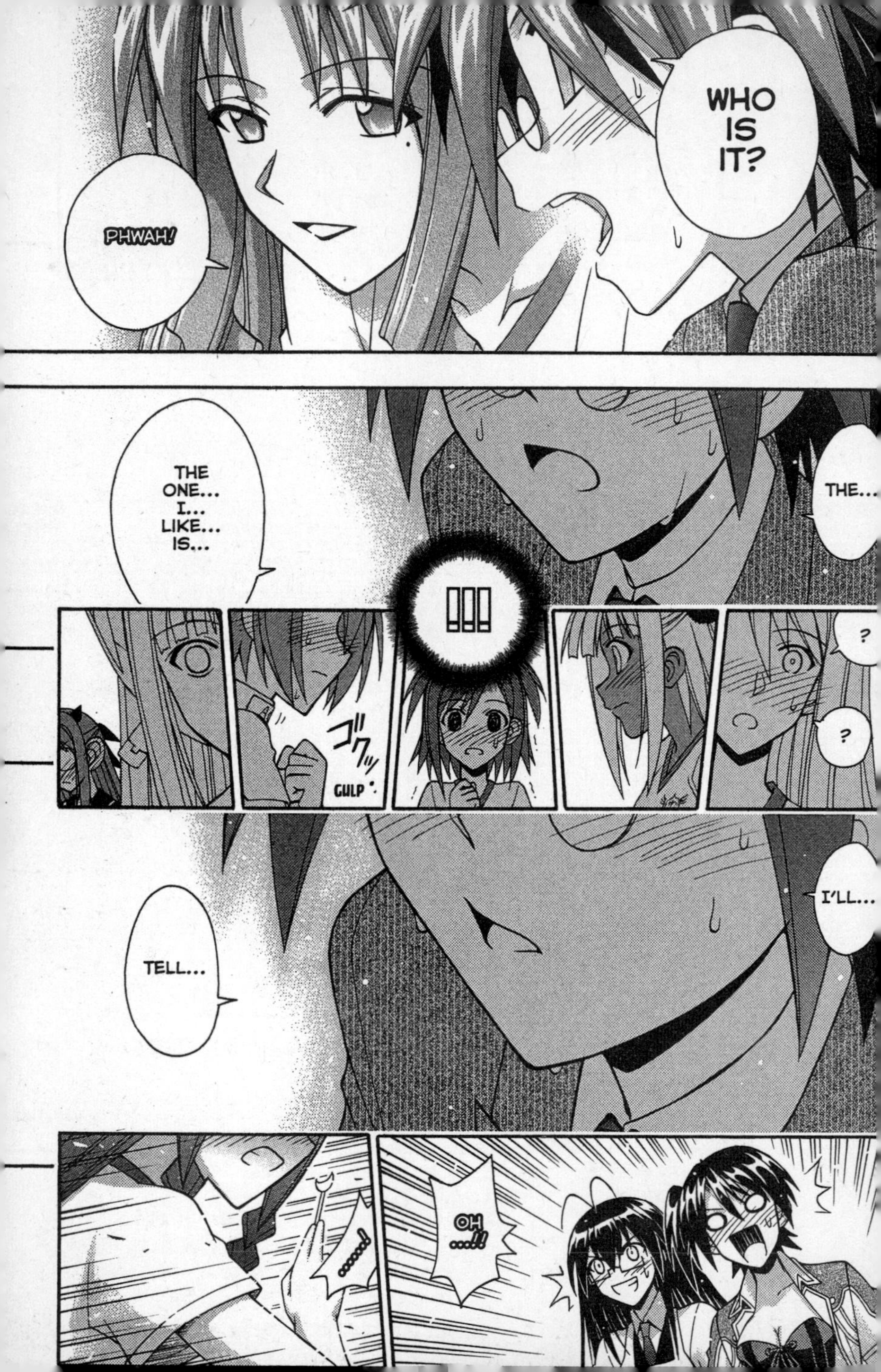
WHO IS IT?
PHWAH!
THE...
THE ONE... I... LIKE... IS...
?
?
!!!
ゴクッ
GULP
I'LL...
TELL...
OH ...!!

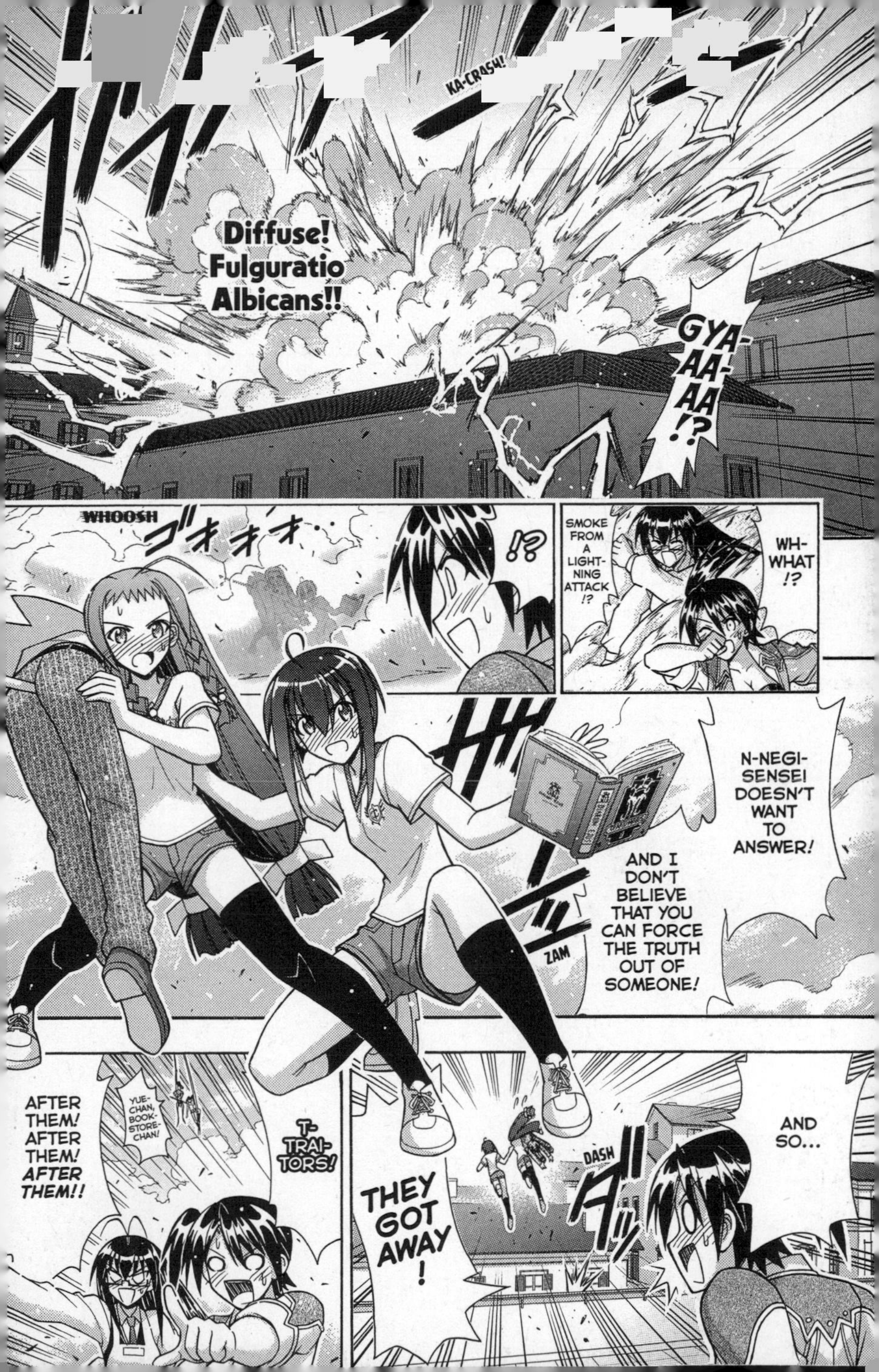
KA-CRASH!
GYAAAAAA!?
Diffuse! Fulguratio Albicans!!
WH-WHAT!?
SMOKE FROM A LIGHTNING ATTACK!?
!?
WHOOSH
N-NEGI-SENSEI DOESN'T WANT TO ANSWER!
AND I DON'T BELIEVE THAT YOU CAN FORCE THE TRUTH OUT OF SOMEONE!
ZAM
AND SO...
DASH
THEY GOT AWAY!
T-TRAITORS!
YUE-CHAN, BOOKSTORE-CHAN!
AFTER THEM! AFTER THEM! AFTER THEM!!

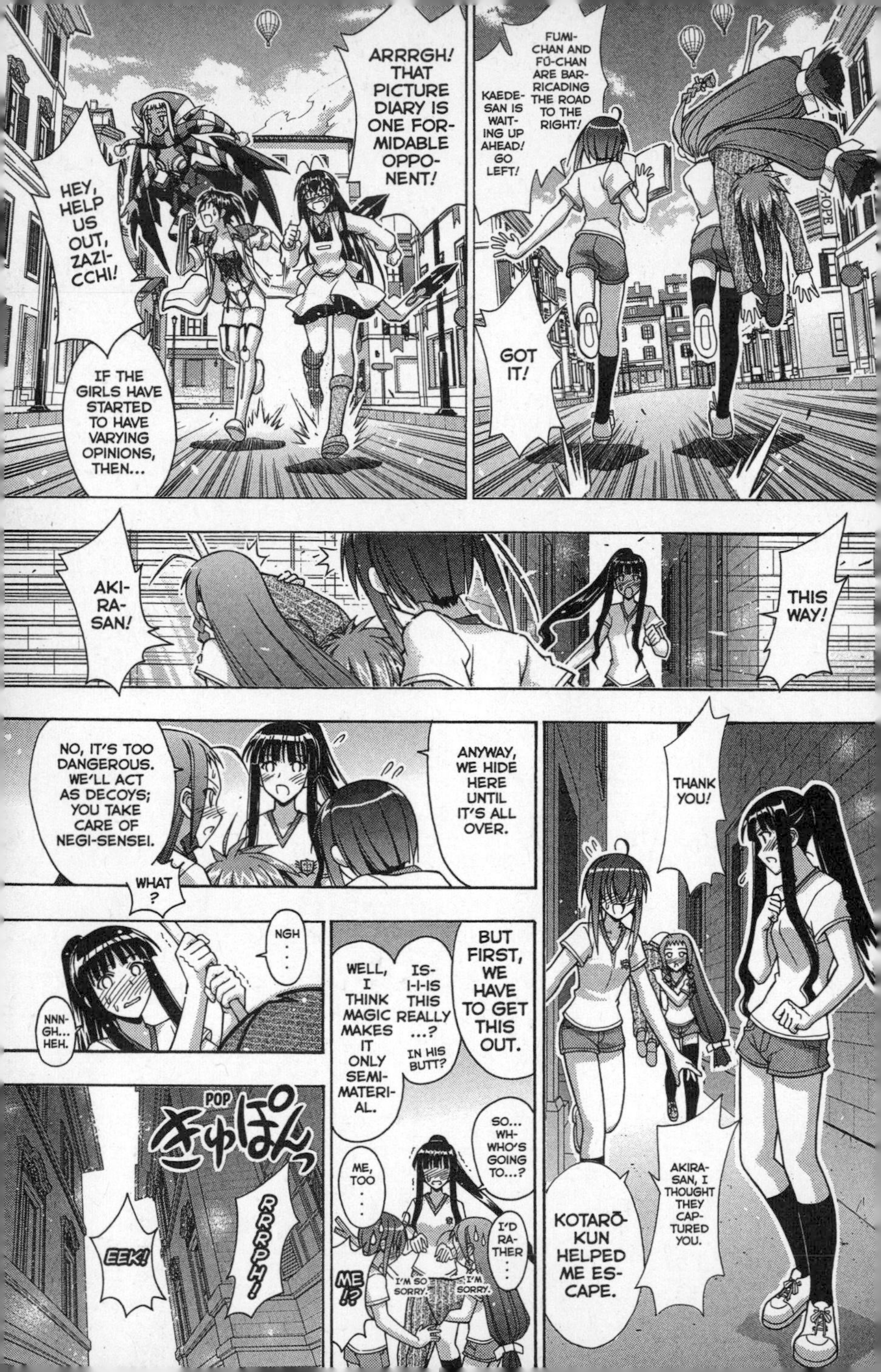
FUMI-CHAN AND FŪ-CHAN ARE BARRICADING THE ROAD TO THE RIGHT!
KAEDE-SAN IS WAITING UP AHEAD! GO LEFT!
GOT IT!
ARRRGH! THAT PICTURE DIARY IS ONE FORMIDABLE OPPONENT!
HEY, HELP US OUT, ZAZICCHI!
IF THE GIRLS HAVE STARTED TO HAVE VARYING OPINIONS, THEN...
THIS WAY!
AKI-RA-SAN!
THANK YOU!
AKIRA-SAN, I THOUGHT THEY CAPTURED YOU.
KOTARŌ-KUN HELPED ME ESCAPE.
ANYWAY, WE HIDE HERE UNTIL IT'S ALL OVER.
NO, IT'S TOO DANGEROUS. WE'LL ACT AS DECOYS; YOU TAKE CARE OF NEGI-SENSEI.
WHAT?
BUT FIRST, WE HAVE TO GET THIS OUT.
IS-I-I-IS THIS REALLY...?
IN HIS BUTT?
WELL, I THINK MAGIC MAKES IT ONLY SEMIMATERIAL.
NGH...
NNNGH... HEH.
SO... WH-WHO'S GOING TO...?
I'D RATHER...
ME, TOO...
I'M SORRY.
I'M SO SORRY.
ME!?
POP
RRRPH!
EEK!

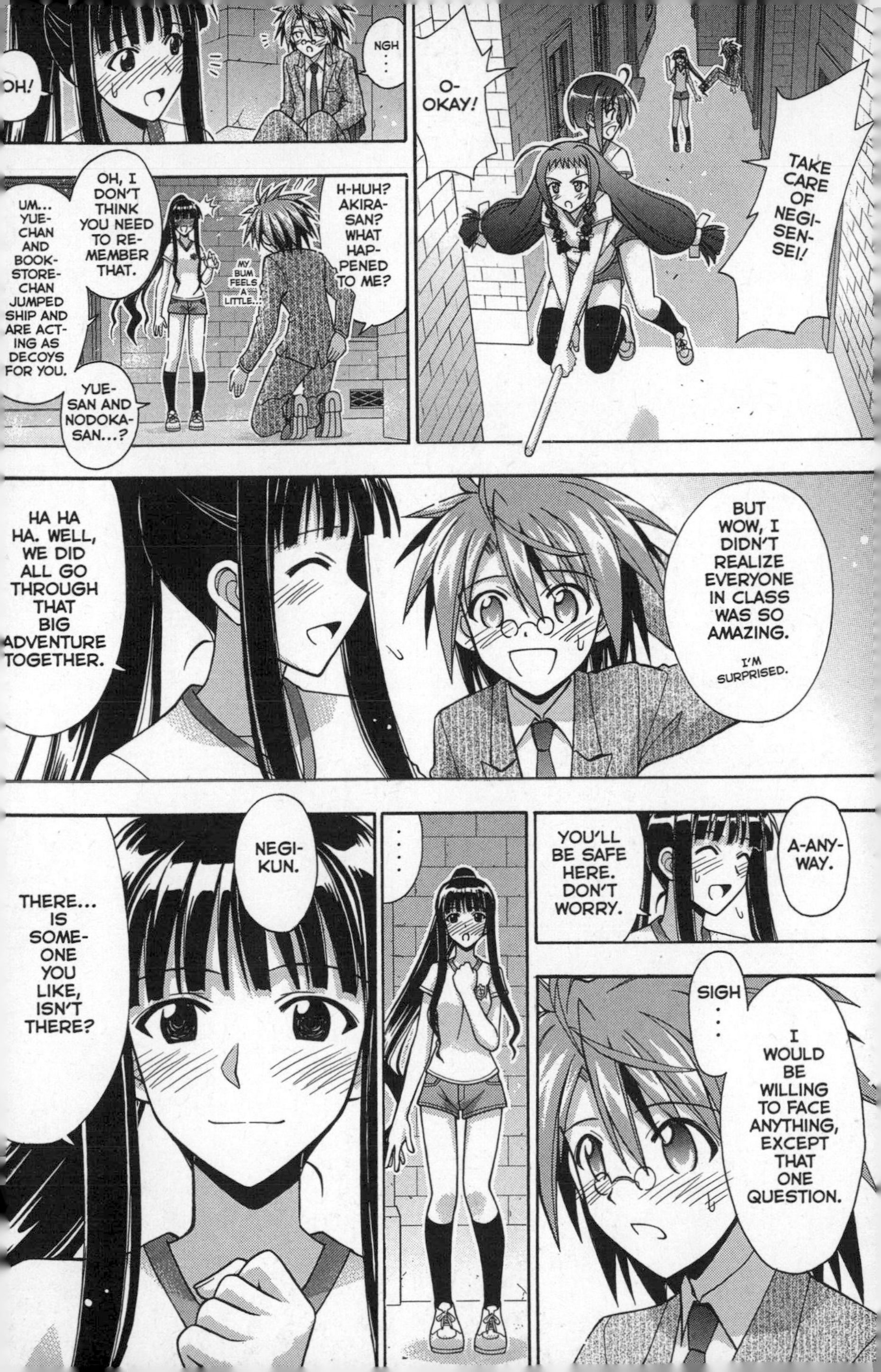
TAKE CARE OF NEGI-SENSEI!
O-OKAY!
NGH...
OH!
H-HUH? AKIRA-SAN? WHAT HAPPENED TO ME?
MY BUM FEELS A LITTLE...
OH, I DON'T THINK YOU NEED TO REMEMBER THAT.
UM... YUE-CHAN AND BOOKSTORE-CHAN JUMPED SHIP AND ARE ACTING AS DECOYS FOR YOU.
YUE-SAN AND NODOKA-SAN...?
BUT WOW, I DIDN'T REALIZE EVERYONE IN CLASS WAS SO AMAZING.
I'M SURPRISED.
HA HA HA. WELL, WE DID ALL GO THROUGH THAT BIG ADVENTURE TOGETHER.
A-ANYWAY.
YOU'LL BE SAFE HERE. DON'T WORRY.
SIGH...
I WOULD BE WILLING TO FACE ANYTHING, EXCEPT THAT ONE QUESTION.
...
NEGI-KUN.
THERE... IS SOMEONE YOU LIKE, ISN'T THERE?

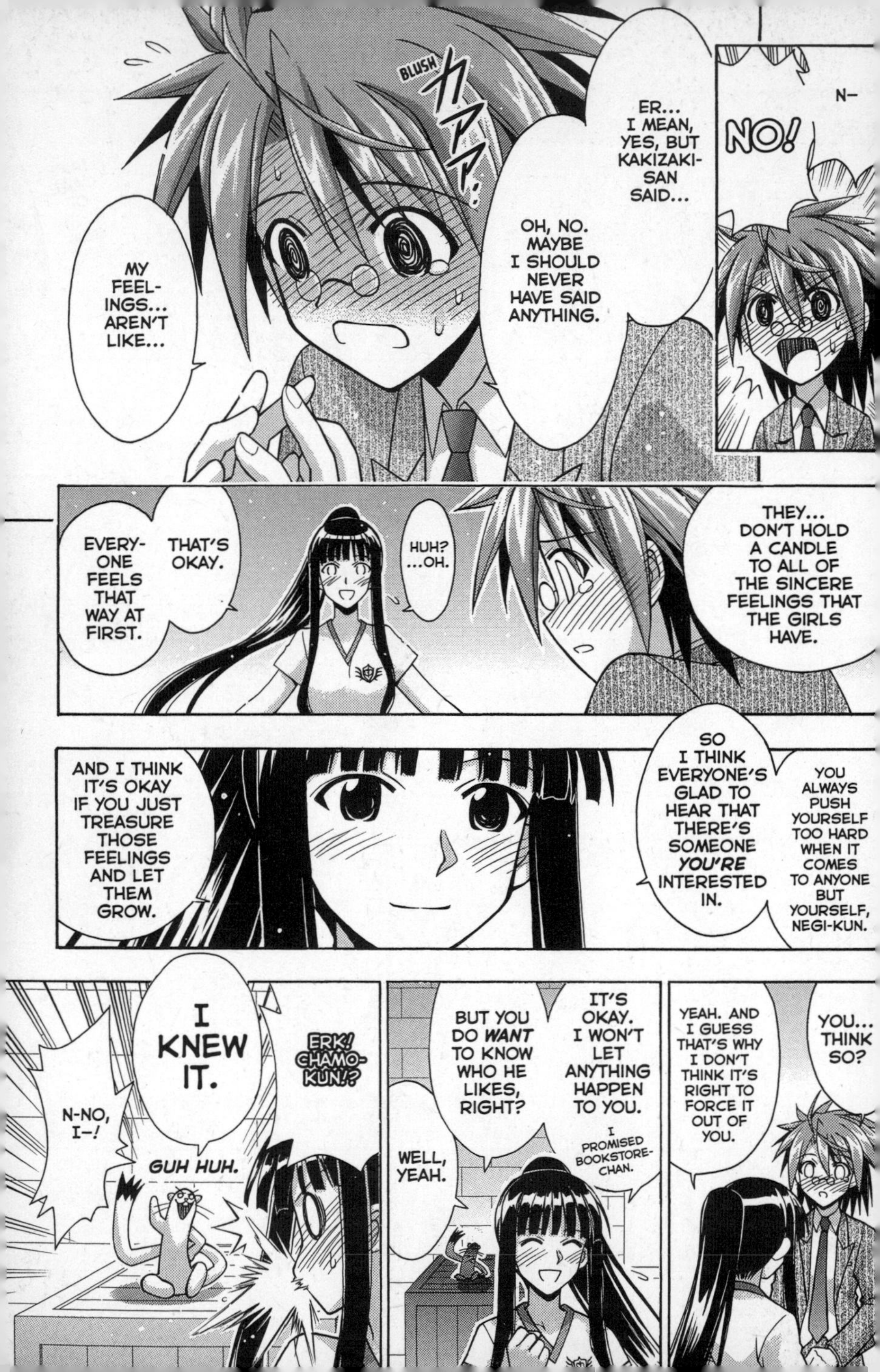
N–
NO!
BLUSH
ER... I MEAN, YES, BUT KAKIZAKI-SAN SAID...
OH, NO. MAYBE I SHOULD NEVER HAVE SAID ANYTHING.
MY FEEL-INGS... AREN'T LIKE...
THEY... DON'T HOLD A CANDLE TO ALL OF THE SINCERE FEELINGS THAT THE GIRLS HAVE.
HUH? ...OH.
THAT'S OKAY.
EVERY-ONE FEELS THAT WAY AT FIRST.
YOU ALWAYS PUSH YOURSELF TOO HARD WHEN IT COMES TO ANYONE BUT YOURSELF, NEGI-KUN.
SO I THINK EVERYONE'S GLAD TO HEAR THAT THERE'S SOMEONE *YOU'RE* INTERESTED IN.
AND I THINK IT'S OKAY IF YOU JUST TREASURE THOSE FEELINGS AND LET THEM GROW.
YOU... THINK SO?
YEAH. AND I GUESS THAT'S WHY I DON'T THINK IT'S RIGHT TO FORCE IT OUT OF YOU.
IT'S OKAY. I WON'T LET ANYTHING HAPPEN TO YOU.
I PROMISED BOOKSTORE-CHAN.
BUT YOU DO *WANT* TO KNOW WHO HE LIKES, RIGHT?
WELL, YEAH.
I KNEW IT.
ERK! CHAMO-KUN!?
GUH HUH.
N-NO, I–!

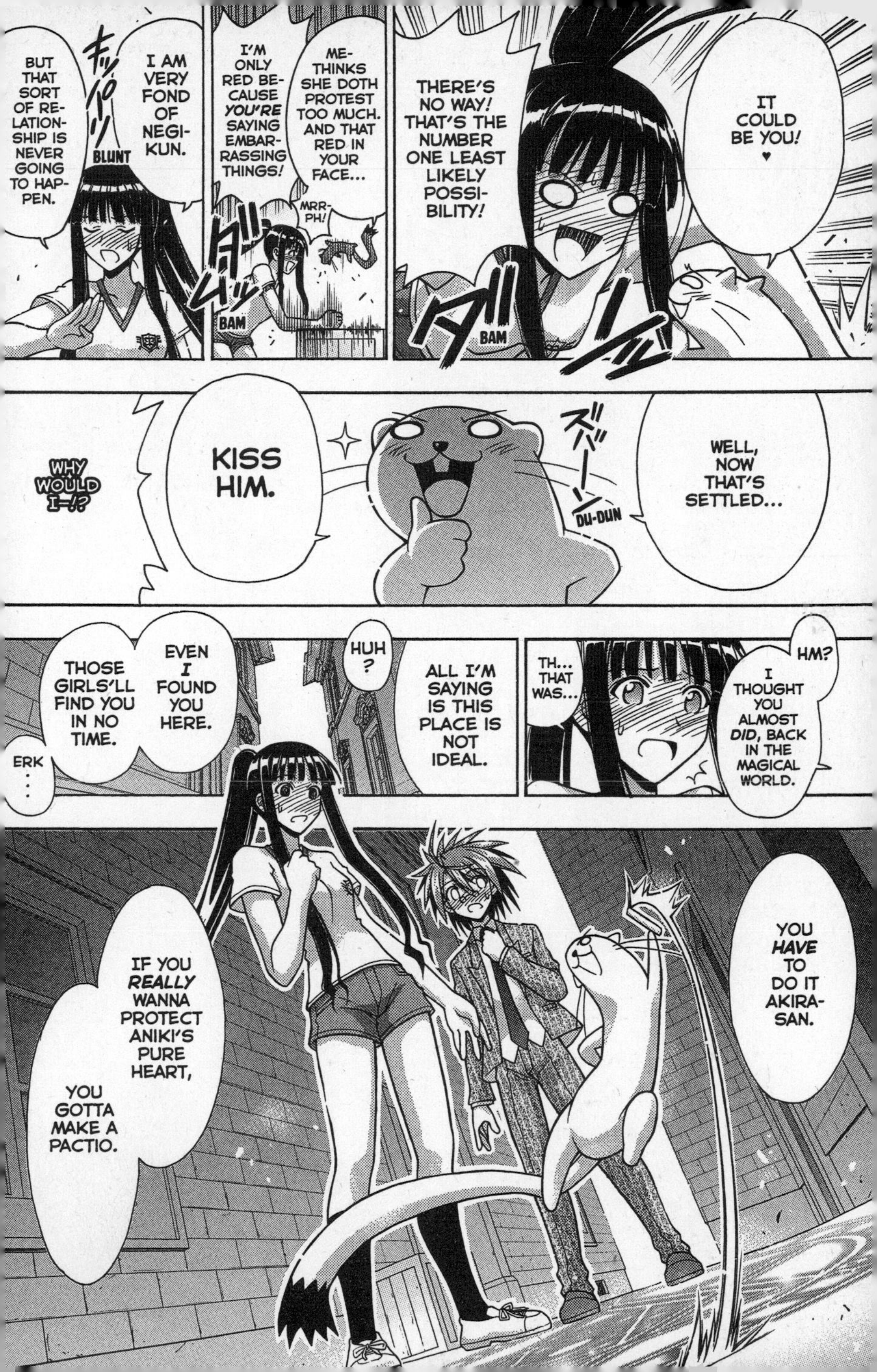
IT COULD BE YOU! ♥
THERE'S NO WAY! THAT'S THE NUMBER ONE LEAST LIKELY POSSIBILITY!
BAM
ME-THINKS SHE DOTH PROTEST TOO MUCH. AND THAT RED IN YOUR FACE...
I'M ONLY RED BECAUSE *YOU'RE* SAYING EMBARRASSING THINGS!
MRR-PH!
BAM
I AM VERY FOND OF NEGI-KUN.
BLUNT
BUT THAT SORT OF RELATIONSHIP IS NEVER GOING TO HAPPEN.
WELL, NOW THAT'S SETTLED...
DU-DUN
KISS HIM.
WHY WOULD I—!?
HM?
I THOUGHT YOU ALMOST *DID*, BACK IN THE MAGICAL WORLD.
TH... THAT WAS...
HUH?
ALL I'M SAYING IS THIS PLACE IS NOT IDEAL.
EVEN *I* FOUND YOU HERE.
THOSE GIRLS'LL FIND YOU IN NO TIME.
ERK...
YOU *HAVE* TO DO IT AKIRA-SAN.
IF YOU *REALLY* WANNA PROTECT ANIKI'S PURE HEART,
YOU GOTTA MAKE A PACTIO.

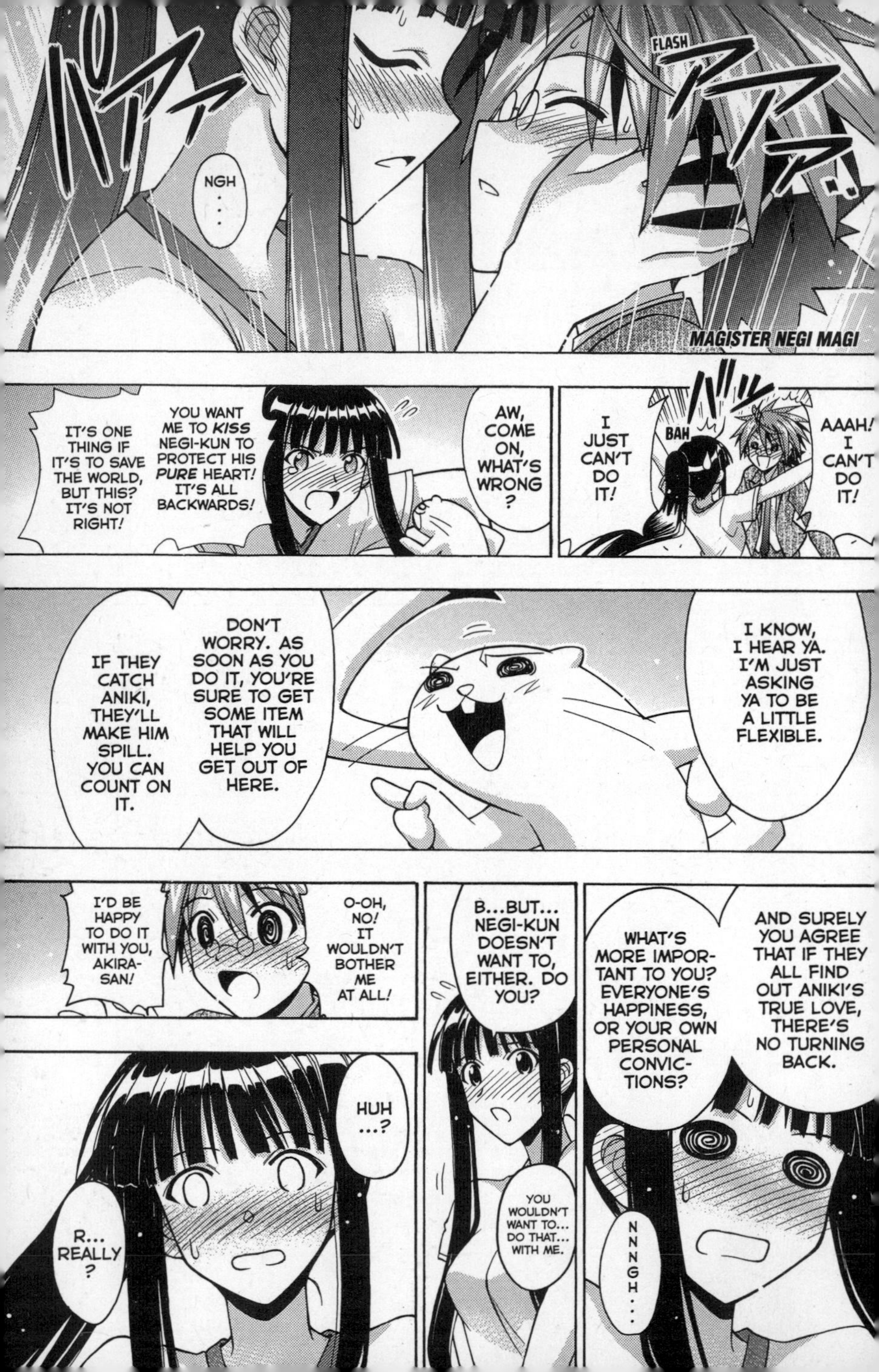
FLASH
NGH...
MAGISTER NEGI MAGI
AAAH! I CAN'T DO IT!
BAH
I JUST CAN'T DO IT!
AW, COME ON, WHAT'S WRONG?
YOU WANT ME TO *KISS* NEGI-KUN TO PROTECT HIS *PURE* HEART! IT'S ALL BACKWARDS!
IT'S ONE THING IF IT'S TO SAVE THE WORLD, BUT THIS? IT'S NOT RIGHT!
I KNOW, I HEAR YA. I'M JUST ASKING YA TO BE A LITTLE FLEXIBLE.
DON'T WORRY. AS SOON AS YOU DO IT, YOU'RE SURE TO GET SOME ITEM THAT WILL HELP YOU GET OUT OF HERE.
IF THEY CATCH ANIKI, THEY'LL MAKE HIM SPILL. YOU CAN COUNT ON IT.
AND SURELY YOU AGREE THAT IF THEY ALL FIND OUT ANIKI'S TRUE LOVE, THERE'S NO TURNING BACK.
WHAT'S MORE IMPORTANT TO YOU? EVERYONE'S HAPPINESS, OR YOUR OWN PERSONAL CONVICTIONS?
NNNGH...
B...BUT... NEGI-KUN DOESN'T WANT TO, EITHER. DO YOU?
YOU WOULDN'T WANT TO... DO THAT... WITH ME.
O-OH, NO! IT WOULDN'T BOTHER ME AT ALL!
I'D BE HAPPY TO DO IT WITH YOU, AKIRA-SAN!
HUH...?
R... REALLY?

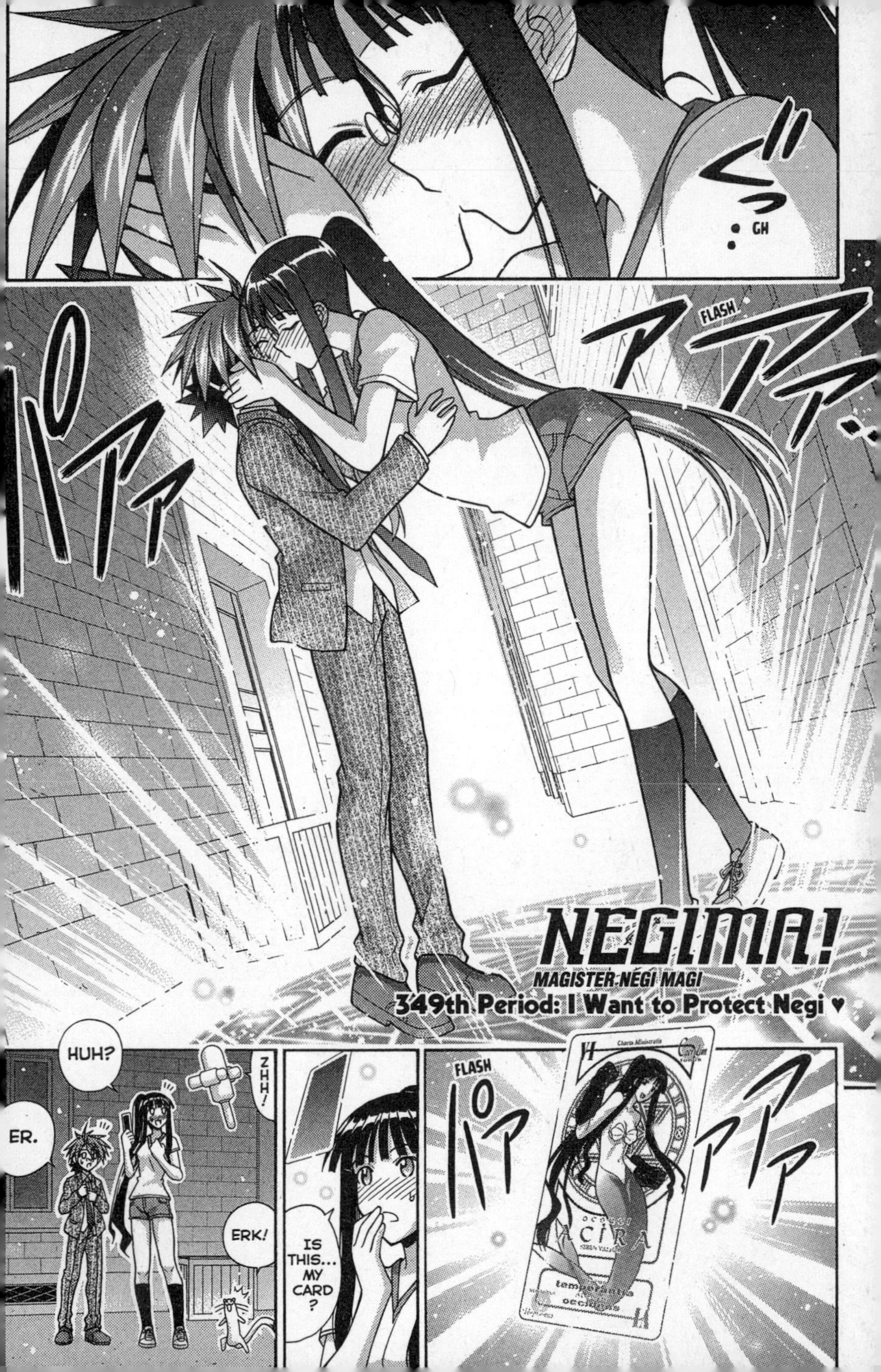
GH
FLASH
NEGIMA!
MAGISTER NEGI MAGI
349th Period: I Want to Protect Negi ♥
FLASH
IS THIS... MY CARD?
ZHH!
HUH?
ER.
ERK!

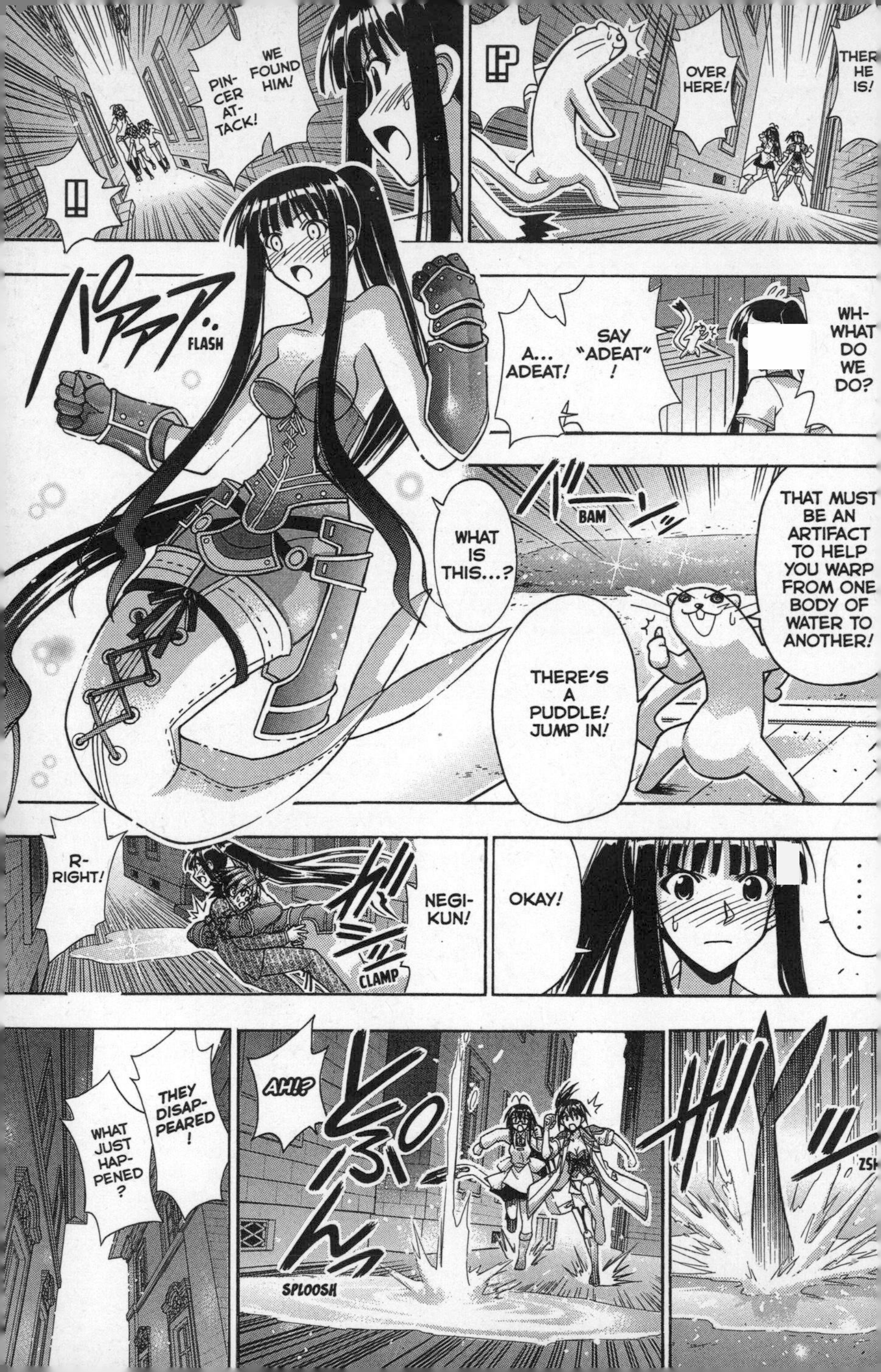
THER HE IS!
OVER HERE!
!?
WE FOUND HIM!
PINCER ATTACK!
!!
WH-WHAT DO WE DO?
SAY "ADEAT"!
A... ADEAT!
THAT MUST BE AN ARTIFACT TO HELP YOU WARP FROM ONE BODY OF WATER TO ANOTHER!
BAM
WHAT IS THIS...?
THERE'S A PUDDLE! JUMP IN!
FLASH
......
OKAY!
NEGI-KUN!
CLAMP
R-RIGHT!
ZSH
AH!?
SPLOOSH
THEY DISAPPEARED!
WHAT JUST HAPPENED?

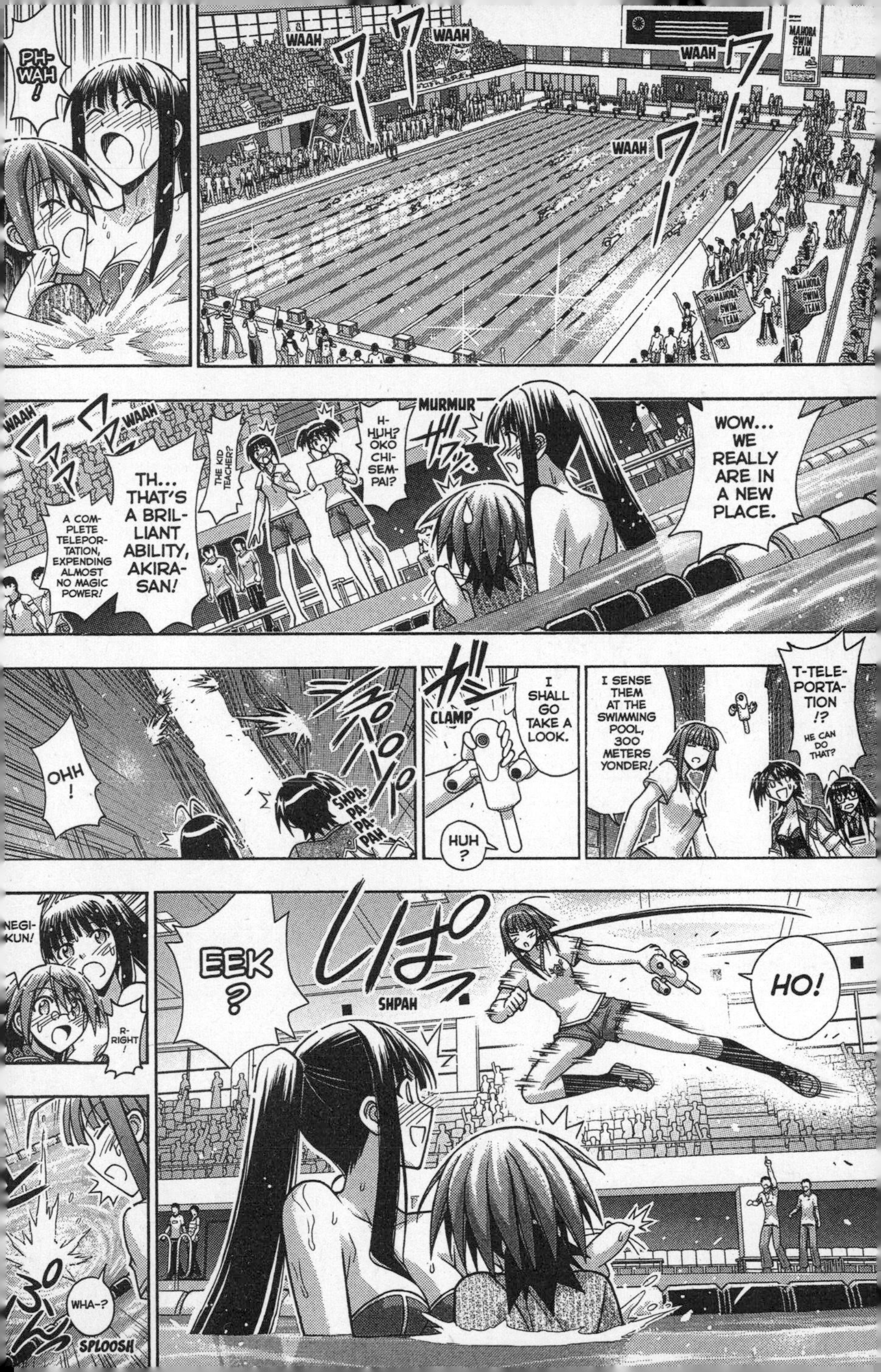
WAAH
WAAH
WAAH
WAAH
MAHORA SWIM TEAM
MAHORA SWIM TEAM
MAHORA SWIM TEAM
PH-WAH!
WOW... WE REALLY ARE IN A NEW PLACE.
MURMUR
H-HUH? OKOCHI-SEMPAI?
THE KID TEACHER?
TH... THAT'S A BRILLIANT ABILITY, AKIRA-SAN!
A COMPLETE TELEPORTATION, EXPENDING ALMOST NO MAGIC POWER!
WAAH
WAAH
T-TELEPORTATION!?
HE CAN DO THAT?
I SENSE THEM AT THE SWIMMING POOL, 300 METERS YONDER!
I SHALL GO TAKE A LOOK.
CLAMP
HUH?
SHPAPAPAPAH
OHH!
HO!
SHPAH
EEK?
NEGI-KUN!
R-RIGHT!
WHA-?
SPLOOSH

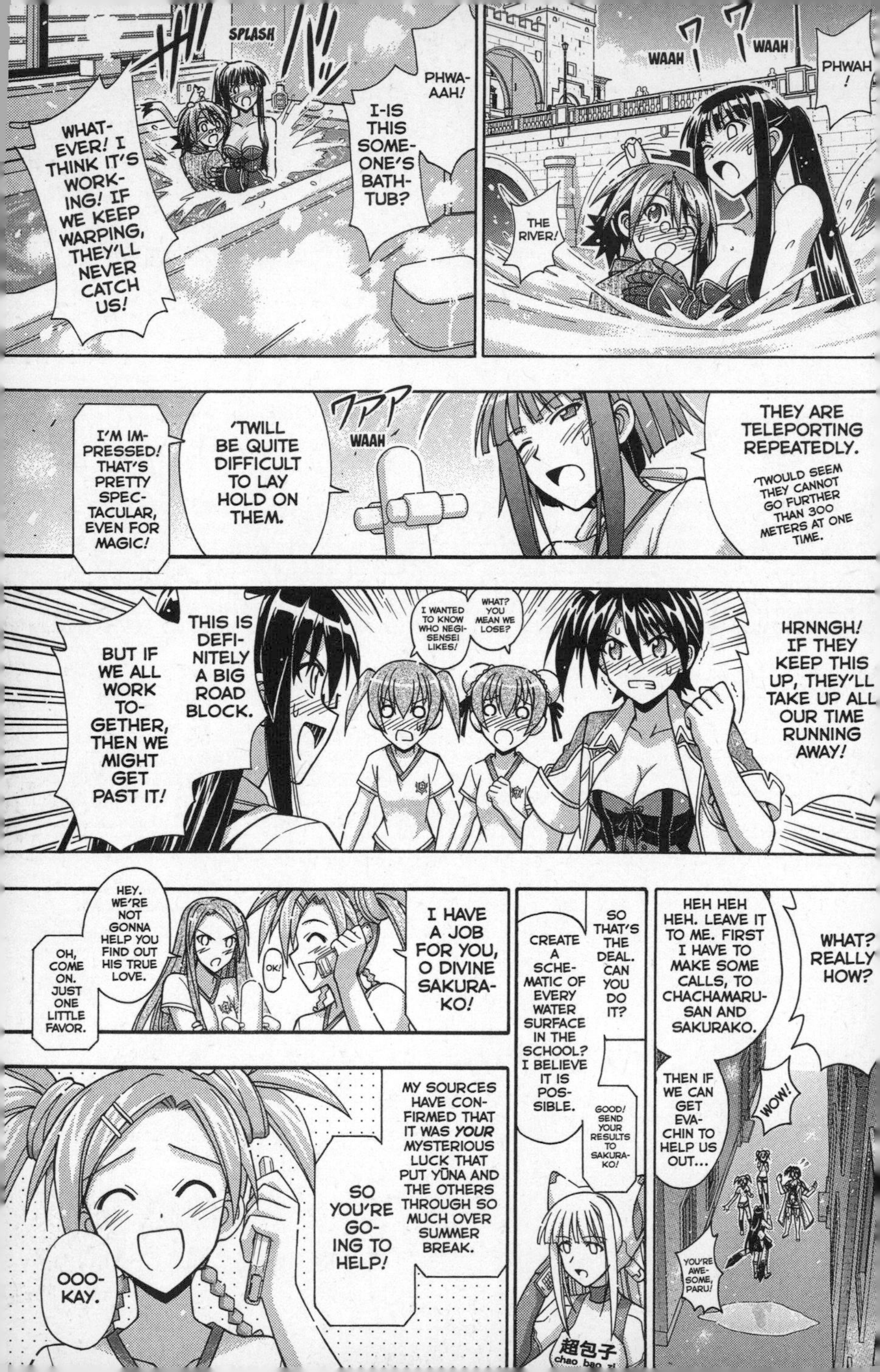
WAAH
WAAH
PHWAH!
THE RIVER!
PHWA-AAH!
I-IS THIS SOMEONE'S BATHTUB?
SPLASH
WHATEVER! I THINK IT'S WORKING! IF WE KEEP WARPING, THEY'LL NEVER CATCH US!
THEY ARE TELEPORTING REPEATEDLY.
'TWOULD SEEM THEY CANNOT GO FURTHER THAN 300 METERS AT ONE TIME.
WAAH
'TWILL BE QUITE DIFFICULT TO LAY HOLD ON THEM.
I'M IMPRESSED! THAT'S PRETTY SPECTACULAR, EVEN FOR MAGIC!
HRNNGH! IF THEY KEEP THIS UP, THEY'LL TAKE UP ALL OUR TIME RUNNING AWAY!
WHAT? YOU MEAN WE LOSE?
I WANTED TO KNOW WHO NEGI-SENSEI LIKES!
THIS IS DEFINITELY A BIG ROAD BLOCK.
BUT IF WE ALL WORK TOGETHER, THEN WE MIGHT GET PAST IT!
WHAT? REALLY HOW?
HEH HEH HEH. LEAVE IT TO ME. FIRST I HAVE TO MAKE SOME CALLS, TO CHACHAMARU-SAN AND SAKURAKO.
THEN IF WE CAN GET EVA-CHIN TO HELP US OUT...
WOW!
YOU'RE AWESOME, PARU!
SO THAT'S THE DEAL. CAN YOU DO IT?
CREATE A SCHEMATIC OF EVERY WATER SURFACE IN THE SCHOOL? I BELIEVE IT IS POSSIBLE.
GOOD! SEND YOUR RESULTS TO SAKURAKO!
超包子
chao bao zi
I HAVE A JOB FOR YOU, O DIVINE SAKURAKO!
OK!
HEY. WE'RE NOT GONNA HELP YOU FIND OUT HIS TRUE LOVE.
OH, COME ON. JUST ONE LITTLE FAVOR.
MY SOURCES HAVE CONFIRMED THAT IT WAS *YOUR* MYSTERIOUS LUCK THAT PUT YŪNA AND THE OTHERS THROUGH SO MUCH OVER SUMMER BREAK.
SO YOU'RE GOING TO HELP!
OOO-KAY.

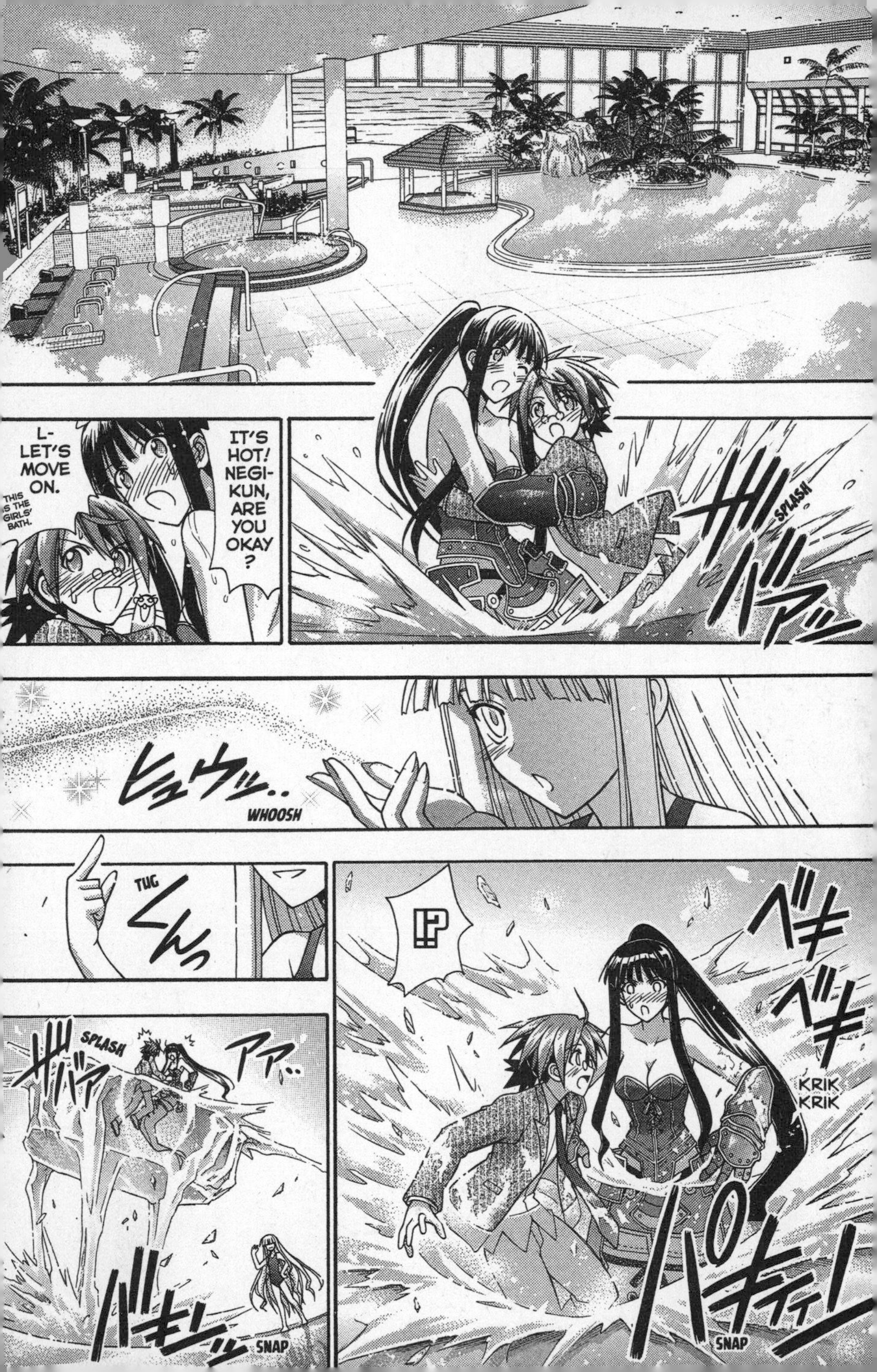
SPLASH
IT'S HOT! NEGI-KUN, ARE YOU OKAY?
L-LET'S MOVE ON.
THIS IS THE GIRLS' BATH.
WHOOSH
!?
KRIK KRIK
SNAP
TUG
SPLASH
SNAP

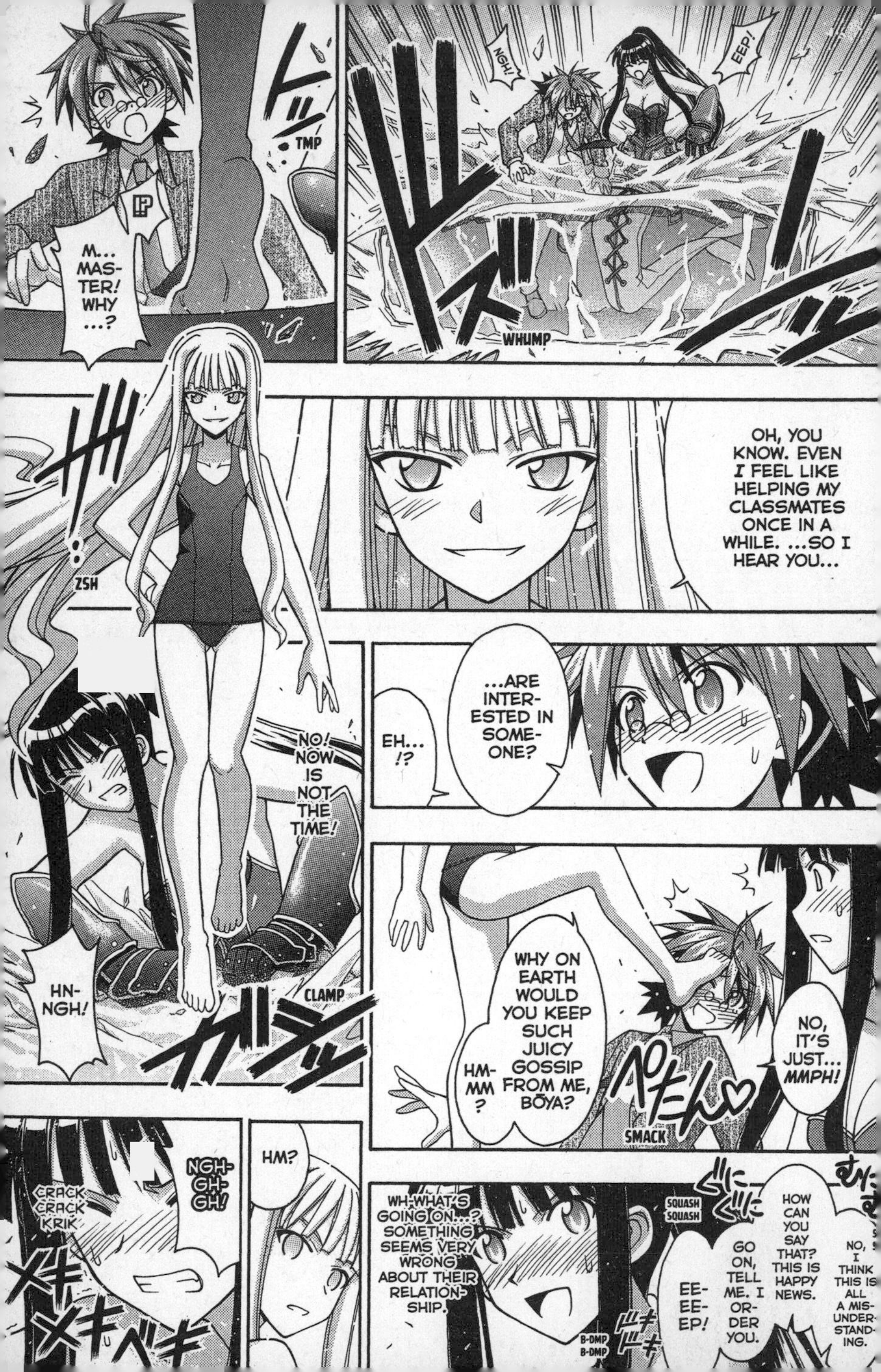
NGH!
EEP!
WHUMP
TMP
!?
M... MASTER! WHY ...?
OH, YOU KNOW. EVEN I FEEL LIKE HELPING MY CLASSMATES ONCE IN A WHILE. ...SO I HEAR YOU...
...ARE INTERESTED IN SOMEONE?
EH... !?
WHY ON EARTH WOULD YOU KEEP SUCH JUICY GOSSIP FROM ME, BŌYA?
HM-MM?
NO, IT'S JUST... MMPH!
SMACK
ZSH
NO! NOW IS NOT THE TIME!
HN-NGH!
CLAMP
NO, I THINK THIS IS ALL A MISUNDERSTANDING.
HOW CAN YOU SAY THAT? THIS IS HAPPY NEWS.
SQUASH SQUASH
GO ON, TELL ME. I ORDER YOU.
EE-EE-EP!
WH-WHAT'S GOING ON...? SOMETHING SEEMS VERY WRONG ABOUT THEIR RELATIONSHIP.
B-DMP B-DMP
HM?
NGH-GH-GH!
CRACK CRACK KRIK

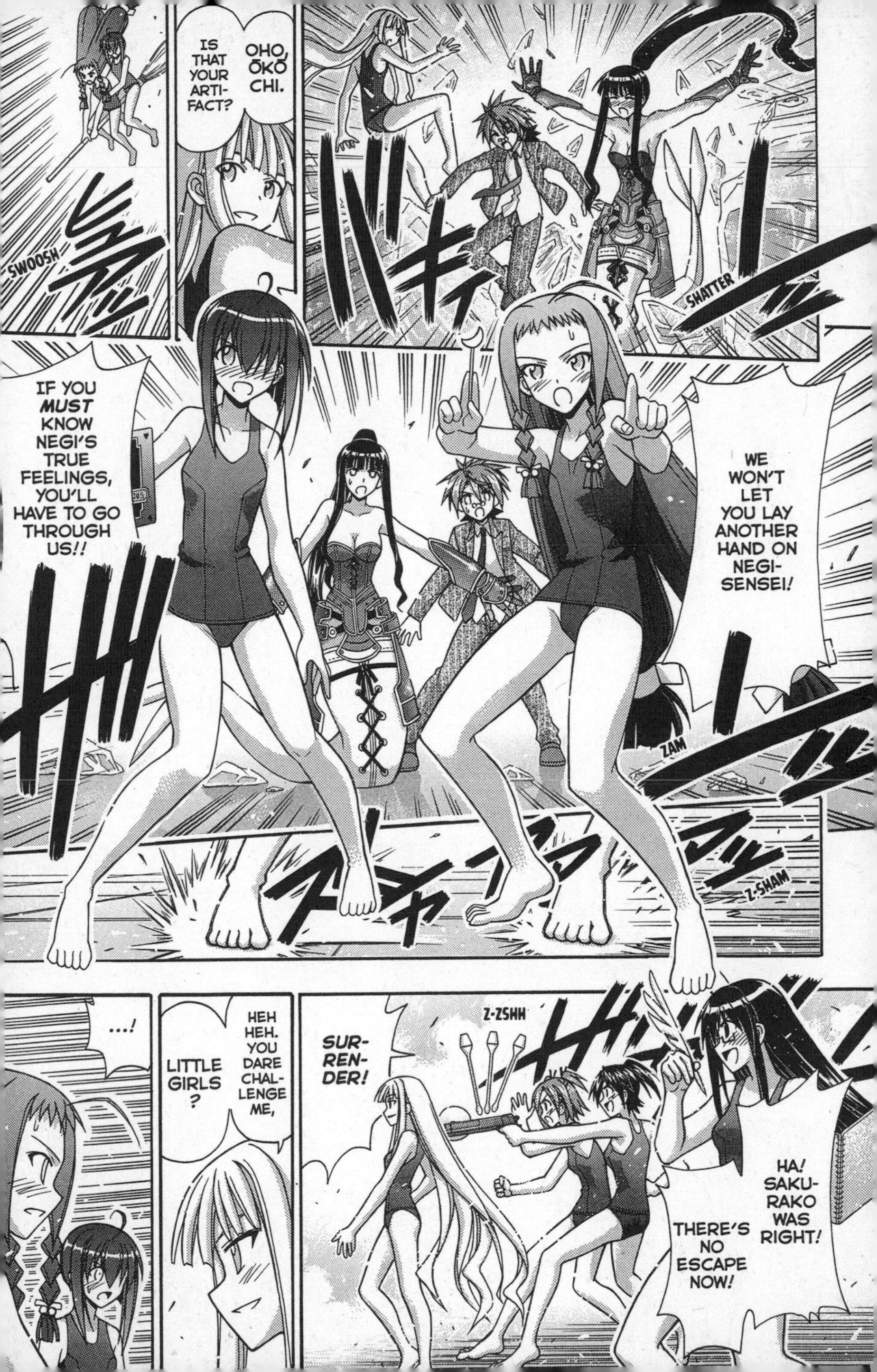
SHATTER
OHO, ŌKŌCHI.
IS THAT YOUR ARTIFACT?
SWOOSH
WE WON'T LET YOU LAY ANOTHER HAND ON NEGI-SENSEI!
IF YOU MUST KNOW NEGI'S TRUE FEELINGS, YOU'LL HAVE TO GO THROUGH US!!
ZAM
Z-SHAM
Z-ZSHH
HA! SAKURAKO WAS RIGHT!
THERE'S NO ESCAPE NOW!
SURRENDER!
HEH HEH. YOU DARE CHALLENGE ME,
LITTLE GIRLS?
...!

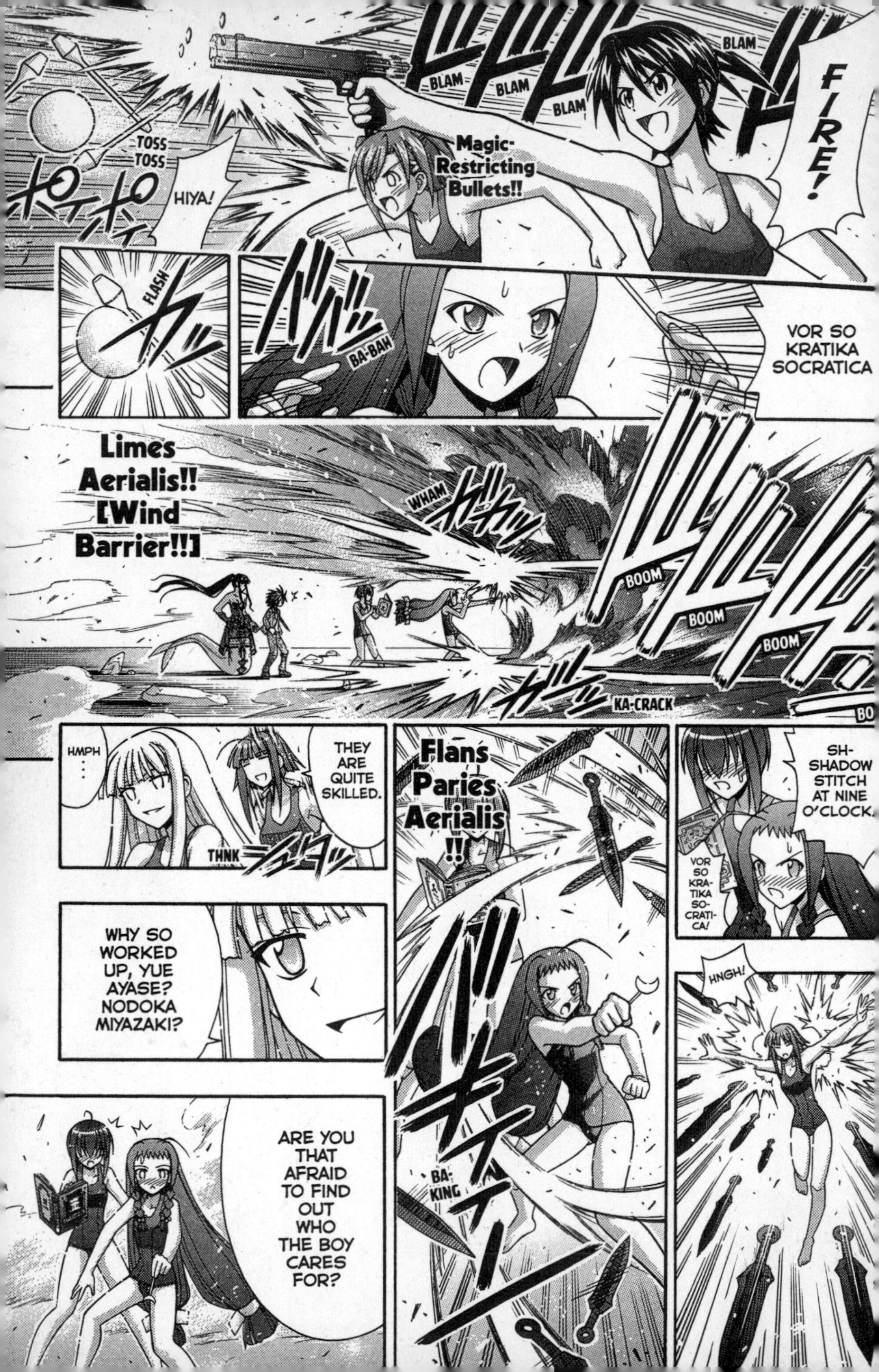
FIRE!
BLAM
BLAM
BLAM
BLAM
Magic-Restricting Bullets!!
HIYA!
TOSS TOSS
VOR SO KRATIKA SOCRATICA
BA-BAH
FLASH
Limes Aerialis!! [Wind Barrier!!]
WHAM
BOOM
BOOM
BOOM
KA-CRACK
BO
SH-SHADOW STITCH AT NINE O'CLOCK.
VOR SO KRA-TIKA SO-CRATI-CA!
HNGH!
Flans Paries Aerialis!!
BA-KING
THEY ARE QUITE SKILLED.
HMPH...
THNK
WHY SO WORKED UP, YUE AYASE? NODOKA MIYAZAKI?
ARE YOU THAT AFRAID TO FIND OUT WHO THE BOY CARES FOR?

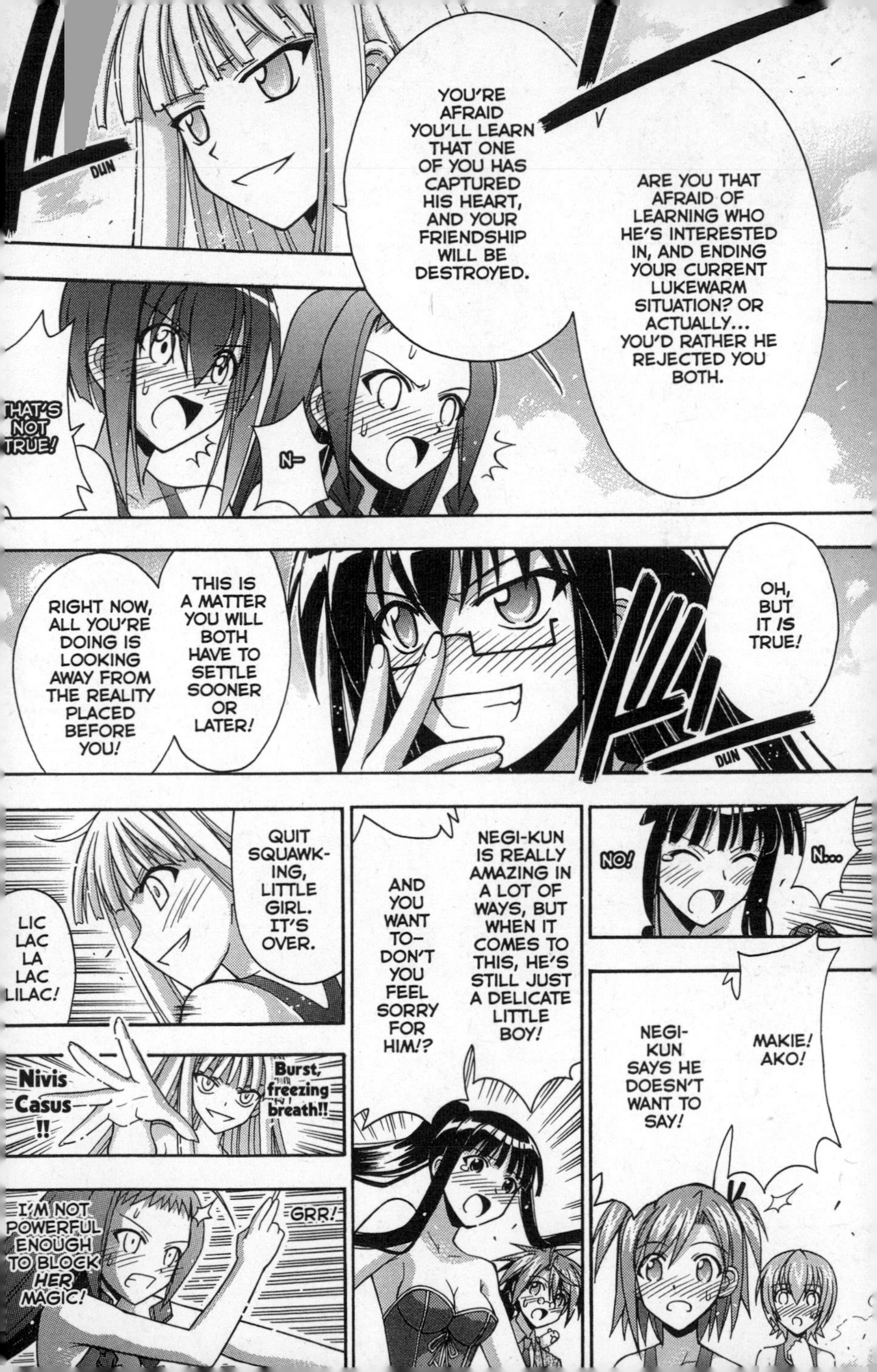
ARE YOU THAT AFRAID OF LEARNING WHO HE'S INTERESTED IN, AND ENDING YOUR CURRENT LUKEWARM SITUATION? OR ACTUALLY... YOU'D RATHER HE REJECTED YOU BOTH.
YOU'RE AFRAID YOU'LL LEARN THAT ONE OF YOU HAS CAPTURED HIS HEART, AND YOUR FRIENDSHIP WILL BE DESTROYED.
DUN
N–
THAT'S NOT TRUE!
OH, BUT IT IS TRUE!
DUN
THIS IS A MATTER YOU WILL BOTH HAVE TO SETTLE SOONER OR LATER!
RIGHT NOW, ALL YOU'RE DOING IS LOOKING AWAY FROM THE REALITY PLACED BEFORE YOU!
N...
NO!
MAKIE! AKO!
NEGI-KUN SAYS HE DOESN'T WANT TO SAY!
NEGI-KUN IS REALLY AMAZING IN A LOT OF WAYS, BUT WHEN IT COMES TO THIS, HE'S STILL JUST A DELICATE LITTLE BOY!
AND YOU WANT TO– DON'T YOU FEEL SORRY FOR HIM!?
QUIT SQUAWK-ING, LITTLE GIRL. IT'S OVER.
LIC LAC LA LAC LILAC!
Burst, freezing breath!!
Nivis Casus!!
GRR!
I'M NOT POWERFUL ENOUGH TO BLOCK HER MAGIC!

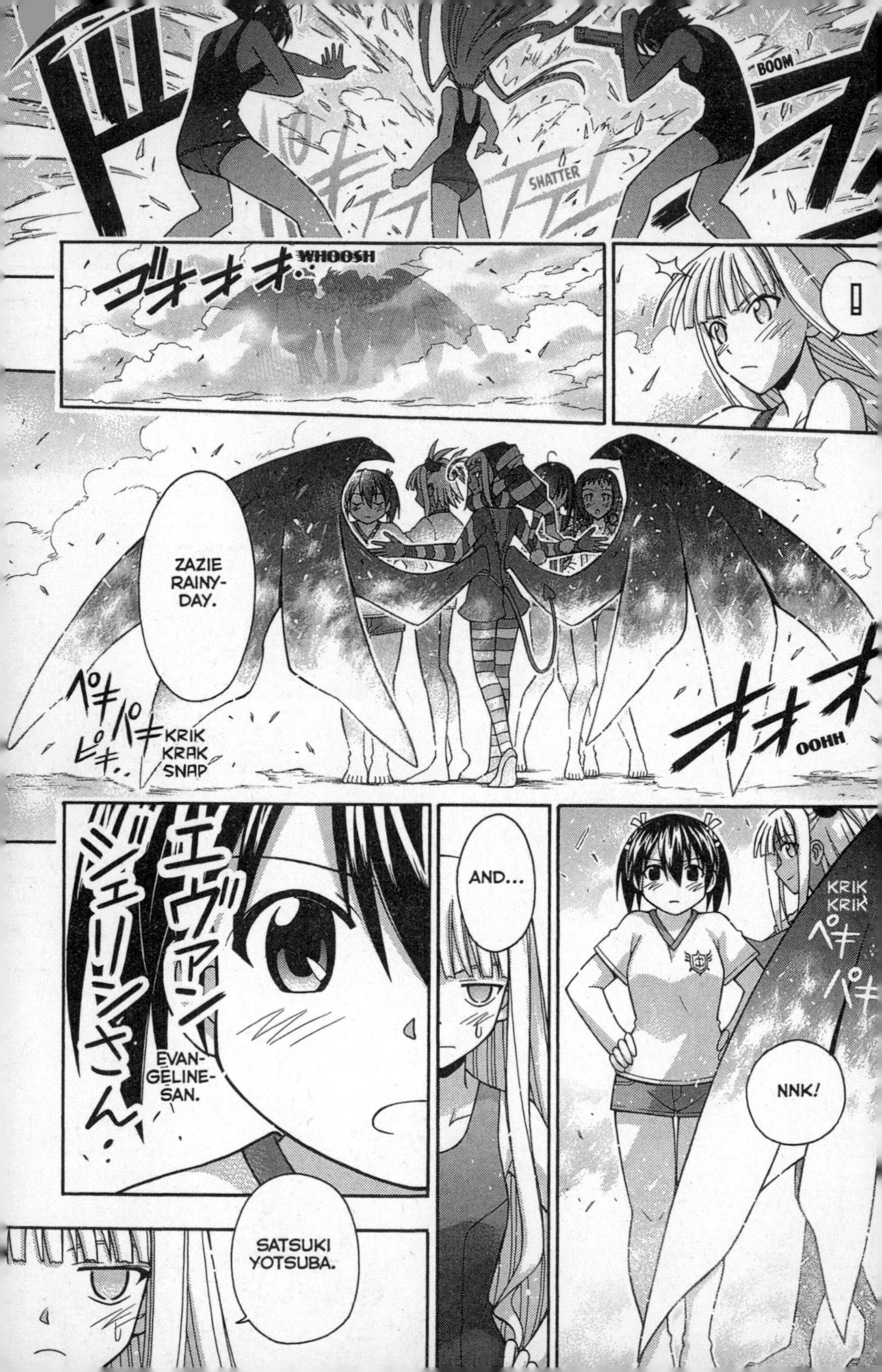
BOOM
SHATTER
!
WHOOSH
ZAZIE RAINY-DAY.
OOHH
KRIK KRAK SNAP
KRIK KRIK
NNK!
AND...
SATSUKI YOTSUBA.
EVANGELINE-SAN.

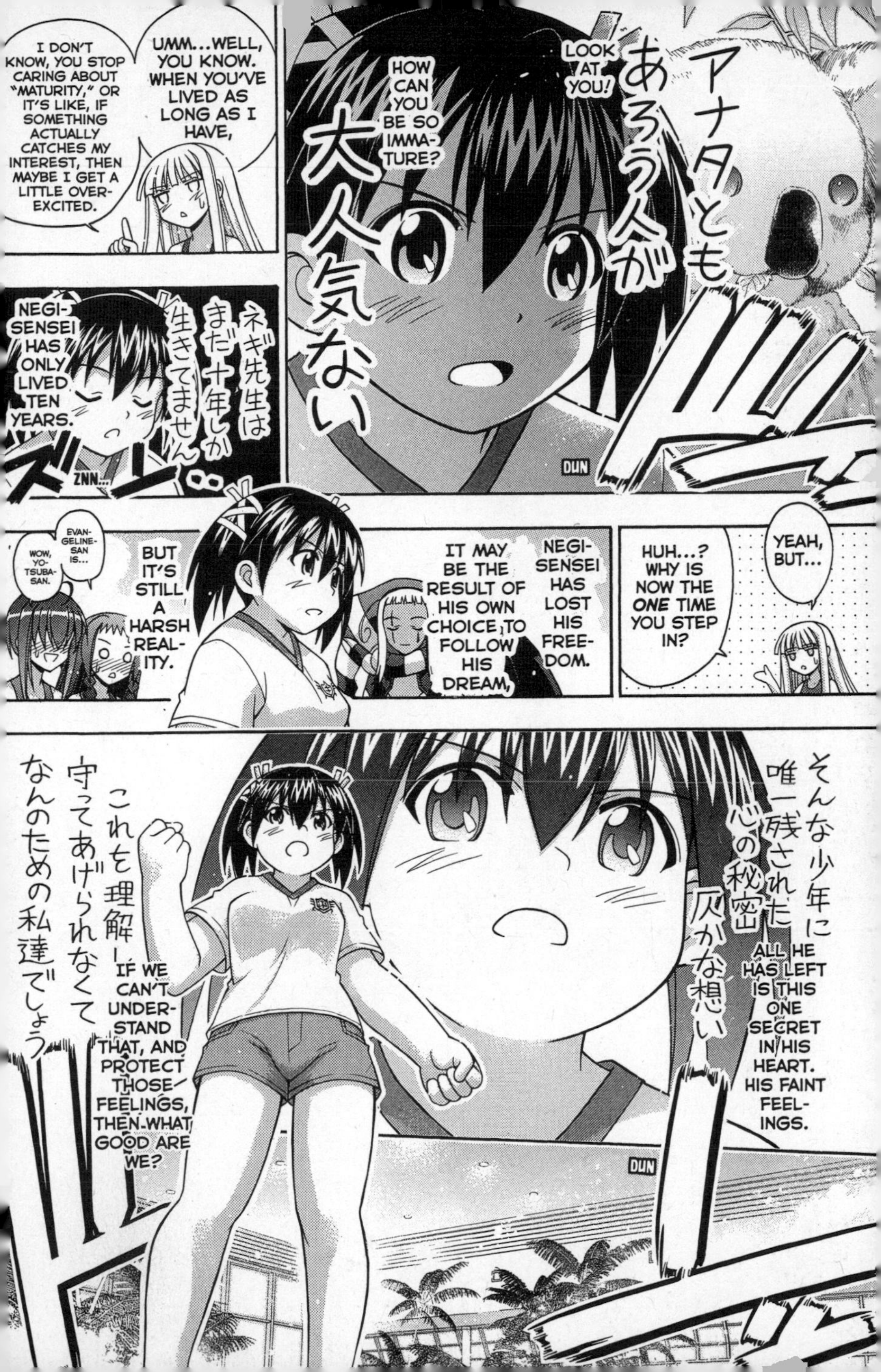

LOOK AT YOU!
アナタともあろう人が大人気ない
HOW CAN YOU BE SO IMMA-TURE?
DUN
UMM...WELL, YOU KNOW. WHEN YOU'VE LIVED AS LONG AS I HAVE,
I DON'T KNOW, YOU STOP CARING ABOUT "MATURITY," OR IT'S LIKE, IF SOMETHING ACTUALLY CATCHES MY INTEREST, THEN MAYBE I GET A LITTLE OVER-EXCITED.
ネギ先生はまだ十年しか生きてません
NEGI-SENSEI HAS ONLY LIVED TEN YEARS.
ZNN...
YEAH, BUT...
HUH...? WHY IS NOW THE *ONE* TIME YOU STEP IN?
NEGI-SENSEI HAS LOST HIS FREE-DOM.
IT MAY BE THE RESULT OF HIS OWN CHOICE TO FOLLOW HIS DREAM,
BUT IT'S STILL A HARSH REAL-ITY.
EVAN-GELINE-SAN IS...
WOW, YO-TSUBA-SAN.
そんな少年に唯一残された心の秘密仄かな想い
ALL HE HAS LEFT IS THIS ONE SECRET IN HIS HEART. HIS FAINT FEEL-INGS.
これを理解し守ってあげられなくてなんのための私達でしょう
IF WE CAN'T UNDER-STAND THAT, AND PROTECT THOSE FEELINGS, THEN WHAT GOOD ARE WE?
DUN

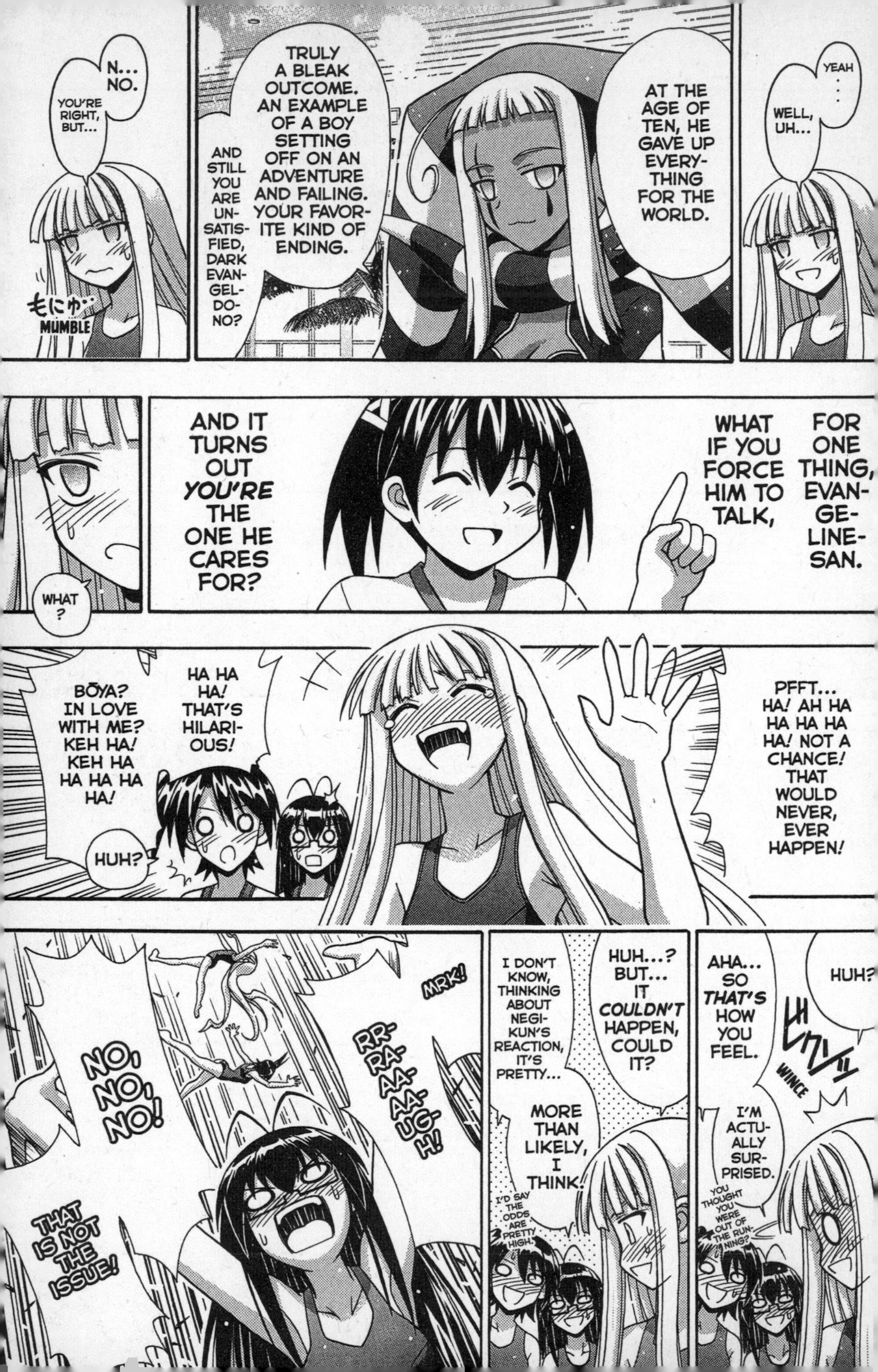
YEAH...
WELL, UH...
AT THE AGE OF TEN, HE GAVE UP EVERYTHING FOR THE WORLD.
TRULY A BLEAK OUTCOME. AN EXAMPLE OF A BOY SETTING OFF ON AN ADVENTURE AND FAILING. YOUR FAVORITE KIND OF ENDING.
AND STILL YOU ARE UNSATISFIED, DARK EVANGEL-DONO?
N... NO.
YOU'RE RIGHT, BUT...
もにゅ‥
MUMBLE
FOR ONE THING, EVANGELINE-SAN.
WHAT IF YOU FORCE HIM TO TALK,
AND IT TURNS OUT *YOU'RE* THE ONE HE CARES FOR?
WHAT?
PFFT... HA! AH HA HA HA HA HA! NOT A CHANCE! THAT WOULD NEVER, EVER HAPPEN!
HA HA HA! THAT'S HILARIOUS!
BŌYA? IN LOVE WITH ME? KEH HA! KEH HA HA HA HA HA!
HUH?
HUH?
WINCE
AHA... SO *THAT'S* HOW YOU FEEL.
I'M ACTUALLY SURPRISED.
YOU THOUGHT YOU WERE OUT OF THE RUNNING?
HUH...? BUT... IT *COULDN'T* HAPPEN, COULD IT?
I DON'T KNOW, THINKING ABOUT NEGI-KUN'S REACTION, IT'S PRETTY...
MORE THAN LIKELY, I THINK.
I'D SAY THE ODDS ARE PRETTY HIGH.
MRK!
RR-RA-AA-AUGH!
NO, NO, NO!
THAT IS NOT THE ISSUE!

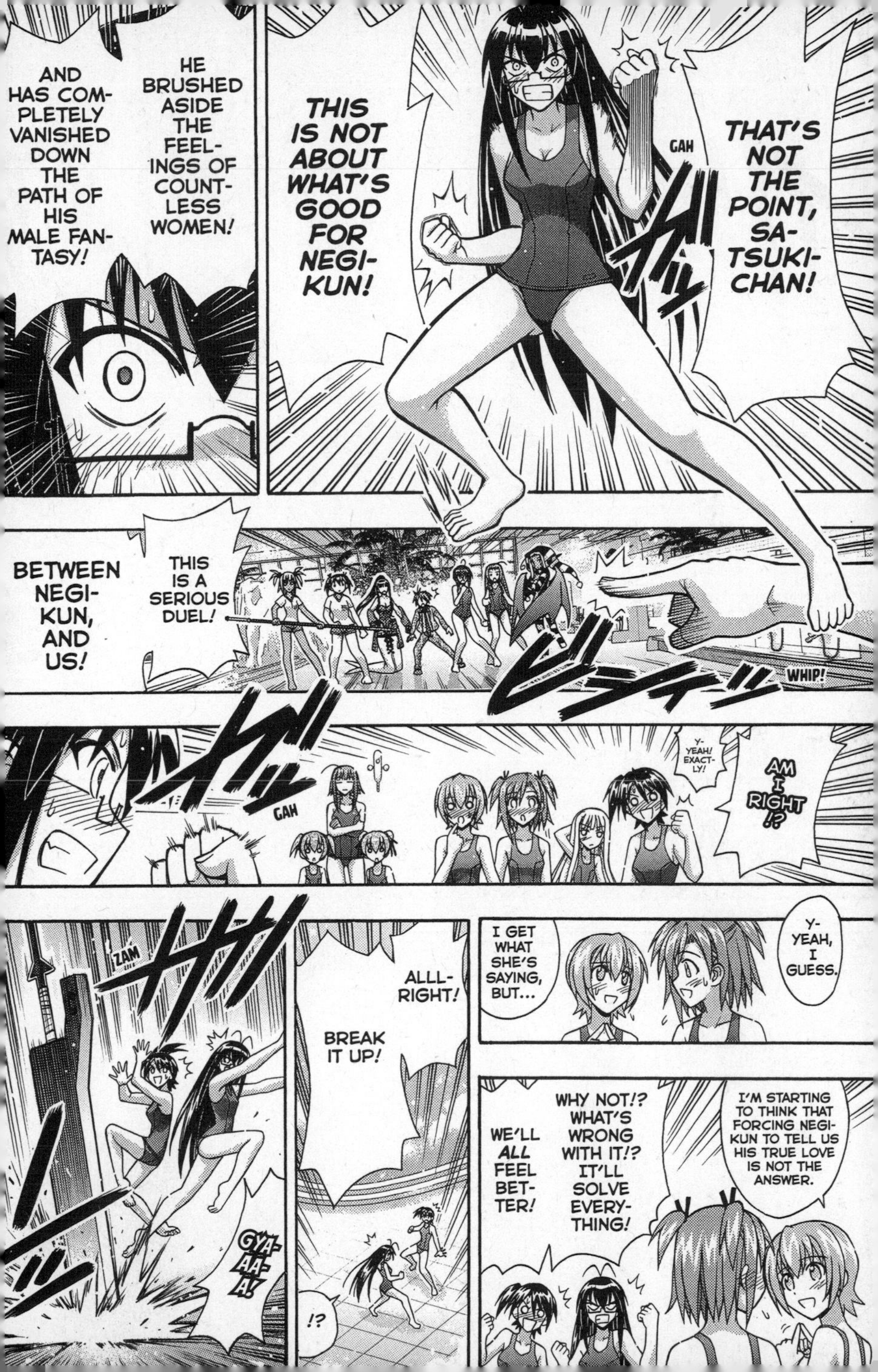

THAT'S NOT THE POINT, SA-TSUKI-CHAN!
GAH
THIS IS NOT ABOUT WHAT'S GOOD FOR NEGI-KUN!
HE BRUSHED ASIDE THE FEEL-INGS OF COUNT-LESS WOMEN!
AND HAS COM-PLETELY VANISHED DOWN THE PATH OF HIS MALE FAN-TASY!
WHIP!
THIS IS A SERIOUS DUEL!
BETWEEN NEGI-KUN, AND US!
AM I RIGHT!?
Y-YEAH! EXACT-LY!
GAH
Y-YEAH, I GUESS.
I GET WHAT SHE'S SAYING, BUT...
I'M STARTING TO THINK THAT FORCING NEGI-KUN TO TELL US HIS TRUE LOVE IS NOT THE ANSWER.
WHY NOT!? WHAT'S WRONG WITH IT!? IT'LL SOLVE EVERY-THING!
WE'LL ALL FEEL BET-TER!
ALLL-RIGHT!
BREAK IT UP!
!?
ZAM
GYA-AA-A!

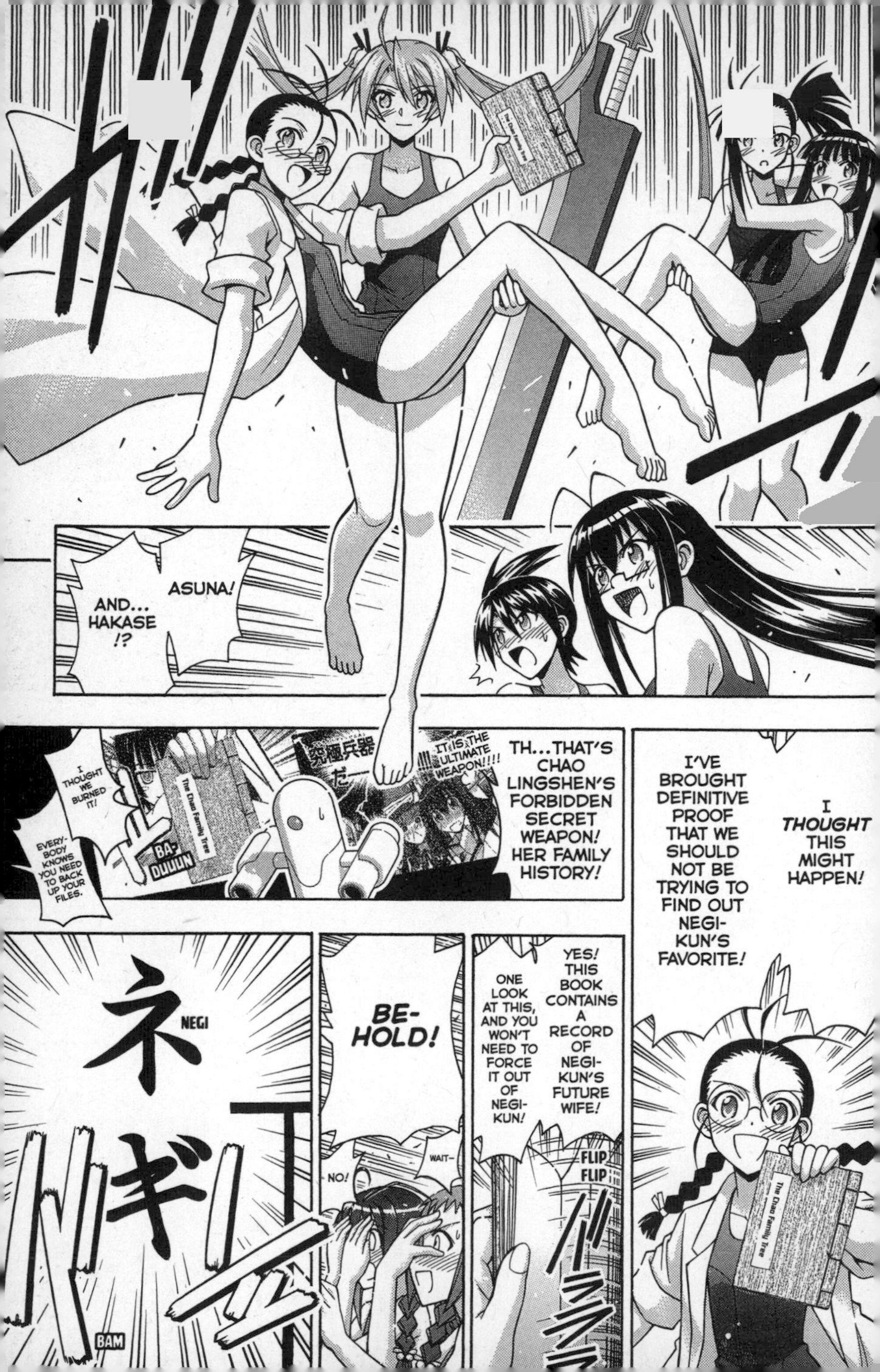

ASUNA!
AND... HAKASE !?
I THOUGHT THIS MIGHT HAPPEN!
I'VE BROUGHT DEFINITIVE PROOF THAT WE SHOULD NOT BE TRYING TO FIND OUT NEGI-KUN'S FAVORITE!
TH...THAT'S CHAO LINGSHEN'S FORBIDDEN SECRET WEAPON! HER FAMILY HISTORY!
IT IS THE ULTIMATE WEAPON!!!!
究極兵器だ――
The Chao Family Tree
I THOUGHT WE BURNED IT!
BA-DUUUN
EVERY-BODY KNOWS YOU NEED TO BACK UP YOUR FILES.
YES! THIS BOOK CONTAINS A RECORD OF NEGI-KUN'S FUTURE WIFE!
ONE LOOK AT THIS, AND YOU WON'T NEED TO FORCE IT OUT OF NEGI-KUN!
FLIP FLIP
BE-HOLD!
WAIT-
NO!
ネ
NEGI
ギ
BAM
The Chao Family Tree

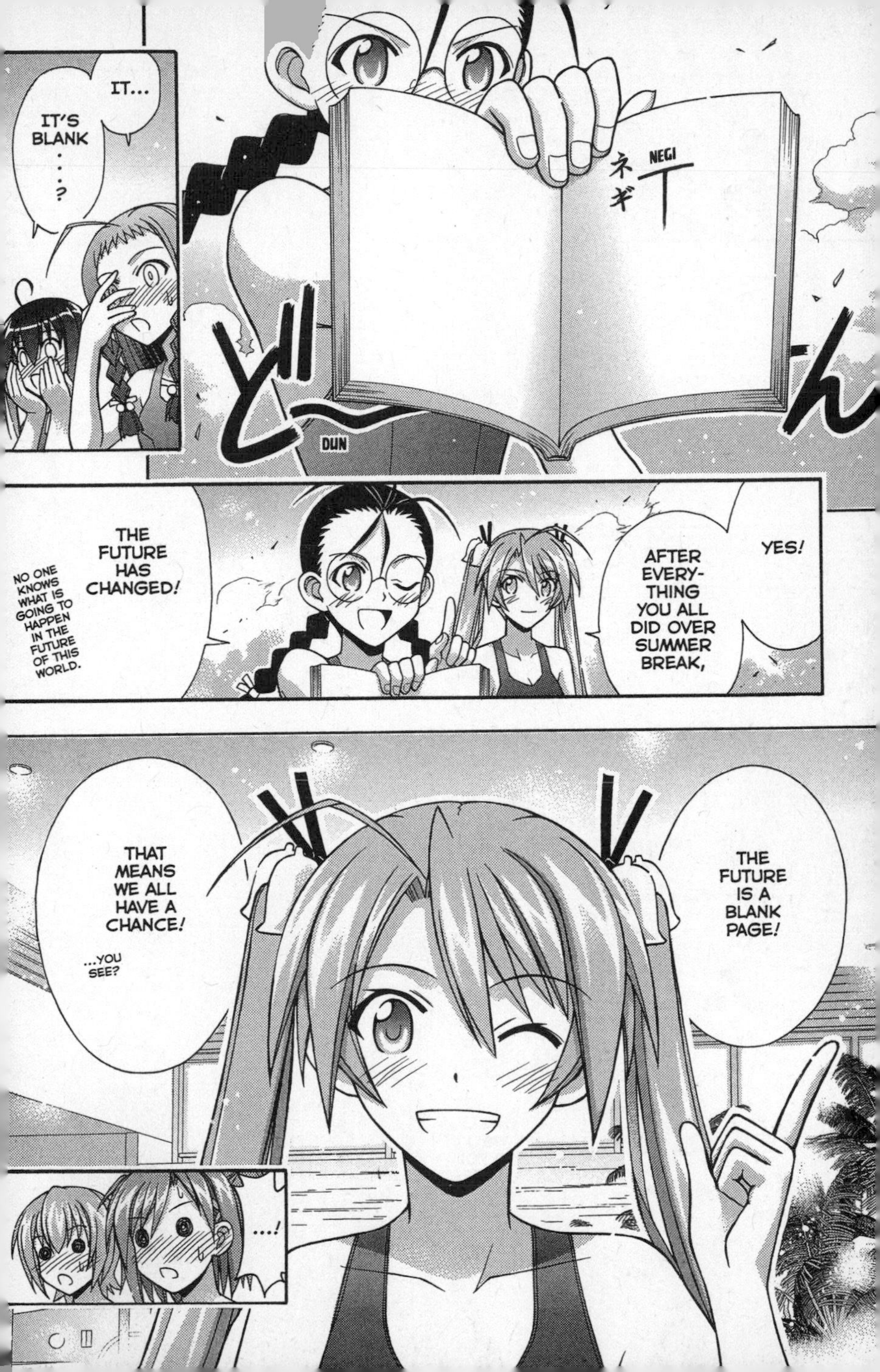
ネギ
NEGI
DUN
IT... IT'S BLANK...?
YES!
AFTER EVERYTHING YOU ALL DID OVER SUMMER BREAK,
THE FUTURE HAS CHANGED!
NO ONE KNOWS WHAT IS GOING TO HAPPEN IN THE FUTURE OF THIS WORLD.
THE FUTURE IS A BLANK PAGE!
THAT MEANS WE ALL HAVE A CHANCE!
...YOU SEE?
...!

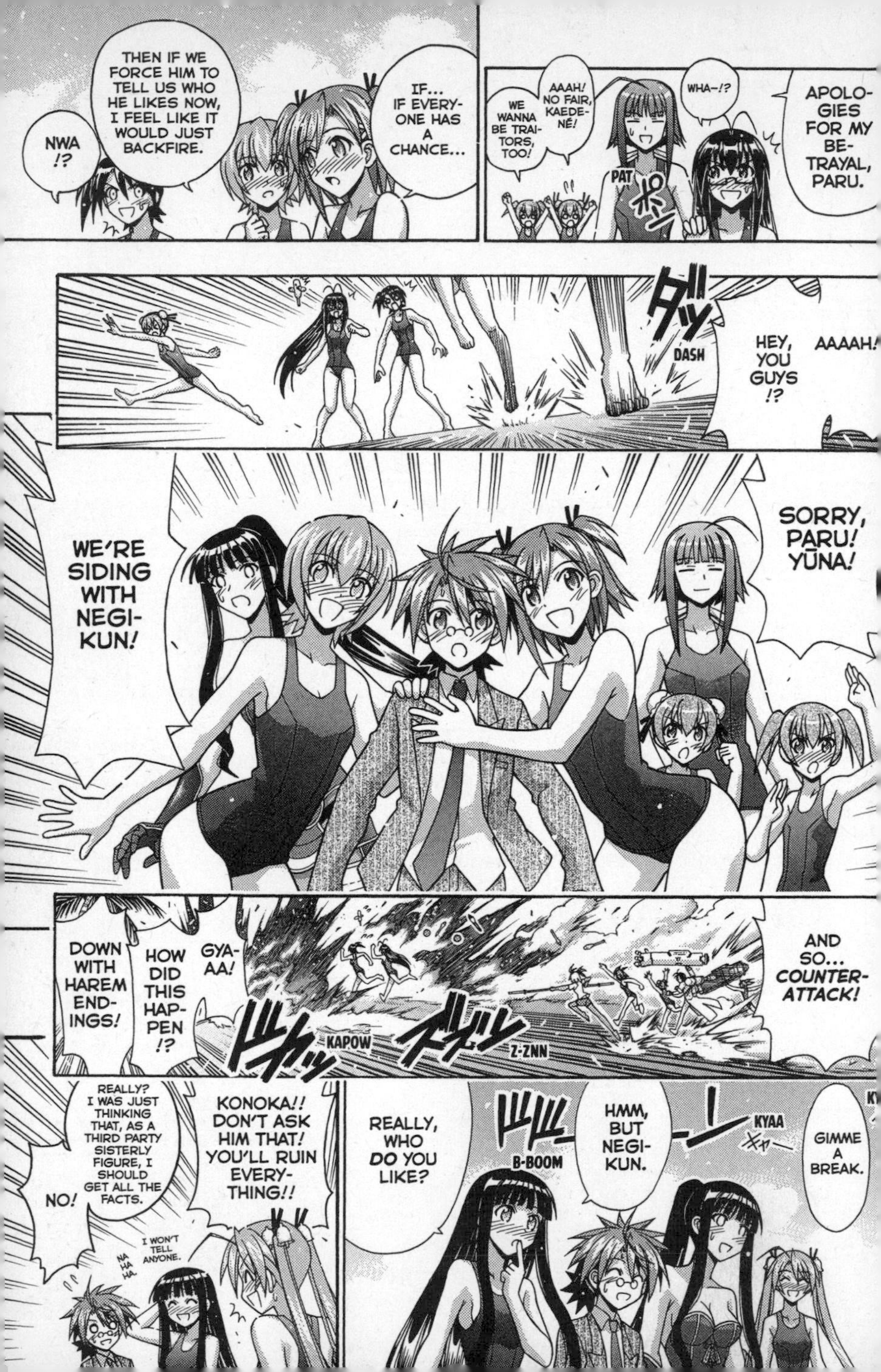
APOLOGIES FOR MY BETRAYAL, PARU.
WHA–!?
AAAH! NO FAIR, KAEDE-NÉ!
WE WANNA BE TRAITORS, TOO!
PAT
IF... IF EVERYONE HAS A CHANCE...
THEN IF WE FORCE HIM TO TELL US WHO HE LIKES NOW, I FEEL LIKE IT WOULD JUST BACKFIRE.
NWA!?
AAAAH!
HEY, YOU GUYS!?
DASH
SORRY, PARU! YŪNA!
WE'RE SIDING WITH NEGI-KUN!
AND SO... COUNTER-ATTACK!
Z-ZNN
KAPOW
GYA-AA!
HOW DID THIS HAPPEN!?
DOWN WITH HAREM ENDINGS!
GIMME A BREAK.
KYAA
HMM, BUT NEGI-KUN.
B-BOOM
REALLY, WHO DO YOU LIKE?
KONOKA!! DON'T ASK HIM THAT! YOU'LL RUIN EVERYTHING!!
REALLY? I WAS JUST THINKING THAT, AS A THIRD PARTY SISTERLY FIGURE, I SHOULD GET ALL THE FACTS.
NO!
I WON'T TELL ANYONE.
NA HA HA.

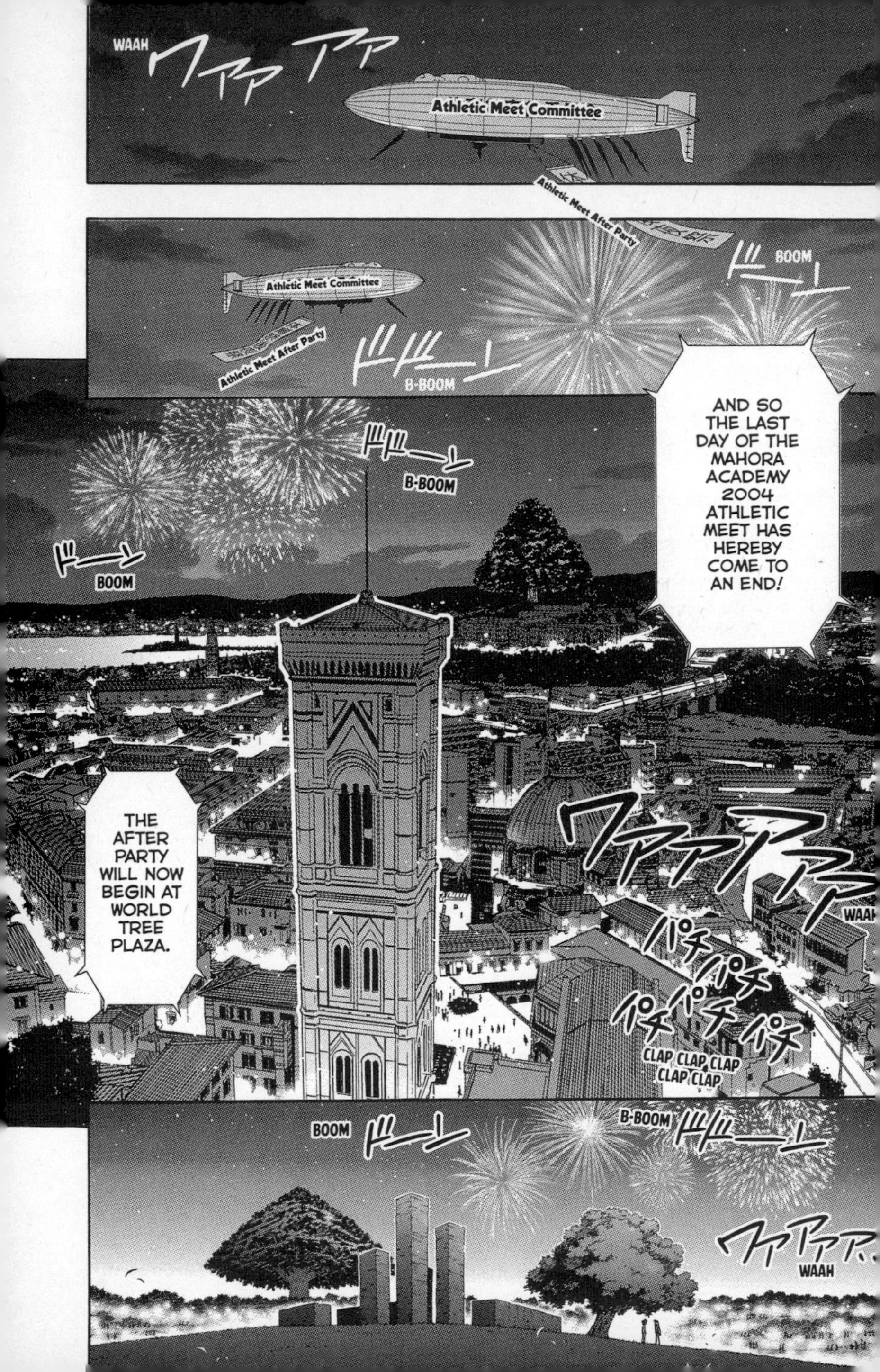

WAAH ワァアア
Athletic Meet Committee
Athletic Meet After Party
ドーン BOOM
Athletic Meet Committee
Athletic Meet After Party
ドドーン B-BOOM
AND SO THE LAST DAY OF THE MAHORA ACADEMY 2004 ATHLETIC MEET HAS HEREBY COME TO AN END!
ドドーン B-BOOM
ドーン BOOM
ワァアアア WAAH
パチパチパチパチパチ CLAP CLAP CLAP CLAP CLAP
THE AFTER PARTY WILL NOW BEGIN AT WORLD TREE PLAZA.
B-BOOM ドドーン
BOOM ドーン
ワァアア WAAH

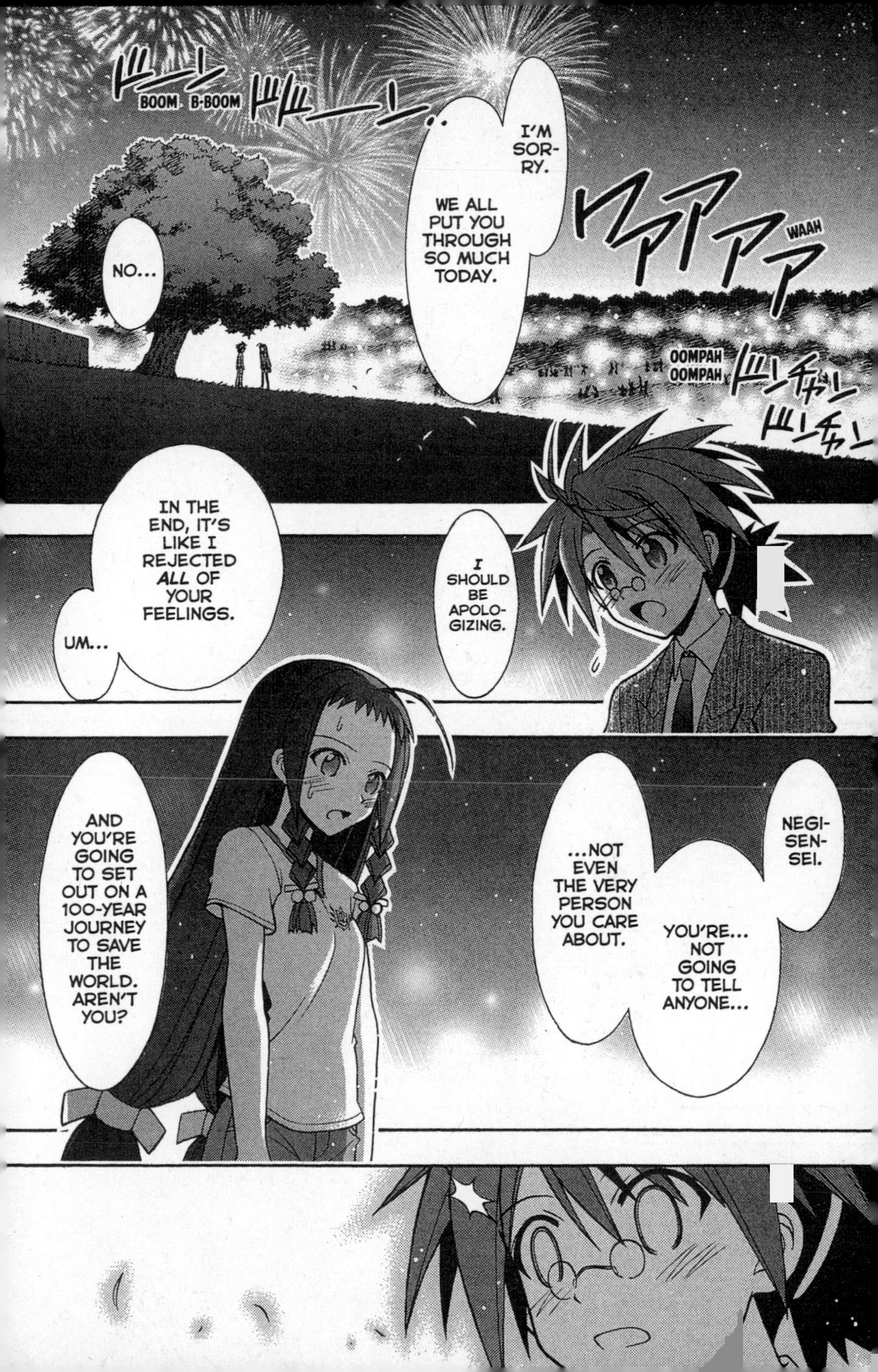
BOOM B-BOOM
I'M SORRY.
WE ALL PUT YOU THROUGH SO MUCH TODAY.
WAAH
NO...
OOMPAH OOMPAH
I SHOULD BE APOLOGIZING.
IN THE END, IT'S LIKE I REJECTED *ALL* OF YOUR FEELINGS.
UM...
NEGI-SENSEI.
YOU'RE... NOT GOING TO TELL ANYONE...
...NOT EVEN THE VERY PERSON YOU CARE ABOUT.
AND YOU'RE GOING TO SET OUT ON A 100-YEAR JOURNEY TO SAVE THE WORLD. AREN'T YOU?

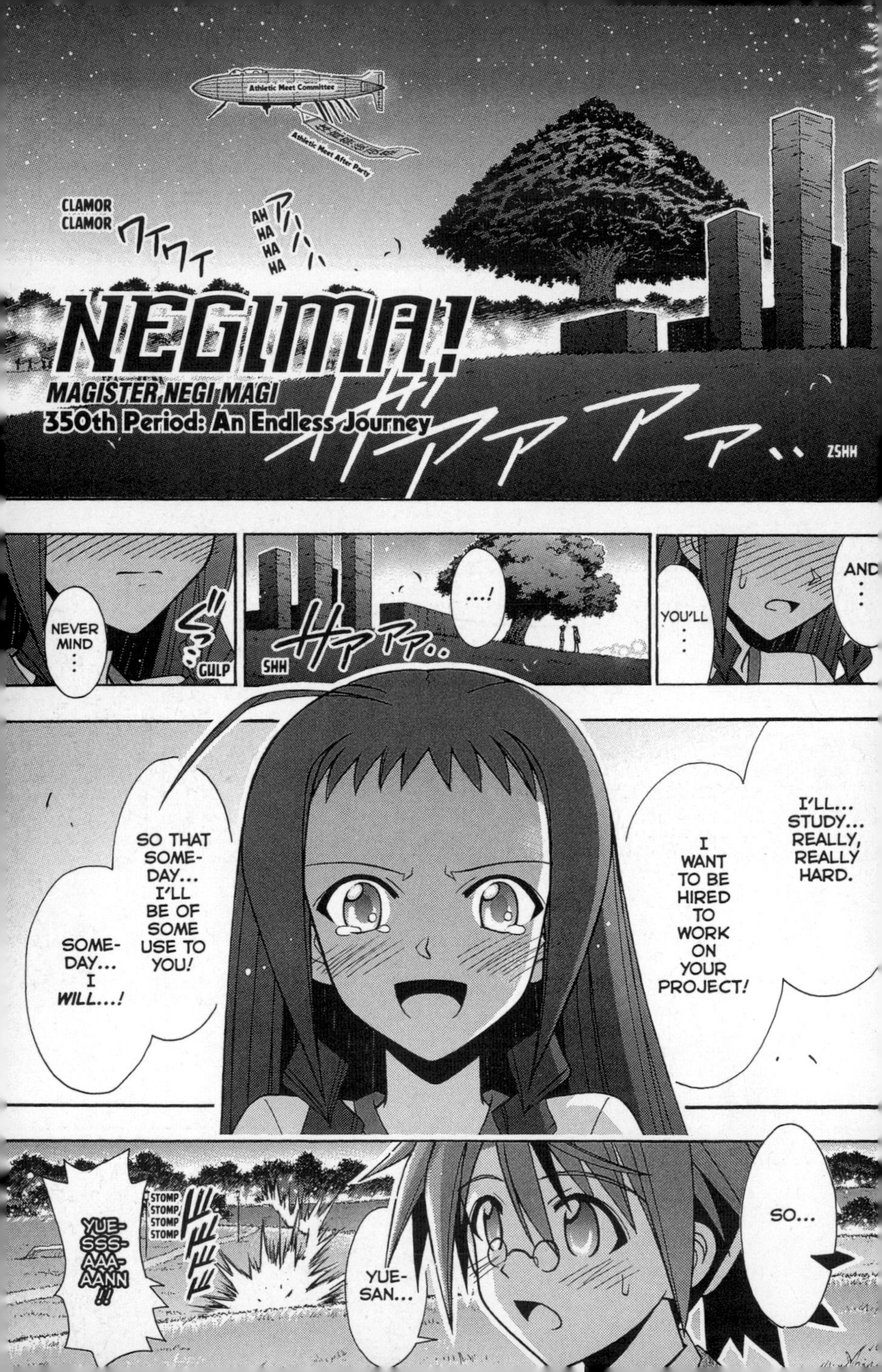
Athletic Meet Committee
Athletic Meet After Party
AH HA HA HA
CLAMOR CLAMOR
NEGIMA!
MAGISTER NEGI MAGI
350th Period: An Endless Journey
ZSHH
AND...
YOU'LL...
...!
SHH
NEVER MIND...
GULP
I'LL... STUDY... REALLY, REALLY HARD.
I WANT TO BE HIRED TO WORK ON YOUR PROJECT!
SO THAT SOME-DAY... I'LL BE OF SOME USE TO YOU!
SOME-DAY... I WILL...!
SO...
YUE-SAN...
STOMP STOMP STOMP STOMP
YUE-SSS-AAA-AANN!!

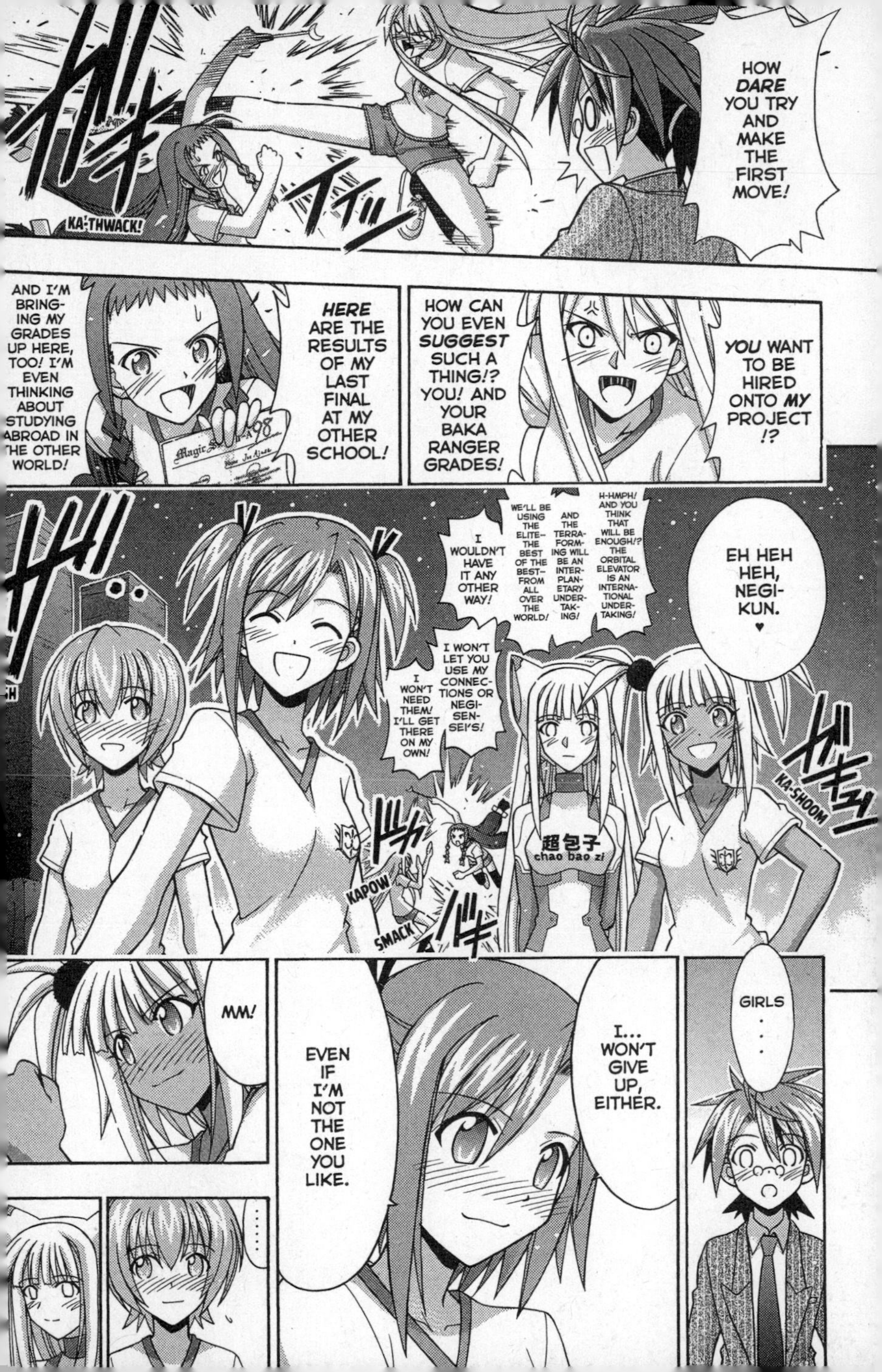

HOW DARE YOU TRY AND MAKE THE FIRST MOVE!
KA-THWACK!
YOU WANT TO BE HIRED ONTO MY PROJECT!?
HOW CAN YOU EVEN SUGGEST SUCH A THING!? YOU! AND YOUR BAKA RANGER GRADES!
HERE ARE THE RESULTS OF MY LAST FINAL AT MY OTHER SCHOOL!
AND I'M BRINGING MY GRADES UP HERE, TOO! I'M EVEN THINKING ABOUT STUDYING ABROAD IN THE OTHER WORLD!
EH HEH HEH, NEGI-KUN. ♥
H-HMPH! AND YOU THINK THAT WILL BE ENOUGH!? THE ORBITAL ELEVATOR IS AN INTERNATIONAL UNDERTAKING!
AND THE TERRAFORMING WILL BE AN INTERPLANETARY UNDERTAKING!
WE'LL BE USING THE ELITE—THE BEST OF THE BEST—FROM ALL OVER THE WORLD!
I WOULDN'T HAVE IT ANY OTHER WAY!
KA-SHOOM
I WON'T LET YOU USE MY CONNECTIONS OR NEGI-SENSEI'S!
I WON'T NEED THEM! I'LL GET THERE ON MY OWN!
超包子
chao bao zi
KAPOW
SMACK
GIRLS . . . .
I... WON'T GIVE UP, EITHER.
EVEN IF I'M NOT THE ONE YOU LIKE.
MM!
......

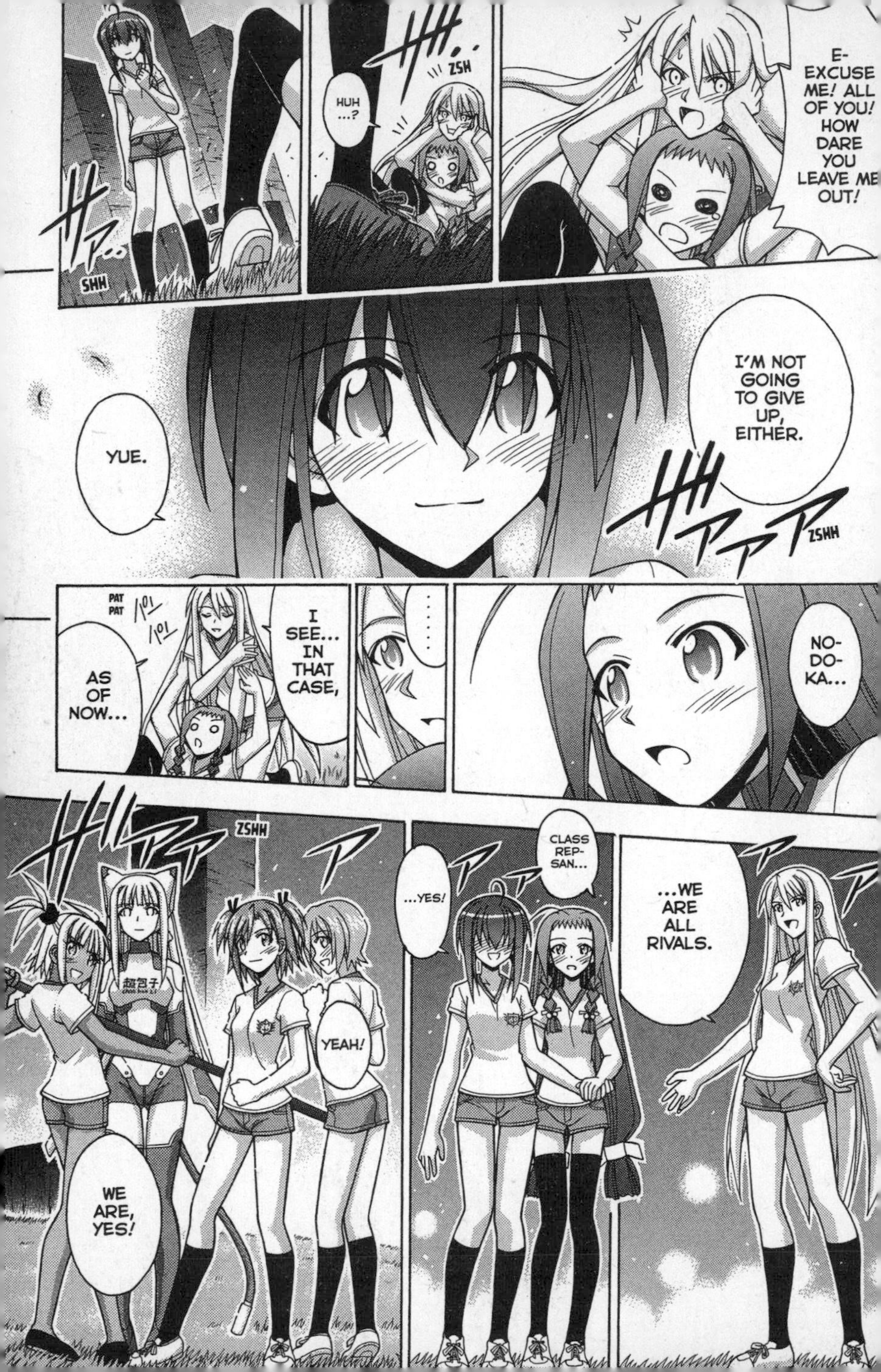
E-
EXCUSE ME! ALL OF YOU! HOW DARE YOU LEAVE ME OUT!
ZSH
HUH ...?
SHH
I'M NOT GOING TO GIVE UP, EITHER.
ZSHH
YUE.
NO-DO-KA...
......
I SEE... IN THAT CASE,
PAT PAT
AS OF NOW...
...WE ARE ALL RIVALS.
CLASS REP-SAN...
...YES!
YEAH!
ZSHH
WE ARE, YES!

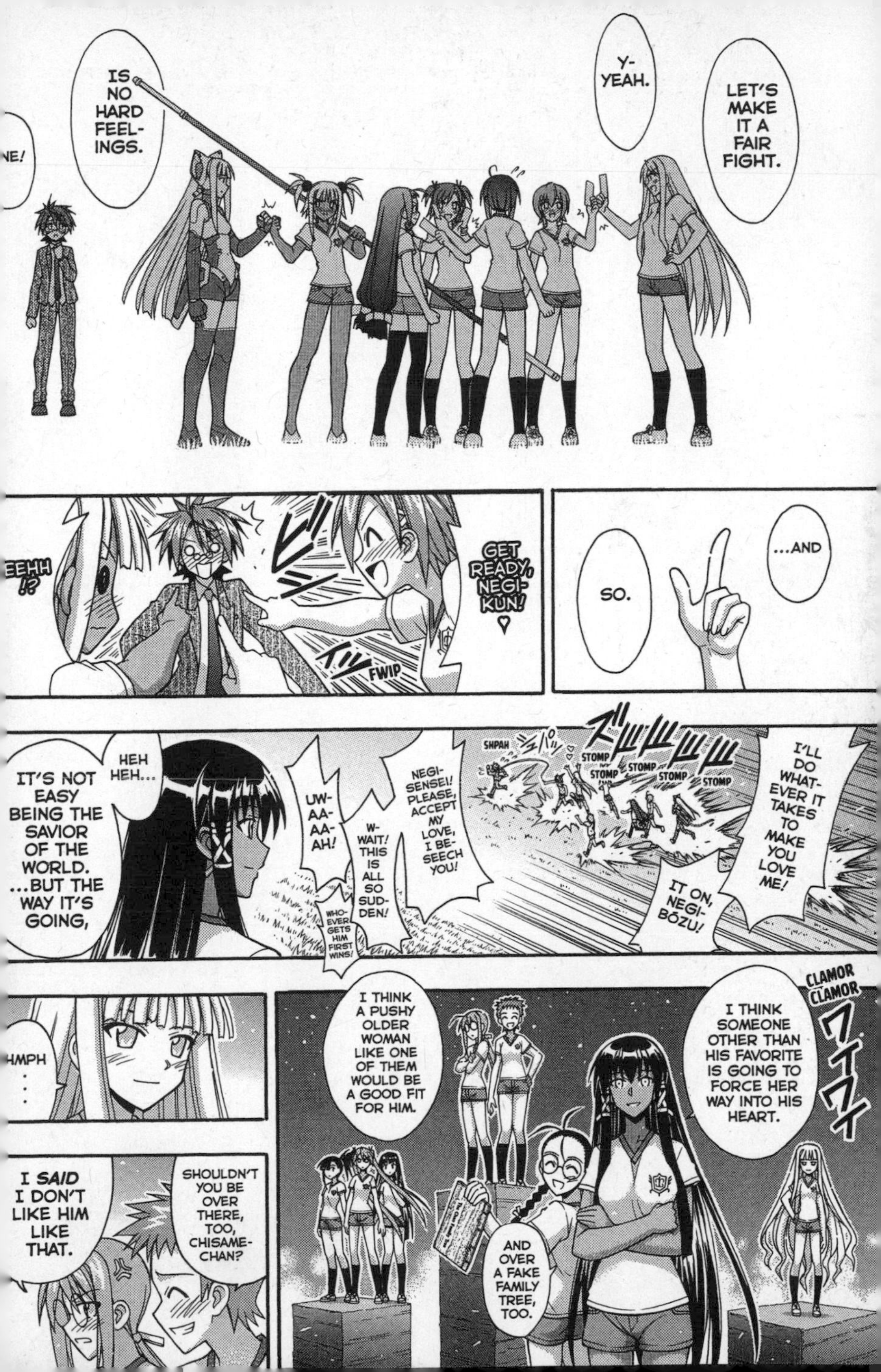
LET'S MAKE IT A FAIR FIGHT.
Y-YEAH.
IS NO HARD FEEL-INGS.
NE!
...AND
SO.
GET READY, NEGI-KUN! ♥
FWIP
EEHH !?
I'LL DO WHAT-EVER IT TAKES TO MAKE YOU LOVE ME!
STOMP STOMP STOMP STOMP STOMP
SHPAH
IT ON, NEGI-BÔZU!
NEGI-SENSEI! PLEASE, ACCEPT MY LOVE, I BE-SEECH YOU!
W-WAIT! THIS IS ALL SO SUD-DEN!
UW-AA-AA-AH!
WHO-EVER GETS HIM FIRST WINS!
HEH HEH...
IT'S NOT EASY BEING THE SAVIOR OF THE WORLD. ...BUT THE WAY IT'S GOING,
CLAMOR CLAMOR
I THINK SOMEONE OTHER THAN HIS FAVORITE IS GOING TO FORCE HER WAY INTO HIS HEART.
I THINK A PUSHY OLDER WOMAN LIKE ONE OF THEM WOULD BE A GOOD FIT FOR HIM.
AND OVER A FAKE FAMILY TREE, TOO.
HMPH...
SHOULDN'T YOU BE OVER THERE, TOO, CHISAME-CHAN?
I *SAID* I DON'T LIKE HIM LIKE THAT.

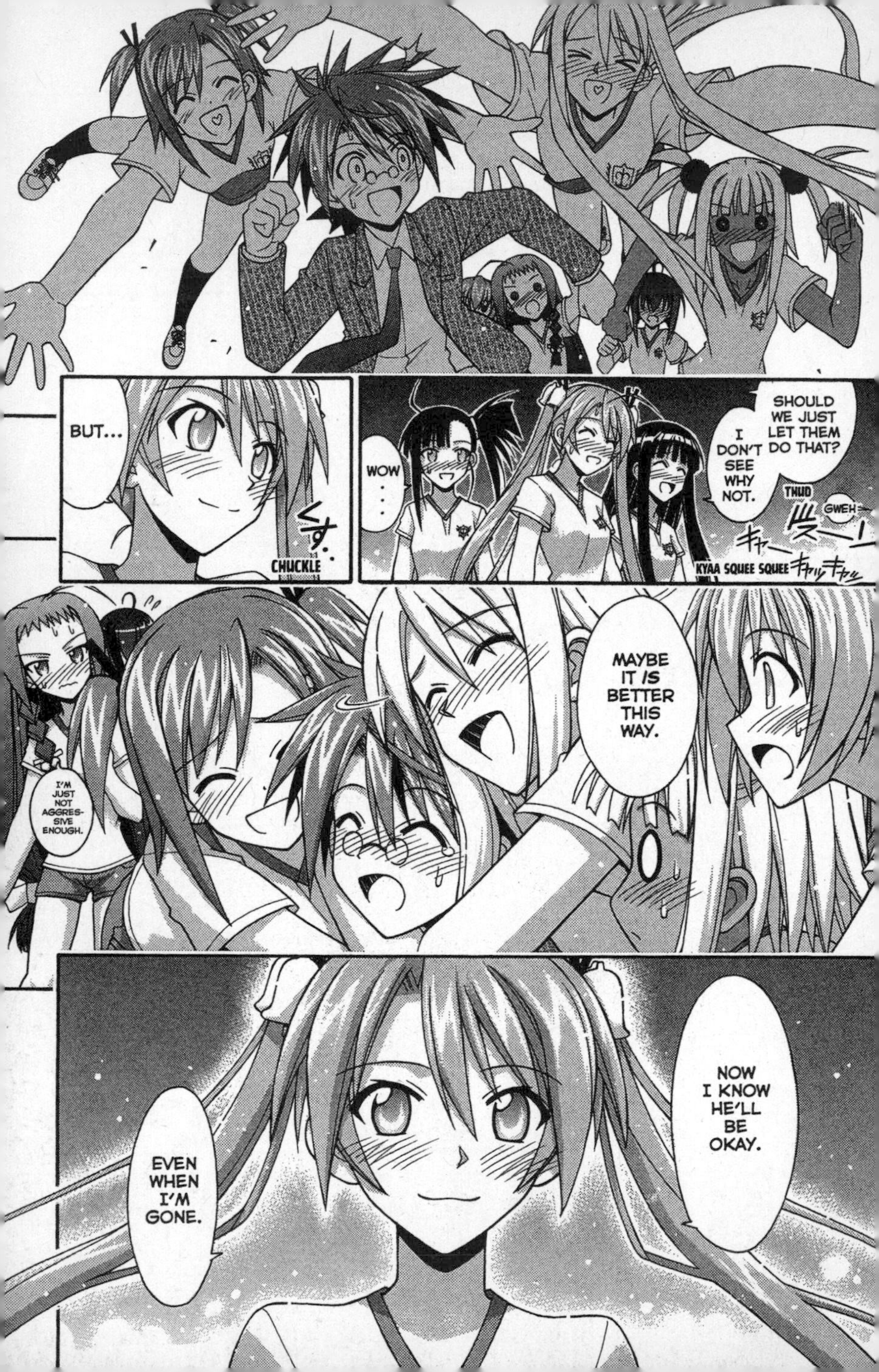
SHOULD WE JUST LET THEM DO THAT?
I DON'T SEE WHY NOT.
WOW . . .
THUD
GWEH
KYAA SQUEE SQUEE
キャー
キャッキャッ
BUT...
くす
CHUCKLE
MAYBE IT *IS* BETTER THIS WAY.
I'M JUST NOT AGGRES-SIVE ENOUGH.
NOW I KNOW HE'LL BE OKAY.
EVEN WHEN I'M GONE.

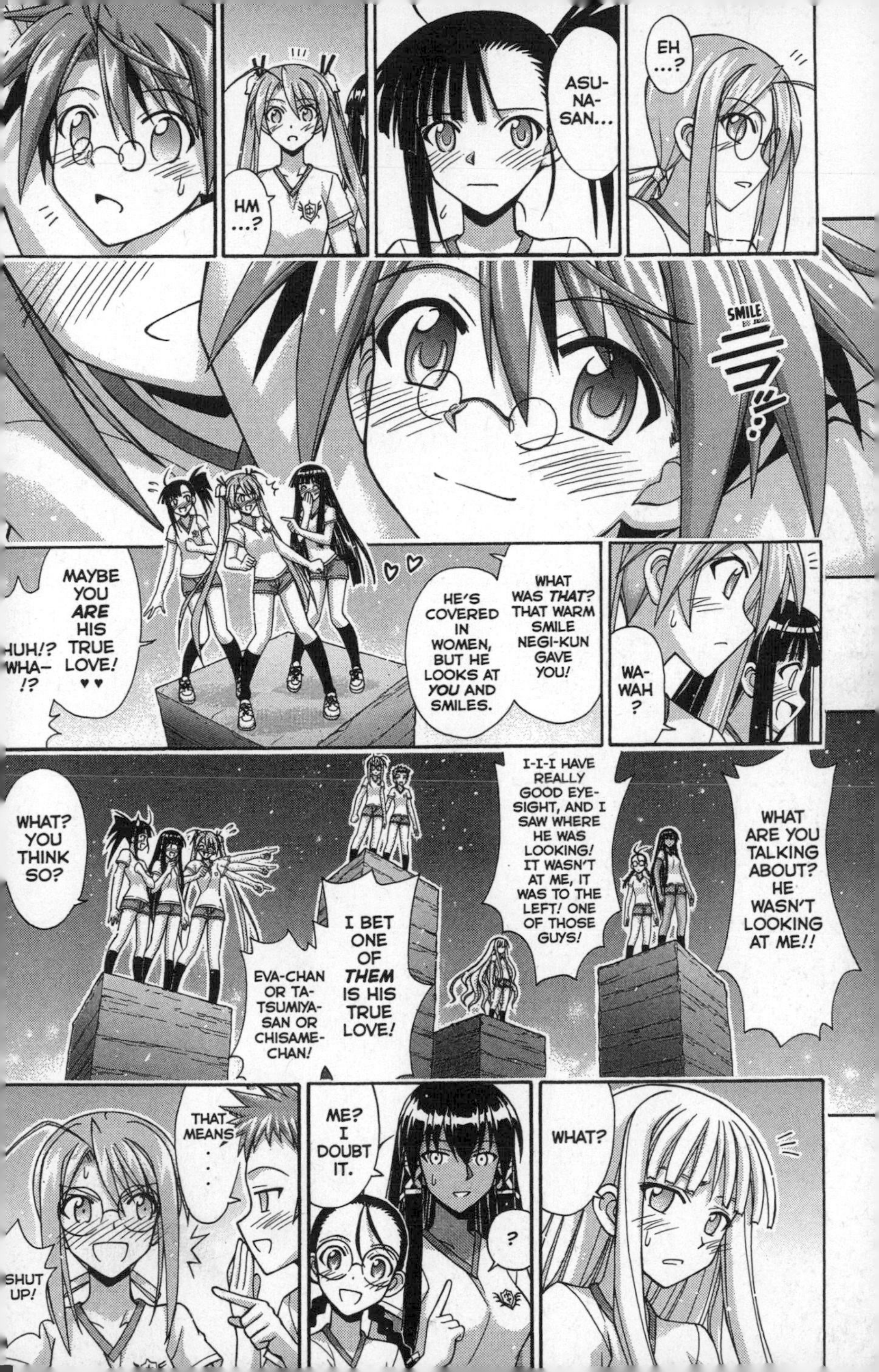
EH ...?
ASUNA-SAN...
HM ...?
SMILE
WA-WAH?
WHAT WAS *THAT*? THAT WARM SMILE NEGI-KUN GAVE YOU!
HE'S COVERED IN WOMEN, BUT HE LOOKS AT *YOU* AND SMILES.
MAYBE YOU ***ARE*** HIS TRUE LOVE! ♥♥
HUH!? WHA-!?
WHAT ARE YOU TALKING ABOUT? HE WASN'T LOOKING AT ME!!
I-I-I HAVE REALLY GOOD EYESIGHT, AND I SAW WHERE HE WAS LOOKING! IT WASN'T AT ME, IT WAS TO THE LEFT! ONE OF THOSE GUYS!
I BET ONE OF ***THEM*** IS HIS TRUE LOVE!
EVA-CHAN OR TATSUMIYA-SAN OR CHISAME-CHAN!
WHAT? YOU THINK SO?
WHAT?
ME? I DOUBT IT.
?
THAT MEANS...
SHUT UP!

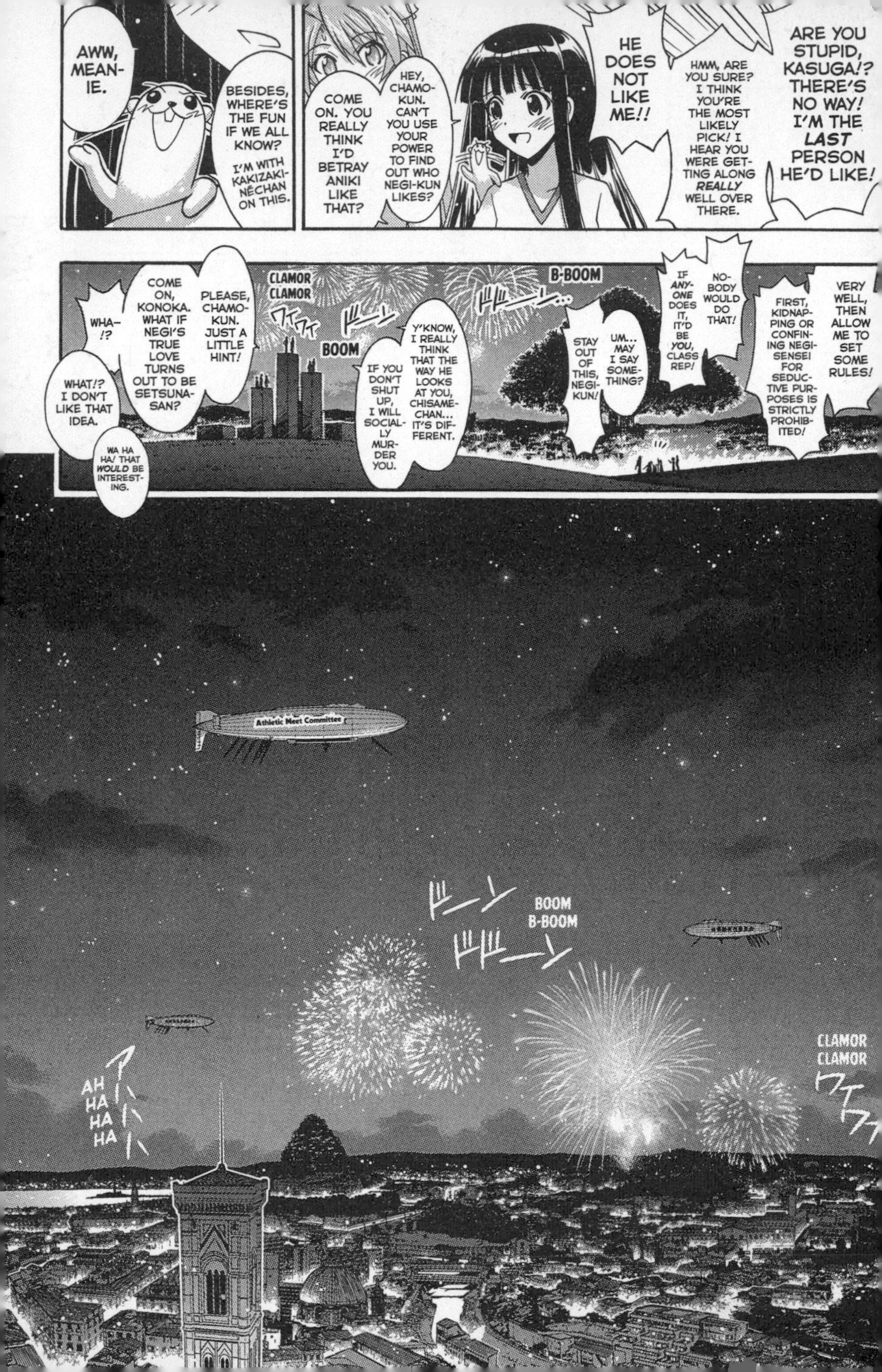
ARE YOU STUPID, KASUGA!? THERE'S NO WAY! I'M THE *LAST* PERSON HE'D LIKE!
HMM, ARE YOU SURE? I THINK YOU'RE THE MOST LIKELY PICK! I HEAR YOU WERE GETTING ALONG *REALLY* WELL OVER THERE.
HE DOES NOT LIKE ME!!
HEY, CHAMO-KUN. CAN'T YOU USE YOUR POWER TO FIND OUT WHO NEGI-KUN LIKES?
COME ON. YOU REALLY THINK I'D BETRAY ANIKI LIKE THAT?
BESIDES, WHERE'S THE FUN IF WE ALL KNOW?
I'M WITH KAKIZAKI-NÉCHAN ON THIS.
AWW, MEANIE.
VERY WELL, THEN ALLOW ME TO SET SOME RULES!
FIRST, KIDNAPPING OR CONFINING NEGI-SENSEI FOR SEDUCTIVE PURPOSES IS STRICTLY PROHIBITED!
NOBODY WOULD DO THAT!
IF *ANYONE* DOES IT, IT'D BE *YOU*, CLASS REP!
UM... MAY I SAY SOMETHING?
STAY OUT OF THIS, NEGI-KUN!
B-BOOM
Y'KNOW, I REALLY THINK THAT THE WAY HE LOOKS AT YOU, CHISAME-CHAN... IT'S DIFFERENT.
IF YOU DON'T SHUT UP, I WILL SOCIALLY MURDER YOU.
BOOM
CLAMOR CLAMOR
PLEASE, CHAMO-KUN. JUST A LITTLE HINT!
COME ON, KONOKA. WHAT IF NEGI'S TRUE LOVE TURNS OUT TO BE SETSUNA-SAN?
WHA-!?
WHAT!? I DON'T LIKE THAT IDEA.
WA HA HA! THAT *WOULD* BE INTERESTING.
Athletic Meet Committee
BOOM
B-BOOM
CLAMOR
CLAMOR
AH
HA
HA
HA

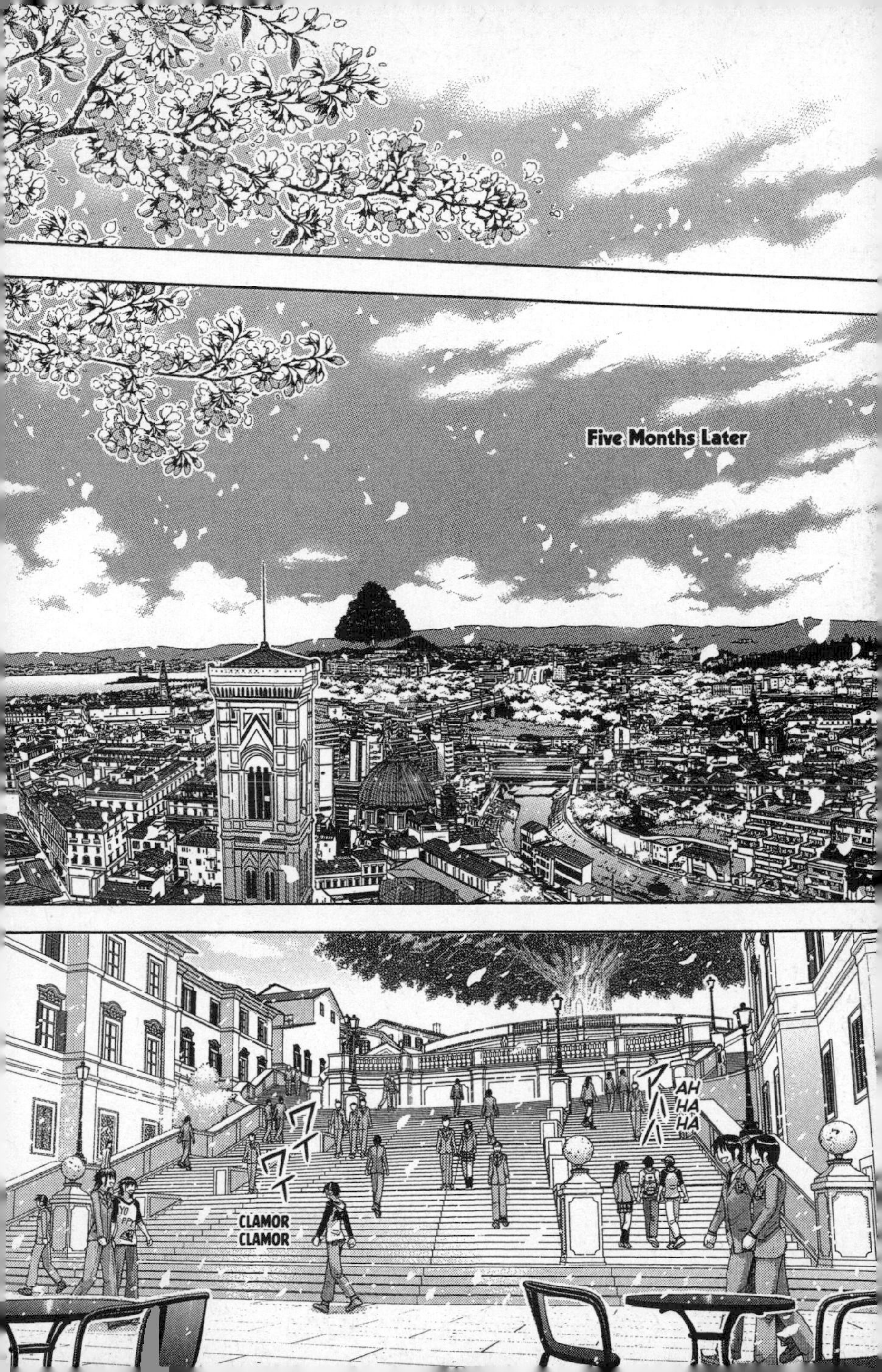
Five Months Later
アハハ
AH HA HA
ワイワイ
CLAMOR CLAMOR

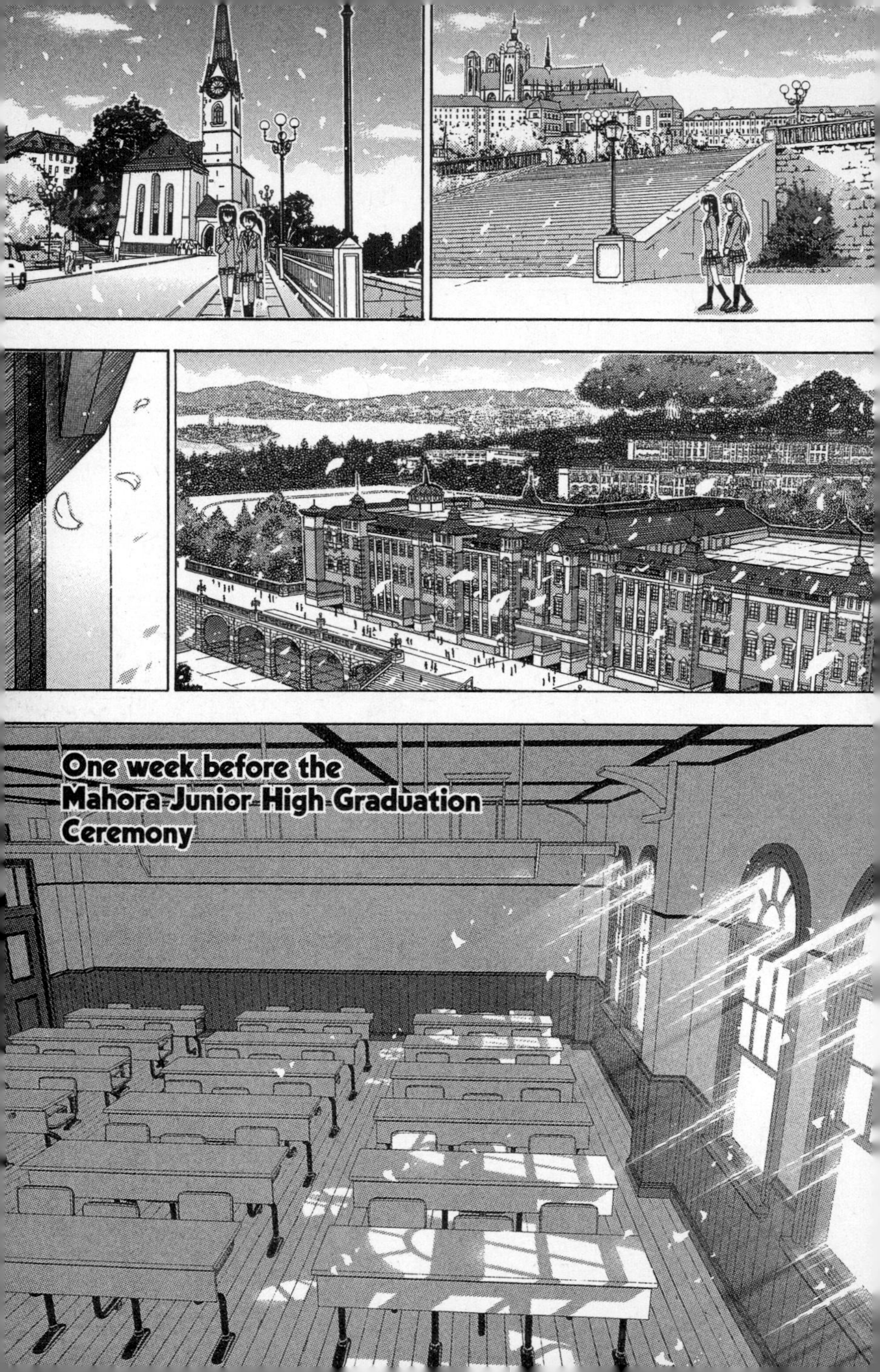
One week before the Mahora Junior High Graduation Ceremony

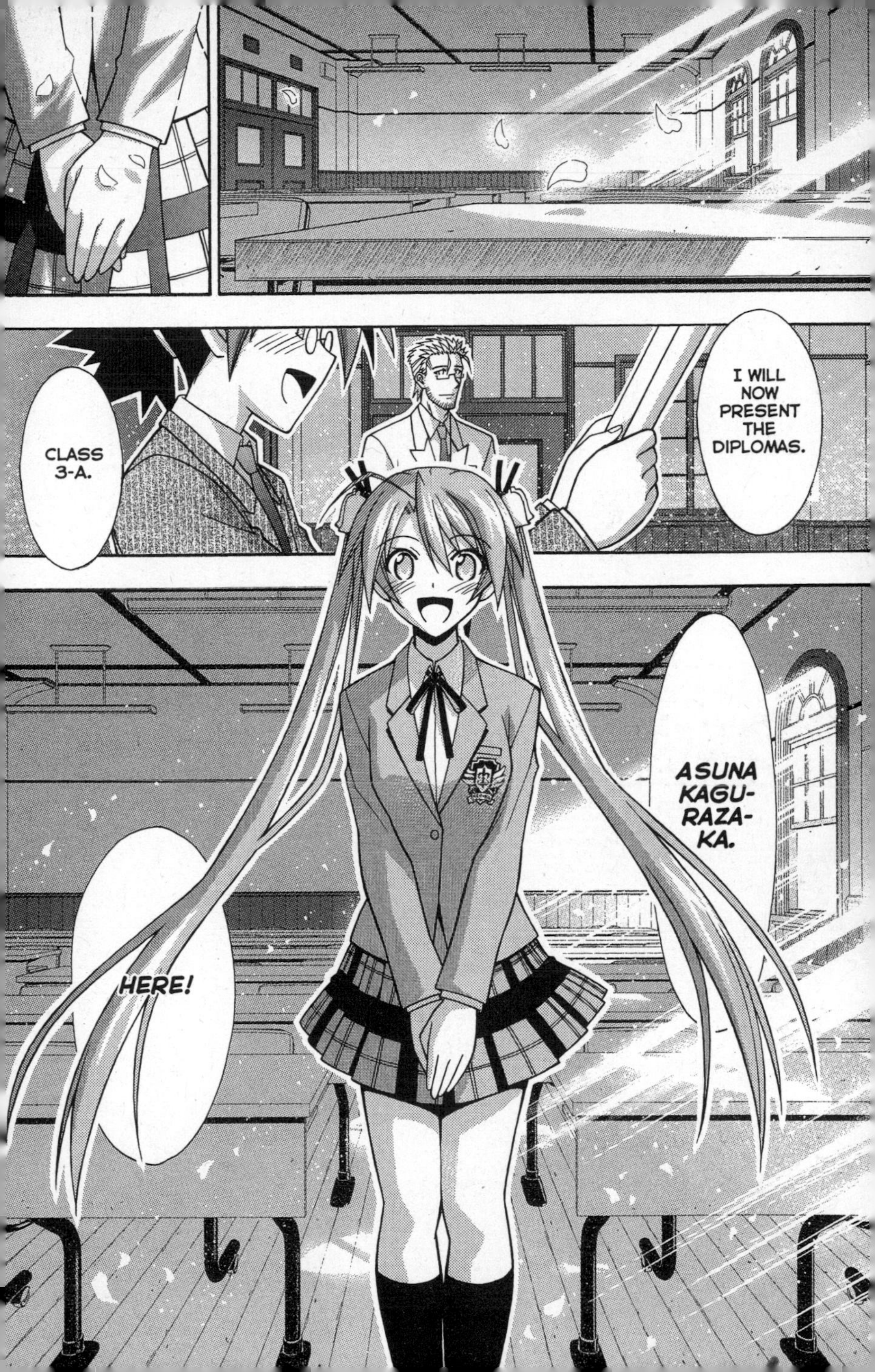
I WILL NOW PRESENT THE DIPLOMAS.
CLASS 3-A.
ASUNA KAGU-RAZA-KA.
HERE!

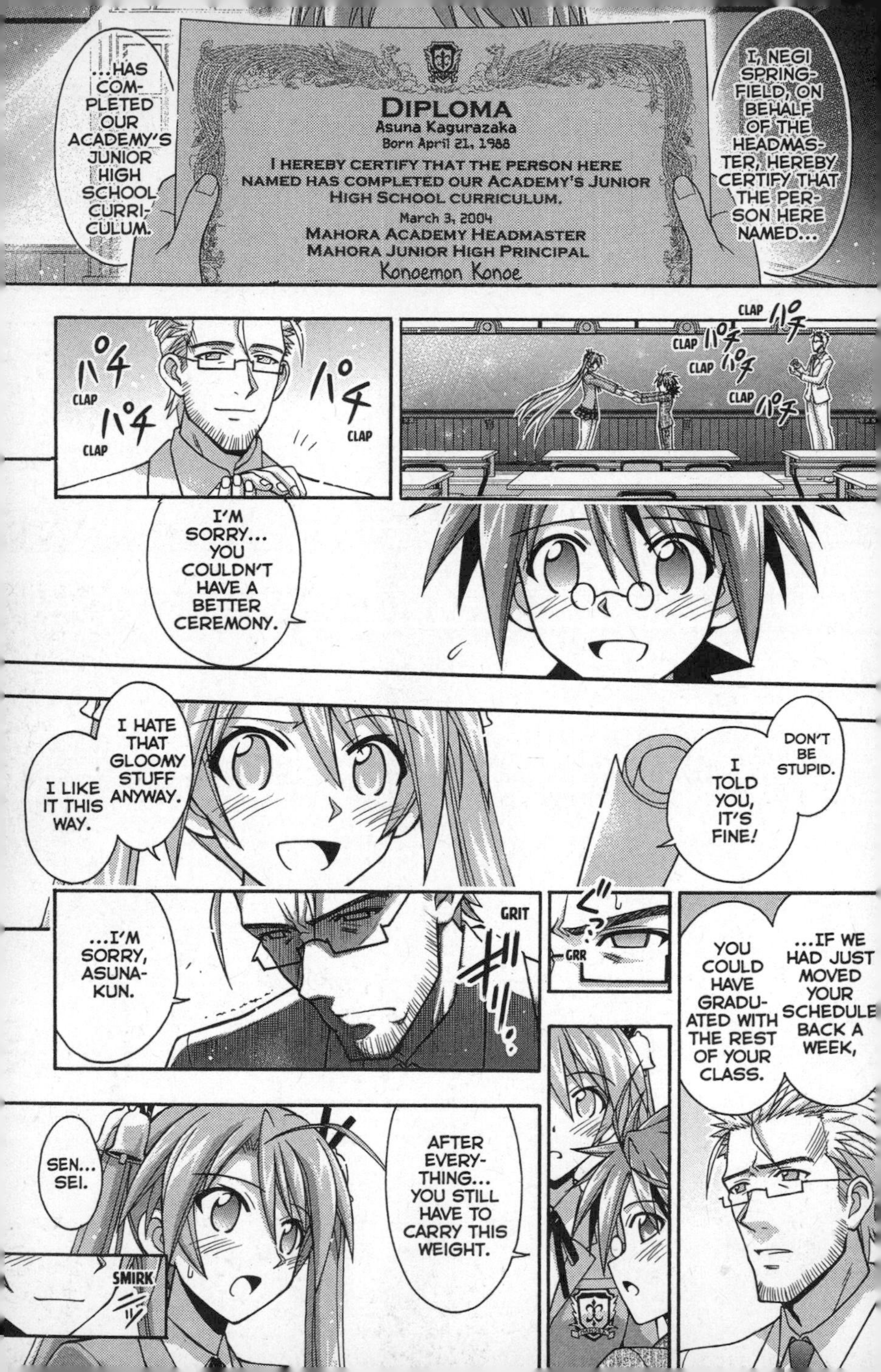
I, NEGI SPRINGFIELD, ON BEHALF OF THE HEADMASTER, HEREBY CERTIFY THAT THE PERSON HERE NAMED...
DIPLOMA
Asuna Kagurazaka
Born April 21, 1988
I HEREBY CERTIFY THAT THE PERSON HERE NAMED HAS COMPLETED OUR ACADEMY'S JUNIOR HIGH SCHOOL CURRICULUM.
March 3, 2004
MAHORA ACADEMY HEADMASTER
MAHORA JUNIOR HIGH PRINCIPAL
Konoemon Konoe
...HAS COMPLETED OUR ACADEMY'S JUNIOR HIGH SCHOOL CURRICULUM.
パチ CLAP
パチ CLAP
パチ CLAP
パチ CLAP
パチ CLAP
パチ CLAP
パチ CLAP
I'M SORRY... YOU COULDN'T HAVE A BETTER CEREMONY.
DON'T BE STUPID.
I TOLD YOU, IT'S FINE!
I HATE THAT GLOOMY STUFF ANYWAY.
I LIKE IT THIS WAY.
...IF WE HAD JUST MOVED YOUR SCHEDULE BACK A WEEK,
YOU COULD HAVE GRADUATED WITH THE REST OF YOUR CLASS.
GRR
GRIT
...I'M SORRY, ASUNA-KUN.
AFTER EVERYTHING... YOU STILL HAVE TO CARRY THIS WEIGHT.
SEN... SEI.
SMIRK

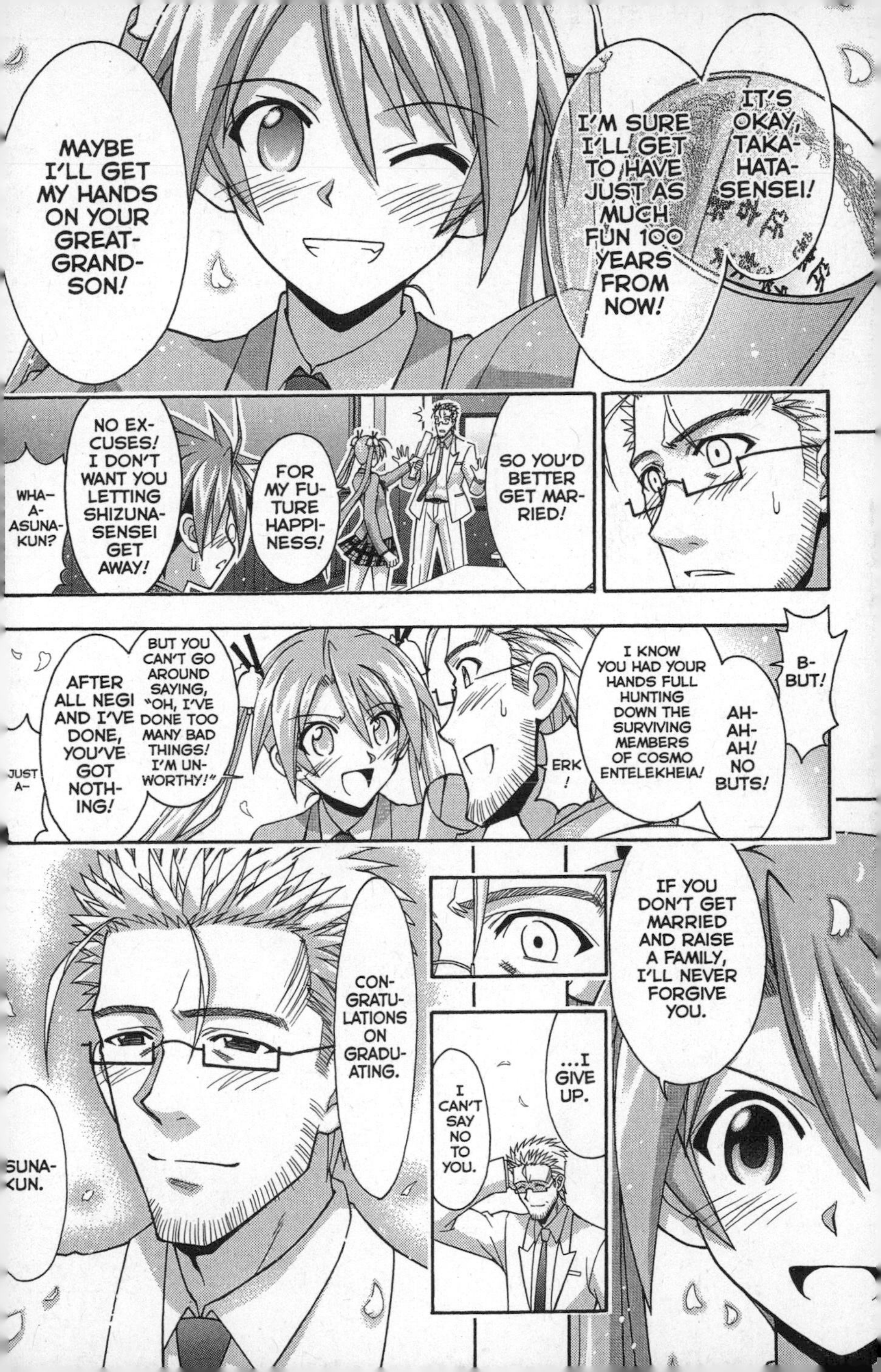
IT'S OKAY, TAKAHATA-SENSEI!
I'M SURE I'LL GET TO HAVE JUST AS MUCH FUN 100 YEARS FROM NOW!
MAYBE I'LL GET MY HANDS ON YOUR GREAT-GRANDSON!
SO YOU'D BETTER GET MARRIED!
FOR MY FUTURE HAPPINESS!
NO EXCUSES! I DON'T WANT YOU LETTING SHIZUNA-SENSEI GET AWAY!
WHA-A-ASUNA-KUN?
B-BUT!
AH-AH-AH! NO BUTS!
I KNOW YOU HAD YOUR HANDS FULL HUNTING DOWN THE SURVIVING MEMBERS OF COSMO ENTELEKHEIA!
ERK!
BUT YOU CAN'T GO AROUND SAYING, "OH, I'VE DONE TOO MANY BAD THINGS! I'M UNWORTHY!"
AFTER ALL NEGI AND I'VE DONE, YOU'VE GOT NOTHING!
JUST A-
IF YOU DON'T GET MARRIED AND RAISE A FAMILY, I'LL NEVER FORGIVE YOU.
...I GIVE UP.
I CAN'T SAY NO TO YOU.
CONGRATULATIONS ON GRADUATING.
SUNA-KUN.

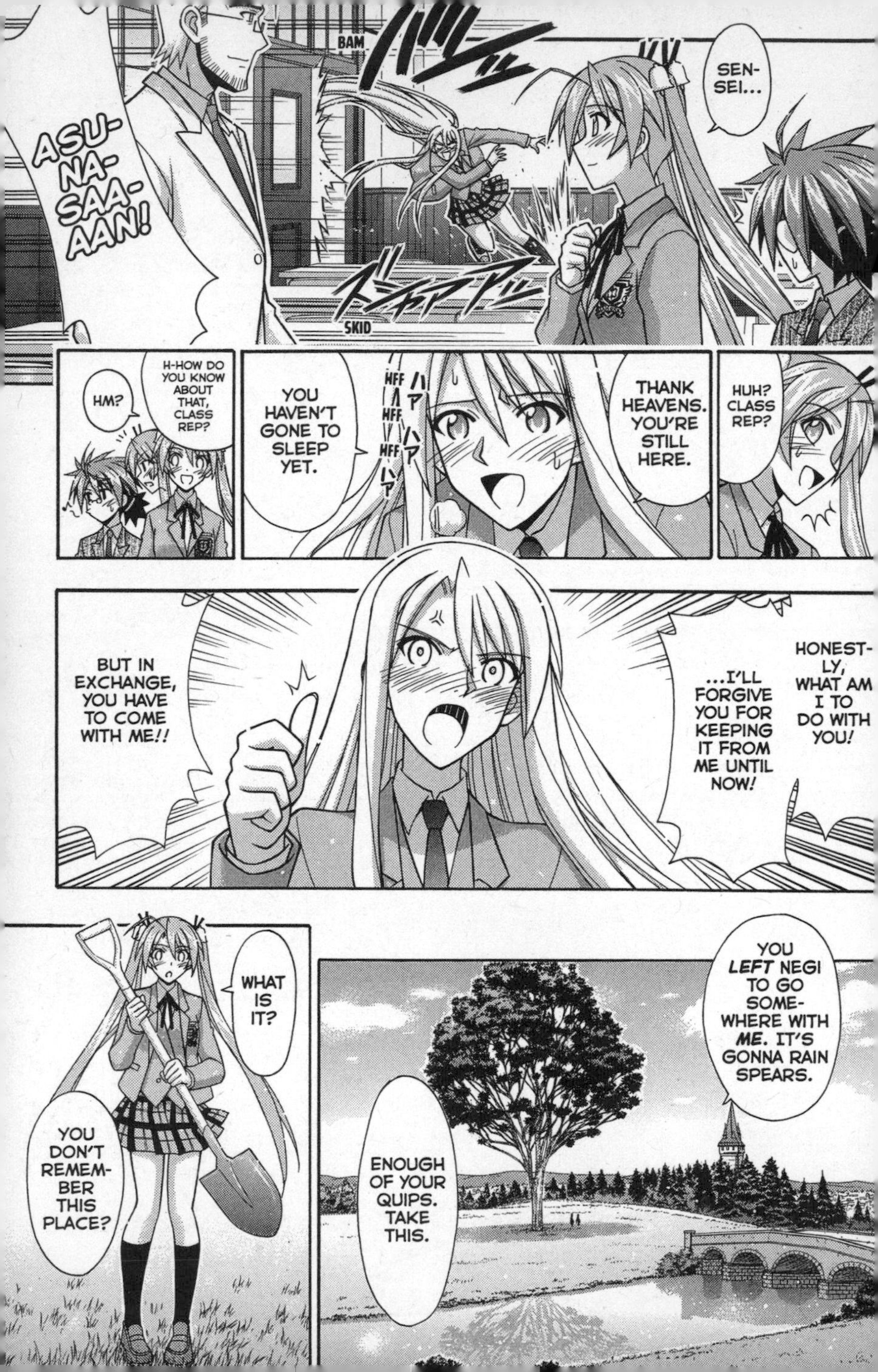
SEN-SEI...
BAM
ASU-NA-SAAA-AAN!
SKID
HUH? CLASS REP?
THANK HEAVENS. YOU'RE STILL HERE.
HFF HFF HFF
YOU HAVEN'T GONE TO SLEEP YET.
H-HOW DO YOU KNOW ABOUT THAT, CLASS REP?
HM?
HONEST-LY, WHAT AM I TO DO WITH YOU!
...I'LL FORGIVE YOU FOR KEEPING IT FROM ME UNTIL NOW!
BUT IN EXCHANGE, YOU HAVE TO COME WITH ME!!
YOU LEFT NEGI TO GO SOME-WHERE WITH ME. IT'S GONNA RAIN SPEARS.
ENOUGH OF YOUR QUIPS. TAKE THIS.
WHAT IS IT?
YOU DON'T REMEM-BER THIS PLACE?

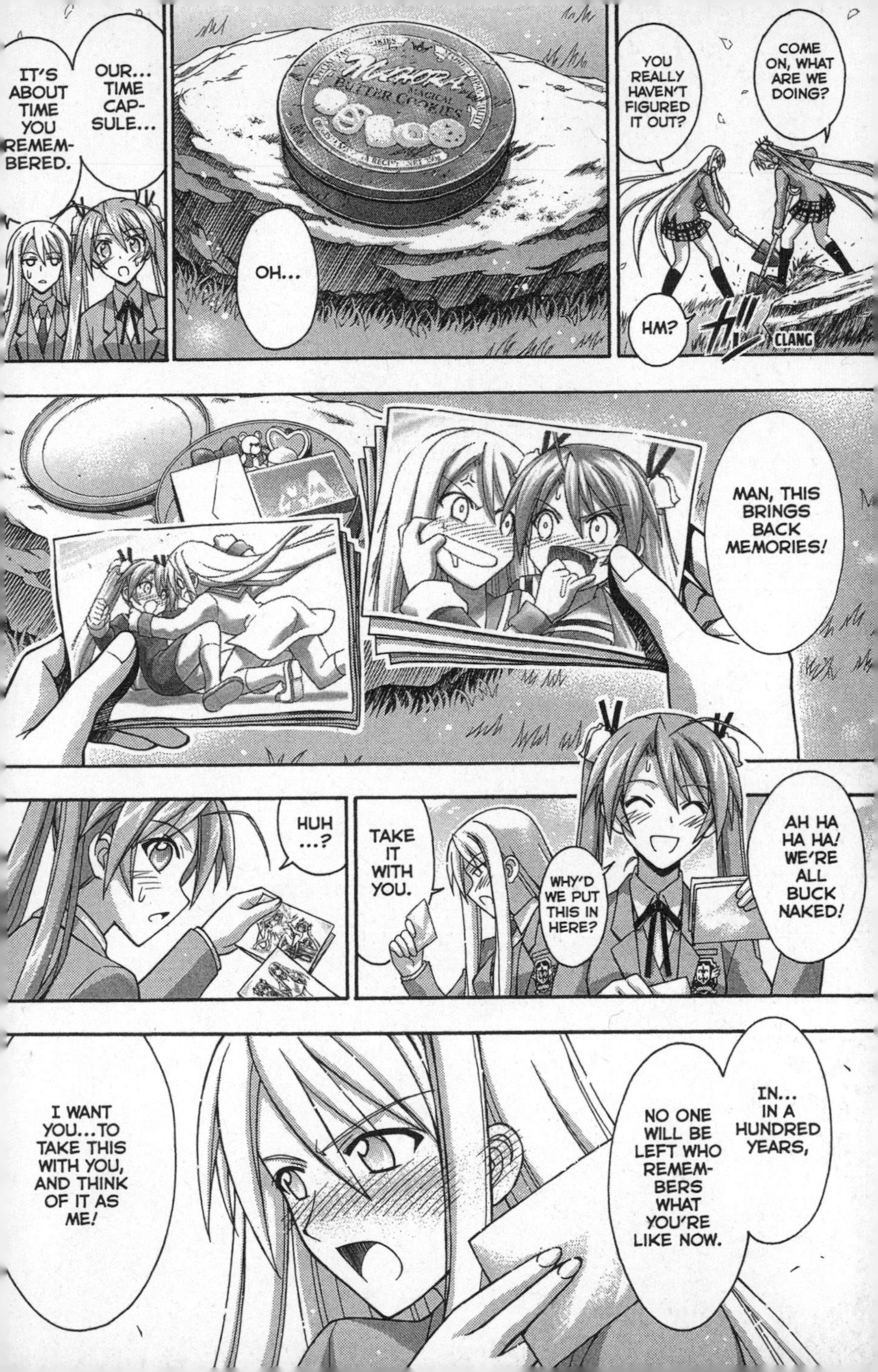
COME ON, WHAT ARE WE DOING?
YOU REALLY HAVEN'T FIGURED IT OUT?
HM?
CLANG
MAGICAL
BUTTER COOKIES
OH...
OUR... TIME CAPSULE...
IT'S ABOUT TIME YOU REMEMBERED.
MAN, THIS BRINGS BACK MEMORIES!
AH HA HA HA! WE'RE ALL BUCK NAKED!
WHY'D WE PUT THIS IN HERE?
TAKE IT WITH YOU.
HUH ...?
IN... IN A HUNDRED YEARS,
NO ONE WILL BE LEFT WHO REMEMBERS WHAT YOU'RE LIKE NOW.
I WANT YOU...TO TAKE THIS WITH YOU, AND THINK OF IT AS ME!

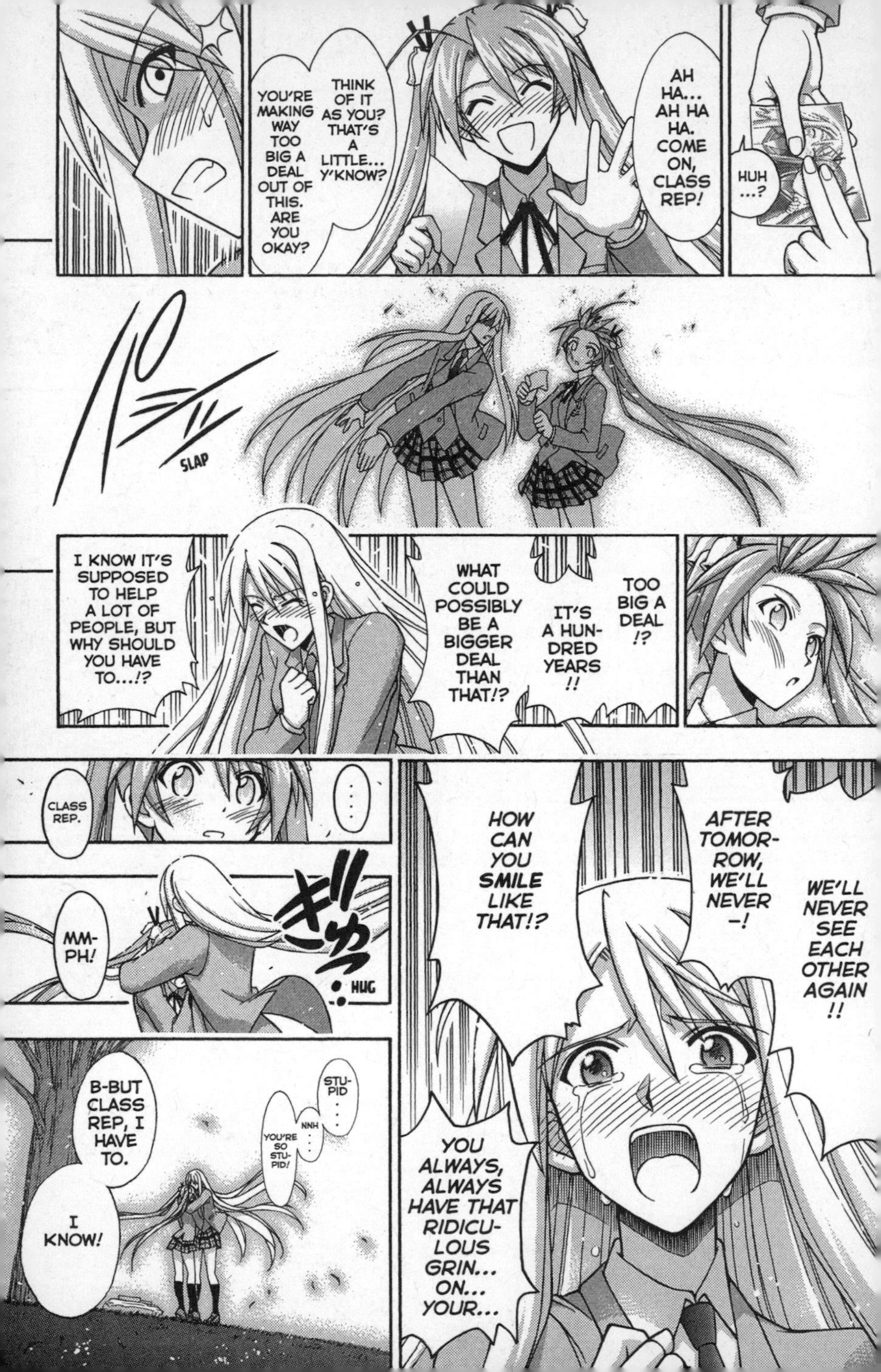
HUH ...?
AH HA... AH HA HA. COME ON, CLASS REP!
THINK OF IT AS YOU? THAT'S A LITTLE... Y'KNOW?
YOU'RE MAKING WAY TOO BIG A DEAL OUT OF THIS. ARE YOU OKAY?
SLAP
TOO BIG A DEAL !?
IT'S A HUN-DRED YEARS !!
WHAT COULD POSSIBLY BE A BIGGER DEAL THAN THAT!?
I KNOW IT'S SUPPOSED TO HELP A LOT OF PEOPLE, BUT WHY SHOULD YOU HAVE TO...!?
WE'LL NEVER SEE EACH OTHER AGAIN !!
AFTER TOMOR-ROW, WE'LL NEVER —!
HOW CAN YOU SMILE LIKE THAT!?
YOU ALWAYS, ALWAYS HAVE THAT RIDICU-LOUS GRIN... ON... YOUR...
...
CLASS REP.
HUG
MM-PH!
STU-PID ...
NNH ...
YOU'RE SO STU-PID!
B-BUT CLASS REP, I HAVE TO.
I KNOW!

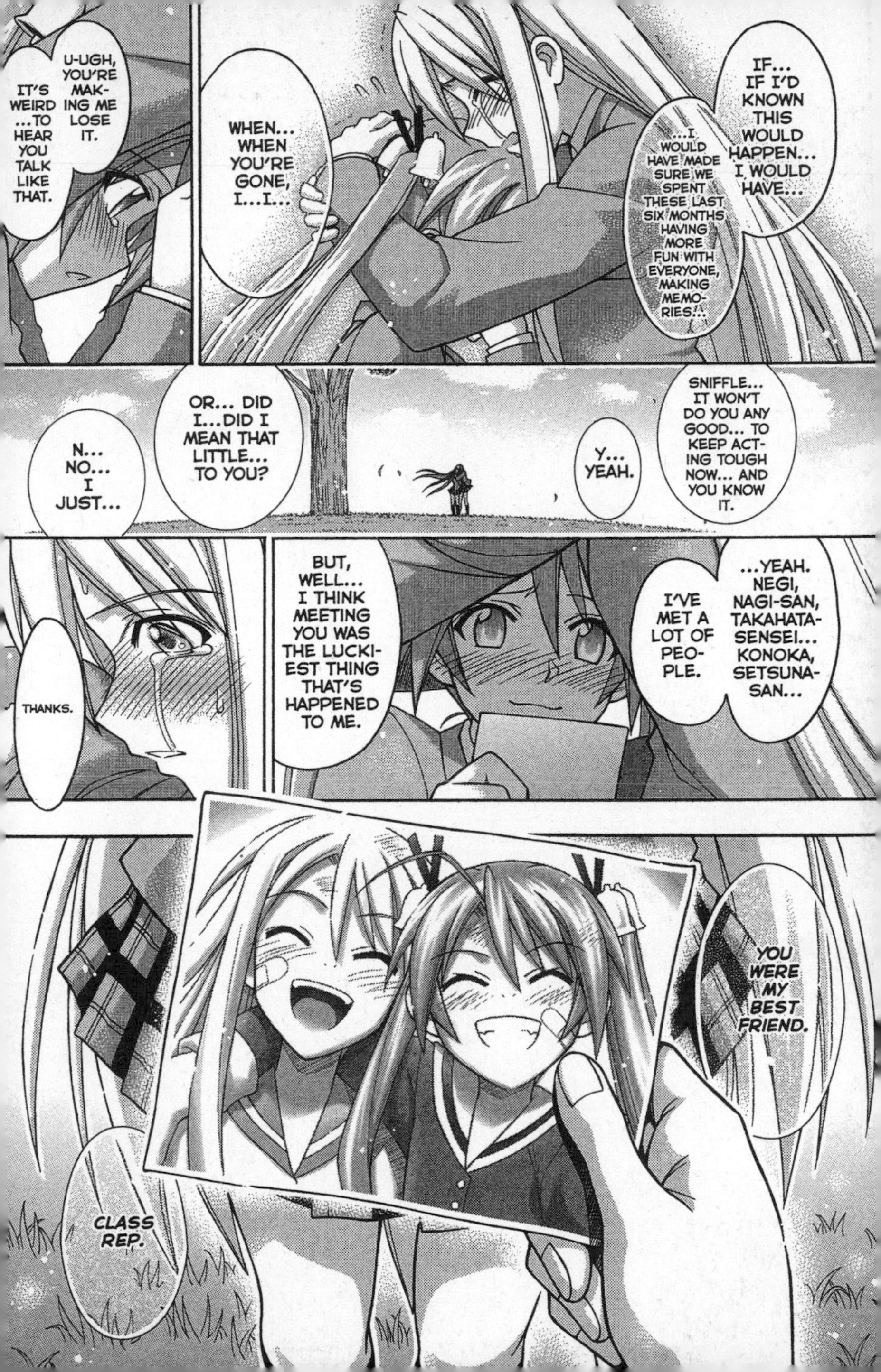
IF... IF I'D KNOWN THIS WOULD HAPPEN... I WOULD HAVE...
...I WOULD HAVE MADE SURE WE SPENT THESE LAST SIX MONTHS HAVING MORE FUN WITH EVERYONE, MAKING MEMORIES...
WHEN... WHEN YOU'RE GONE, I...I...
U-UGH, YOU'RE MAKING ME LOSE IT.
IT'S WEIRD ...TO HEAR YOU TALK LIKE THAT.
SNIFFLE... IT WON'T DO YOU ANY GOOD... TO KEEP ACTING TOUGH NOW... AND YOU KNOW IT.
Y... YEAH.
OR... DID I...DID I MEAN THAT LITTLE... TO YOU?
N... NO... I JUST...
...YEAH. NEGI, NAGI-SAN, TAKAHATA-SENSEI... KONOKA, SETSUNA-SAN...
I'VE MET A LOT OF PEOPLE.
BUT, WELL... I THINK MEETING YOU WAS THE LUCKIEST THING THAT'S HAPPENED TO ME.
THANKS.
YOU WERE MY BEST FRIEND.
CLASS REP.

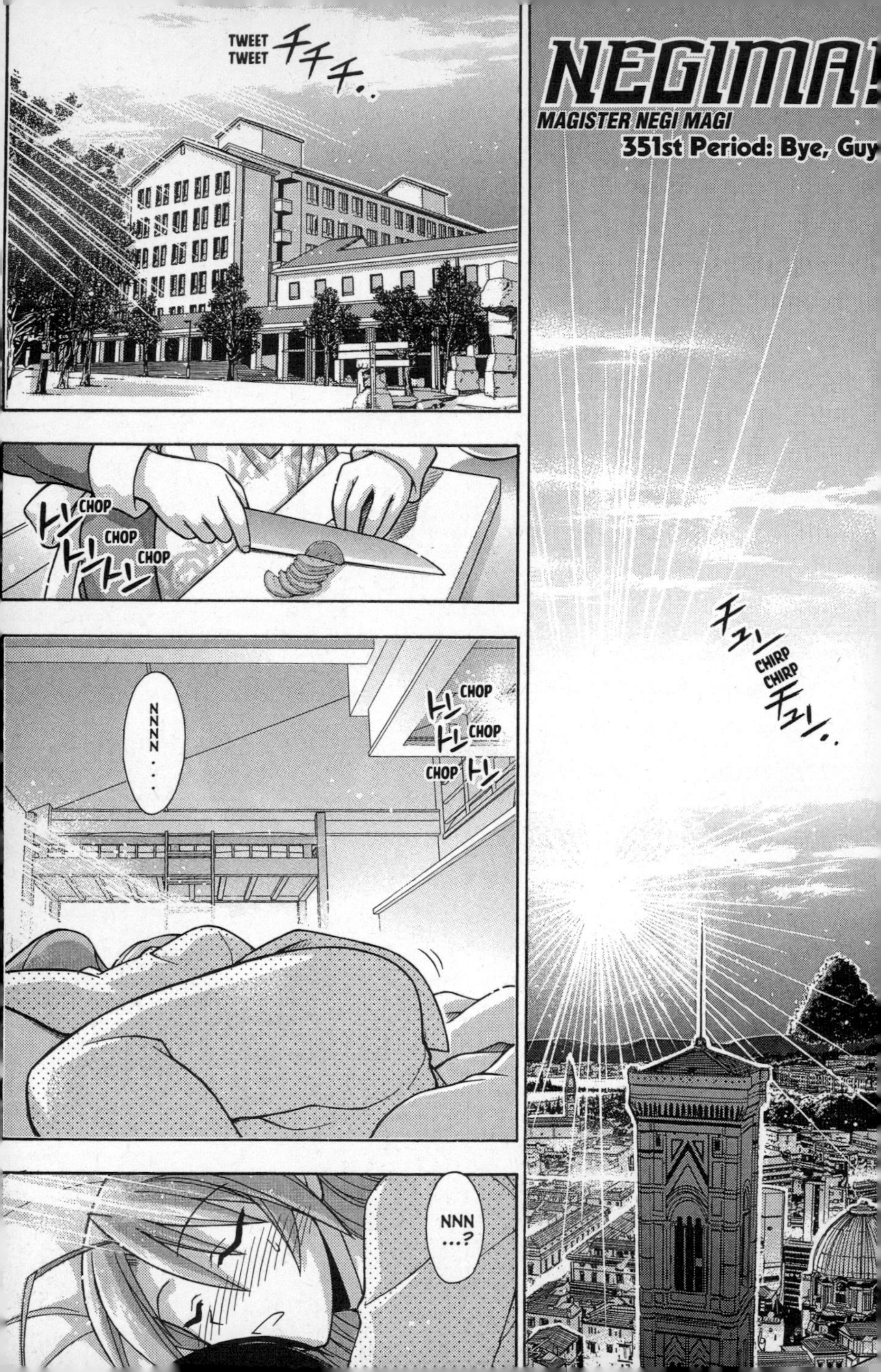
NEGIMA!
MAGISTER NEGI MAGI
351st Period: Bye, Guy
CHIRP CHIRP
TWEET TWEET
チチチ..
CHOP CHOP CHOP
NNNN...
CHOP CHOP CHOP
NNN...?

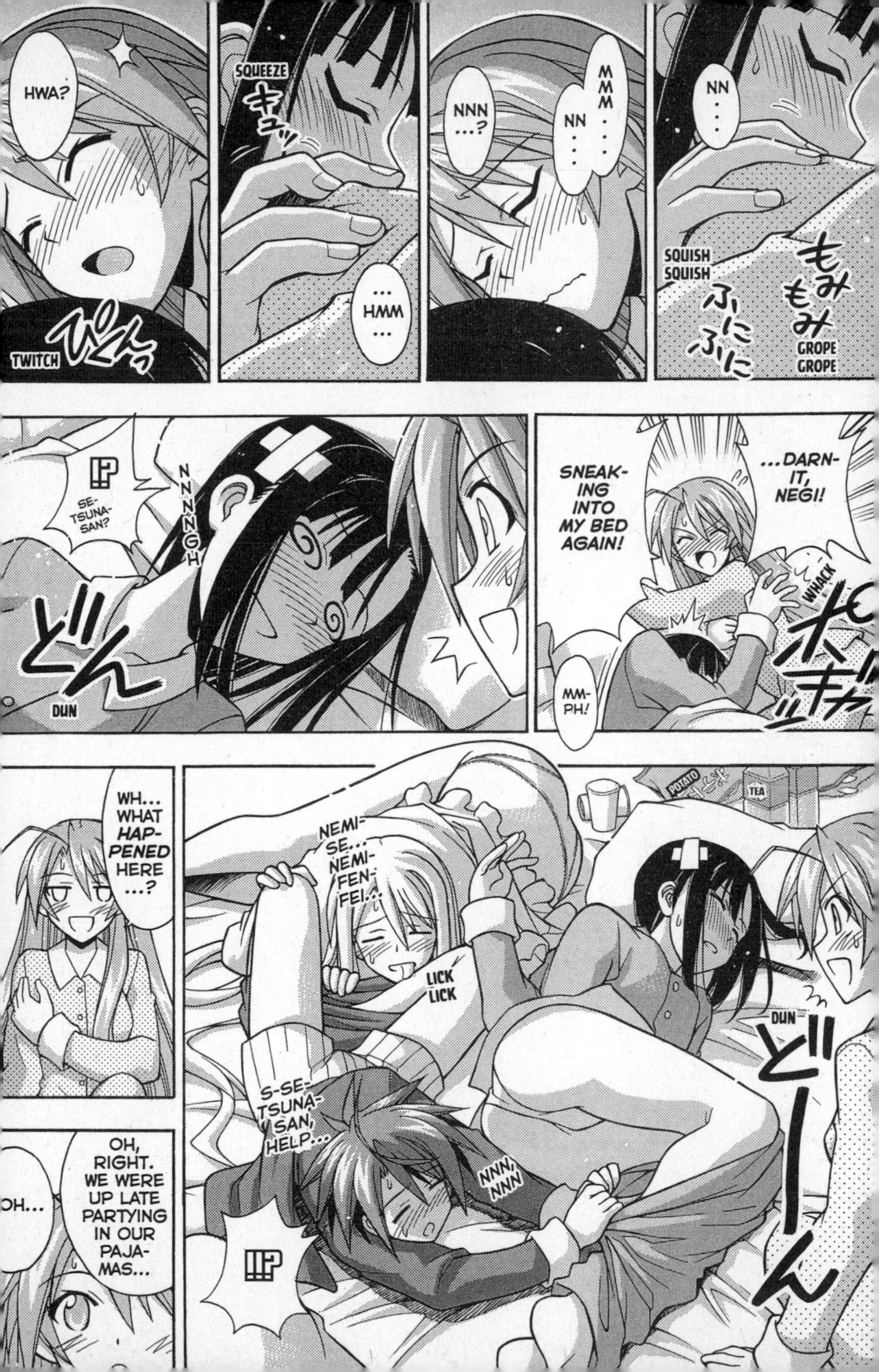
NN . . .
SQUISH SQUISH
もみもみ
GROPE GROPE
ふにふに
MMM . . . NN . . .
NNN . . .?
SQUEEZE
キュッ
. . . HMM . . .
HWA?
TWITCH
ぴくんっ
. . . DARN-IT, NEGI!
SNEAK-ING INTO MY BED AGAIN!
WHACK
MM-PH!
NNNNGH
!?
SE-TSUNA-SAN?
どん
DUN
POTATO
TEA
NEMI-SE. . . NEMI-FEN-FEI. . .
LICK LICK
DUN
どーん
S-SE-TSUNA-SAN, HELP. . .
NNN, NNN
!!?
WH. . . WHAT HAP-PENED HERE . . .?
OH, RIGHT. WE WERE UP LATE PARTYING IN OUR PAJA-MAS. . .
OH. . .

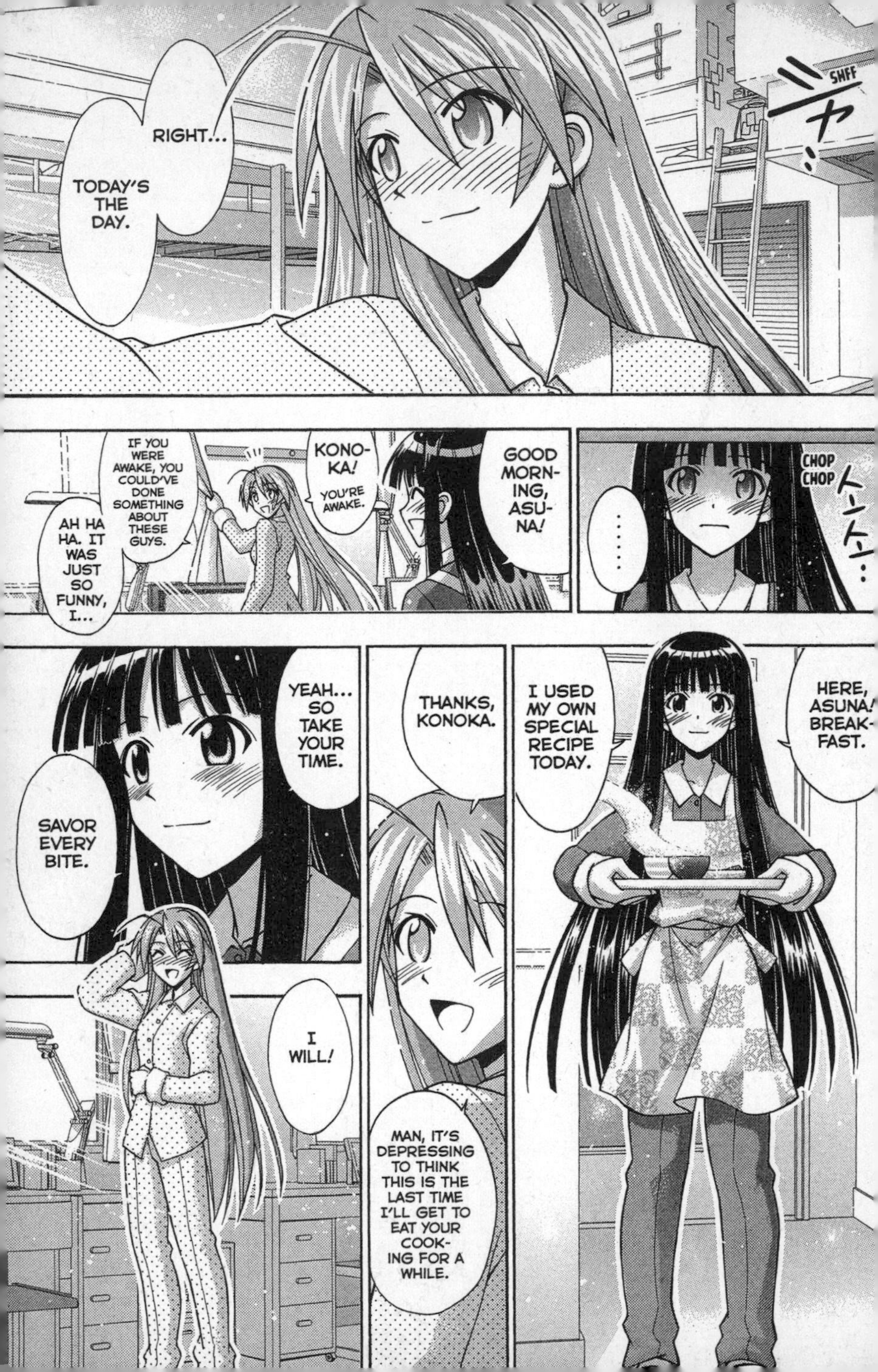
SHFF
RIGHT...
TODAY'S THE DAY.
CHOP CHOP
......
GOOD MORNING, ASUNA!
KONOKA! YOU'RE AWAKE.
IF YOU WERE AWAKE, YOU COULD'VE DONE SOMETHING ABOUT THESE GUYS.
AH HA HA. IT WAS JUST SO FUNNY, I...
HERE, ASUNA! BREAKFAST.
I USED MY OWN SPECIAL RECIPE TODAY.
THANKS, KONOKA.
MAN, IT'S DEPRESSING TO THINK THIS IS THE LAST TIME I'LL GET TO EAT YOUR COOKING FOR A WHILE.
YEAH... SO TAKE YOUR TIME.
SAVOR EVERY BITE.
I WILL!

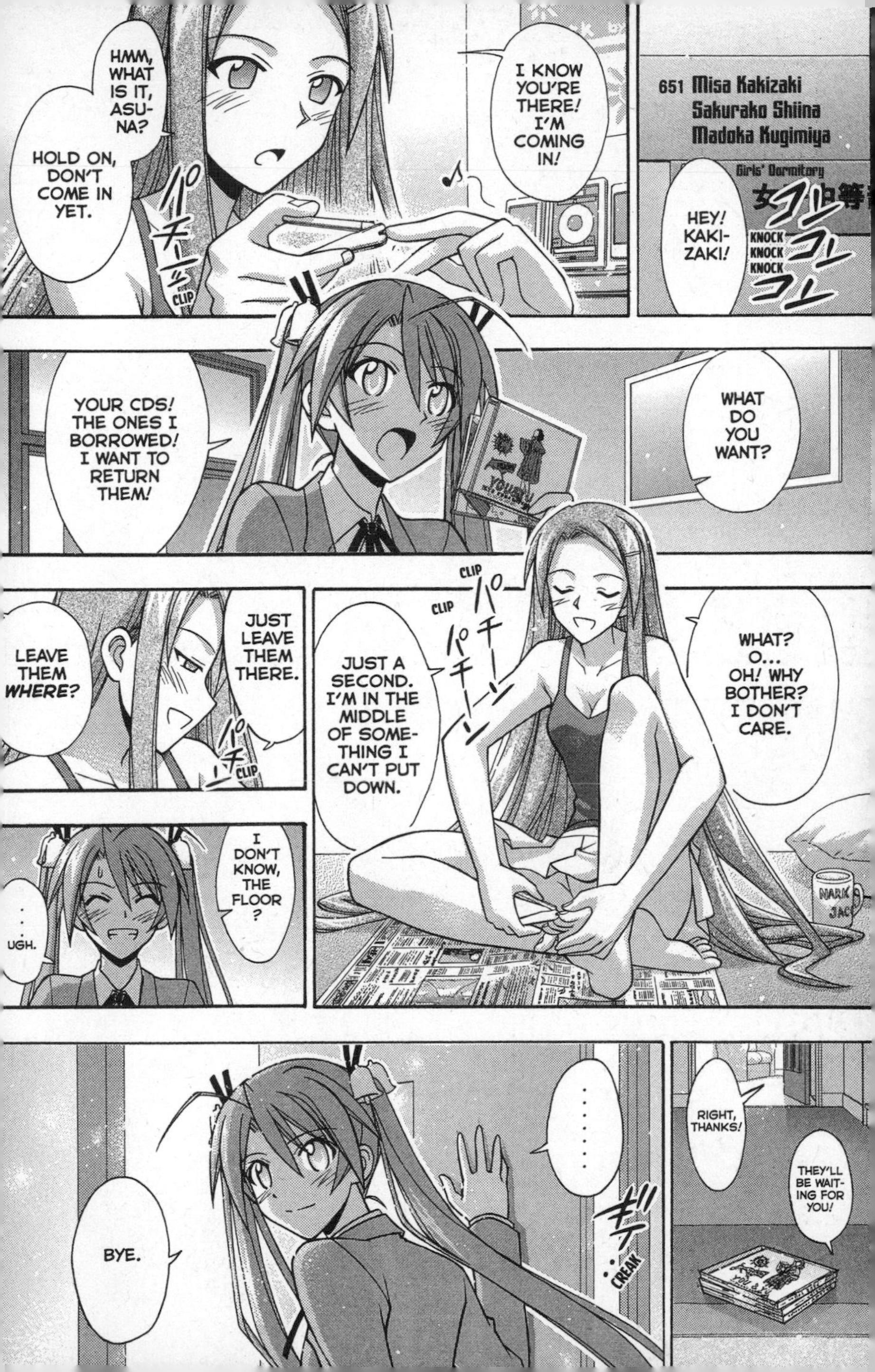
651 Misa Kakizaki
Sakurako Shiina
Madoka Kugimiya
Girls' Dormitory
HEY! KAKI-ZAKI!
KNOCK KNOCK KNOCK
I KNOW YOU'RE THERE! I'M COMING IN!
HMM, WHAT IS IT, ASUNA?
HOLD ON, DON'T COME IN YET.
CLIP
WHAT DO YOU WANT?
YOUR CDS! THE ONES I BORROWED! I WANT TO RETURN THEM!
WHAT? O... OH! WHY BOTHER? I DON'T CARE.
CLIP
CLIP
JUST A SECOND. I'M IN THE MIDDLE OF SOME-THING I CAN'T PUT DOWN.
JUST LEAVE THEM THERE.
LEAVE THEM *WHERE*?
CLIP
I DON'T KNOW, THE FLOOR?
... UGH.
RIGHT, THANKS!
THEY'LL BE WAIT-ING FOR YOU!
......
CREAK
BYE.

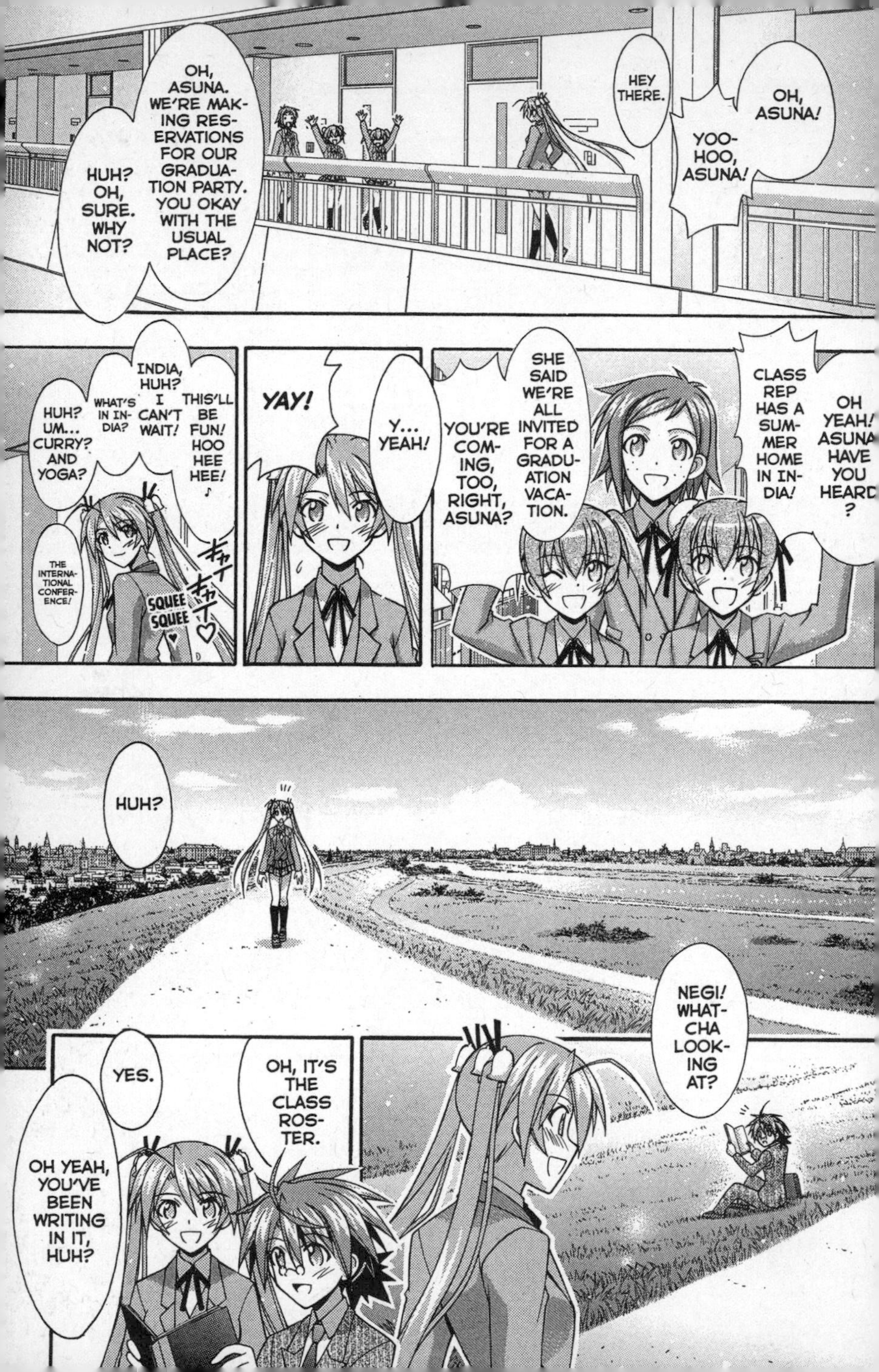
OH, ASUNA!
YOO-HOO, ASUNA!
HEY THERE.
OH, ASUNA. WE'RE MAKING RESERVATIONS FOR OUR GRADUATION PARTY. YOU OKAY WITH THE USUAL PLACE?
HUH? OH, SURE. WHY NOT?
OH YEAH! ASUNA HAVE YOU HEARD?
CLASS REP HAS A SUMMER HOME IN INDIA!
SHE SAID WE'RE ALL INVITED FOR A GRADUATION VACATION.
YOU'RE COMING, TOO, RIGHT, ASUNA?
Y... YEAH!
YAY!
THIS'LL BE FUN! HOO HEE HEE! ♪
INDIA, HUH? I CAN'T WAIT!
WHAT'S IN INDIA?
HUH? UM... CURRY? AND YOGA?
THE INTERNATIONAL CONFERENCE!
SQUEE SQUEE ♥
HUH?
NEGI! WHATCHA LOOKING AT?
OH, IT'S THE CLASS ROSTER.
YES.
OH YEAH, YOU'VE BEEN WRITING IN IT, HUH?

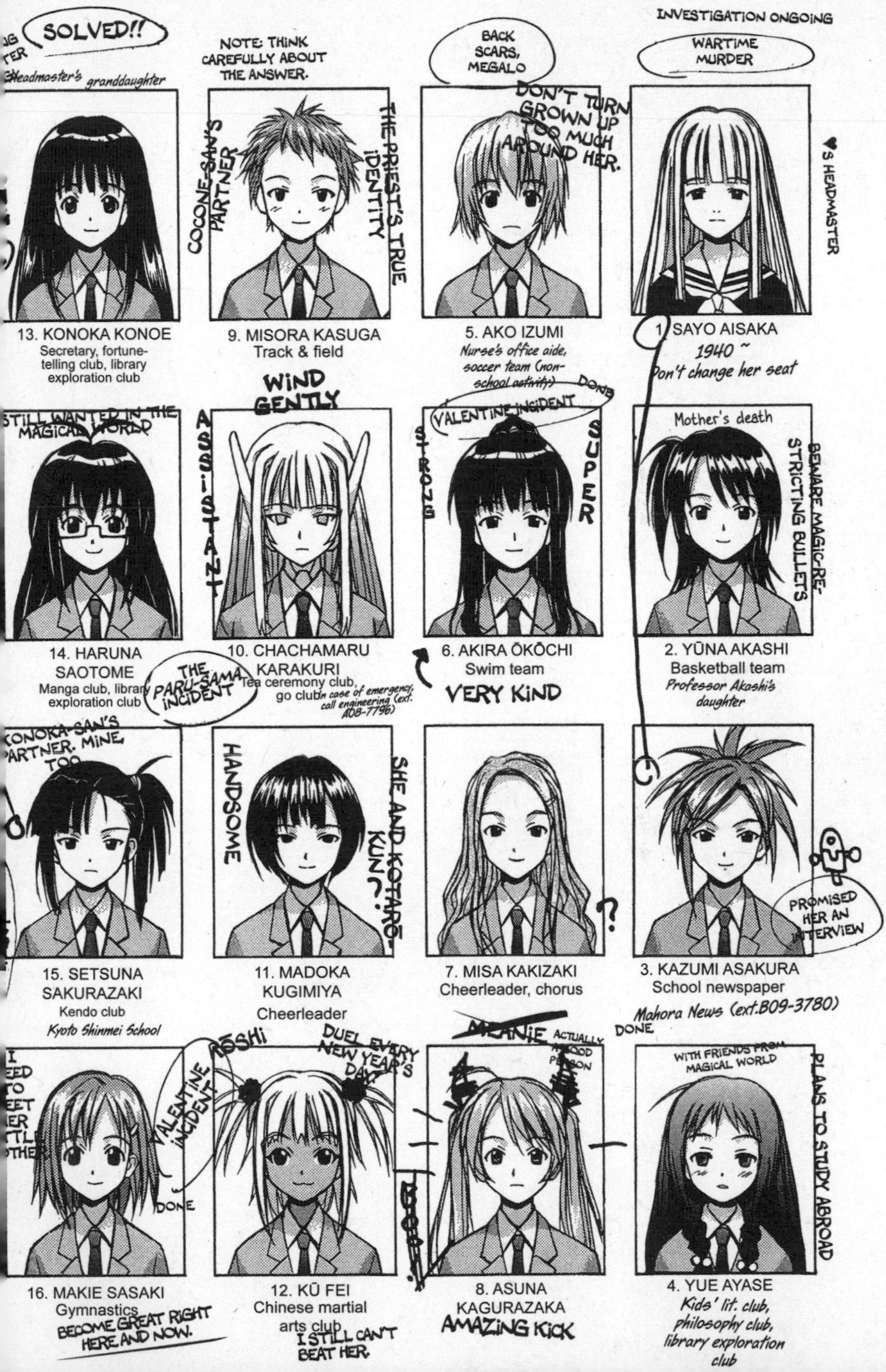
INVESTIGATION ONGOING
WARTIME MURDER
♥s HEADMASTER
1. SAYO AISAKA
1940 ~
Don't change her seat
BACK SCARS, MEGALO
DON'T TURN GROWN UP TOO MUCH AROUND HER.
5. AKO IZUMI
Nurse's office aide, soccer team (non-school activity)
NOTE: THINK CAREFULLY ABOUT THE ANSWER.
THE PRIEST'S TRUE IDENTITY
COCONE-SAN'S PARTNER
9. MISORA KASUGA
Track & field
SOLVED!!
Headmaster's granddaughter
13. KONOKA KONOE
Secretary, fortune-telling club, library exploration club
Mother's death
BEWARE MAGIC-RESTRICTING BULLETS
2. YŪNA AKASHI
Basketball team
Professor Akashi's daughter
VALENTINE INCIDENT
DONE
SUPER
STRONG
6. AKIRA ŌKŌCHI
Swim team
VERY KIND
WIND GENTLY
ASSISTANT
10. CHACHAMARU KARAKURI
Tea ceremony club, go club
In case of emergency, call engineering (ext. A08-7796)
STILL WANTED IN THE MAGICAL WORLD
14. HARUNA SAOTOME
Manga club, library exploration club
THE PARU-SAMA INCIDENT
PROMISED HER AN INTERVIEW
3. KAZUMI ASAKURA
School newspaper
Mahora News (ext.B09-3780)
?
7. MISA KAKIZAKI
Cheerleader, chorus
HANDSOME
SHE AND KOTARŌ-KUN?
11. MADOKA KUGIMIYA
Cheerleader
KONOKA-SAN'S PARTNER. MINE, TOO
15. SETSUNA SAKURAZAKI
Kendo club
Kyoto Shinmei School
WITH FRIENDS FROM MAGICAL WORLD
PLANS TO STUDY ABROAD
4. YUE AYASE
Kids' lit. club, philosophy club, library exploration club
~~MEANIE~~ ACTUALLY A GOOD PERSON
DONE
8. ASUNA KAGURAZAKA
AMAZING KICK
DUEL EVERY NEW YEAR'S DAY
RŌSHI
12. KŪ FEI
Chinese martial arts club
I STILL CAN'T BEAT HER.
VALENTINE INCIDENT
DONE
16. MAKIE SASAKI
Gymnastics
BECOME GREAT RIGHT HERE AND NOW.

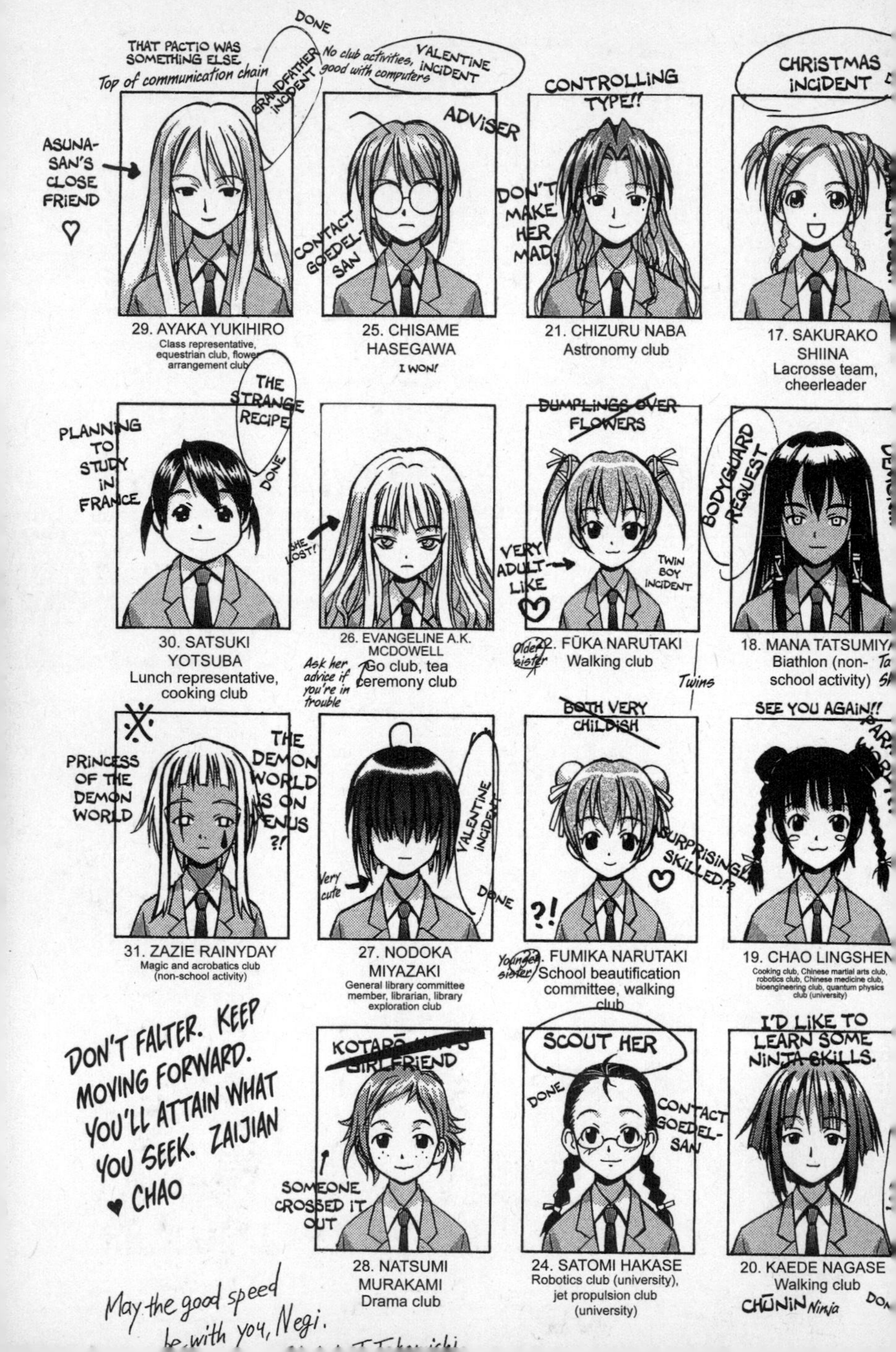
CHRISTMAS INCIDENT
17. SAKURAKO SHIINA
Lacrosse team, cheerleader
CONTROLLING TYPE!!
DON'T MAKE HER MAD
21. CHIZURU NABA
Astronomy club
VALENTINE INCIDENT
No club activities, good with computers
ADVISER
CONTACT GOEDEL-SAN
25. CHISAME HASEGAWA
I WON!
DONE
GRANDFATHER INCIDENT
THAT PACTIO WAS SOMETHING ELSE
Top of communication chain
ASUNA-SAN'S CLOSE FRIEND ♥
29. AYAKA YUKIHIRO
Class representative, equestrian club, flower arrangement club
BODYGUARD REQUEST
18. MANA TATSUMIY
Biathlon (non-school activity)
DUMPLINGS OVER FLOWERS
VERY ADULT-LIKE ♥
TWIN BOY INCIDENT
Older sister
FŪKA NARUTAKI
Walking club
Twins
SHE LOST!
26. EVANGELINE A.K. MCDOWELL
Go club, tea ceremony club
Ask her advice if you're in trouble
THE STRANGE RECIPE
DONE
PLANNING TO STUDY IN FRANCE
30. SATSUKI YOTSUBA
Lunch representative, cooking club
SEE YOU AGAIN!!
19. CHAO LINGSHEN
Cooking club, Chinese martial arts club, robotics club, Chinese medicine club, bioengineering club, quantum physics club (university)
BOTH VERY CHILDISH
SURPRISINGLY SKILLED!? ♥
?!
Younger sister
FUMIKA NARUTAKI
School beautification committee, walking club
VALENTINE INCIDENT
DONE
Very cute
27. NODOKA MIYAZAKI
General library committee member, librarian, library exploration club
THE DEMON WORLD IS ON VENUS ?!
PRINCESS OF THE DEMON WORLD
31. ZAZIE RAINYDAY
Magic and acrobatics club (non-school activity)
I'D LIKE TO LEARN SOME NINJA SKILLS.
20. KAEDE NAGASE
Walking club
CHŪNIN Ninja
SCOUT HER
DONE
CONTACT GOEDEL-SAN
24. SATOMI HAKASE
Robotics club (university), jet propulsion club (university)
KOTARŌ [redacted]
SOMEONE CROSSED IT OUT
28. NATSUMI MURAKAMI
Drama club
DON'T FALTER. KEEP MOVING FORWARD. YOU'LL ATTAIN WHAT YOU SEEK. ZAIJIAN ♥ CHAO
May the good speed be with you, Negi.

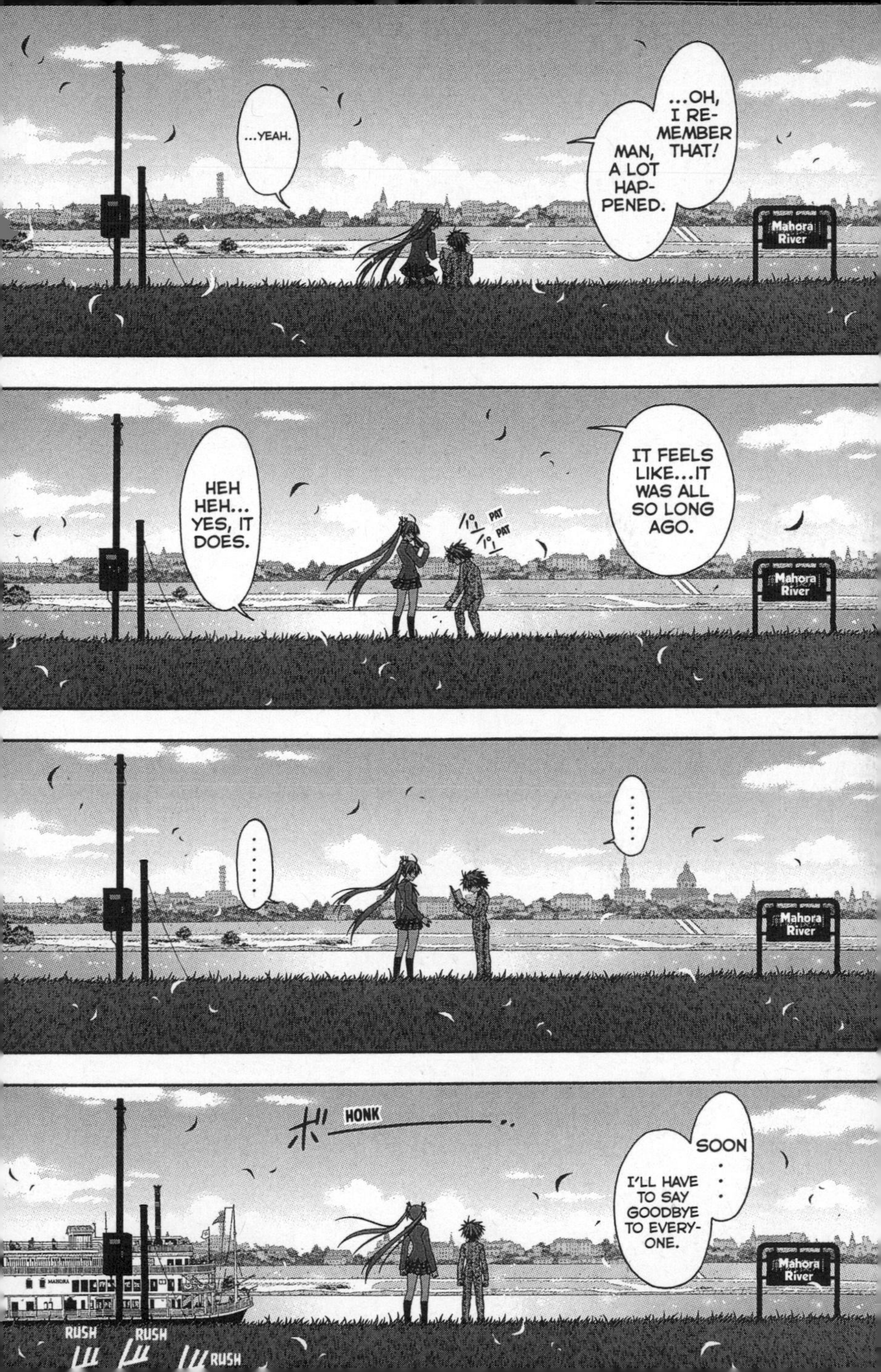
...OH, I REMEMBER THAT!
MAN, A LOT HAPPENED.
...YEAH.
Mahora River
IT FEELS LIKE...IT WAS ALL SO LONG AGO.
PAT
PAT
HEH HEH... YES, IT DOES.
Mahora River
......
......
Mahora River
SOON...
I'LL HAVE TO SAY GOODBYE TO EVERYONE.
Mahora River
HONK
RUSH
RUSH
RUSH

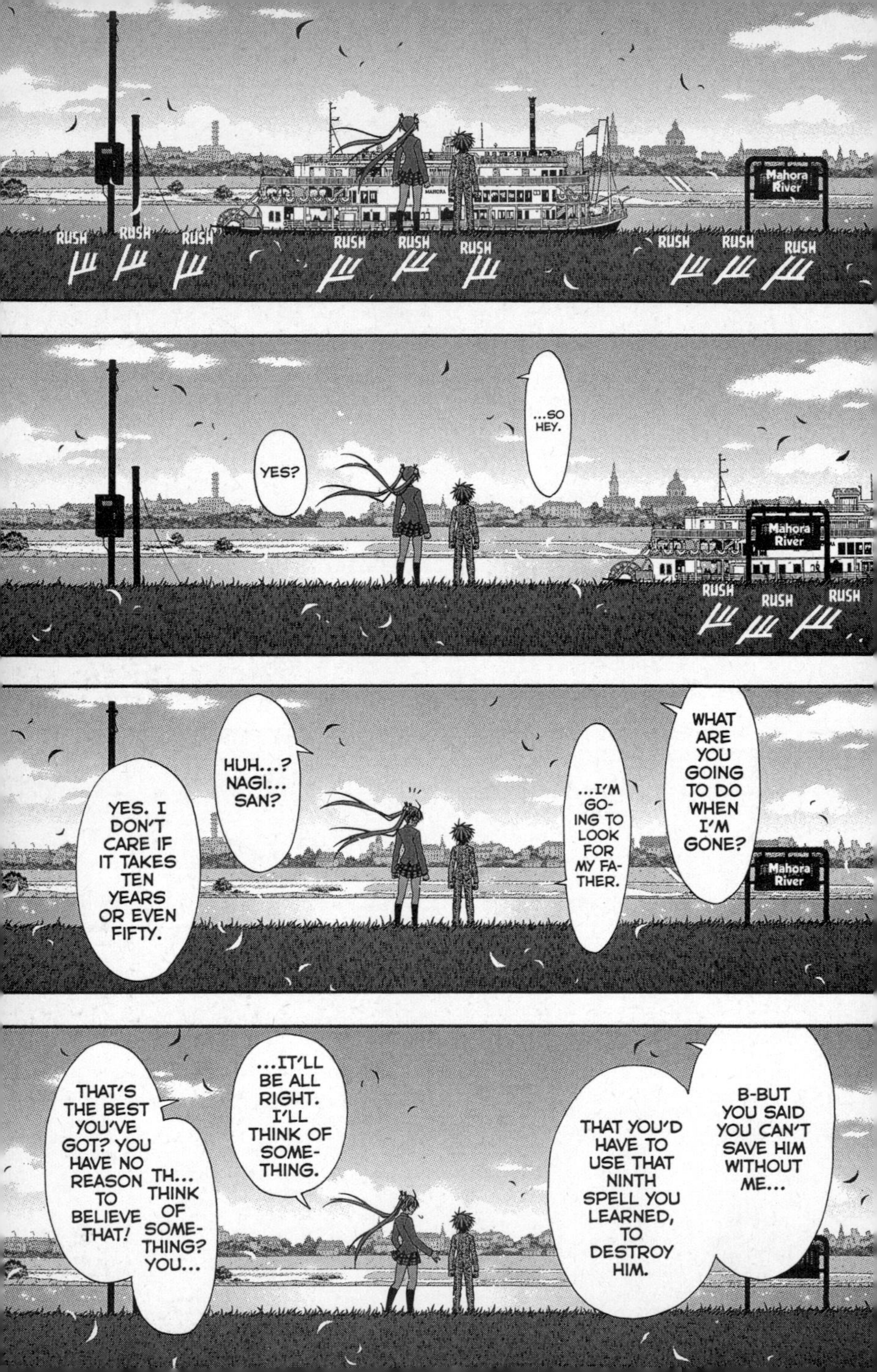
Mahora River
RUSH RUSH RUSH
RUSH RUSH RUSH
RUSH RUSH RUSH
...SO HEY.
YES?
Mahora River
RUSH RUSH RUSH
WHAT ARE YOU GOING TO DO WHEN I'M GONE?
...I'M GO-ING TO LOOK FOR MY FA-THER.
Mahora River
HUH...? NAGI... SAN?
YES. I DON'T CARE IF IT TAKES TEN YEARS OR EVEN FIFTY.
B-BUT YOU SAID YOU CAN'T SAVE HIM WITHOUT ME...
THAT YOU'D HAVE TO USE THAT NINTH SPELL YOU LEARNED, TO DESTROY HIM.
...IT'LL BE ALL RIGHT. I'LL THINK OF SOME-THING.
TH... THINK OF SOME-THING? YOU...
THAT'S THE BEST YOU'VE GOT? YOU HAVE NO REASON TO BELIEVE THAT!

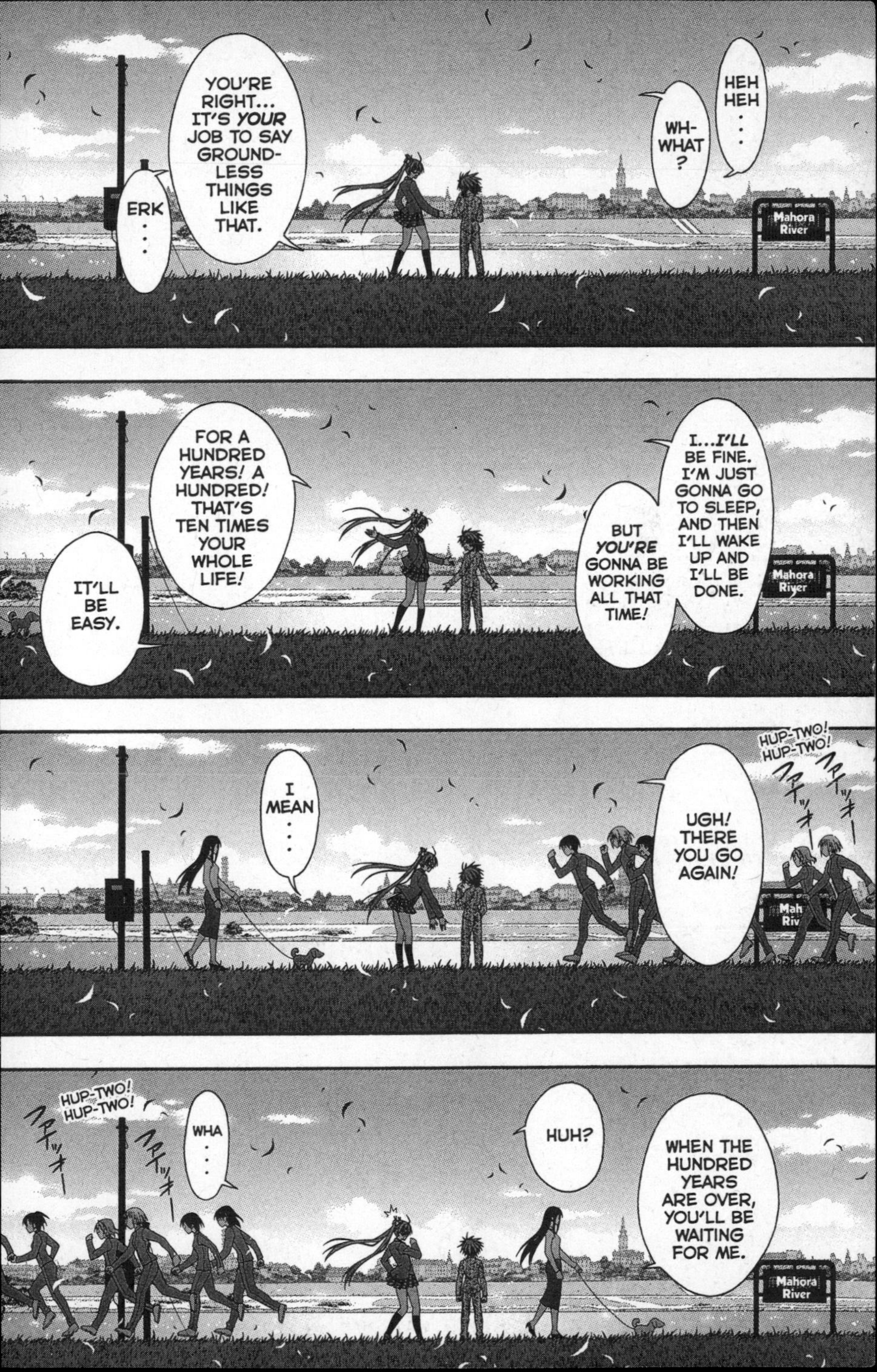
HEH HEH...
WH-WHAT?
YOU'RE RIGHT... IT'S *YOUR* JOB TO SAY GROUNDLESS THINGS LIKE THAT.
ERK...
Mahora River
I...*I'LL* BE FINE. I'M JUST GONNA GO TO SLEEP, AND THEN I'LL WAKE UP AND I'LL BE DONE.
BUT *YOU'RE* GONNA BE WORKING ALL THAT TIME!
FOR A HUNDRED YEARS! A HUNDRED! THAT'S TEN TIMES YOUR WHOLE LIFE!
IT'LL BE EASY.
HUP-TWO! HUP-TWO!
UGH! THERE YOU GO AGAIN!
I MEAN...
WHEN THE HUNDRED YEARS ARE OVER, YOU'LL BE WAITING FOR ME.
HUH?
WHA...
HUP-TWO! HUP-TWO!

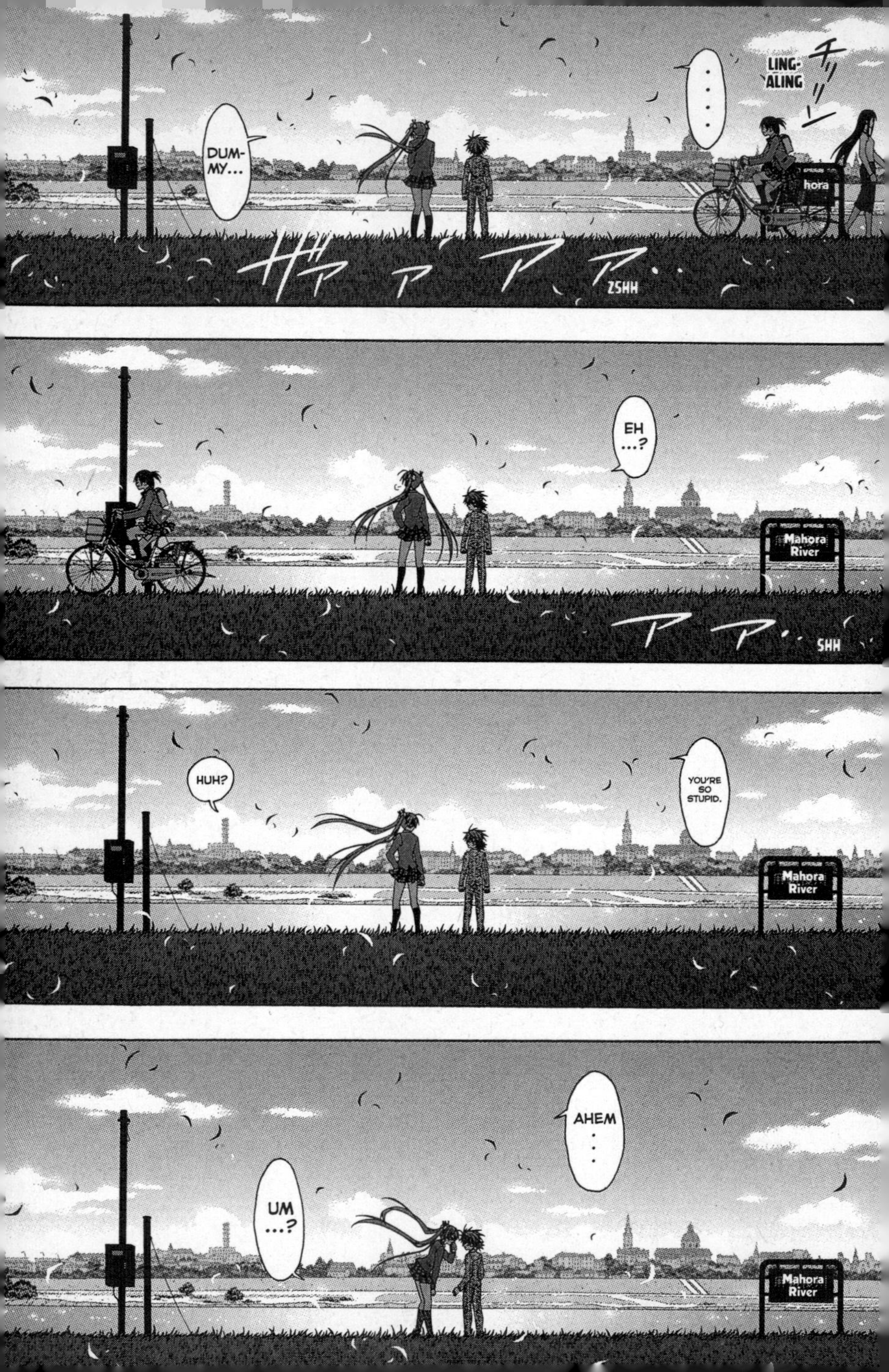

LING-ALING
...
hora
DUM-MY...
ZSHH
EH ...?
Mahora River
SHH
YOU'RE SO STUPID.
Mahora River
HUH?
AHEM ...
Mahora River
UM ...?

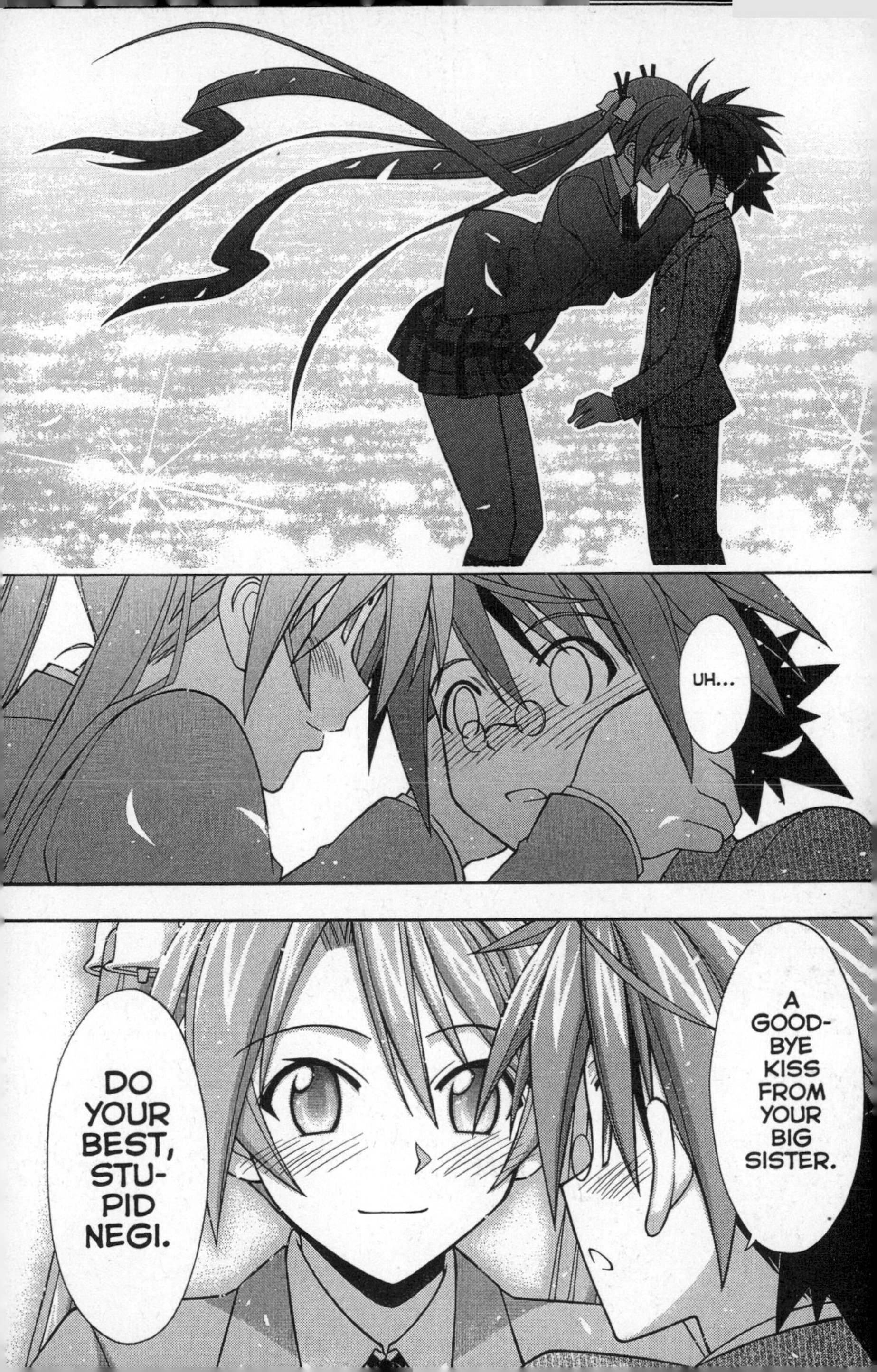
UH...
A GOOD-BYE KISS FROM YOUR BIG SISTER.
DO YOUR BEST, STU-PID NEGI.

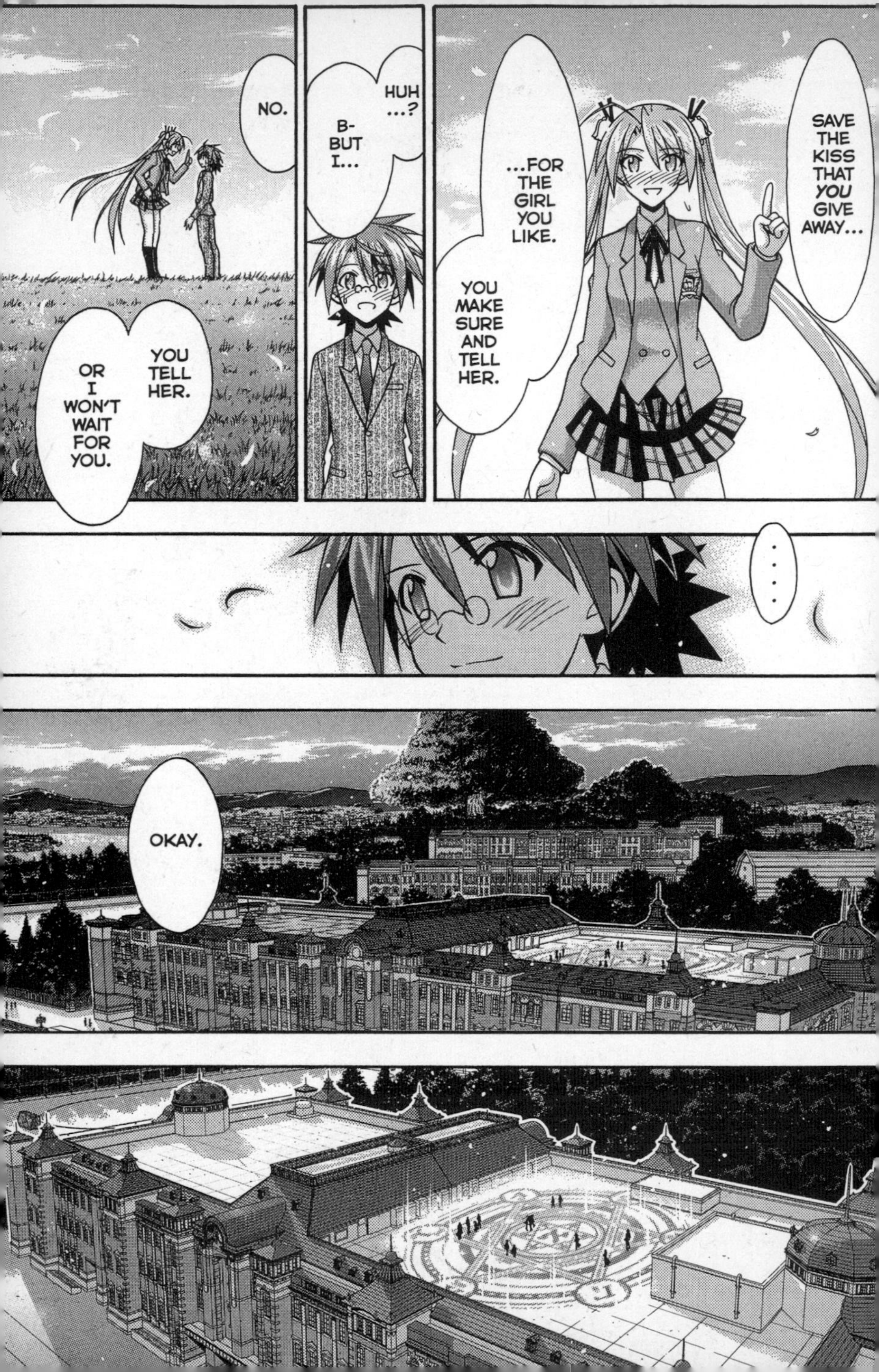
SAVE THE KISS THAT *YOU* GIVE AWAY...
...FOR THE GIRL YOU LIKE.
YOU MAKE SURE AND TELL HER.
HUH ...?
B-BUT I...
NO.
YOU TELL HER.
OR I WON'T WAIT FOR YOU.
.....
OKAY.

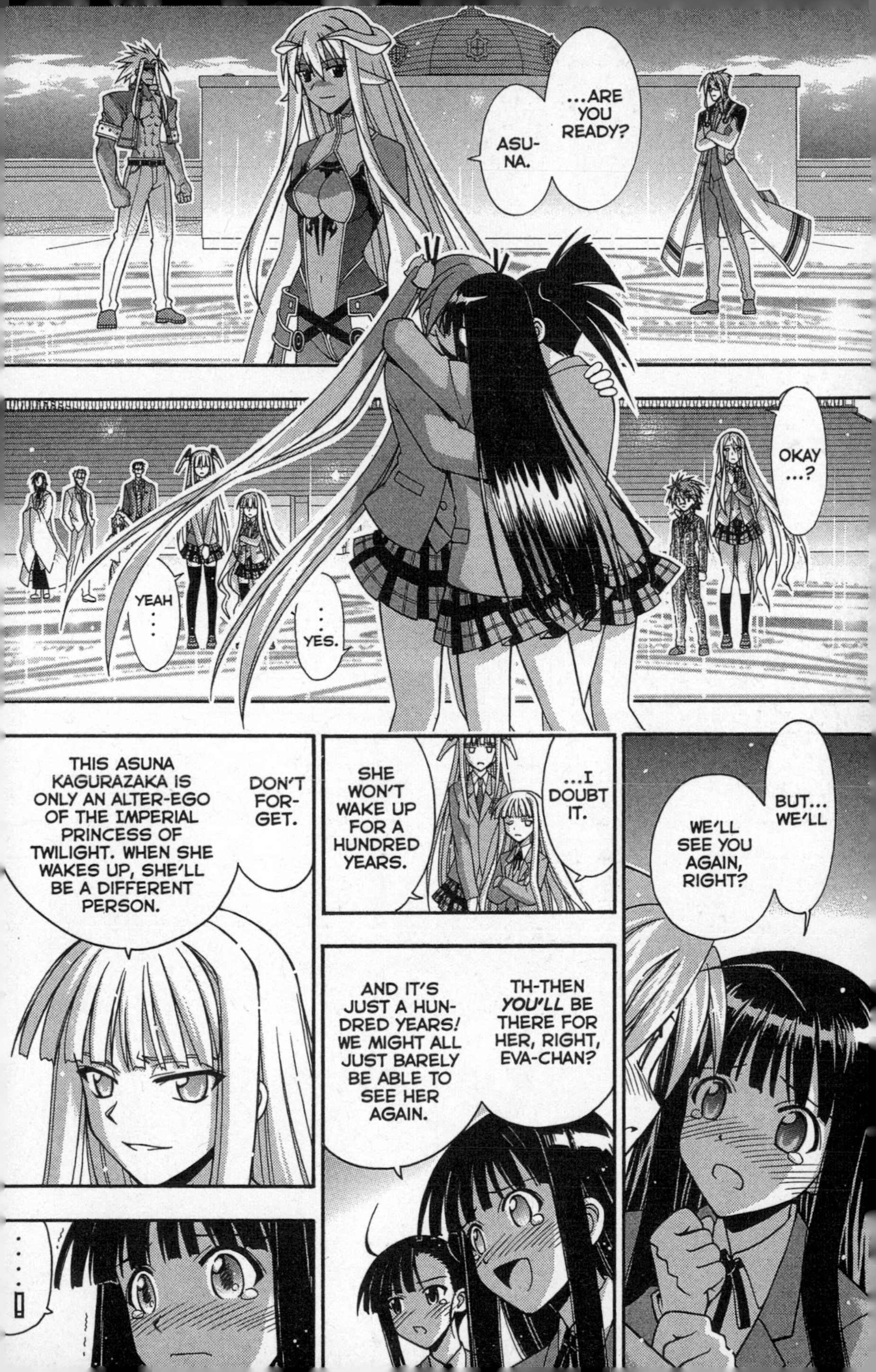
...ARE YOU READY?
ASU-NA.
OKAY ...?
...YES.
YEAH ...
BUT... WE'LL
WE'LL SEE YOU AGAIN, RIGHT?
...I DOUBT IT.
SHE WON'T WAKE UP FOR A HUNDRED YEARS.
DON'T FOR-GET.
THIS ASUNA KAGURAZAKA IS ONLY AN ALTER-EGO OF THE IMPERIAL PRINCESS OF TWILIGHT. WHEN SHE WAKES UP, SHE'LL BE A DIFFERENT PERSON.
TH-THEN *YOU'LL* BE THERE FOR HER, RIGHT, EVA-CHAN?
AND IT'S JUST A HUN-DRED YEARS! WE MIGHT ALL JUST BARELY BE ABLE TO SEE HER AGAIN.
.....!

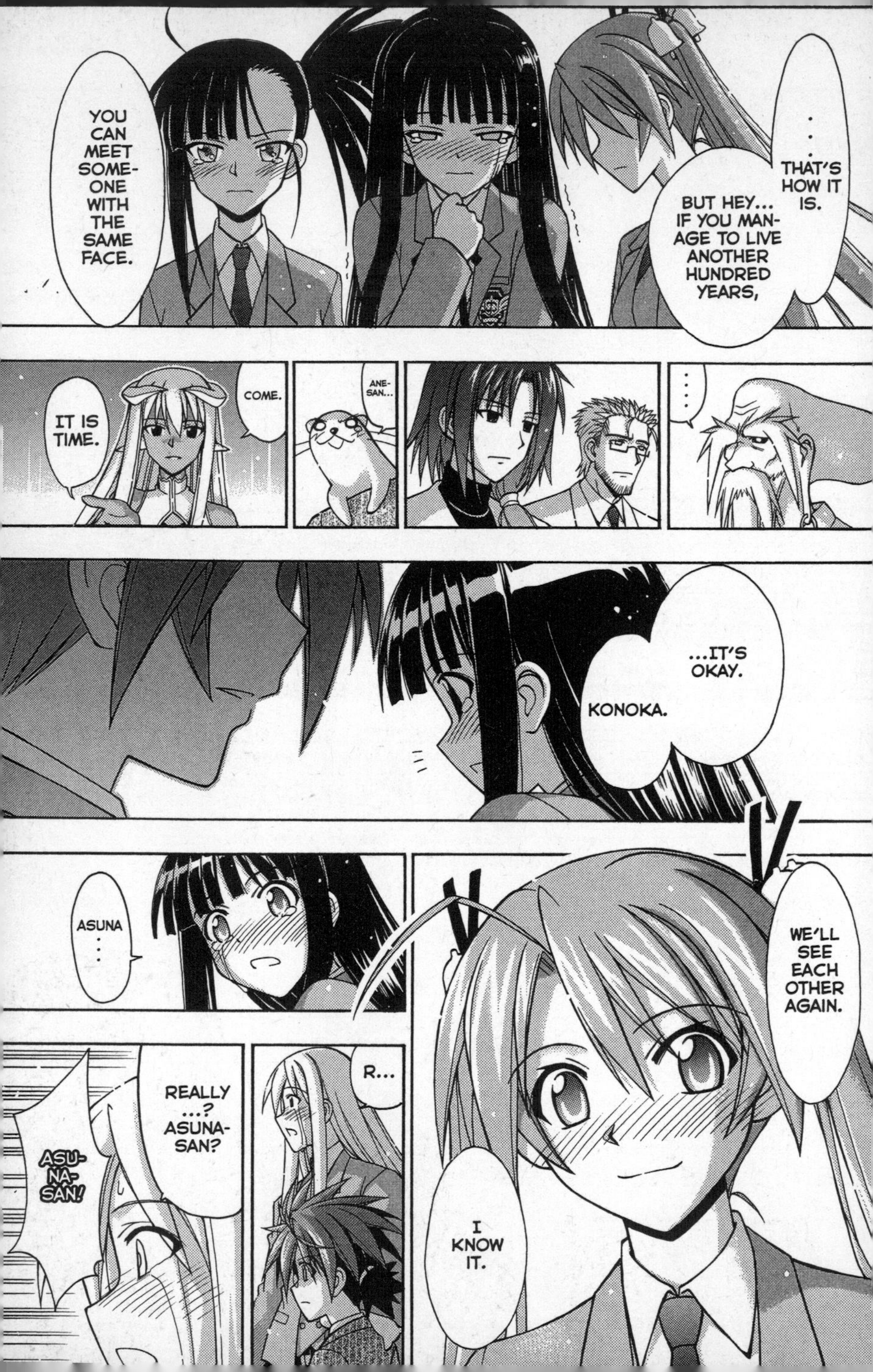
. . . THAT'S HOW IT IS.
BUT HEY... IF YOU MANAGE TO LIVE ANOTHER HUNDRED YEARS,
YOU CAN MEET SOMEONE WITH THE SAME FACE.
. . . .
ANE-SAN...
COME.
IT IS TIME.
...IT'S OKAY.
KONOKA.
WE'LL SEE EACH OTHER AGAIN.
I KNOW IT.
ASUNA . . .
R...
REALLY ...? ASUNA-SAN?
ASUNA-SAN!

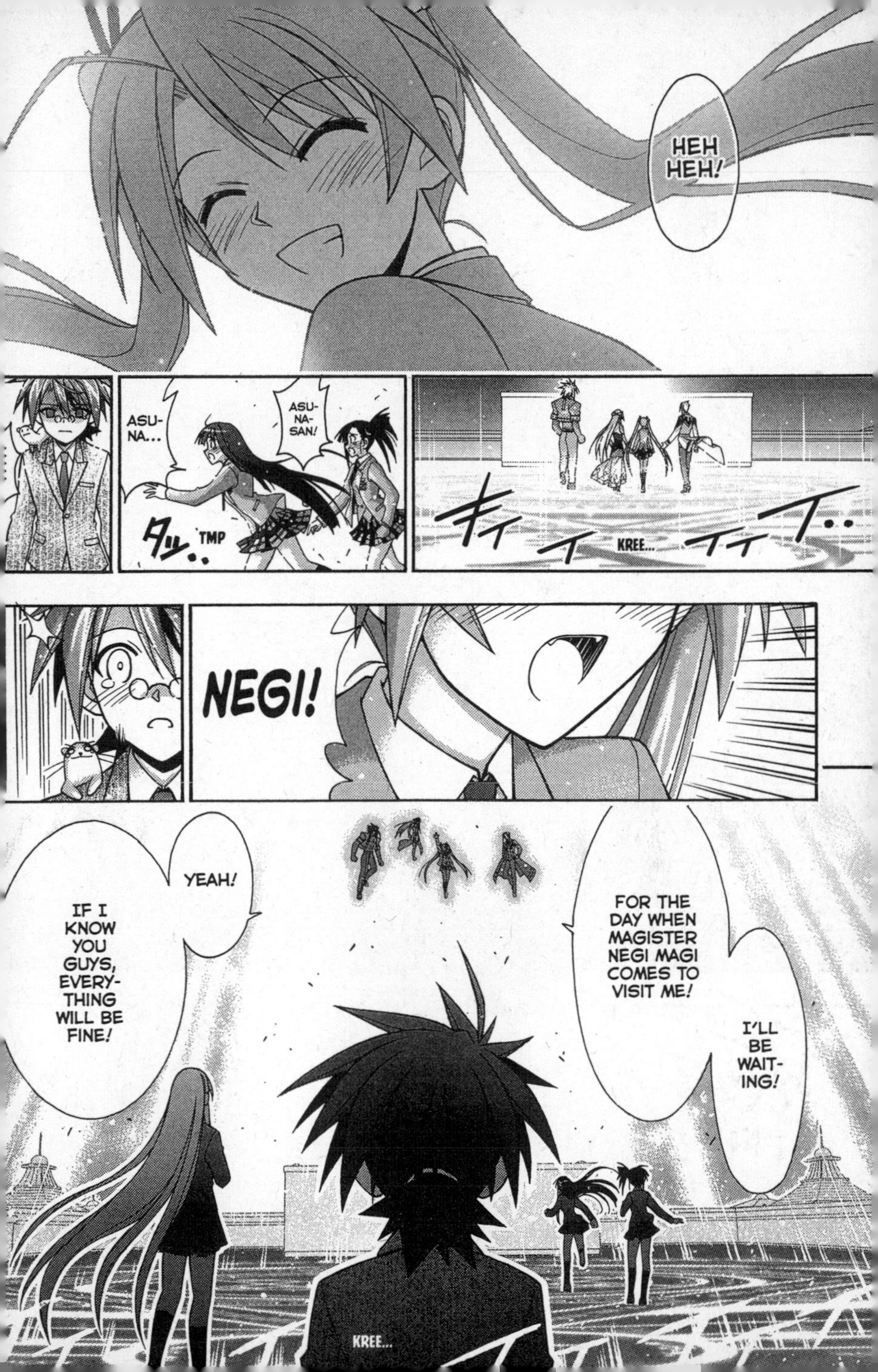

HEH HEH!
キィィィィィ..
KREE...
ASU-NA-SAN!
ASU-NA...
タッ..
TMP
NEGI!
I'LL BE WAIT-ING!
FOR THE DAY WHEN MAGISTER NEGI MAGI COMES TO VISIT ME!
YEAH!
IF I KNOW YOU GUYS, EVERY-THING WILL BE FINE!
KREE...

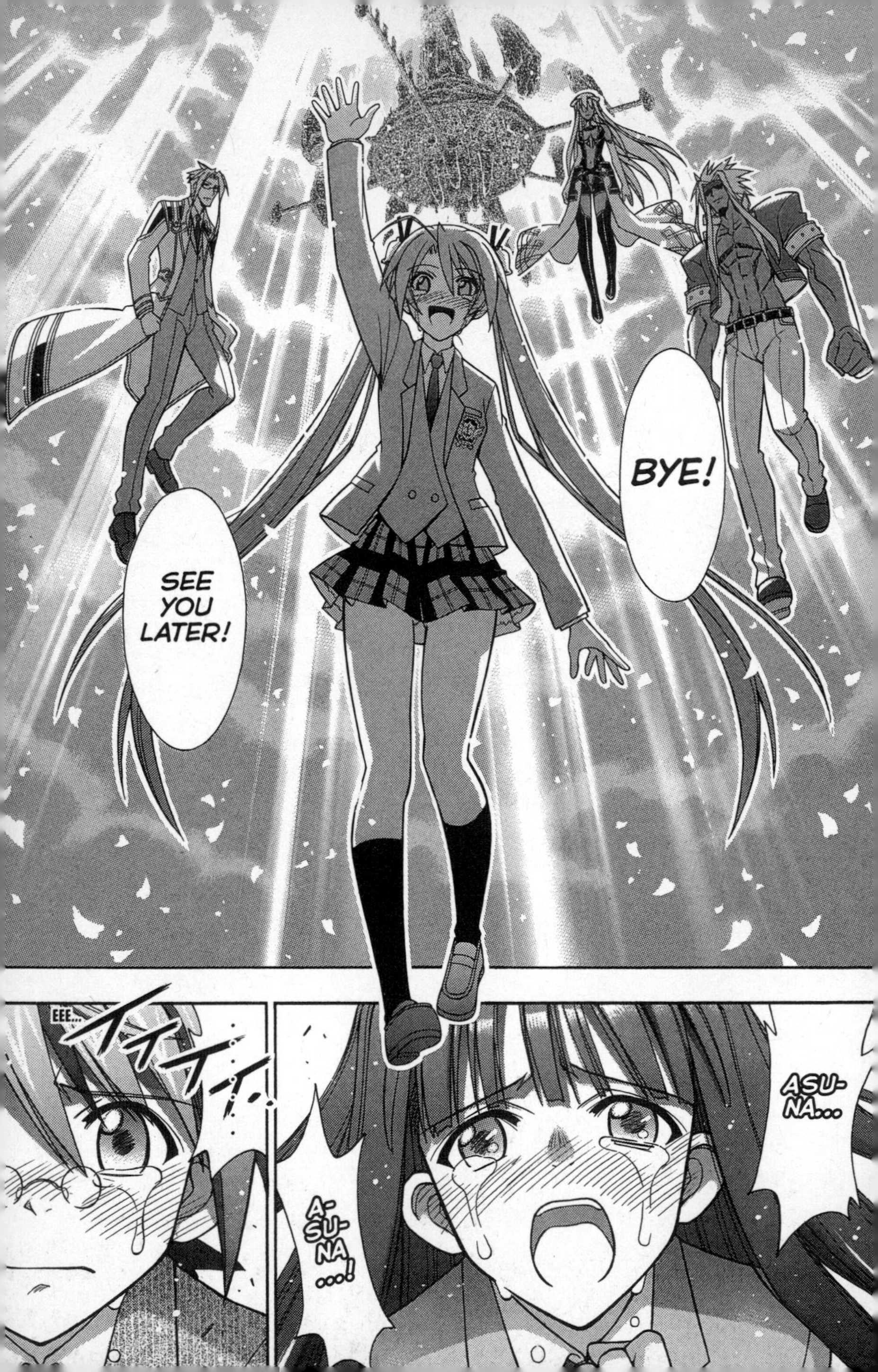
BYE!
SEE YOU LATER!
ASU-NA...
A-SU-NA...!
EEE...

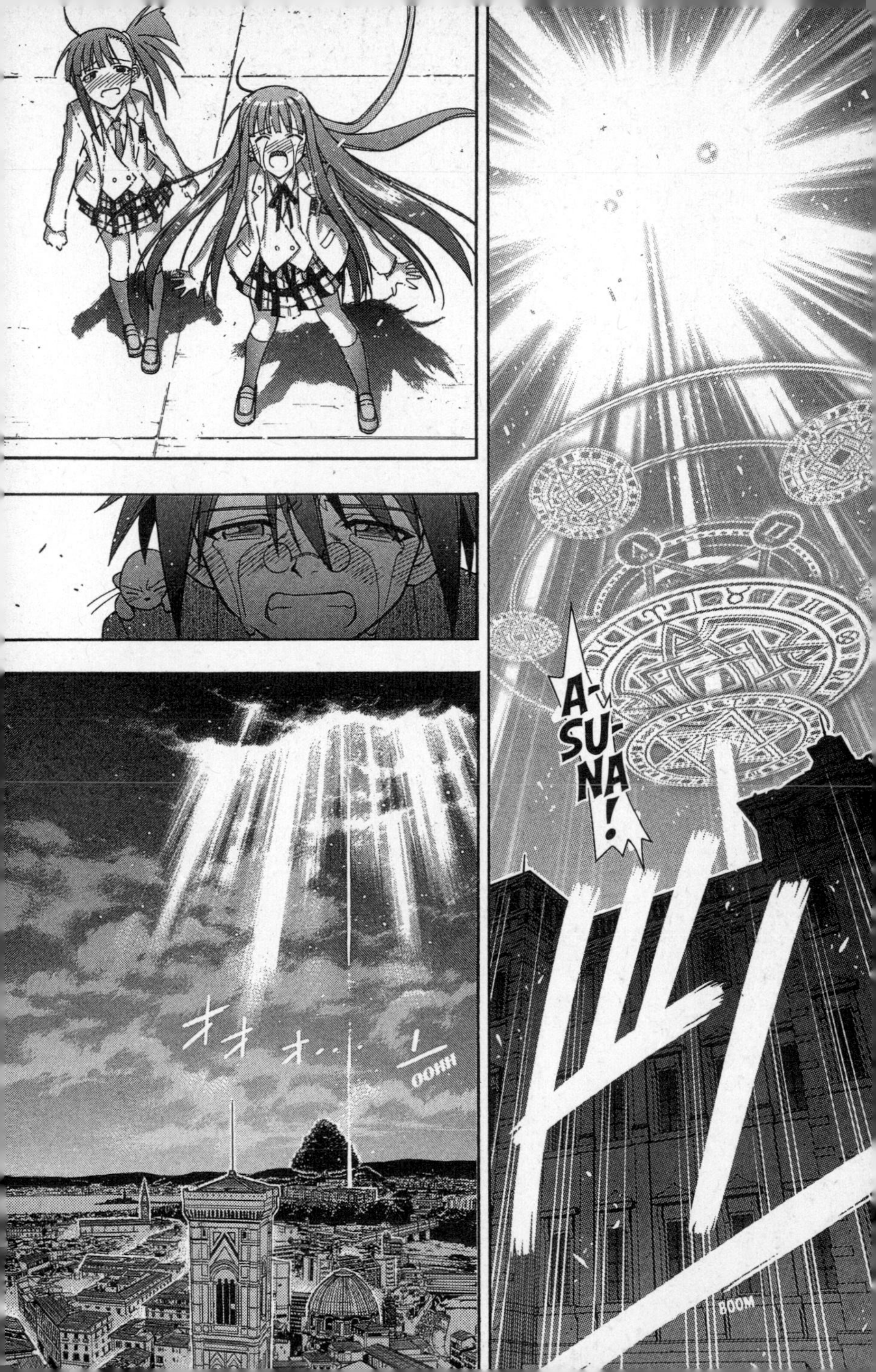
A-SU-NA!
BOOM
オオ オ…!
OOHH

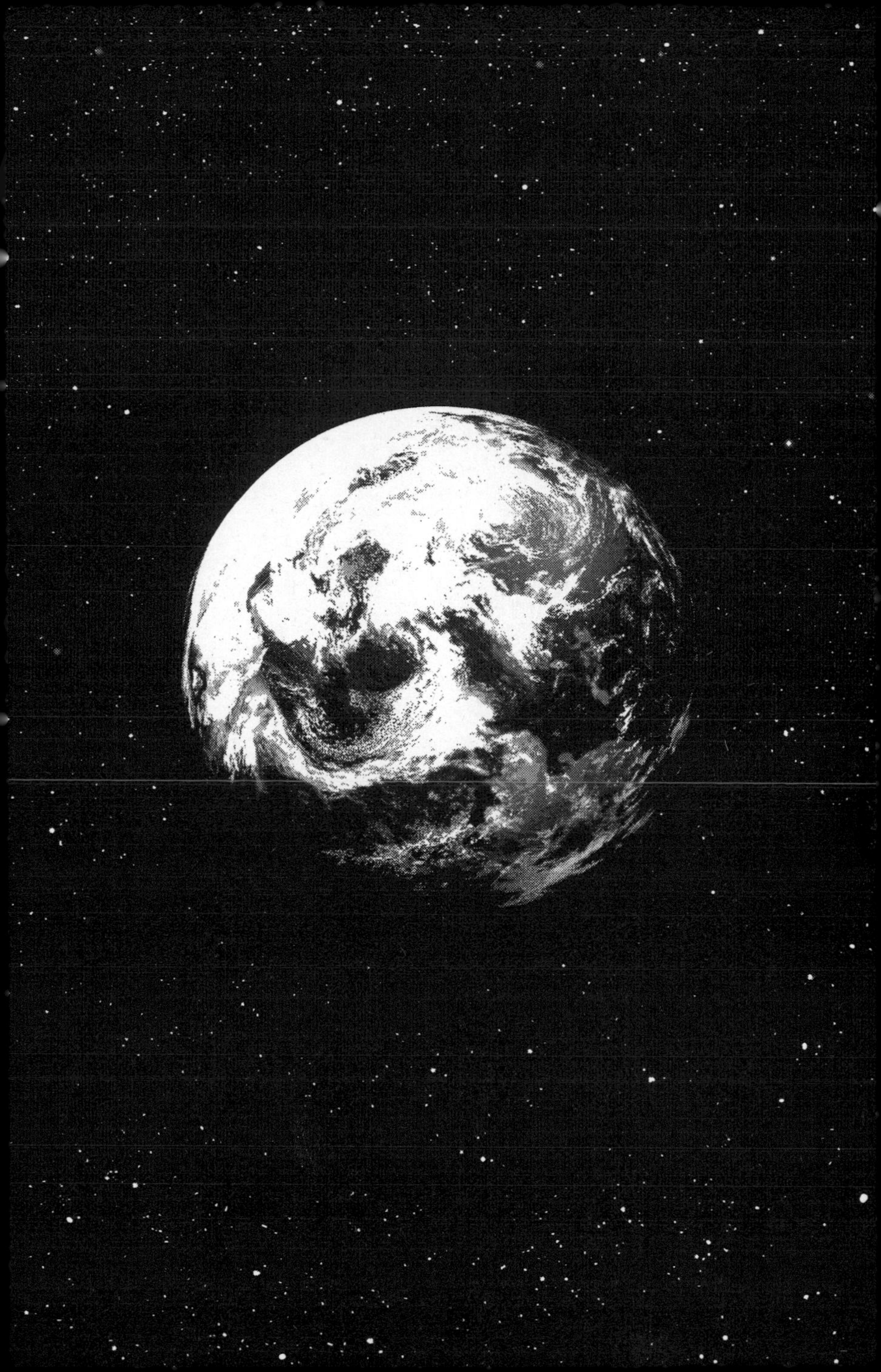

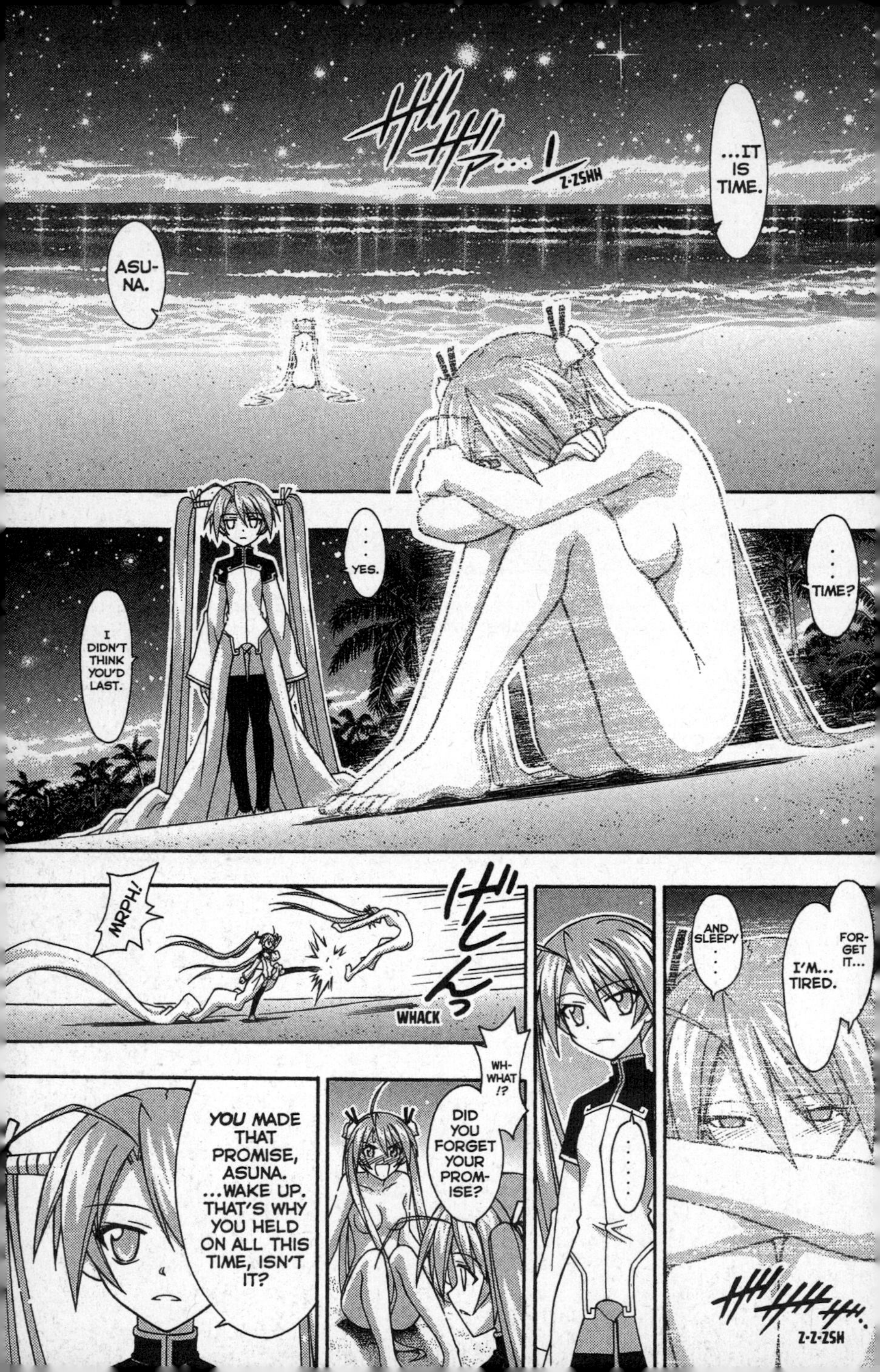
...IT IS TIME.
Z-ZSHH
ASUNA.
... TIME?
... YES.
I DIDN'T THINK YOU'D LAST.
FORGET IT... I'M... TIRED.
AND SLEEPY...
Z-Z-ZSH
......
WHACK
MRPH!
WH-WHAT!?
DID YOU FORGET YOUR PROMISE?
YOU MADE THAT PROMISE, ASUNA. ...WAKE UP. THAT'S WHY YOU HELD ON ALL THIS TIME, ISN'T IT?

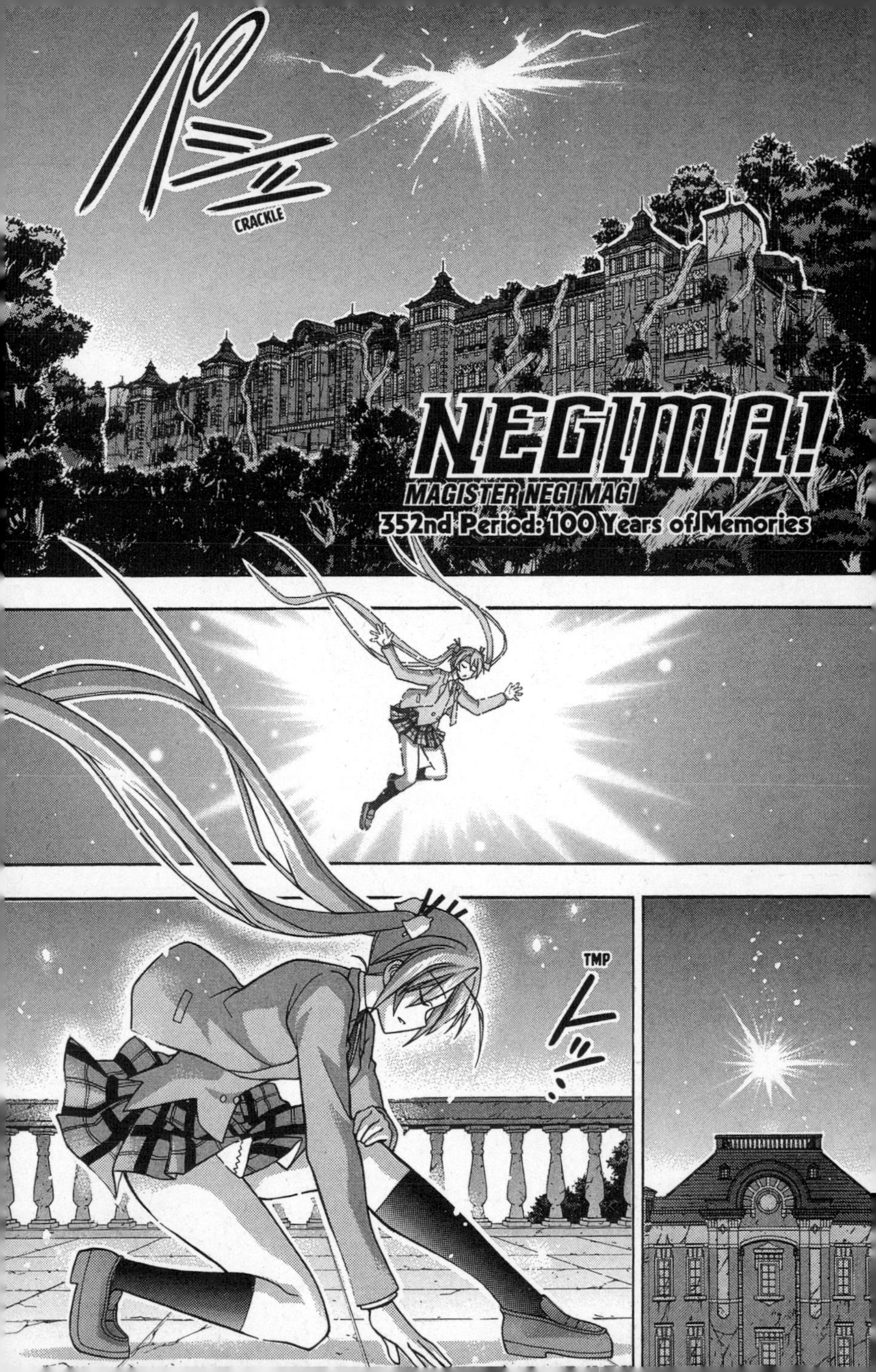
CRACKLE
NEGIMA!
MAGISTER NEGI MAGI
352nd Period: 100 Years of Memories
TMP

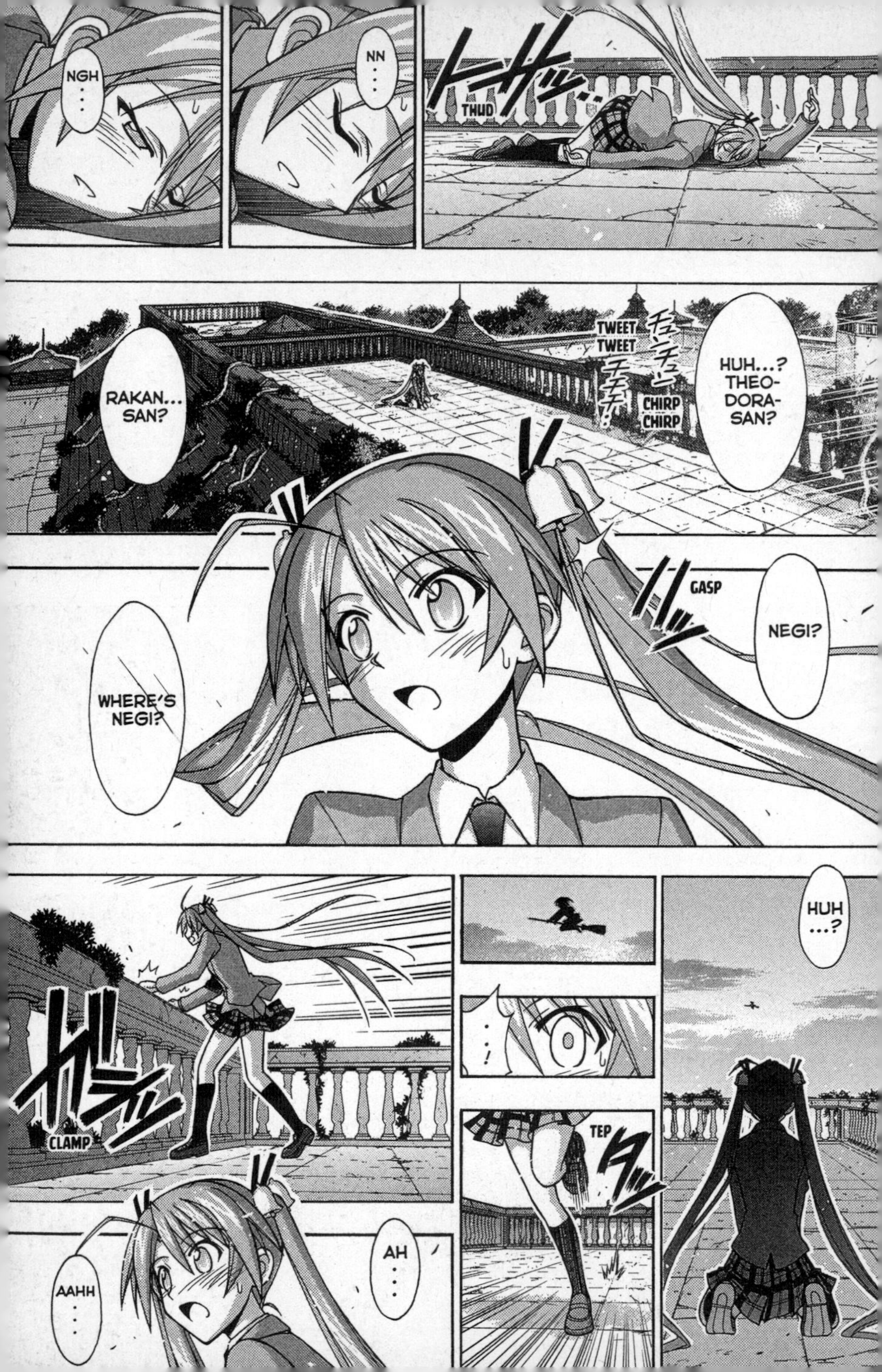
THUD
NN . . . .
NGH . . .
HUH...? THEODORA-SAN?
TWEET TWEET
チュンチュン
CHIRP CHIRP
チチチ…
RAKAN... SAN?
GASP
NEGI?
WHERE'S NEGI?
HUH ...?
. . !
TEP
CLAMP
AH . . . .
AAHH . . .

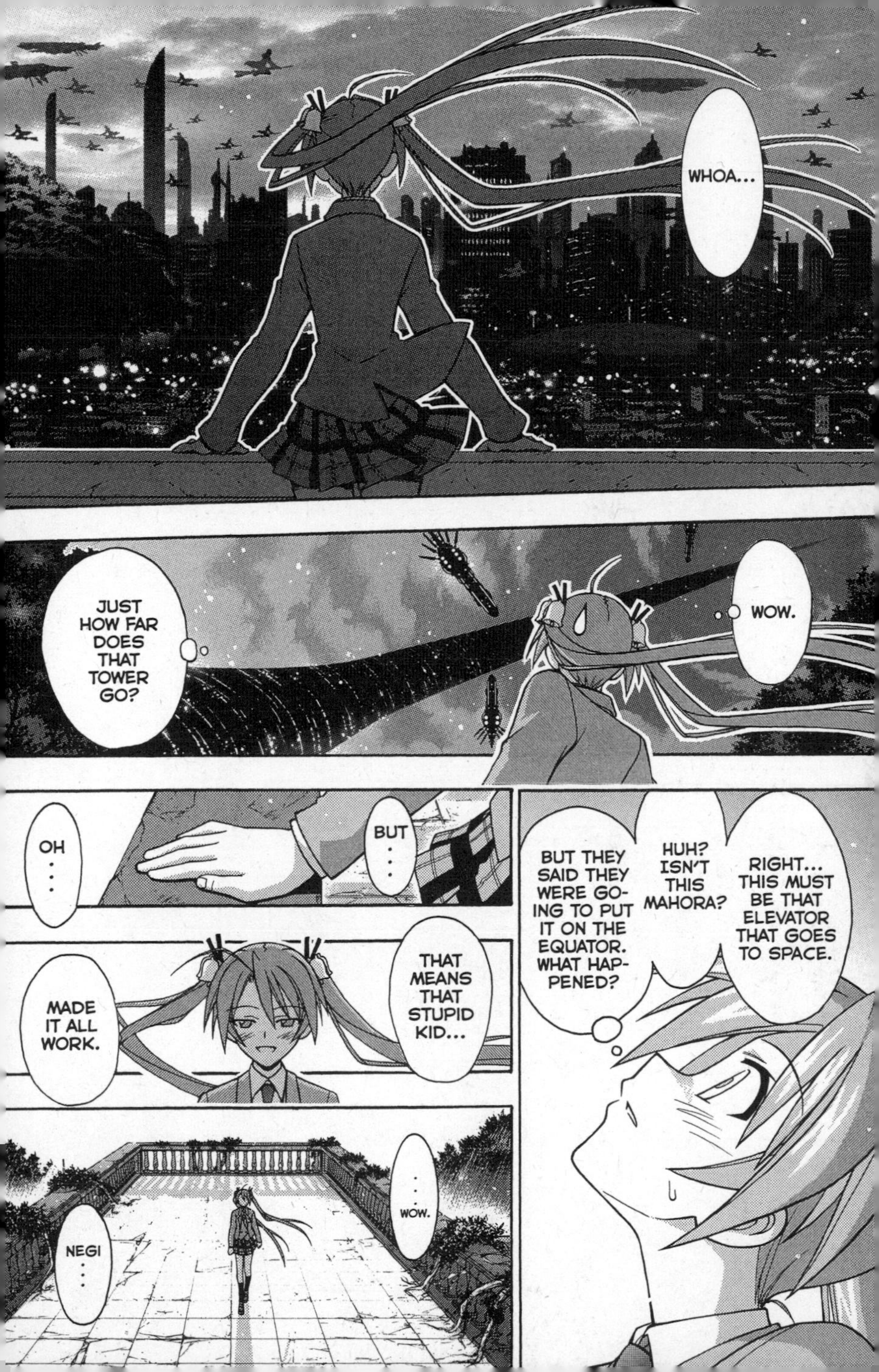
WHOA...
WOW.
JUST HOW FAR DOES THAT TOWER GO?
RIGHT... THIS MUST BE THAT ELEVATOR THAT GOES TO SPACE.
HUH? ISN'T THIS MAHORA?
BUT THEY SAID THEY WERE GOING TO PUT IT ON THE EQUATOR. WHAT HAPPENED?
BUT...
OH...
THAT MEANS THAT STUPID KID...
MADE IT ALL WORK.
...WOW.
NEGI...

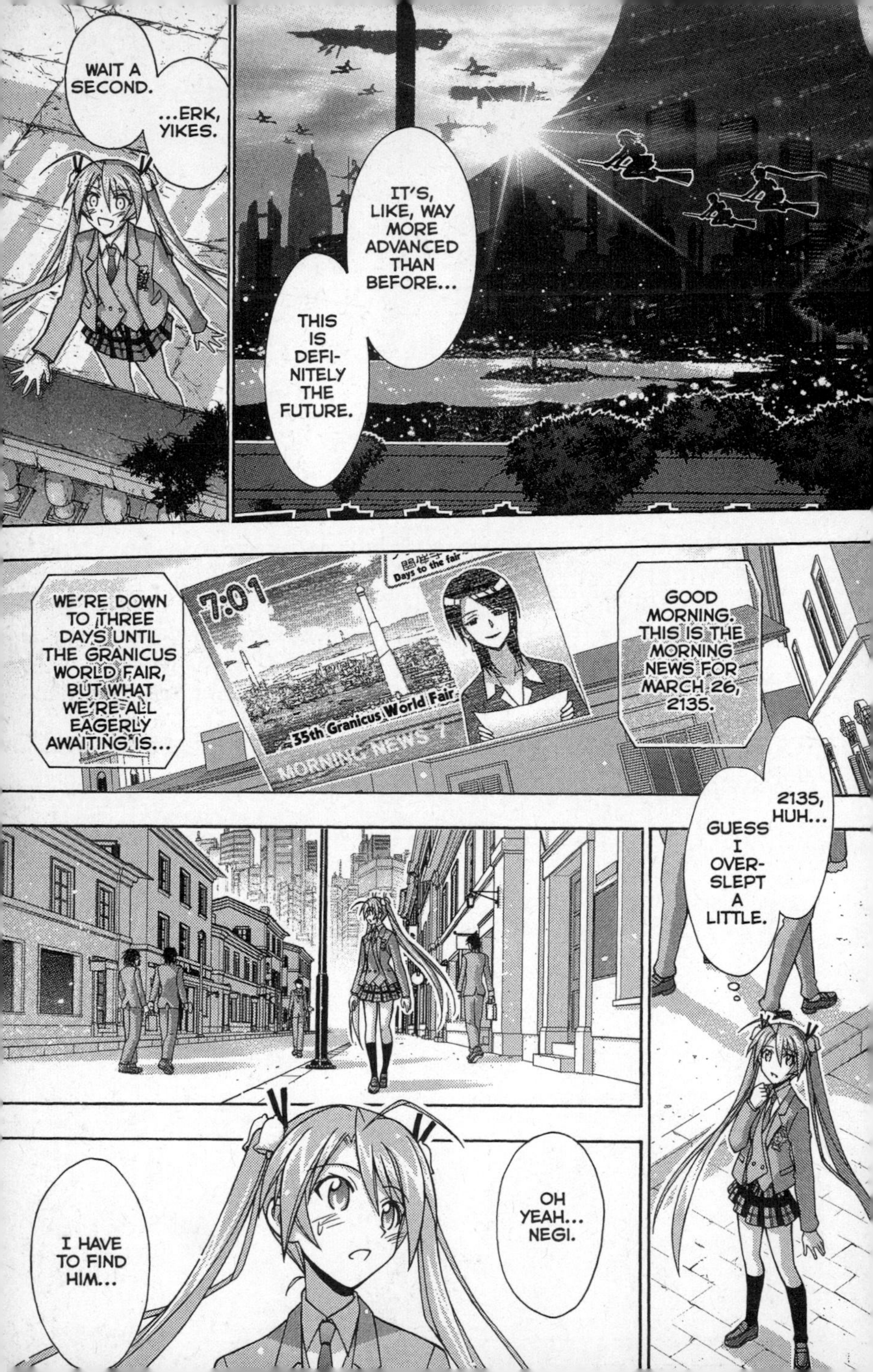

IT'S, LIKE, WAY MORE ADVANCED THAN BEFORE...
THIS IS DEFI-NITELY THE FUTURE.
WAIT A SECOND.
...ERK, YIKES.
GOOD MORNING. THIS IS THE MORNING NEWS FOR MARCH 26, 2135.
Days to the fair
7:01
35th Granicus World Fair
MORNING NEWS 7
WE'RE DOWN TO THREE DAYS UNTIL THE GRANICUS WORLD FAIR, BUT WHAT WE'RE ALL EAGERLY AWAITING IS...
2135, HUH... GUESS I OVER-SLEPT A LITTLE.
OH YEAH... NEGI.
I HAVE TO FIND HIM...

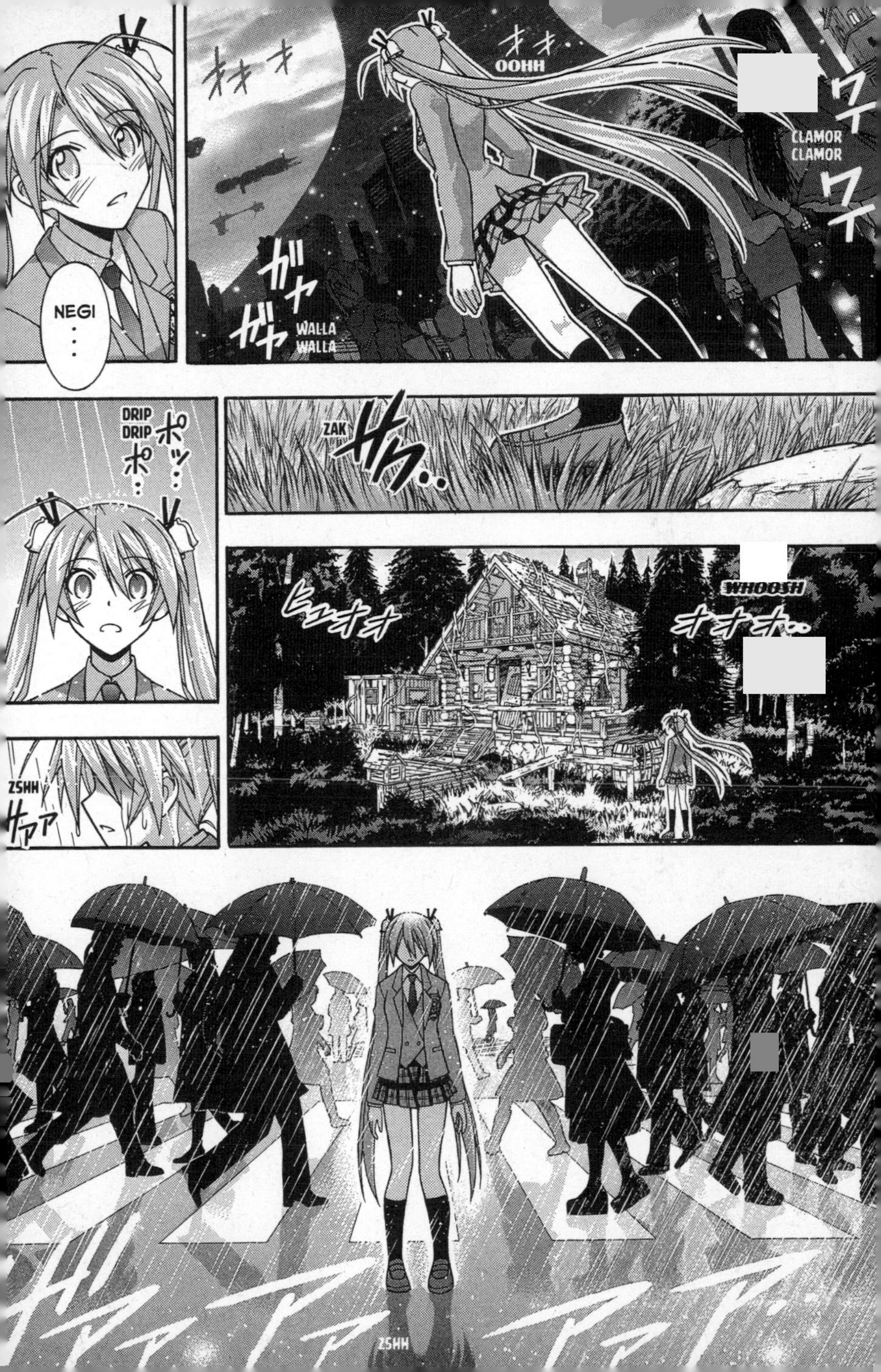

オオ
OOHH
ワイワイ
CLAMOR
CLAMOR
オオオ
ガヤガヤ
WALLA
WALLA
NEGI
...
ZAK
ザク..
ヒュオオ
WHOOSH
オオオ..
DRIP
DRIP
ポツ..ポ..
ZSHH
ザァア
ZSHH

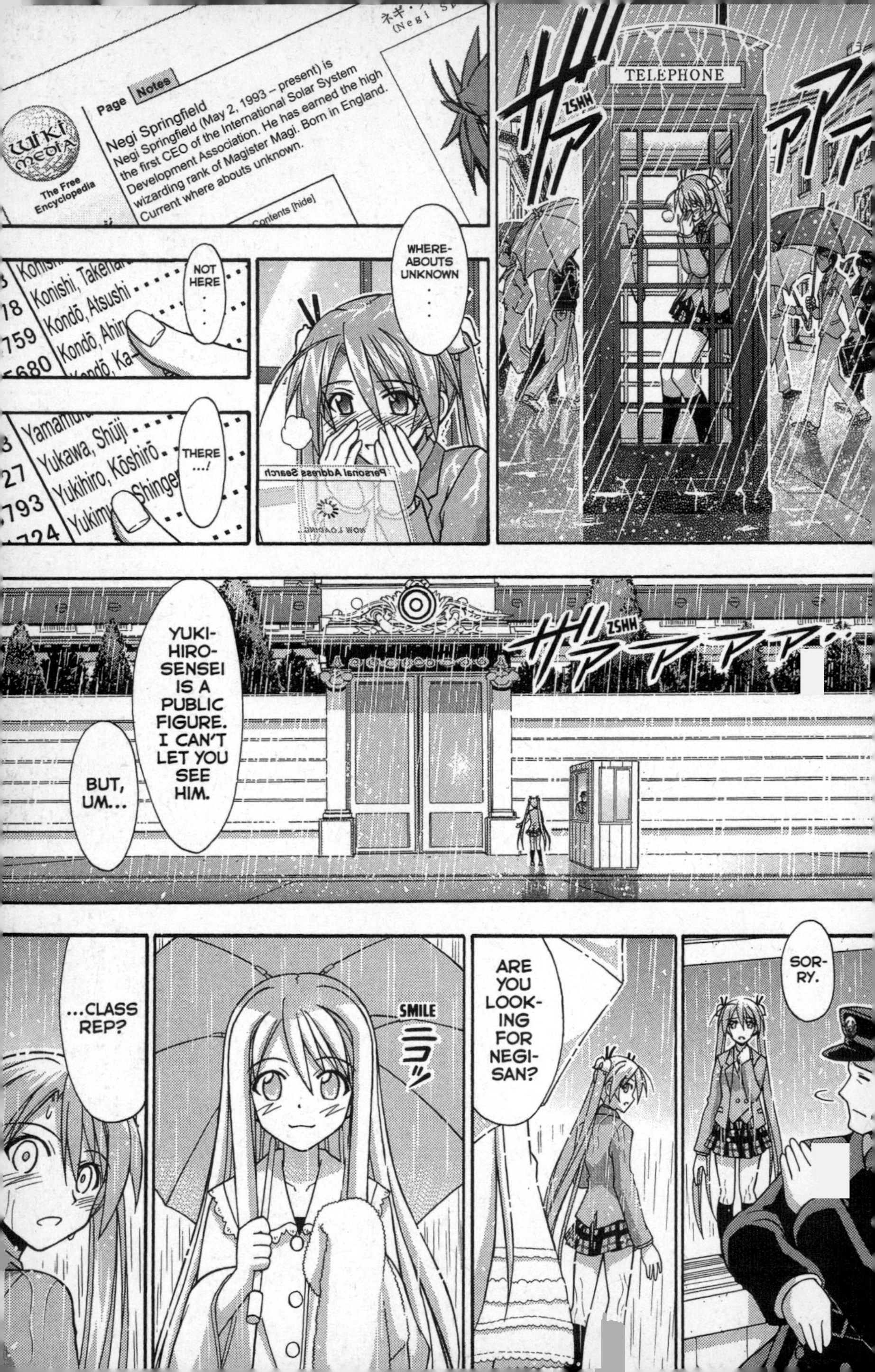
ZSHH
TELEPHONE
Page Notes
Negi Springfield
Negi Springfield (May 2, 1993 – present) is the first CEO of the International Solar System Development Association. He has earned the high wizarding rank of Magister Magi. Born in England. Current where abouts unknown.
Contents [hide]
WikiMedia The Free Encyclopedia
WHERE-ABOUTS UNKNOWN . . .
Personal Address Search
NOT HERE . . .
Konishi, Takenari
Kondō, Atsushi
THERE ...!
Yukawa, Shūji
Yukihiro, Kōshirō
ZSHH
YUKI-HIRO-SENSEI IS A PUBLIC FIGURE. I CAN'T LET YOU SEE HIM.
BUT, UM...
SORRY.
ARE YOU LOOKING FOR NEGI-SAN?
SMILE
...CLASS REP?

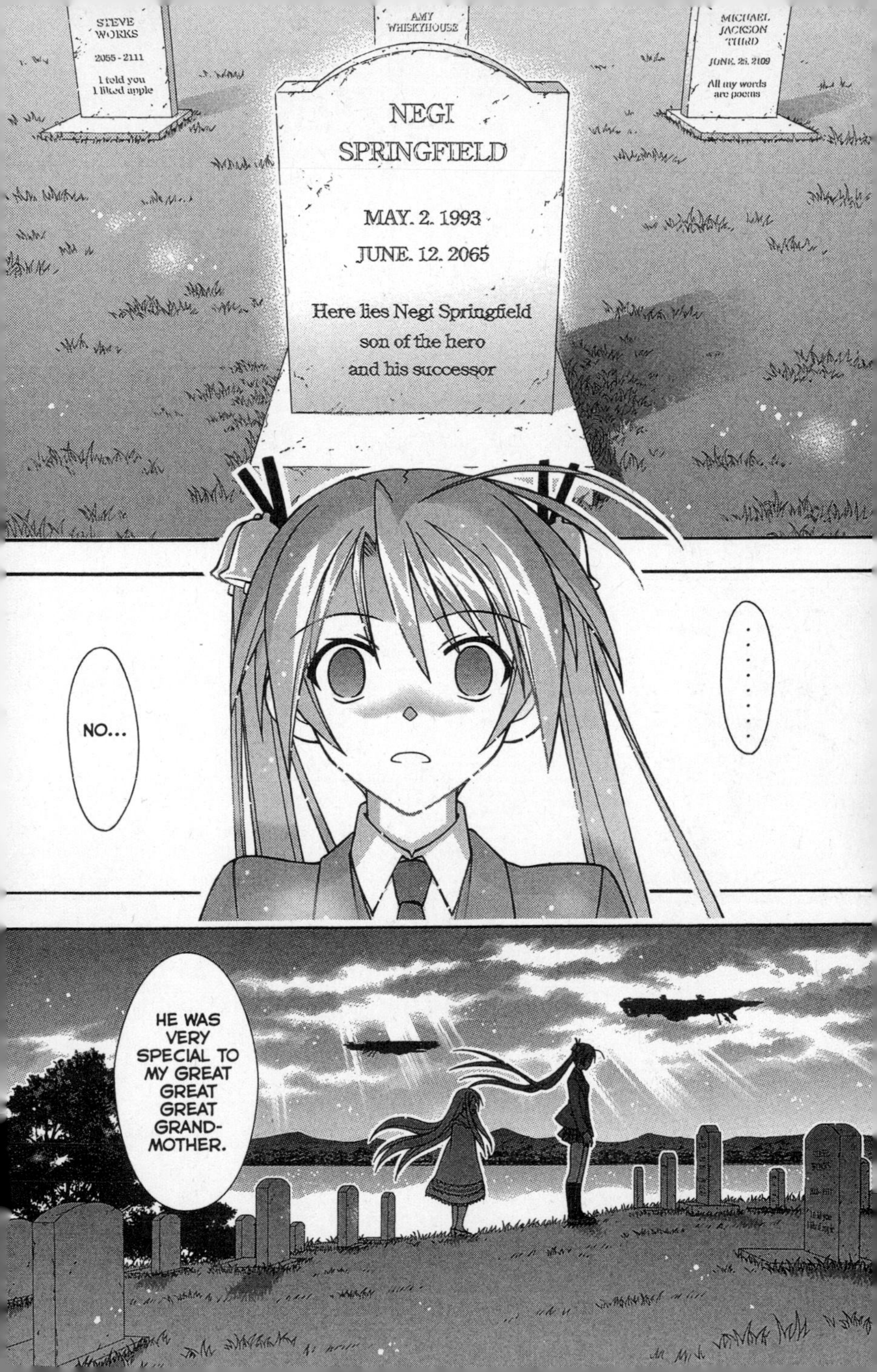
MICHAEL JACKSON THIRD
JUNE. 25. 2109
All my words are poems
AMY WHISKYHOUSE
STEVE WORKS
2055 - 2111
I told you I liked apple
NEGI SPRINGFIELD
MAY. 2. 1993
JUNE. 12. 2065
Here lies Negi Springfield son of the hero and his successor
......
NO...
HE WAS VERY SPECIAL TO MY GREAT GREAT GREAT GRAND-MOTHER.

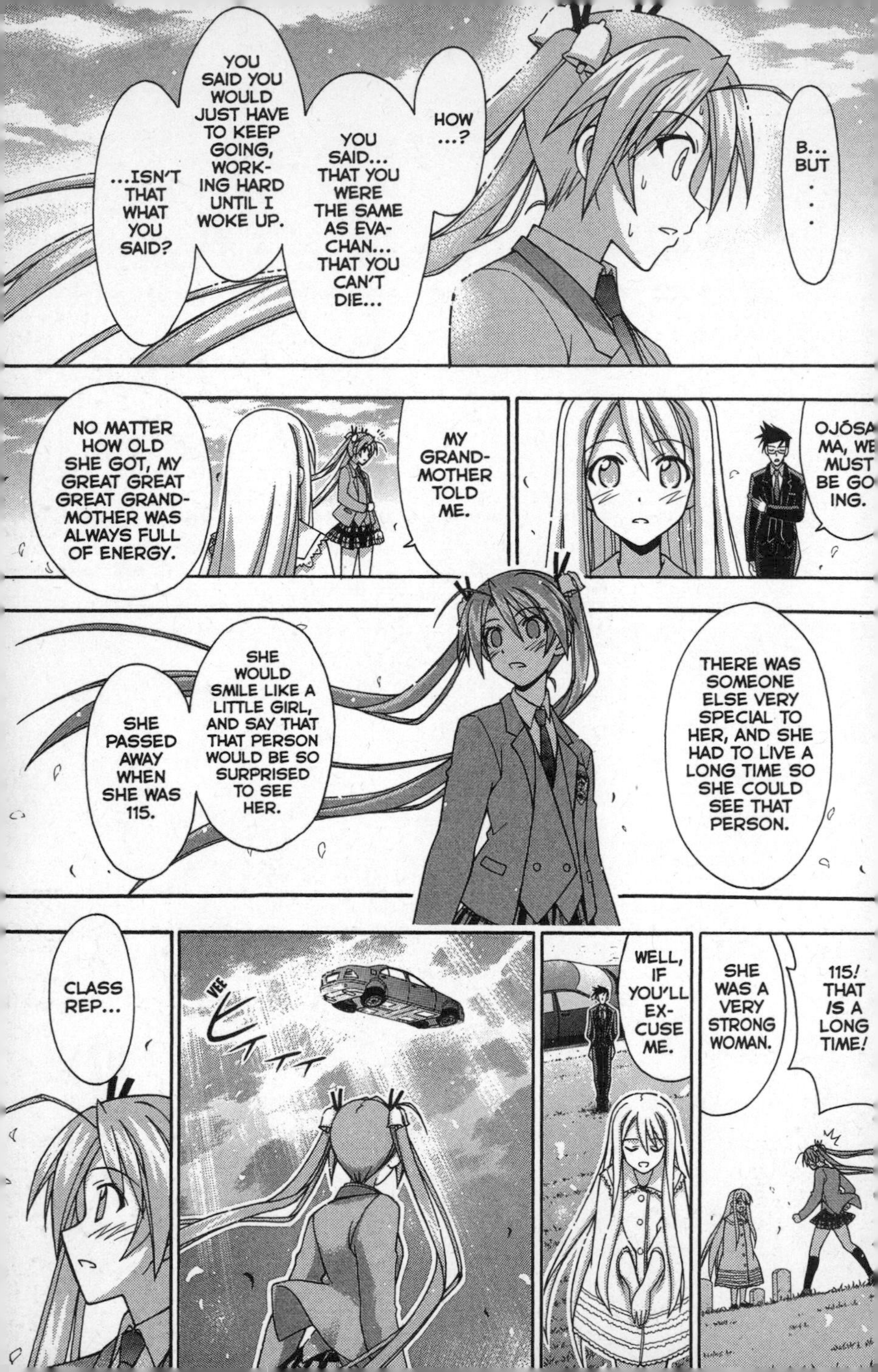
B... BUT . . .
HOW ...?
YOU SAID... THAT YOU WERE THE SAME AS EVA-CHAN... THAT YOU CAN'T DIE...
YOU SAID YOU WOULD JUST HAVE TO KEEP GOING, WORKING HARD UNTIL I WOKE UP.
...ISN'T THAT WHAT YOU SAID?
OJŌSAMA, WE MUST BE GOING.
MY GRANDMOTHER TOLD ME.
NO MATTER HOW OLD SHE GOT, MY GREAT GREAT GREAT GRANDMOTHER WAS ALWAYS FULL OF ENERGY.
THERE WAS SOMEONE ELSE VERY SPECIAL TO HER, AND SHE HAD TO LIVE A LONG TIME SO SHE COULD SEE THAT PERSON.
SHE WOULD SMILE LIKE A LITTLE GIRL, AND SAY THAT THAT PERSON WOULD BE SO SURPRISED TO SEE HER.
SHE PASSED AWAY WHEN SHE WAS 115.
115! THAT *IS* A LONG TIME!
SHE WAS A VERY STRONG WOMAN.
WELL, IF YOU'LL EXCUSE ME.
VEE
TTT
CLASS REP...

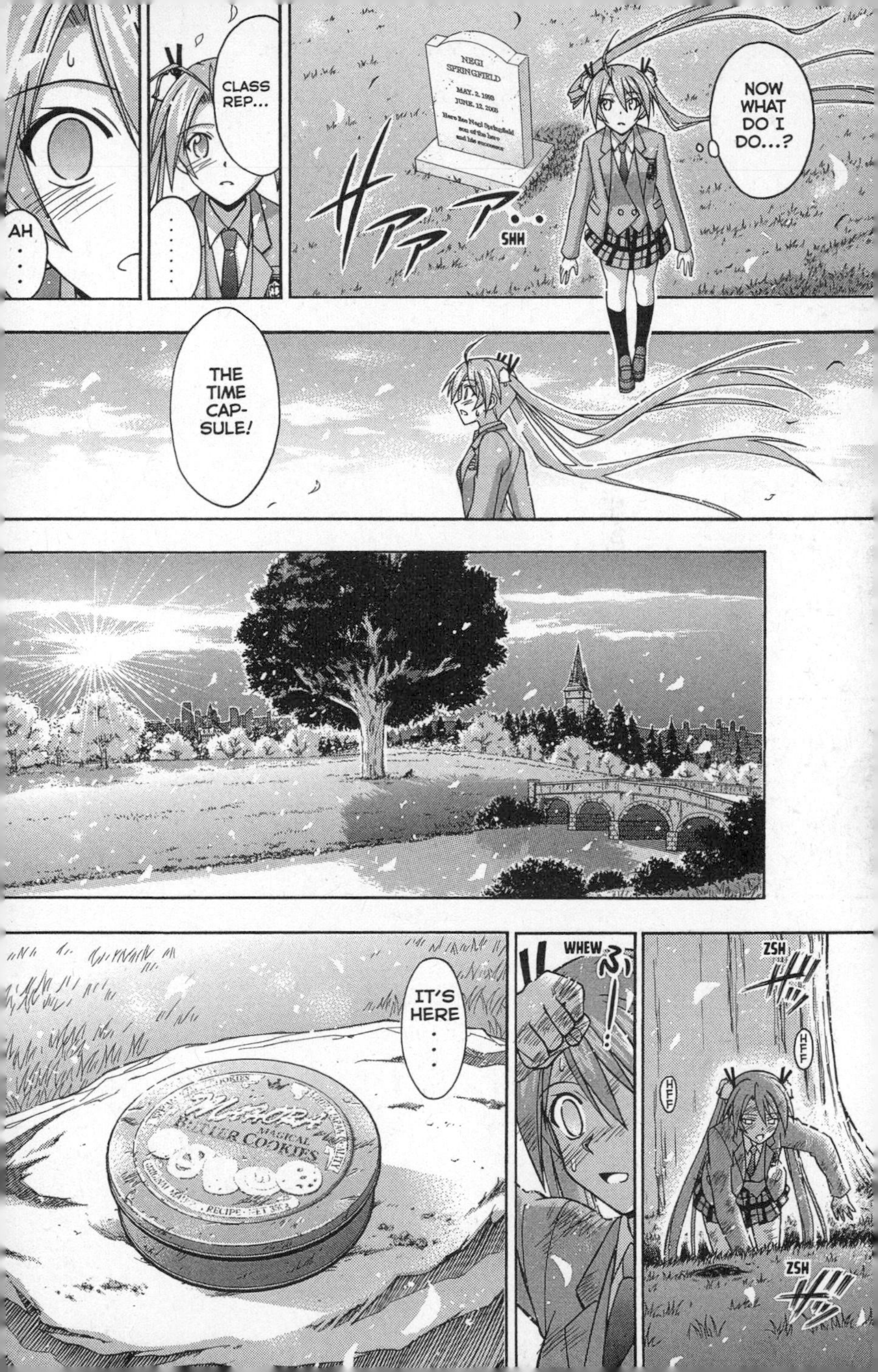
NOW WHAT DO I DO...?
NEGI SPRINGFIELD
SHH
CLASS REP...
......
AH ...
THE TIME CAP-SULE!
ZSH
HFF
HFF
ZSH
WHEW
IT'S HERE ...
MAGICAL
BUTTER COOKIES
RECIPE

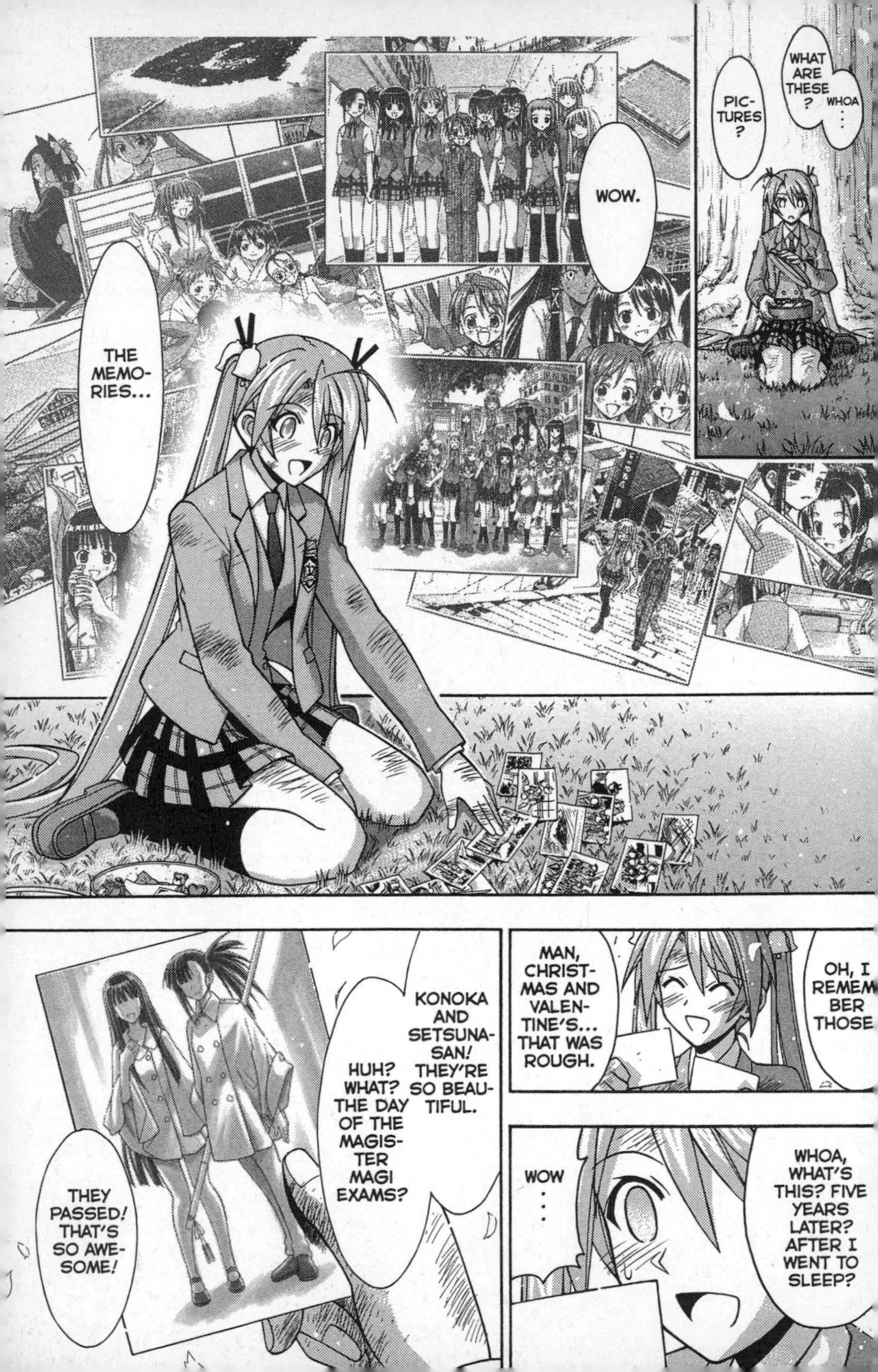
WHAT ARE THESE?
WHOA...
PICTURES?
WOW.
THE MEMORIES...
OH, I REMEMBER THOSE
MAN, CHRISTMAS AND VALENTINE'S... THAT WAS ROUGH.
WHOA, WHAT'S THIS? FIVE YEARS LATER? AFTER I WENT TO SLEEP?
WOW...
KONOKA AND SETSUNA-SAN! THEY'RE SO BEAUTIFUL.
HUH? WHAT? THE DAY OF THE MAGISTER MAGI EXAMS?
THEY PASSED! THAT'S SO AWESOME!

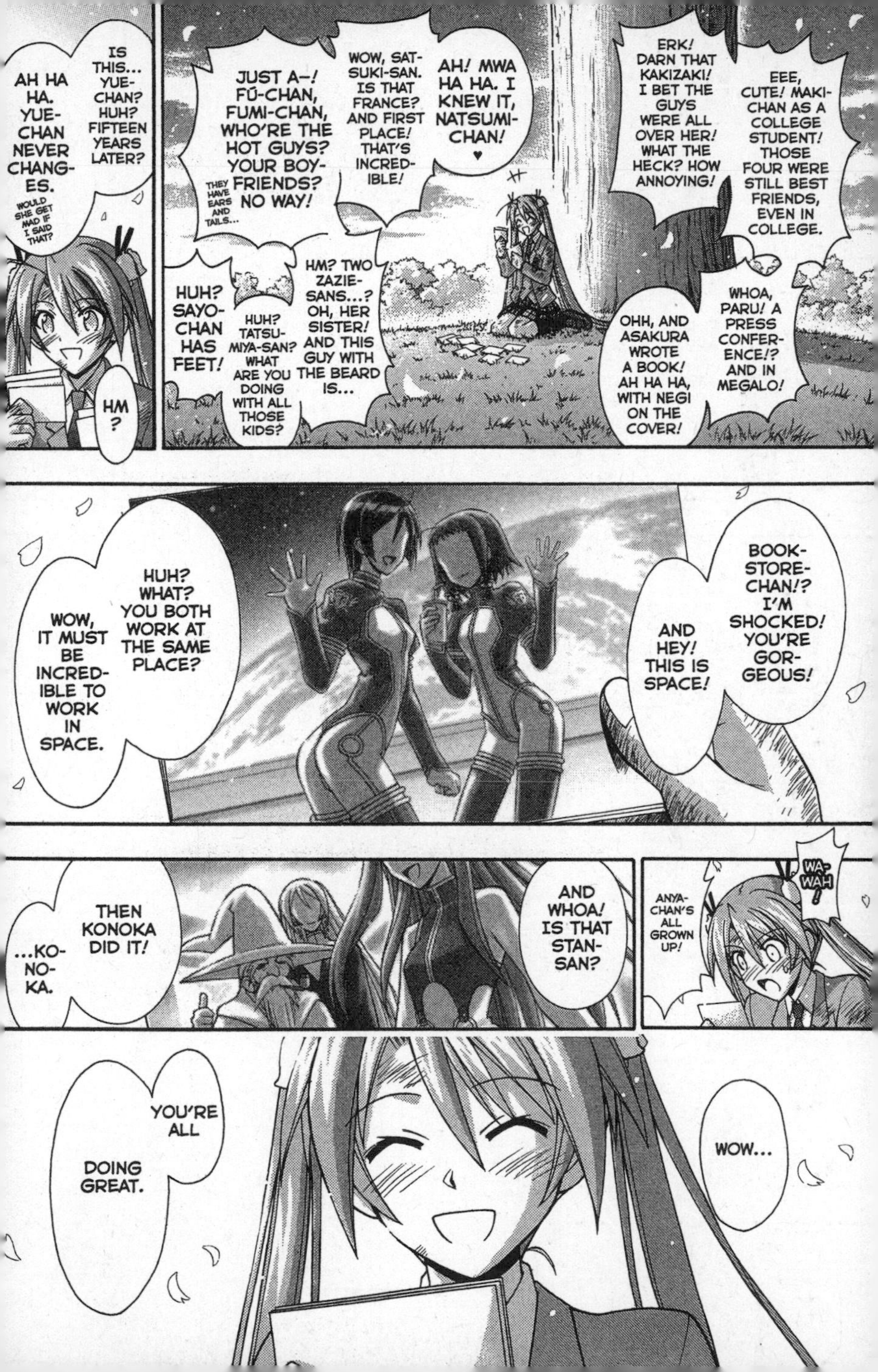
EEE, CUTE! MAKI-CHAN AS A COLLEGE STUDENT! THOSE FOUR WERE STILL BEST FRIENDS, EVEN IN COLLEGE.
ERK! DARN THAT KAKIZAKI! I BET THE GUYS WERE ALL OVER HER! WHAT THE HECK? HOW ANNOYING!
AH! MWA HA HA. I KNEW IT, NATSUMI-CHAN! ♥
WOW, SATSUKI-SAN. IS THAT FRANCE? AND FIRST PLACE! THAT'S INCREDIBLE!
JUST A-! FŪ-CHAN, FUMI-CHAN, WHO'RE THE HOT GUYS? YOUR BOYFRIENDS? NO WAY!
THEY HAVE EARS AND TAILS...
WHOA, PARU! A PRESS CONFERENCE!? AND IN MEGALO!
OHH, AND ASAKURA WROTE A BOOK! AH HA HA, WITH NEGI ON THE COVER!
HM? TWO ZAZIE-SANS...? OH, HER SISTER! AND THIS GUY WITH THE BEARD IS...
HUH? TATSUMIYA-SAN? WHAT ARE YOU DOING WITH ALL THOSE KIDS?
HUH? SAYO-CHAN HAS FEET!
IS THIS... YUE-CHAN? HUH? FIFTEEN YEARS LATER?
AH HA HA. YUE-CHAN NEVER CHANGES.
WOULD SHE GET MAD IF I SAID THAT?
HM?
BOOKSTORE-CHAN!? I'M SHOCKED! YOU'RE GORGEOUS!
AND HEY! THIS IS SPACE!
HUH? WHAT? YOU BOTH WORK AT THE SAME PLACE?
WOW, IT MUST BE INCREDIBLE TO WORK IN SPACE.
WA-WAH!
ANYA-CHAN'S ALL GROWN UP!
AND WHOA! IS THAT STAN-SAN?
THEN KONOKA DID IT!
...KO-NO-KA.
WOW...
YOU'RE ALL DOING GREAT.

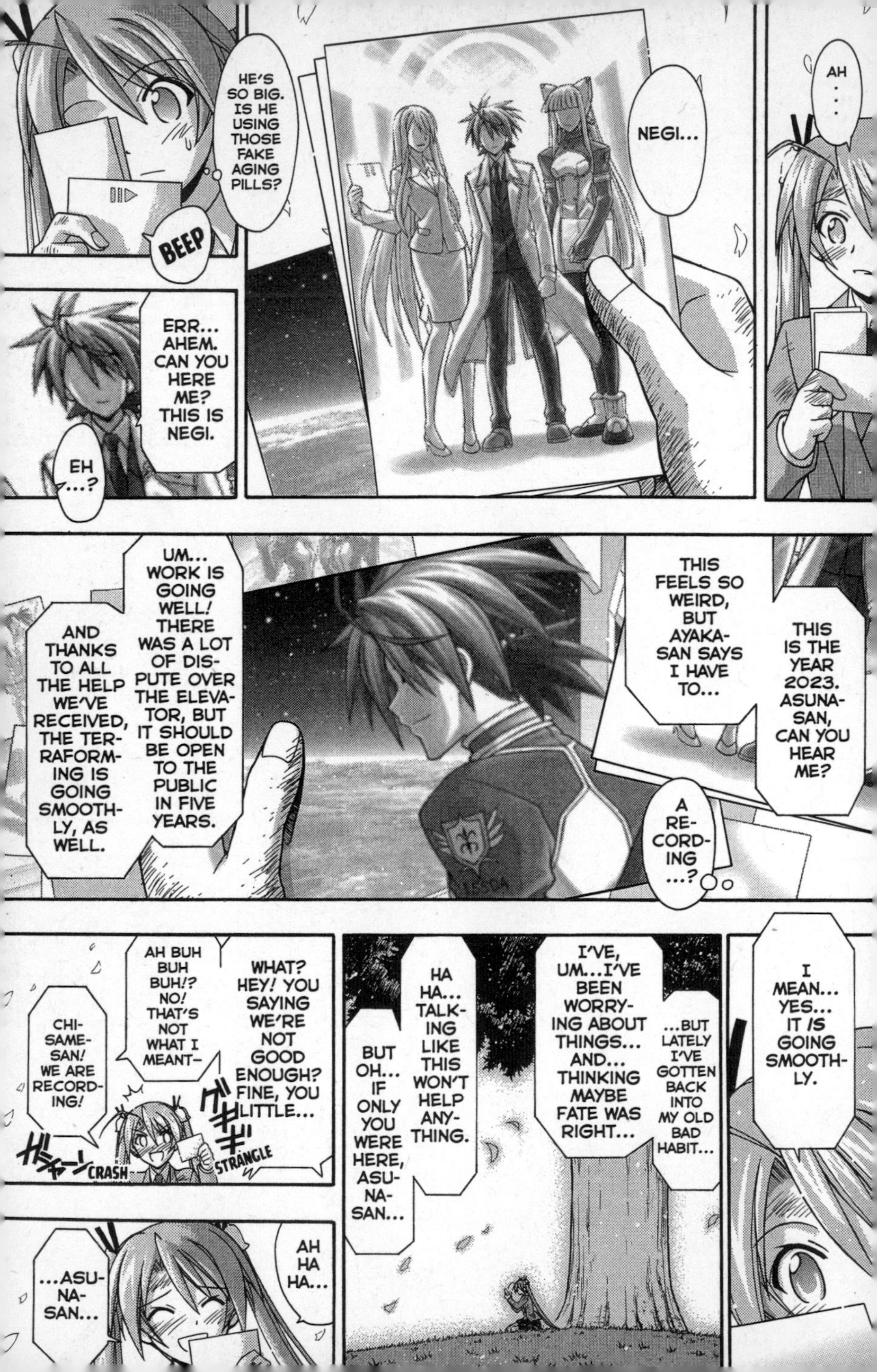
AH...
NEGI...
HE'S SO BIG. IS HE USING THOSE FAKE AGING PILLS?
BEEP
ERR... AHEM. CAN YOU HERE ME? THIS IS NEGI.
EH...?
THIS IS THE YEAR 2023. ASUNA-SAN, CAN YOU HEAR ME?
THIS FEELS SO WEIRD, BUT AYAKA-SAN SAYS I HAVE TO...
A RECORDING...?
UM... WORK IS GOING WELL! THERE WAS A LOT OF DISPUTE OVER THE ELEVATOR, BUT IT SHOULD BE OPEN TO THE PUBLIC IN FIVE YEARS.
AND THANKS TO ALL THE HELP WE'VE RECEIVED, THE TERRAFORMING IS GOING SMOOTHLY, AS WELL.
I MEAN... YES... IT IS GOING SMOOTHLY.
I'VE, UM...I'VE BEEN WORRYING ABOUT THINGS... AND... THINKING MAYBE FATE WAS RIGHT...
...BUT LATELY I'VE GOTTEN BACK INTO MY OLD BAD HABIT...
HA HA... TALKING LIKE THIS WON'T HELP ANYTHING.
BUT OH... IF ONLY YOU WERE HERE, ASUNA-SAN...
WHAT? HEY! YOU SAYING WE'RE NOT GOOD ENOUGH? FINE, YOU LITTLE...
AH BUH BUH!? NO! THAT'S NOT WHAT I MEANT—
CHI-SAME-SAN! WE ARE RECORDING!
CRASH
STRANGLE
AH HA HA...
...ASUNA-SAN...

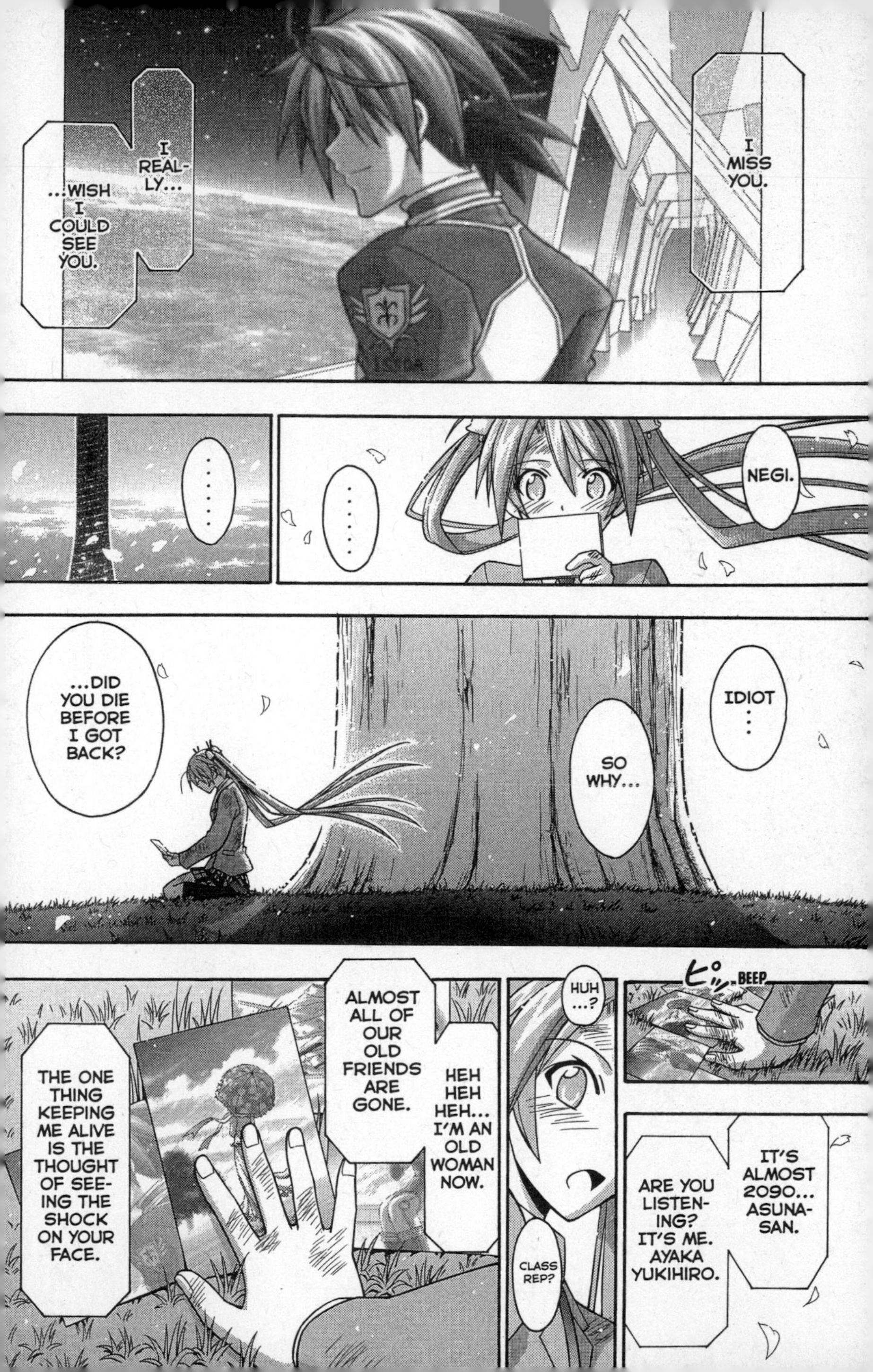
I MISS YOU.
I REALLY...
...WISH I COULD SEE YOU.
NEGI.
......
......
IDIOT...
SO WHY...
...DID YOU DIE BEFORE I GOT BACK?
ピッ BEEP
IT'S ALMOST 2090... ASUNA-SAN.
ARE YOU LISTENING? IT'S ME. AYAKA YUKIHIRO.
HUH...?
CLASS REP?
ALMOST ALL OF OUR OLD FRIENDS ARE GONE.
HEH HEH HEH... I'M AN OLD WOMAN NOW.
THE ONE THING KEEPING ME ALIVE IS THE THOUGHT OF SEEING THE SHOCK ON YOUR FACE.

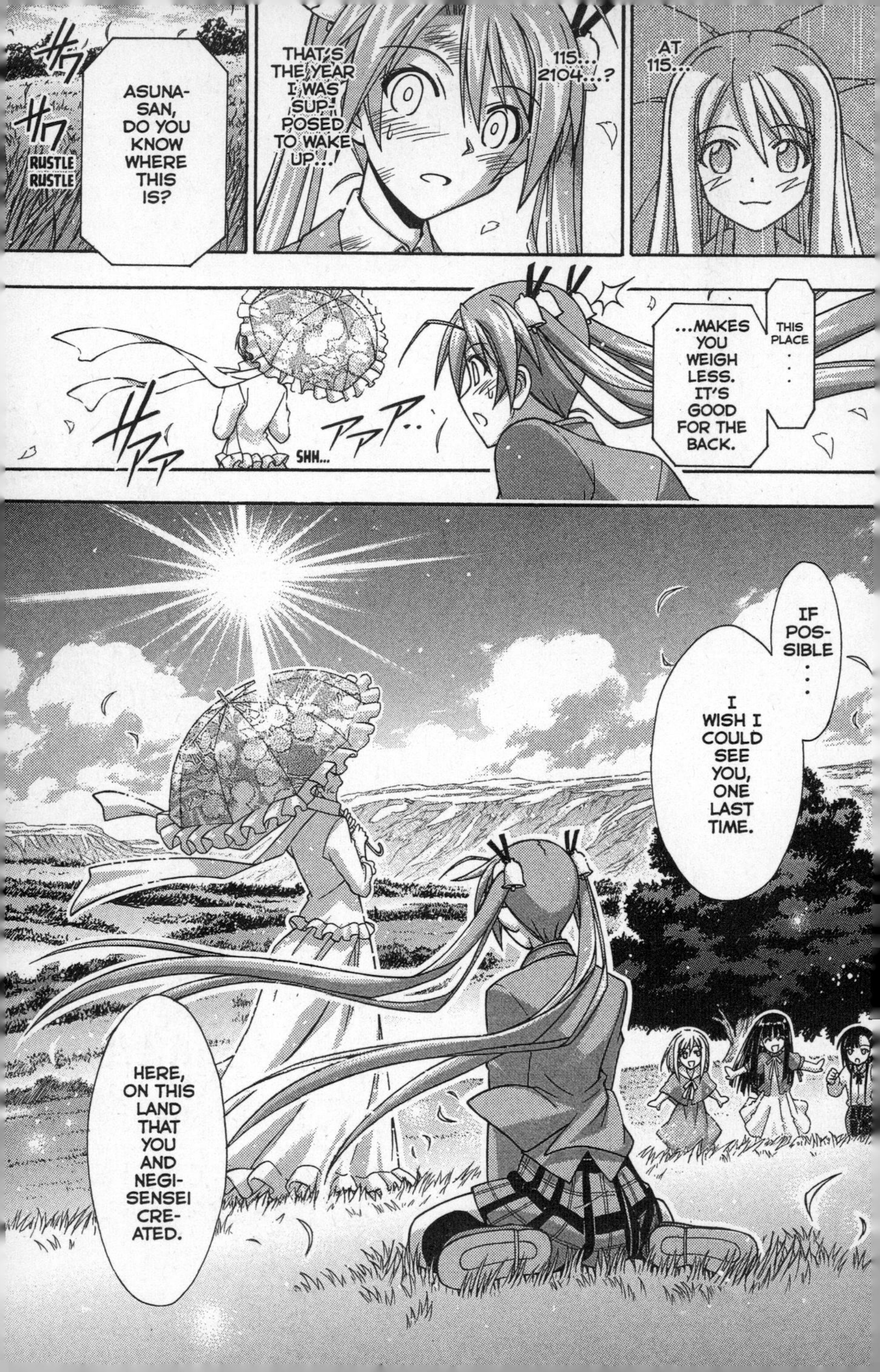
AT 115...
115... 2104...?
THAT'S THE YEAR I WAS SUP-POSED TO WAKE UP...!
ASUNA-SAN, DO YOU KNOW WHERE THIS IS?
RUSTLE RUSTLE
THIS PLACE...
...MAKES YOU WEIGH LESS. IT'S GOOD FOR THE BACK.
SHH...
IF POS-SIBLE...
I WISH I COULD SEE YOU, ONE LAST TIME.
HERE, ON THIS LAND THAT YOU AND NEGI-SENSEI CRE-ATED.

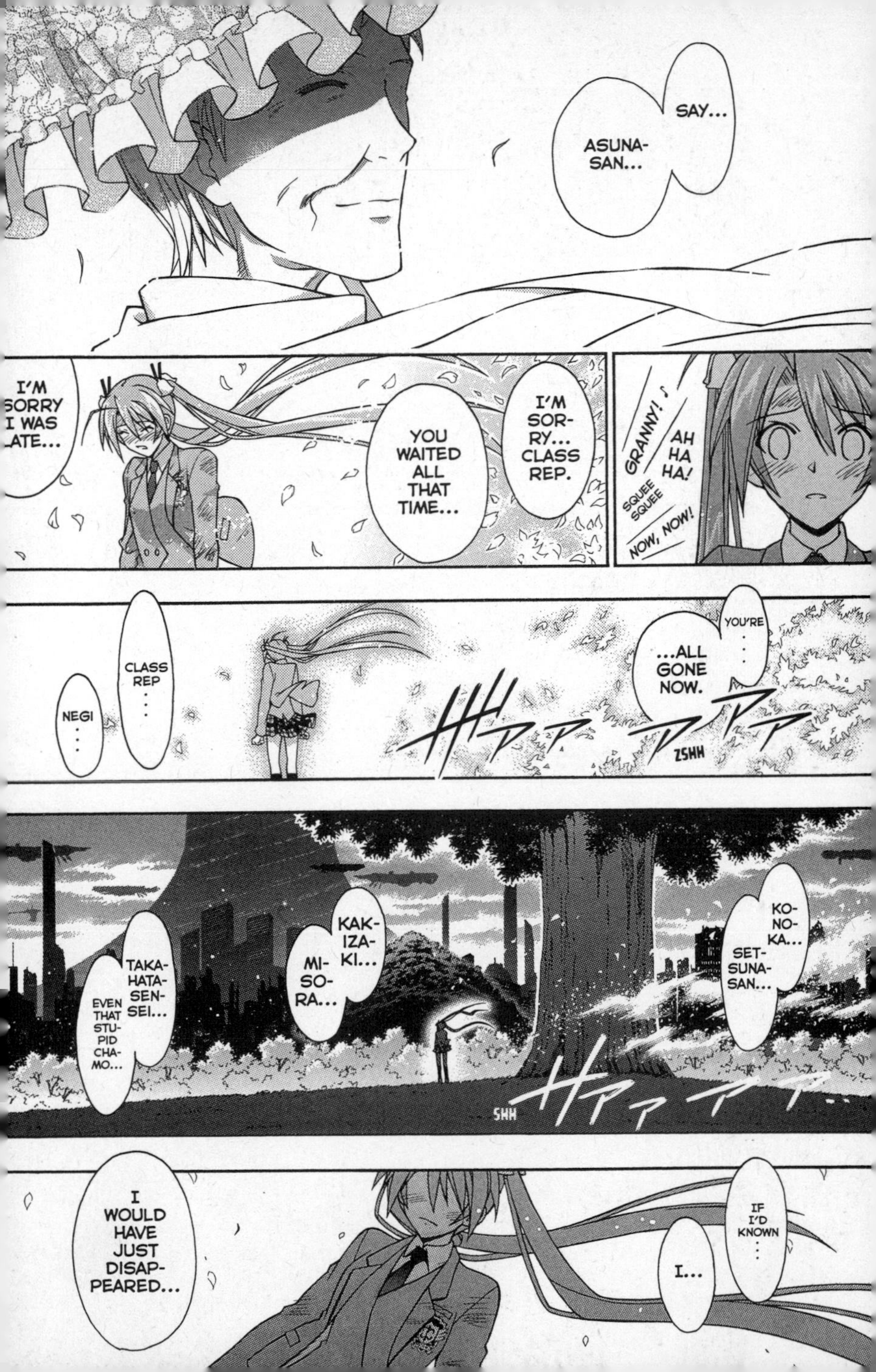
SAY...
ASUNA-SAN...
GRANNY! ♪
AH HA HA!
SQUEE SQUEE
NOW, NOW!
I'M SORRY... CLASS REP.
YOU WAITED ALL THAT TIME...
I'M SORRY I WAS LATE...
YOU'RE...
...ALL GONE NOW.
ZSHH
CLASS REP...
NEGI...
KONOKA...
SETSUNA-SAN...
KAKIZAKI...
MISORA...
TAKAHATA-SENSEI...
EVEN THAT STUPID CHAMO...
SHH
IF I'D KNOWN...
I...
I WOULD HAVE JUST DISAPPEARED...

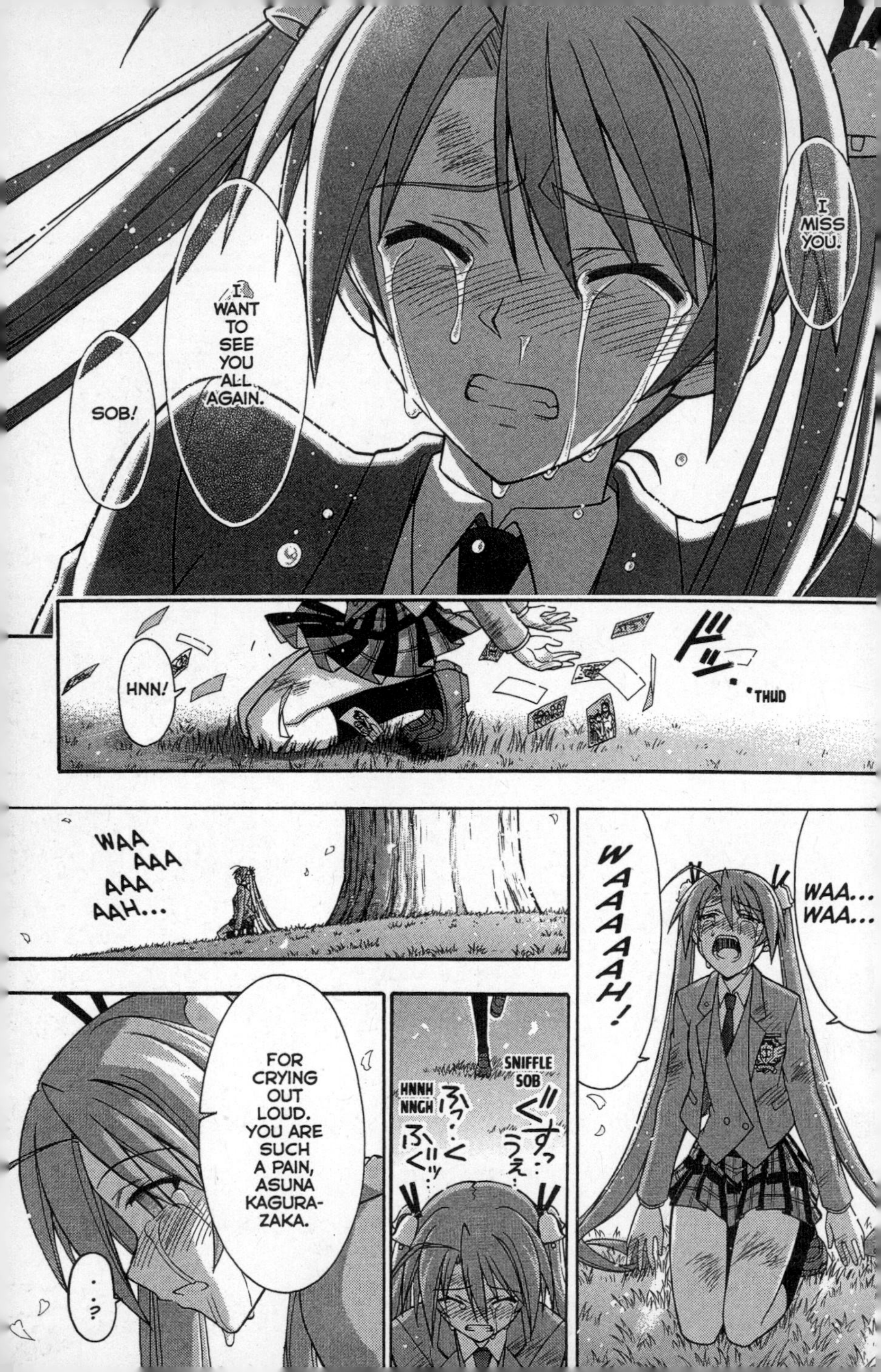
I MISS YOU.
I WANT TO SEE YOU ALL AGAIN.
SOB!
ドッ
THUD
HNN!
WAA... WAA...
WAAAAAAH!
WAA AAA AAA AAH...
SNIFFLE SOB
HNNH NNGH
FOR CRYING OUT LOUD. YOU ARE SUCH A PAIN, ASUNA KAGURAZAKA.
...?

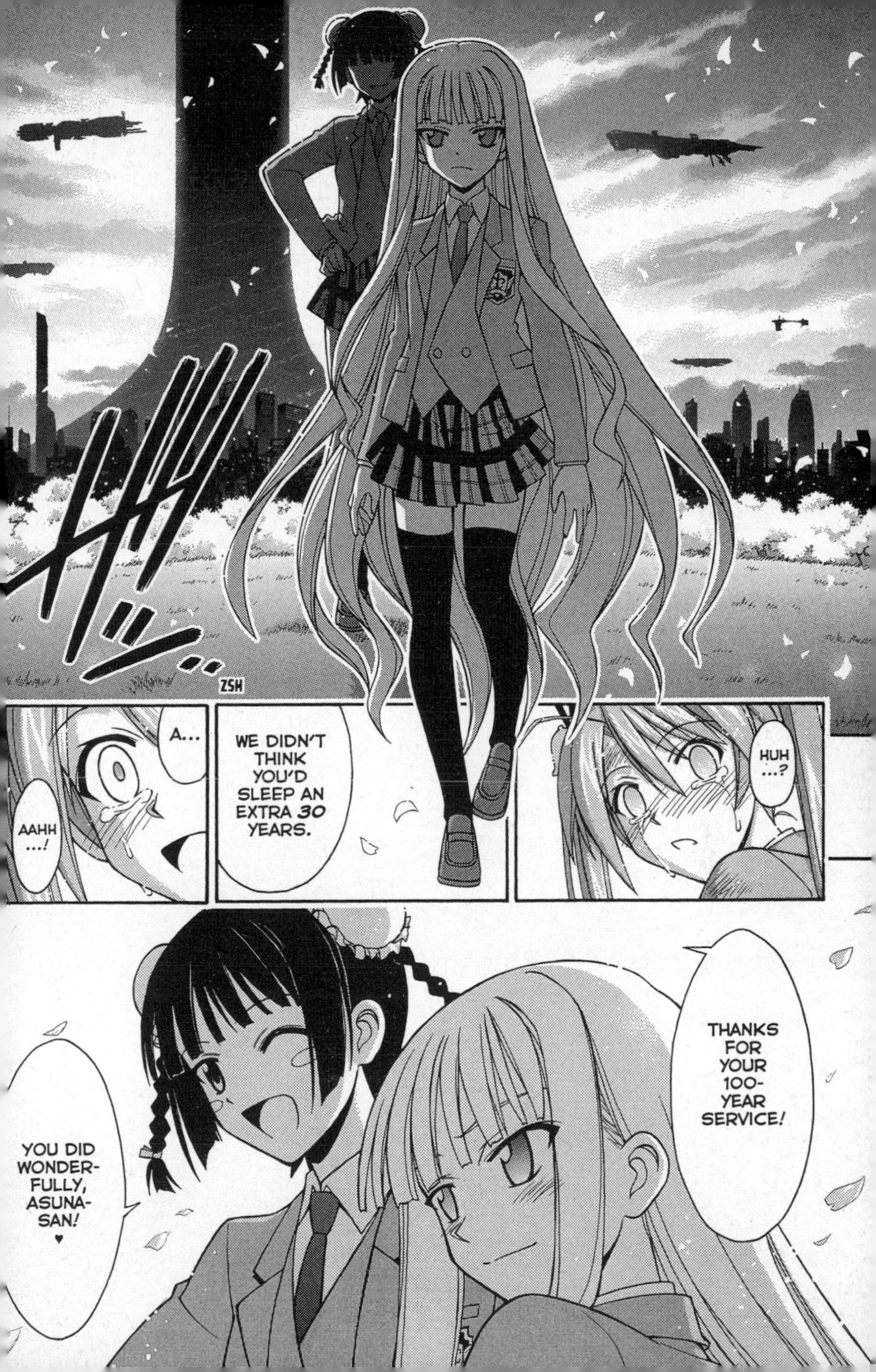
ZSH
HUH ...?
WE DIDN'T THINK YOU'D SLEEP AN EXTRA 30 YEARS.
A...
AAHH ...!
THANKS FOR YOUR 100-YEAR SERVICE!
YOU DID WONDERFULLY, ASUNA-SAN! ♥

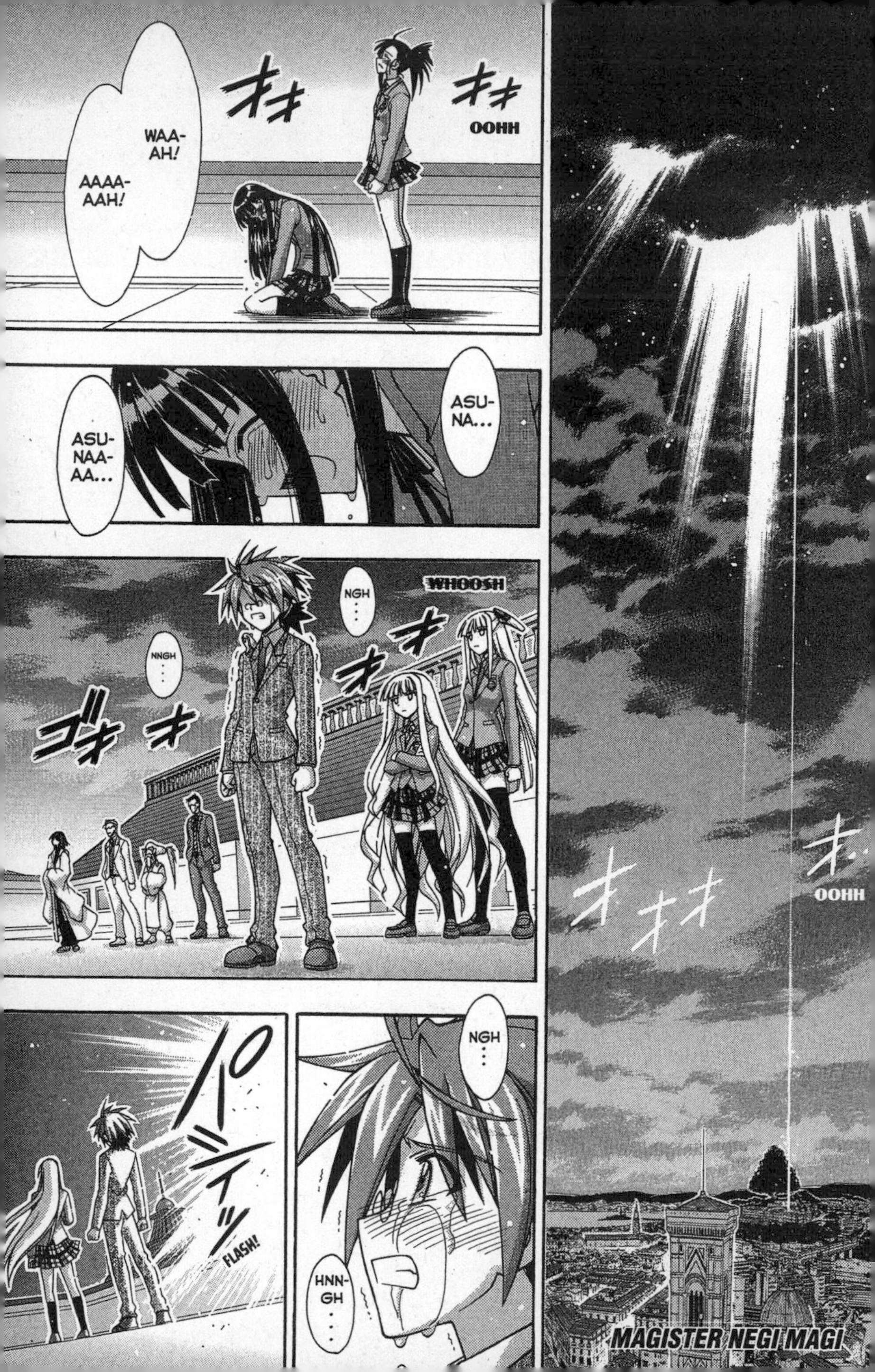
OOHH
MAGISTER NEGI MAGI
OOHH
WAA-AH!
AAAA-AAH!
ASU-NA...
ASU-NAAA-AA...
WHOOSH
NGH...
NNGH...
NGH...
HNN-GH...
FLASH!

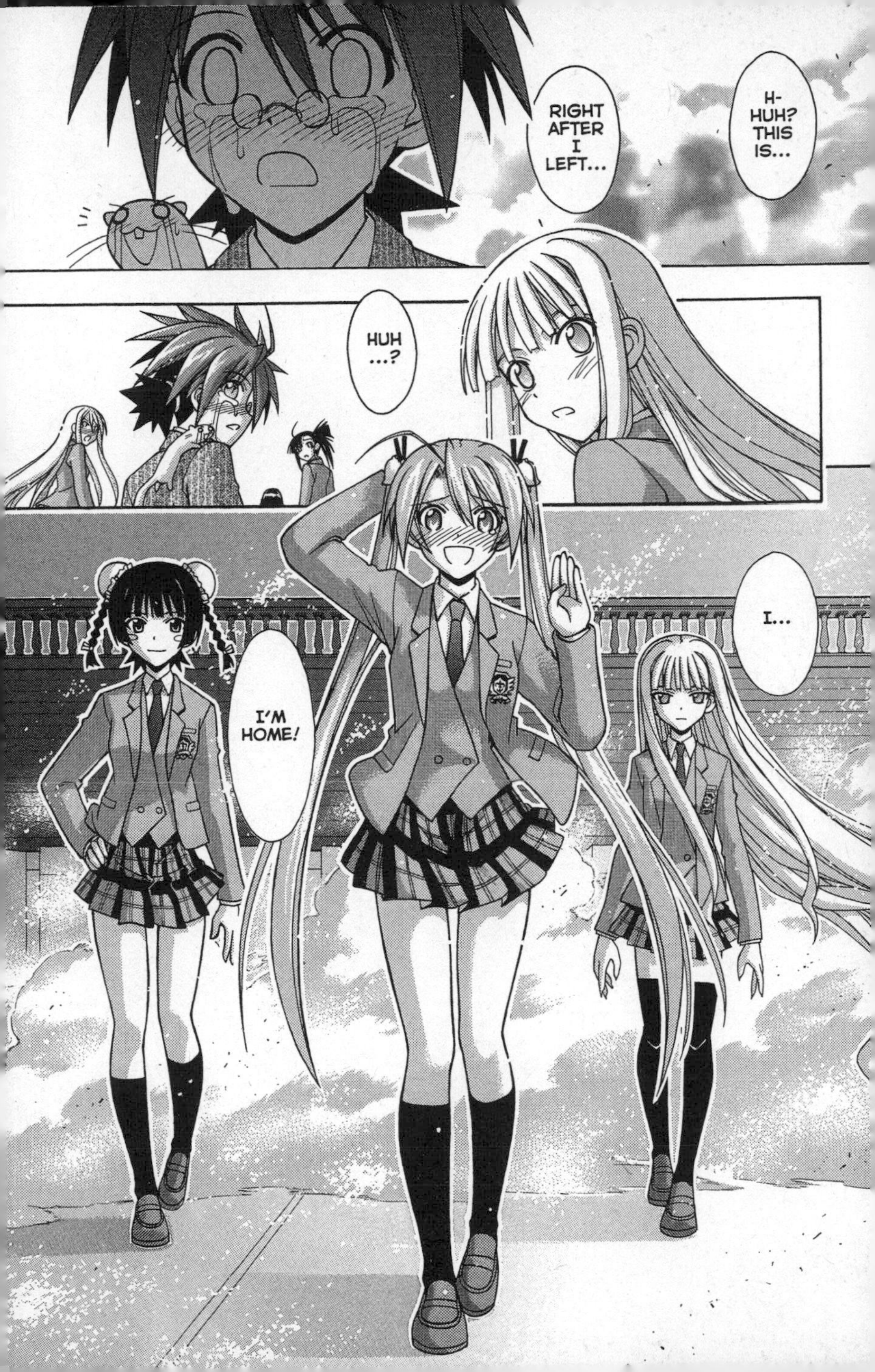
H-HUH? THIS IS...
RIGHT AFTER I LEFT...
HUH ...?
I...
I'M HOME!

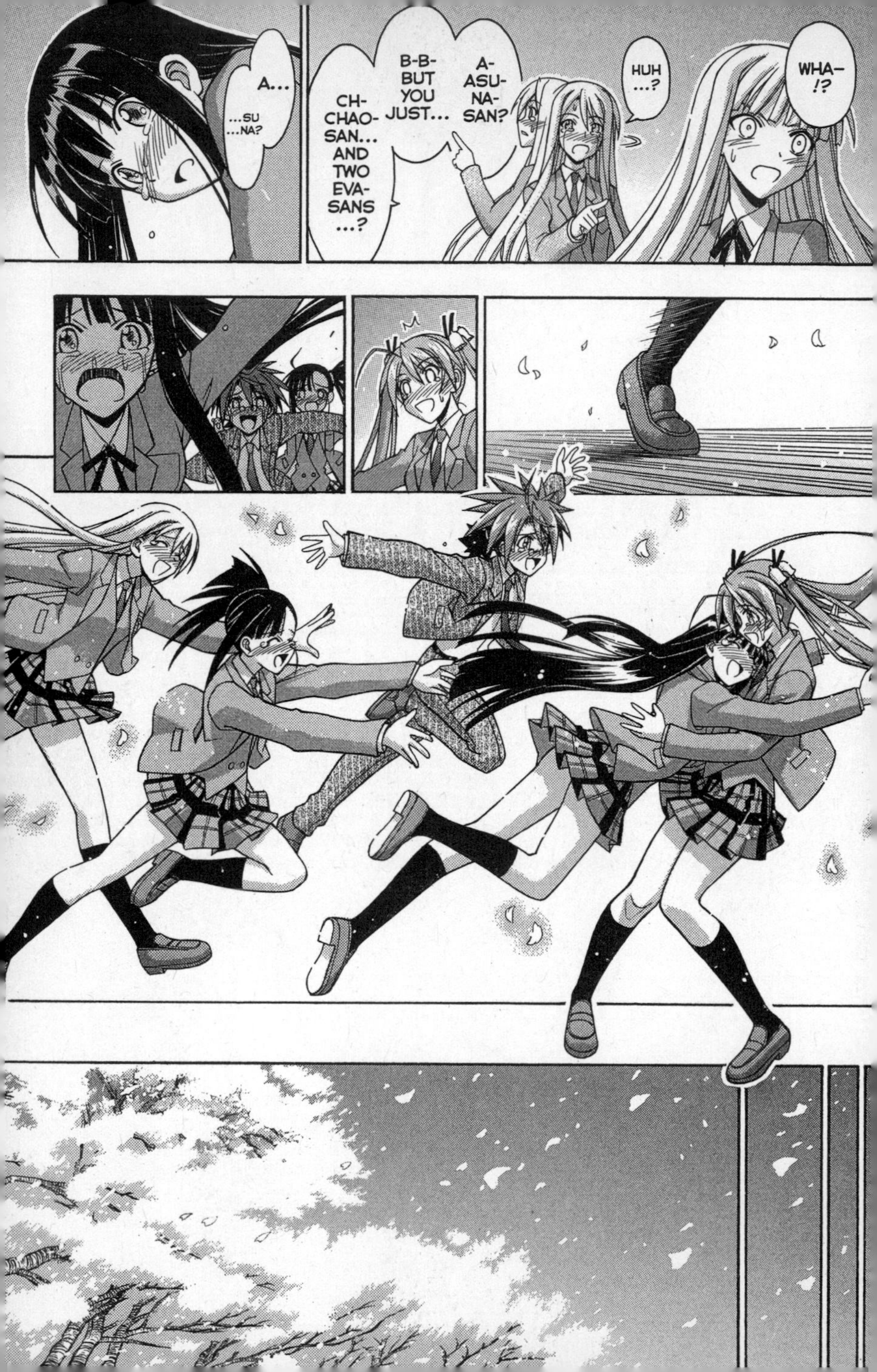
WHA— !?
HUH ...?
A- ASU- NA- SAN?
B-B- BUT YOU JUST...
CH- CHAO- SAN... AND TWO EVA- SANS ...?
A...
...SU ...NA?

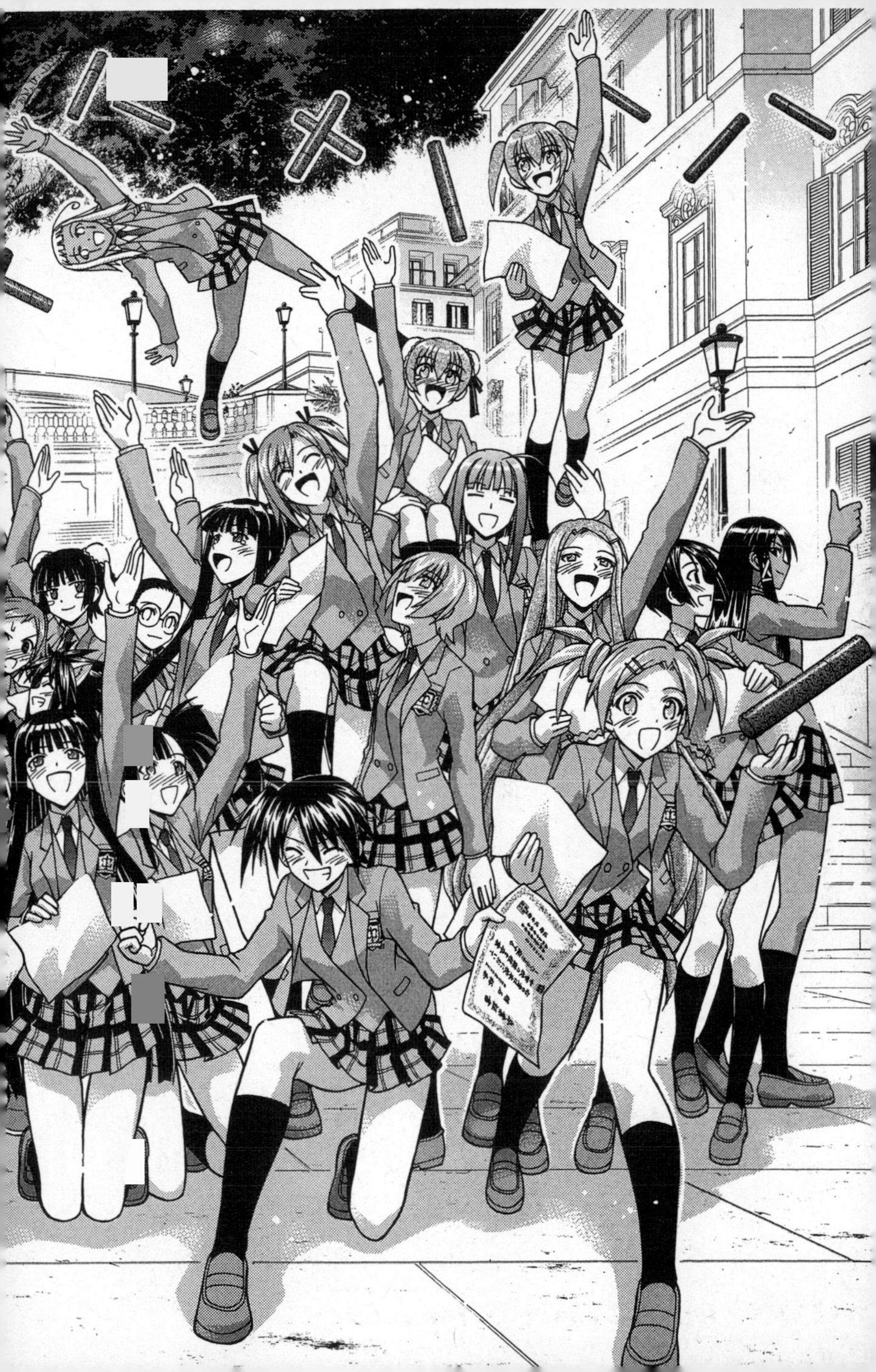

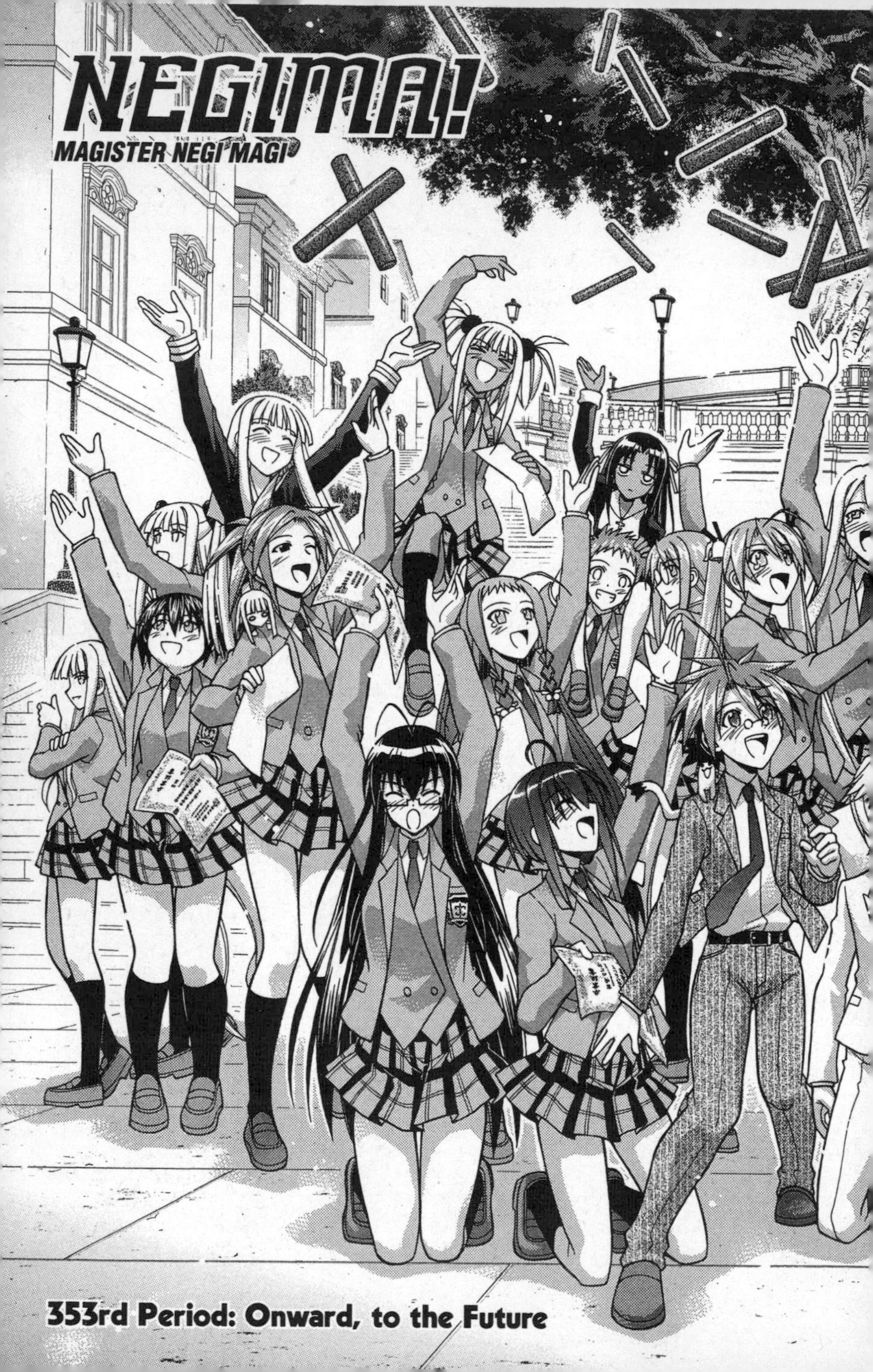
NEGIMA!
MAGISTER NEGI MAGI
353rd Period: Onward, to the Future

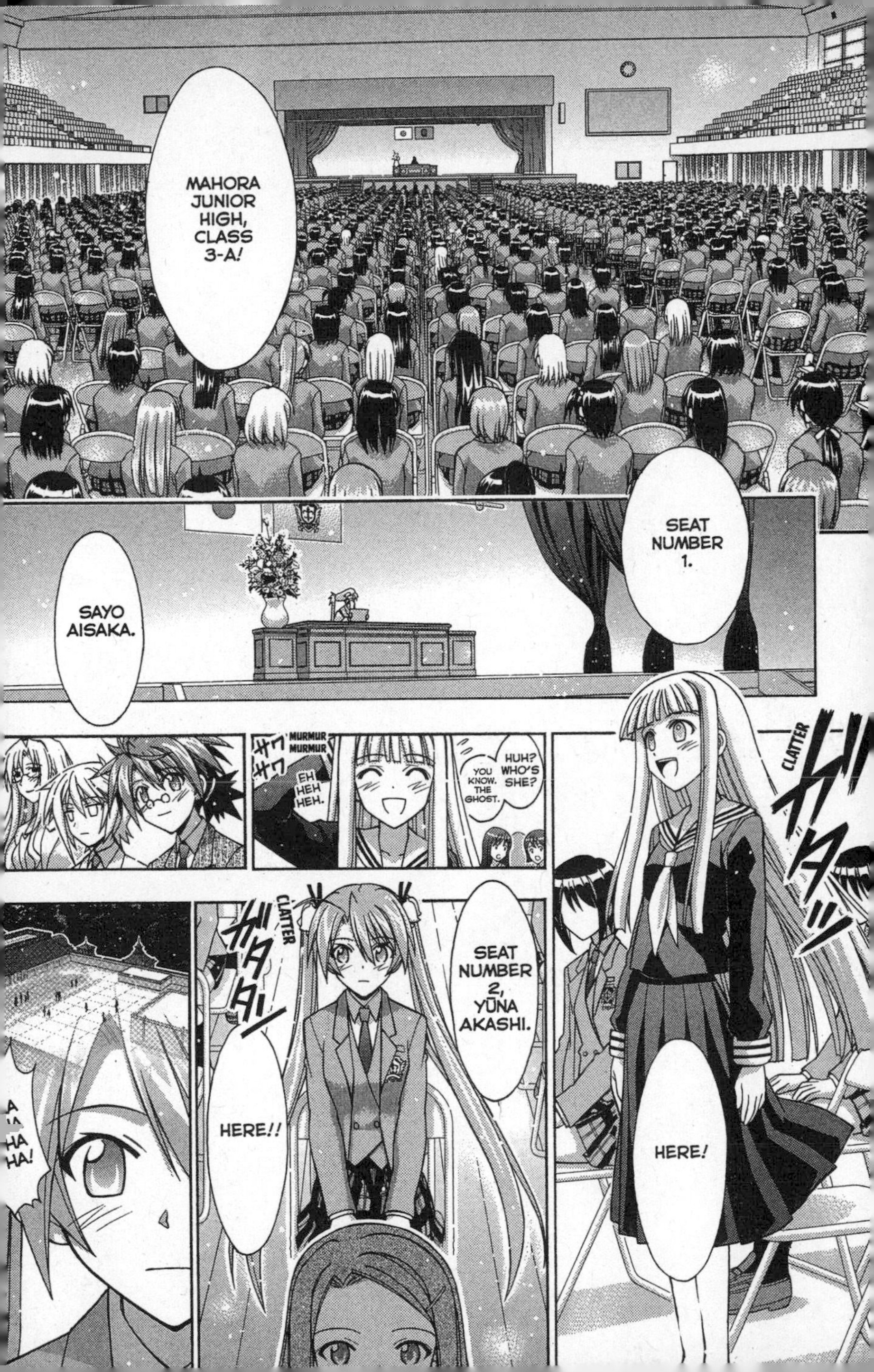
MAHORA JUNIOR HIGH, CLASS 3-A!
SEAT NUMBER 1.
SAYO AISAKA.
CLATTER
HERE!
HUH? WHO'S SHE?
YOU KNOW. THE GHOST.
MURMUR MURMUR
EH HEH HEH.
SEAT NUMBER 2, YŪNA AKASHI.
CLATTER
HERE!!
A HA HA HA!

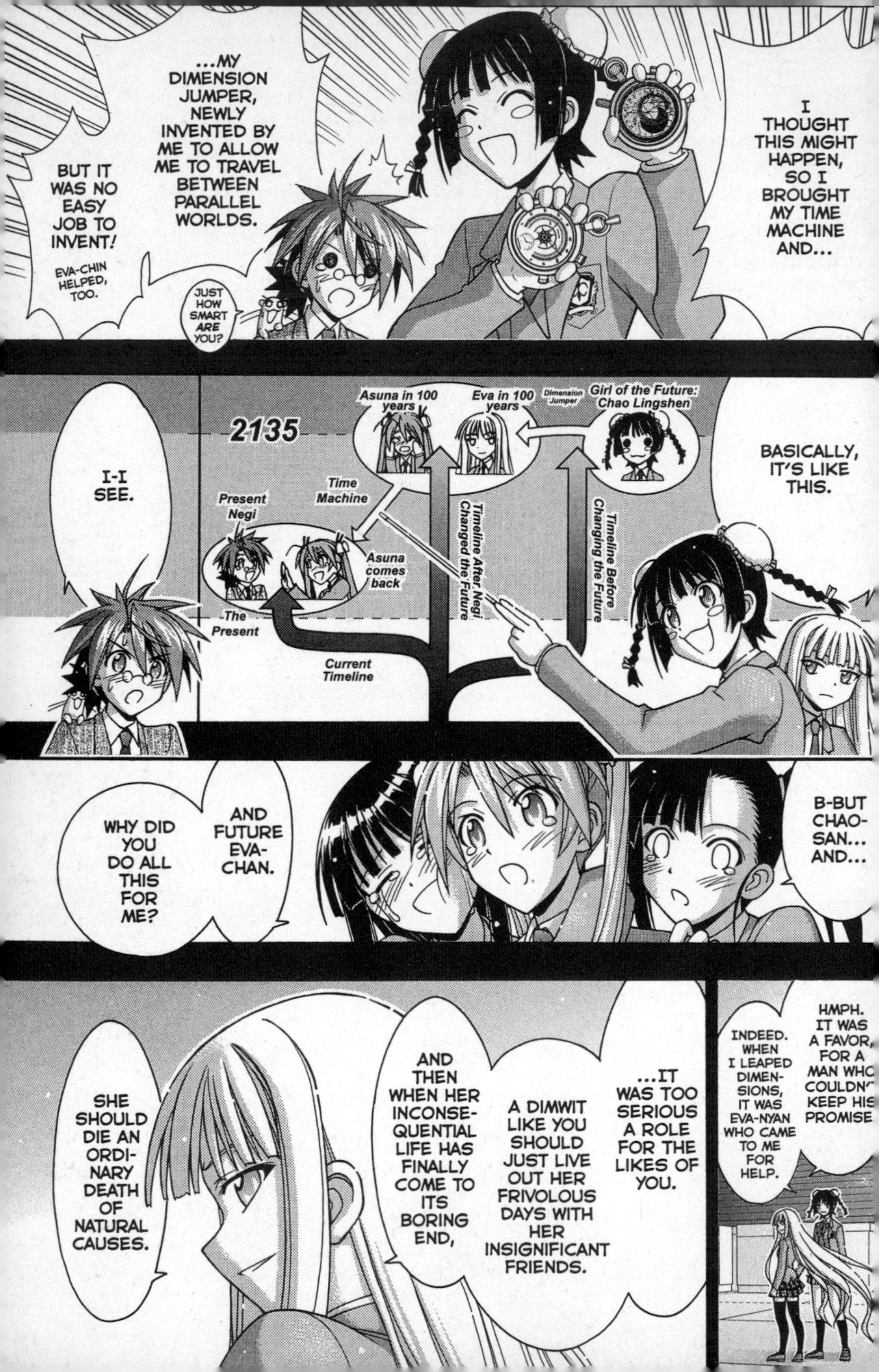
I THOUGHT THIS MIGHT HAPPEN, SO I BROUGHT MY TIME MACHINE AND...
...MY DIMENSION JUMPER, NEWLY INVENTED BY ME TO ALLOW ME TO TRAVEL BETWEEN PARALLEL WORLDS.
BUT IT WAS NO EASY JOB TO INVENT!
EVA-CHIN HELPED, TOO.
JUST HOW SMART ARE YOU?
BASICALLY, IT'S LIKE THIS.
Girl of the Future: Chao Lingshen
Dimension Jumper
Eva in 100 years
Asuna in 100 years
2135
Timeline Before Changing the Future
Timeline After Negi Changed the Future
Time Machine
Present Negi
Asuna comes back
The Present
Current Timeline
I-I SEE.
B-BUT CHAO-SAN... AND...
AND FUTURE EVA-CHAN.
WHY DID YOU DO ALL THIS FOR ME?
HMPH. IT WAS A FAVOR, FOR A MAN WHO COULDN'T KEEP HIS PROMISE.
INDEED. WHEN I LEAPED DIMENSIONS, IT WAS EVA-NYAN WHO CAME TO ME FOR HELP.
...IT WAS TOO SERIOUS A ROLE FOR THE LIKES OF YOU.
A DIMWIT LIKE YOU SHOULD JUST LIVE OUT HER FRIVOLOUS DAYS WITH HER INSIGNIFICANT FRIENDS.
AND THEN WHEN HER INCONSEQUENTIAL LIFE HAS FINALLY COME TO ITS BORING END,
SHE SHOULD DIE AN ORDINARY DEATH OF NATURAL CAUSES.

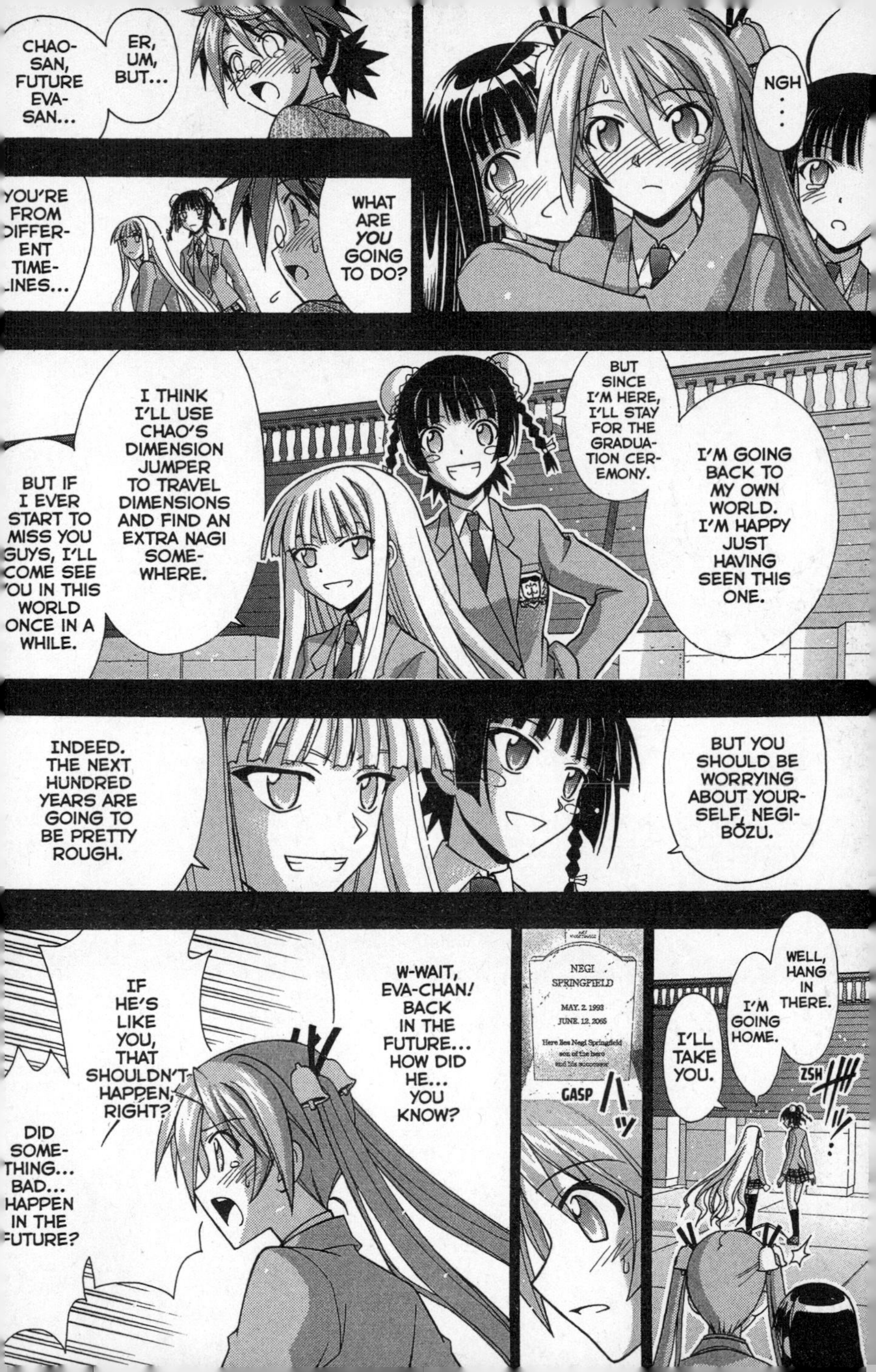
NGH...
ER, UM, BUT...
CHAO-SAN, FUTURE EVA-SAN...
WHAT ARE *YOU* GOING TO DO?
YOU'RE FROM DIFFERENT TIMELINES...
I'M GOING BACK TO MY OWN WORLD. I'M HAPPY JUST HAVING SEEN THIS ONE.
BUT SINCE I'M HERE, I'LL STAY FOR THE GRADUATION CEREMONY.
I THINK I'LL USE CHAO'S DIMENSION JUMPER TO TRAVEL DIMENSIONS AND FIND AN EXTRA NAGI SOMEWHERE.
BUT IF I EVER START TO MISS YOU GUYS, I'LL COME SEE YOU IN THIS WORLD ONCE IN A WHILE.
BUT YOU SHOULD BE WORRYING ABOUT YOURSELF, NEGI-BOZU.
INDEED. THE NEXT HUNDRED YEARS ARE GOING TO BE PRETTY ROUGH.
WELL, HANG IN THERE.
I'M GOING HOME.
I'LL TAKE YOU.
ZSH
NEGI SPRINGFIELD
MAY. 2. 1993
JUNE. 12. 2065
Here lies Negi Springfield son of the hero and his successor
GASP
W-WAIT, EVA-CHAN! BACK IN THE FUTURE... HOW DID HE... YOU KNOW?
IF HE'S LIKE YOU, THAT SHOULDN'T HAPPEN, RIGHT?
DID SOMETHING... BAD... HAPPEN IN THE FUTURE?

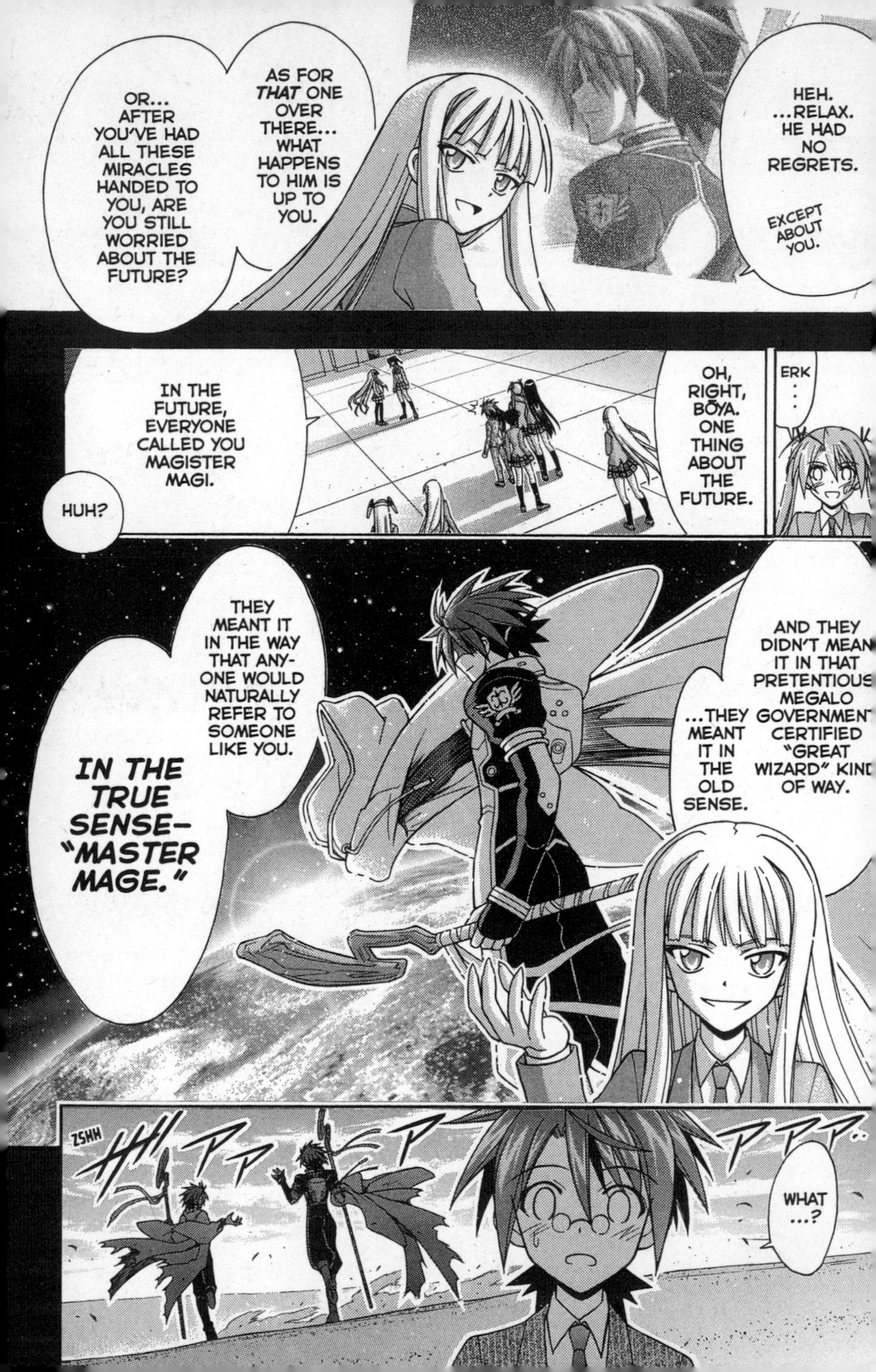
HEH. ...RELAX. HE HAD NO REGRETS.
EXCEPT ABOUT YOU.
AS FOR *THAT* ONE OVER THERE... WHAT HAPPENS TO HIM IS UP TO YOU.
OR... AFTER YOU'VE HAD ALL THESE MIRACLES HANDED TO YOU, ARE YOU STILL WORRIED ABOUT THE FUTURE?
ERK ...
OH, RIGHT, BŌYA. ONE THING ABOUT THE FUTURE.
IN THE FUTURE, EVERYONE CALLED YOU MAGISTER MAGI.
HUH?
AND THEY DIDN'T MEAN IT IN THAT PRETENTIOUS MEGALO GOVERNMENT CERTIFIED "GREAT WIZARD" KIND OF WAY.
...THEY MEANT IT IN THE OLD SENSE.
THEY MEANT IT IN THE WAY THAT ANYONE WOULD NATURALLY REFER TO SOMEONE LIKE YOU.
IN THE TRUE SENSE— "MASTER MAGE."
WHAT ...?
ZSHH

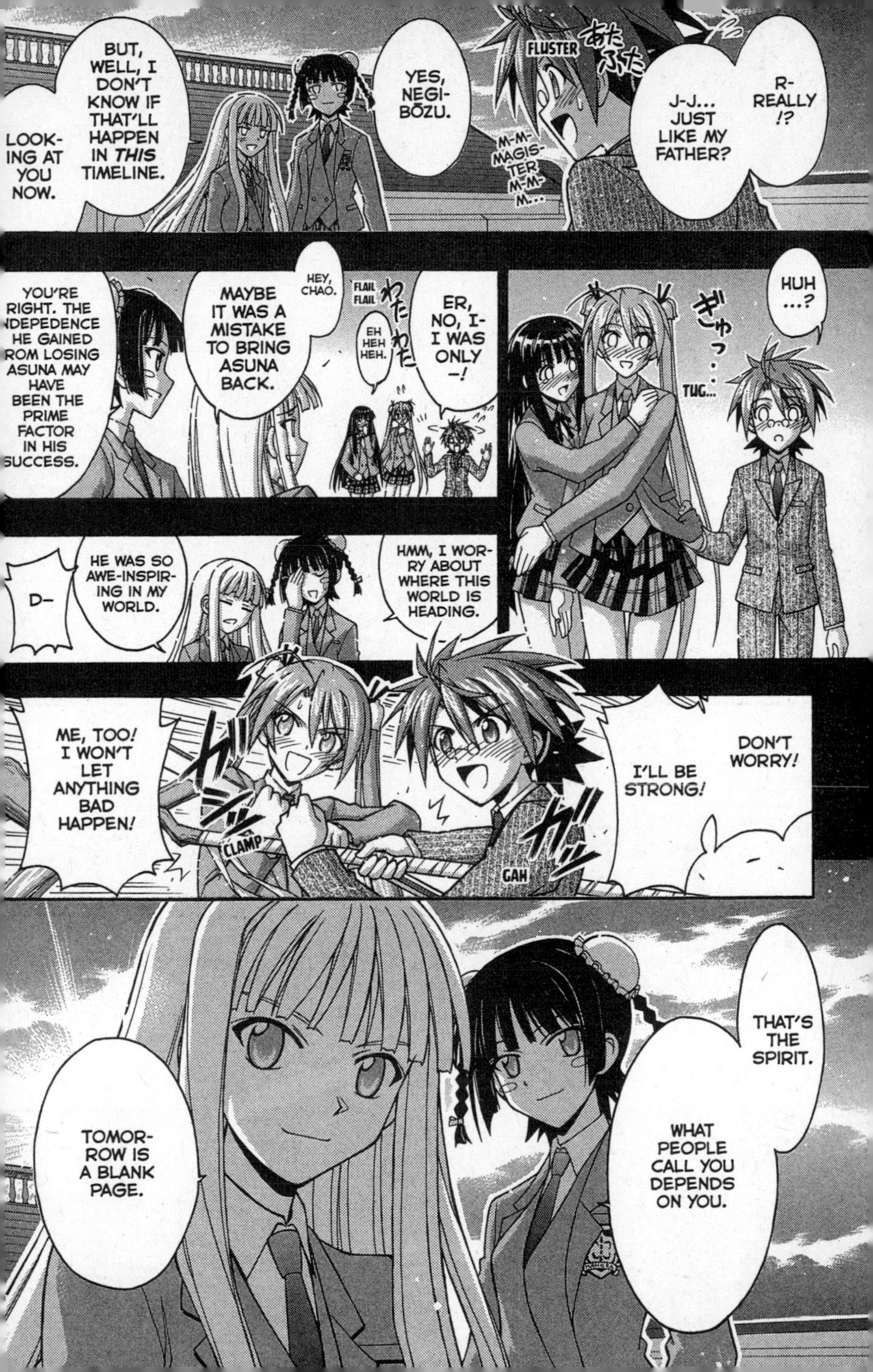
R-REALLY!?
J-J... JUST LIKE MY FATHER?
あたふた
FLUSTER
M-M-MAGISTER M-M-M...
YES, NEGI-BŌZU.
BUT, WELL, I DON'T KNOW IF THAT'LL HAPPEN IN THIS TIMELINE.
LOOKING AT YOU NOW.
HUH...?
ぎゅっ...
TUG...
ER, NO, I- I WAS ONLY-!
わたわた
FLAIL FLAIL
EH HEH HEH.
HEY, CHAO.
MAYBE IT WAS A MISTAKE TO BRING ASUNA BACK.
YOU'RE RIGHT. THE NDEPEDENCE HE GAINED ROM LOSING ASUNA MAY HAVE BEEN THE PRIME FACTOR IN HIS SUCCESS.
HMM, I WORRY ABOUT WHERE THIS WORLD IS HEADING.
HE WAS SO AWE-INSPIRING IN MY WORLD.
D-
DON'T WORRY!
I'LL BE STRONG!
GAH
CLAMP
ME, TOO! I WON'T LET ANYTHING BAD HAPPEN!
THAT'S THE SPIRIT.
WHAT PEOPLE CALL YOU DEPENDS ON YOU.
TOMORROW IS A BLANK PAGE.

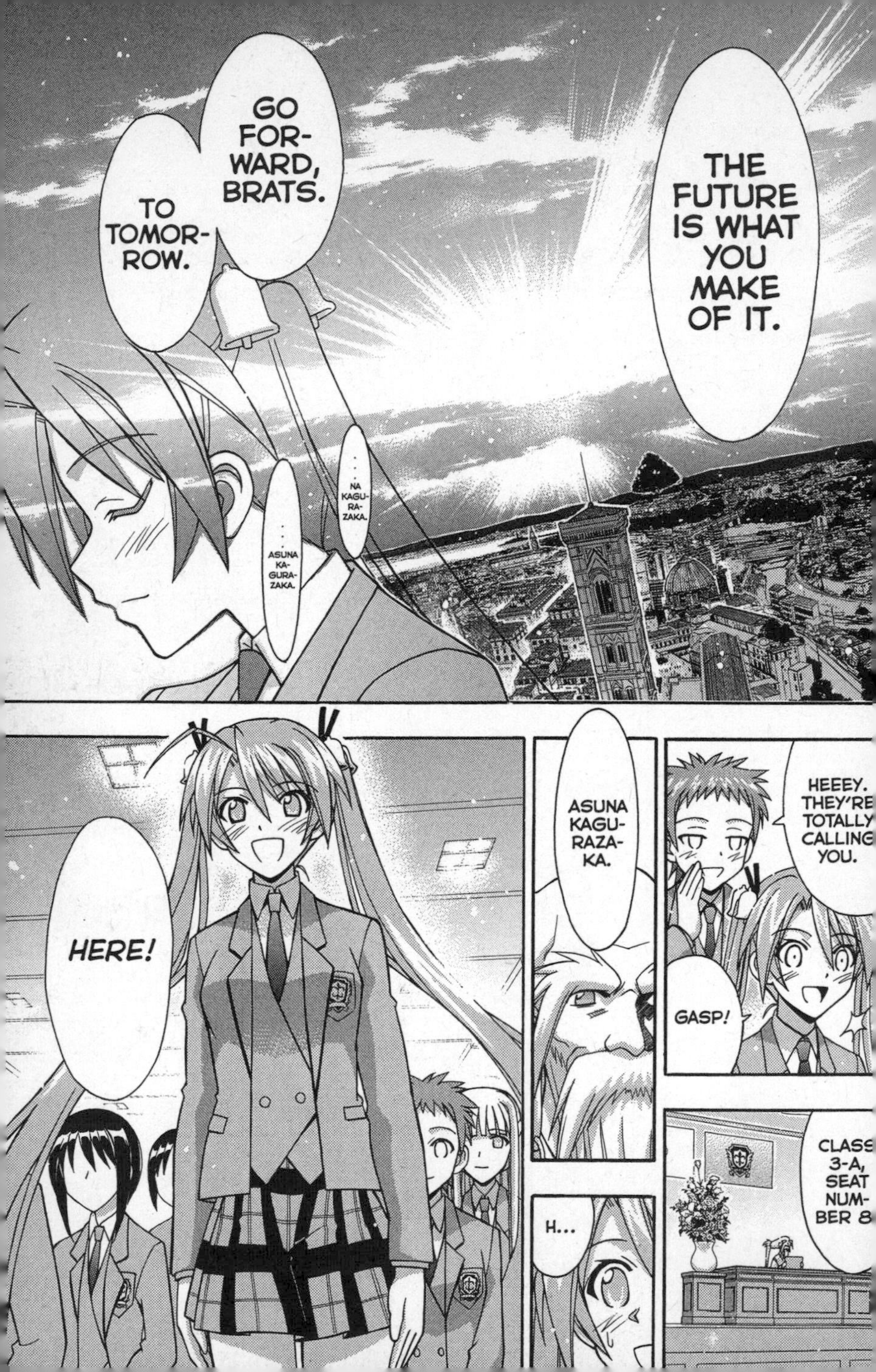
THE FUTURE IS WHAT YOU MAKE OF IT.
GO FOR-WARD, BRATS.
TO TOMOR-ROW.
. . . NA KAGU-RA-ZAKA.
. . . ASUNA KA-GURA-ZAKA.
HEEEY. THEY'RE TOTALLY CALLING YOU.
GASP!
CLASS 3-A, SEAT NUM-BER 8
ASUNA KAGU-RAZA-KA.
H...
HERE!

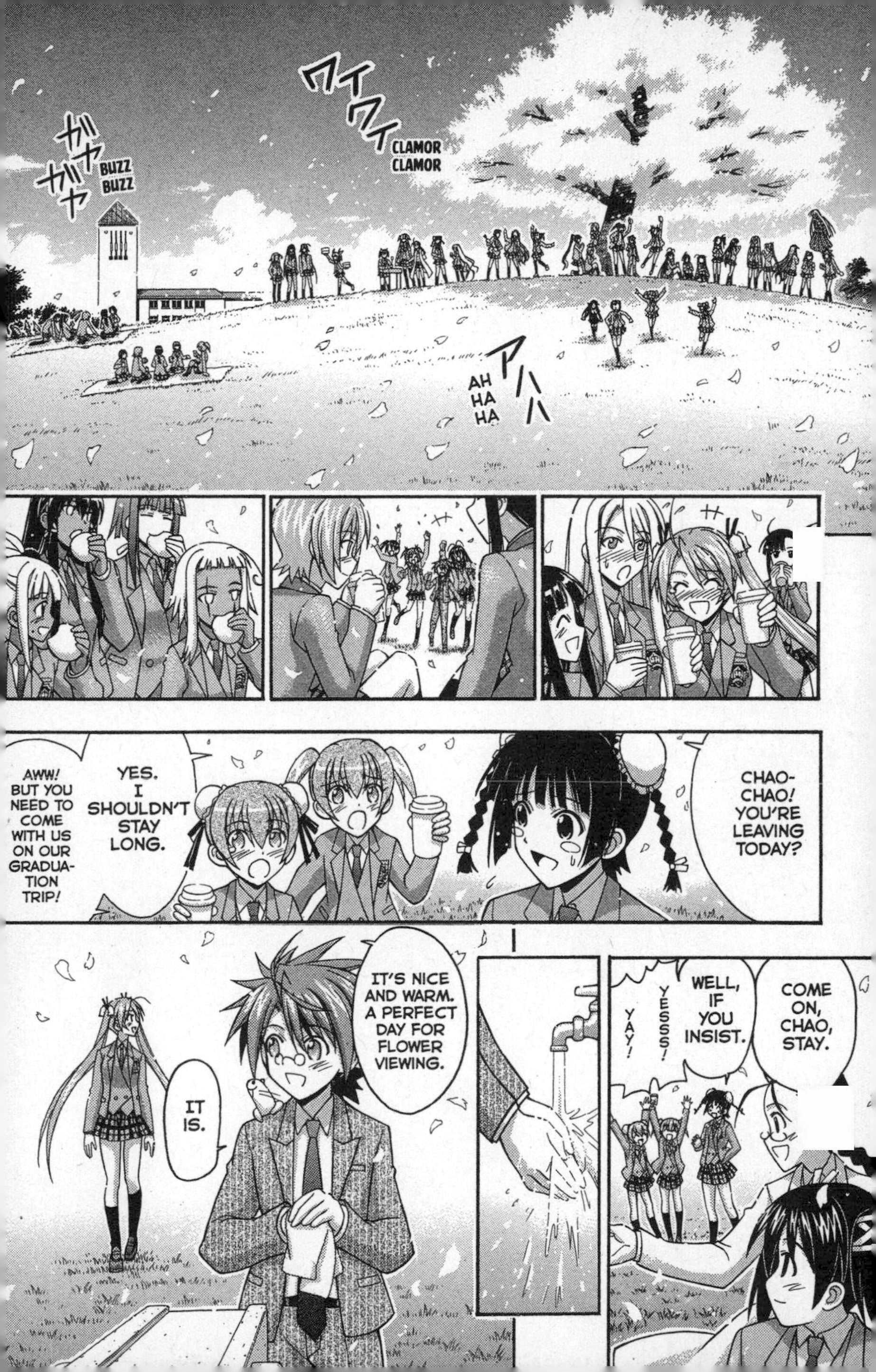
ワイワイ
CLAMOR CLAMOR
ガヤガヤ
BUZZ BUZZ
アハハ
AH HA HA
CHAO-CHAO! YOU'RE LEAVING TODAY?
YES. I SHOULDN'T STAY LONG.
AWW! BUT YOU NEED TO COME WITH US ON OUR GRADUATION TRIP!
COME ON, CHAO, STAY.
WELL, IF YOU INSIST.
YESS!
YAY!
IT'S NICE AND WARM. A PERFECT DAY FOR FLOWER VIEWING.
IT IS.

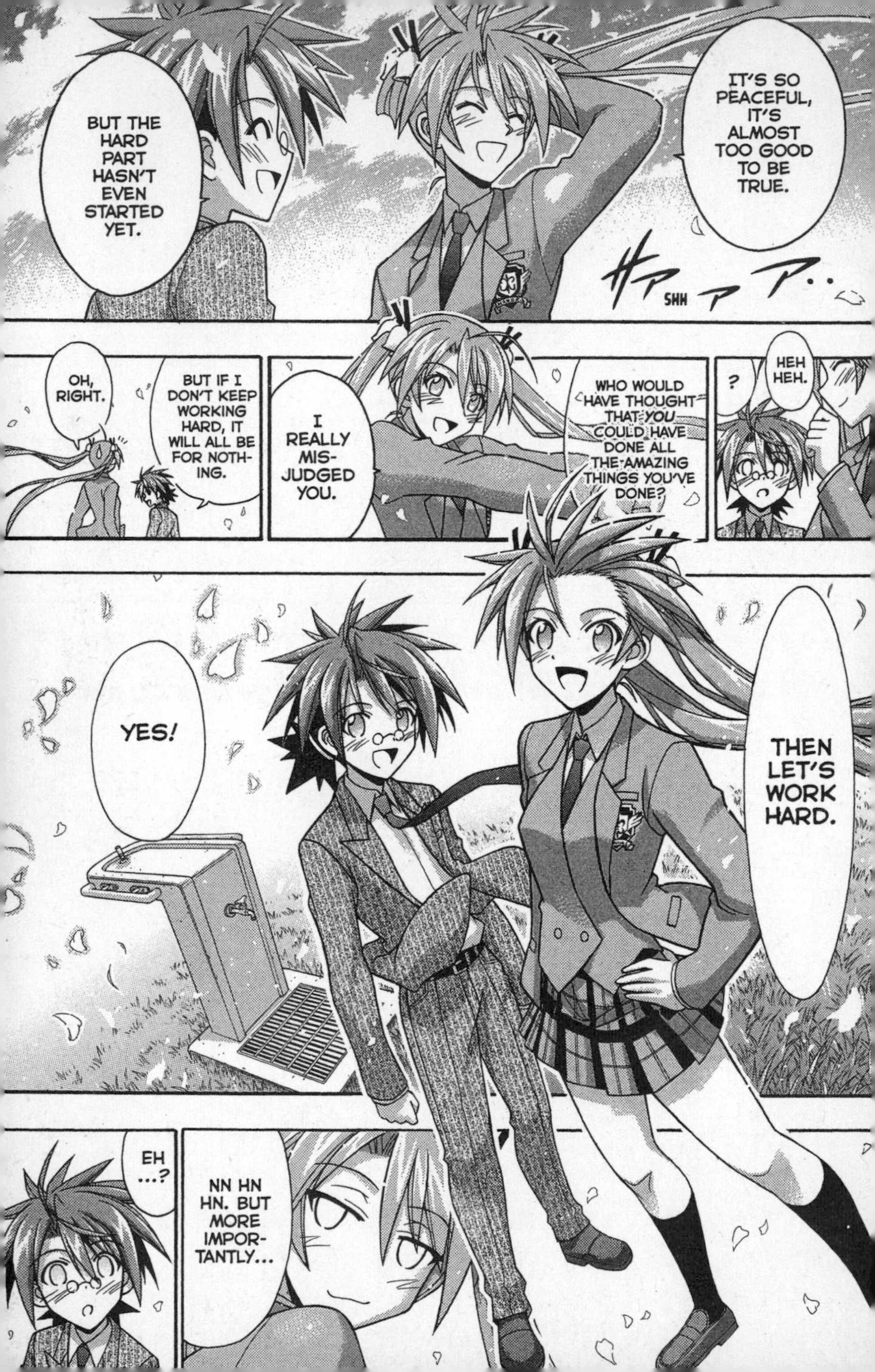
IT'S SO PEACEFUL, IT'S ALMOST TOO GOOD TO BE TRUE.
SHH
BUT THE HARD PART HASN'T EVEN STARTED YET.
HEH HEH.
?
WHO WOULD HAVE THOUGHT THAT *YOU* COULD HAVE DONE ALL THE AMAZING THINGS YOU'VE DONE?
I REALLY MIS-JUDGED YOU.
BUT IF I DON'T KEEP WORKING HARD, IT WILL ALL BE FOR NOTH-ING.
OH, RIGHT.
THEN LET'S WORK HARD.
YES!
NN HN HN. BUT MORE IMPOR-TANTLY...
EH ...?

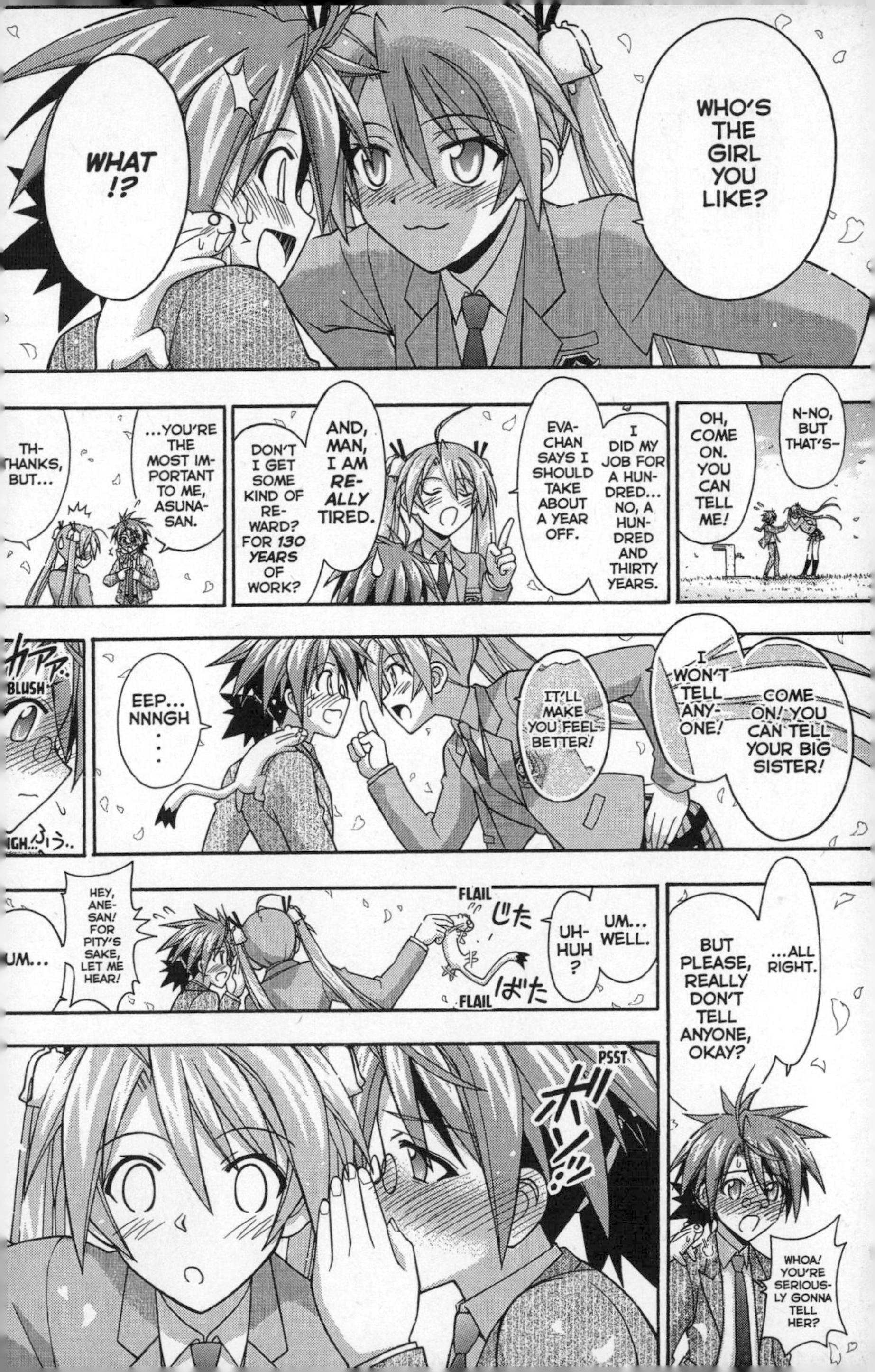
WHO'S THE GIRL YOU LIKE?
WHAT !?
N-NO, BUT THAT'S-
OH, COME ON. YOU CAN TELL ME!
I DID MY JOB FOR A HUN-DRED... NO, A HUN-DRED AND THIRTY YEARS.
EVA-CHAN SAYS I SHOULD TAKE ABOUT A YEAR OFF.
AND, MAN, I AM RE-ALLY TIRED.
DON'T I GET SOME KIND OF RE-WARD? FOR 130 YEARS OF WORK?
...YOU'RE THE MOST IM-PORTANT TO ME, ASUNA-SAN.
TH-THANKS, BUT...
COME ON! YOU CAN TELL YOUR BIG SISTER!
I WON'T TELL ANY-ONE!
IT'LL MAKE YOU FEEL BETTER!
EEP... NNNGH ...
BLUSH
ふう..
...ALL RIGHT.
BUT PLEASE, REALLY DON'T TELL ANYONE, OKAY?
UM... WELL.
UH-HUH ?
FLAIL じた
FLAIL ばた
HEY, ANE-SAN! FOR PITY'S SAKE, LET ME HEAR!
UM...
WHOA! YOU'RE SERIOUS-LY GONNA TELL HER?
PSST

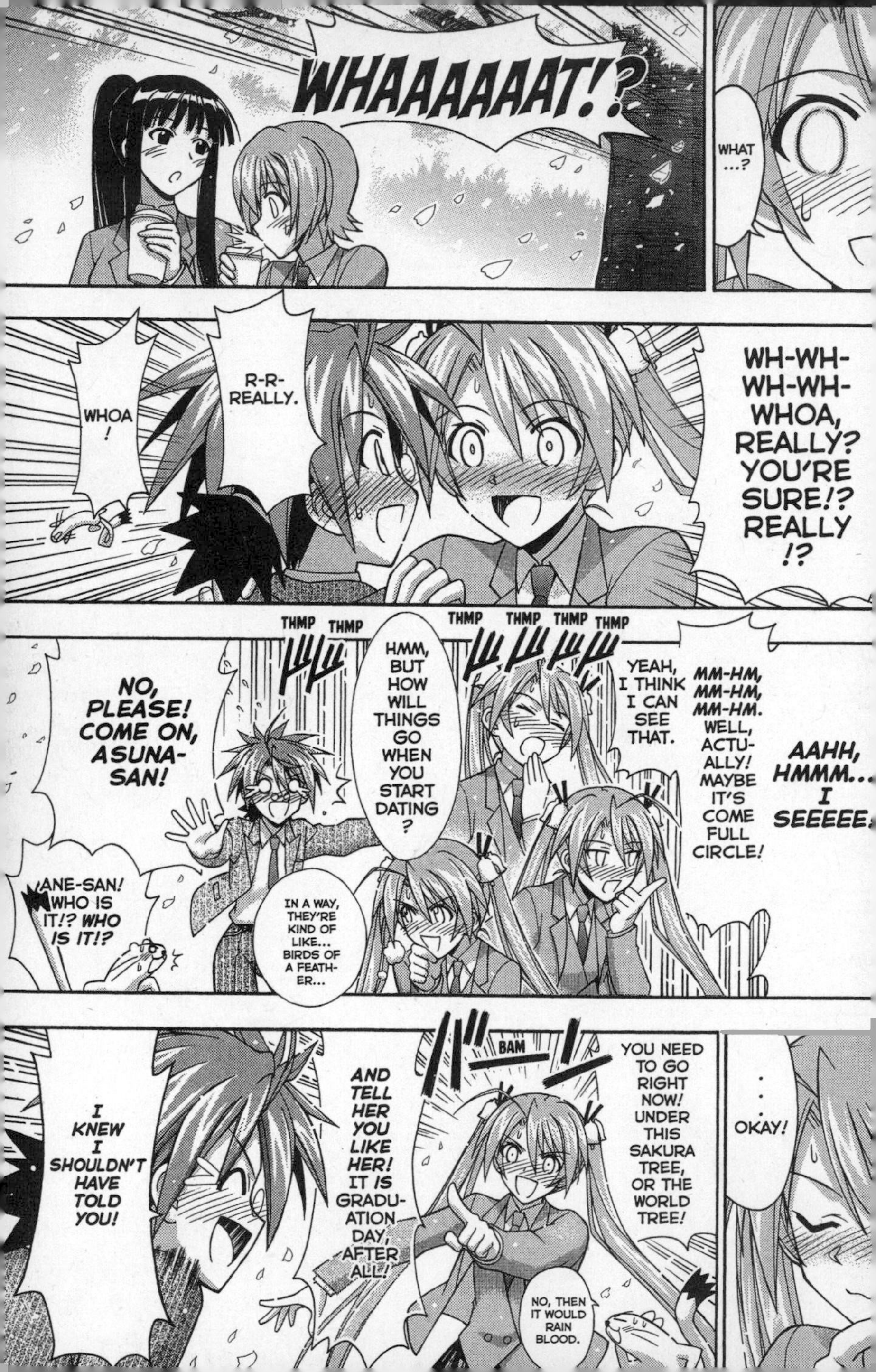
WHAT ...?
WHAAAAAAT!?
WH-WH-WH-WH-WHOA, REALLY? YOU'RE SURE!? REALLY!?
R-R-REALLY.
WHOA!
AAHH, HMMM... I SEEEEE.
MM-HM, MM-HM, MM-HM. WELL, ACTU-ALLY! MAYBE IT'S COME FULL CIRCLE!
YEAH, I THINK I CAN SEE THAT.
THMP THMP THMP THMP
HMM, BUT HOW WILL THINGS GO WHEN YOU START DATING?
THMP THMP
IN A WAY, THEY'RE KIND OF LIKE... BIRDS OF A FEATH-ER...
NO, PLEASE! COME ON, ASUNA-SAN!
ANE-SAN! WHO IS IT!? WHO IS IT!?
...OKAY!
YOU NEED TO GO RIGHT NOW! UNDER THIS SAKURA TREE, OR THE WORLD TREE!
BAM
AND TELL HER YOU LIKE HER! IT IS GRADU-ATION DAY, AFTER ALL!
NO, THEN IT WOULD RAIN BLOOD.
I KNEW I SHOULDN'T HAVE TOLD YOU!

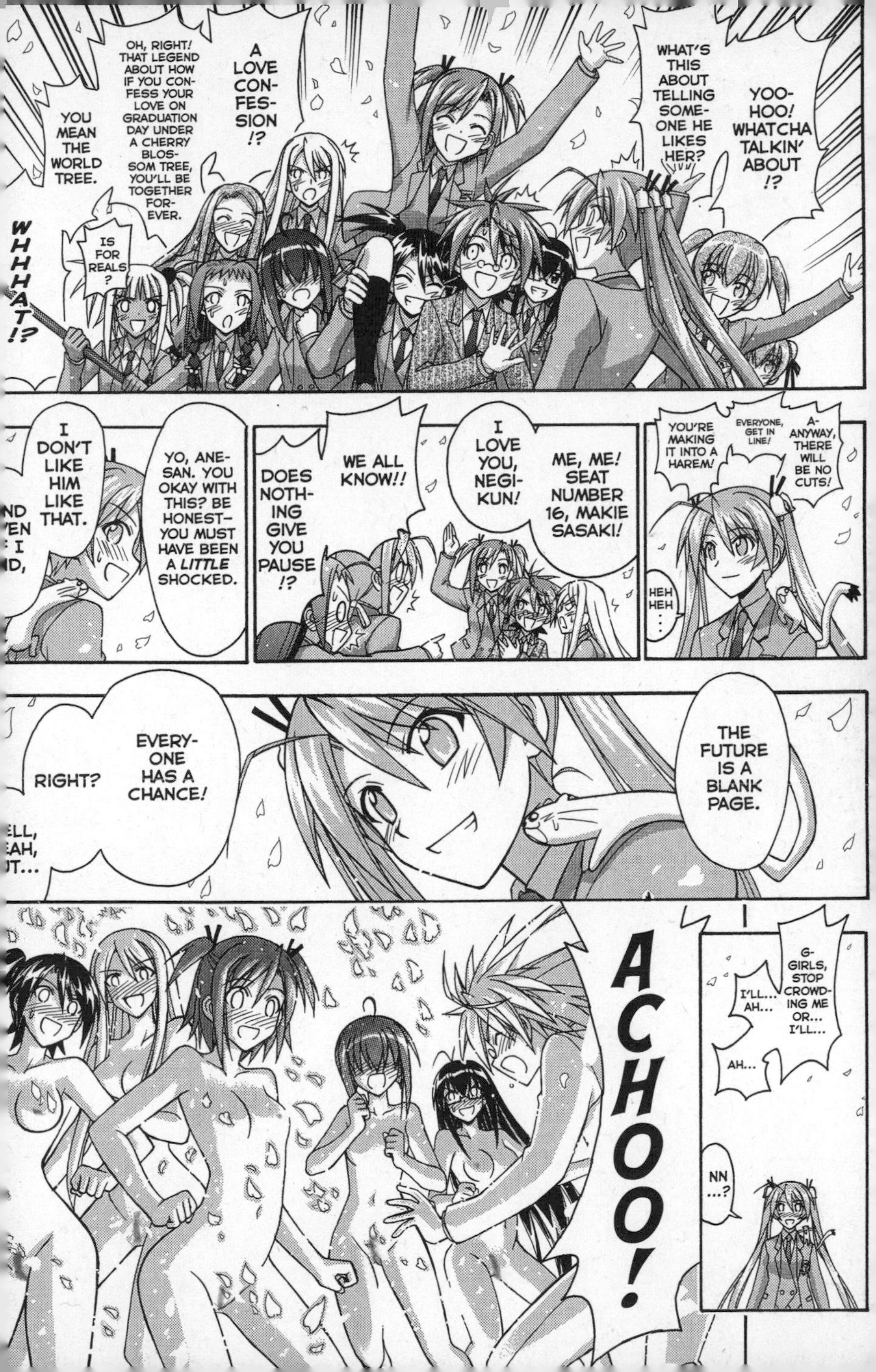
YOO-HOO! WHATCHA TALKIN' ABOUT !?
WHAT'S THIS ABOUT TELLING SOME-ONE HE LIKES HER?
A LOVE CON-FES-SION !?
OH, RIGHT! THAT LEGEND ABOUT HOW IF YOU CON-FESS YOUR LOVE ON GRADUATION DAY UNDER A CHERRY BLOS-SOM TREE, YOU'LL BE TOGETHER FOR-EVER.
YOU MEAN THE WORLD TREE.
IS FOR REALS?
WHHHAT!?
A-ANYWAY, THERE WILL BE NO CUTS!
EVERYONE, GET IN LINE!
YOU'RE MAKING IT INTO A HAREM!
HEH HEH...
ME, ME! SEAT NUMBER 16, MAKIE SASAKI!
I LOVE YOU, NEGI-KUN!
WE ALL KNOW!!
DOES NOTHING GIVE YOU PAUSE !?
YO, ANE-SAN. YOU OKAY WITH THIS? BE HONEST- YOU MUST HAVE BEEN A *LITTLE* SHOCKED.
I DON'T LIKE HIM LIKE THAT.
THE FUTURE IS A BLANK PAGE.
EVERY-ONE HAS A CHANCE!
RIGHT?
G-GIRLS, STOP CROWD-ING ME OR... I'LL...
I'LL... AH...
AH...
NN ...?
ACHOO!

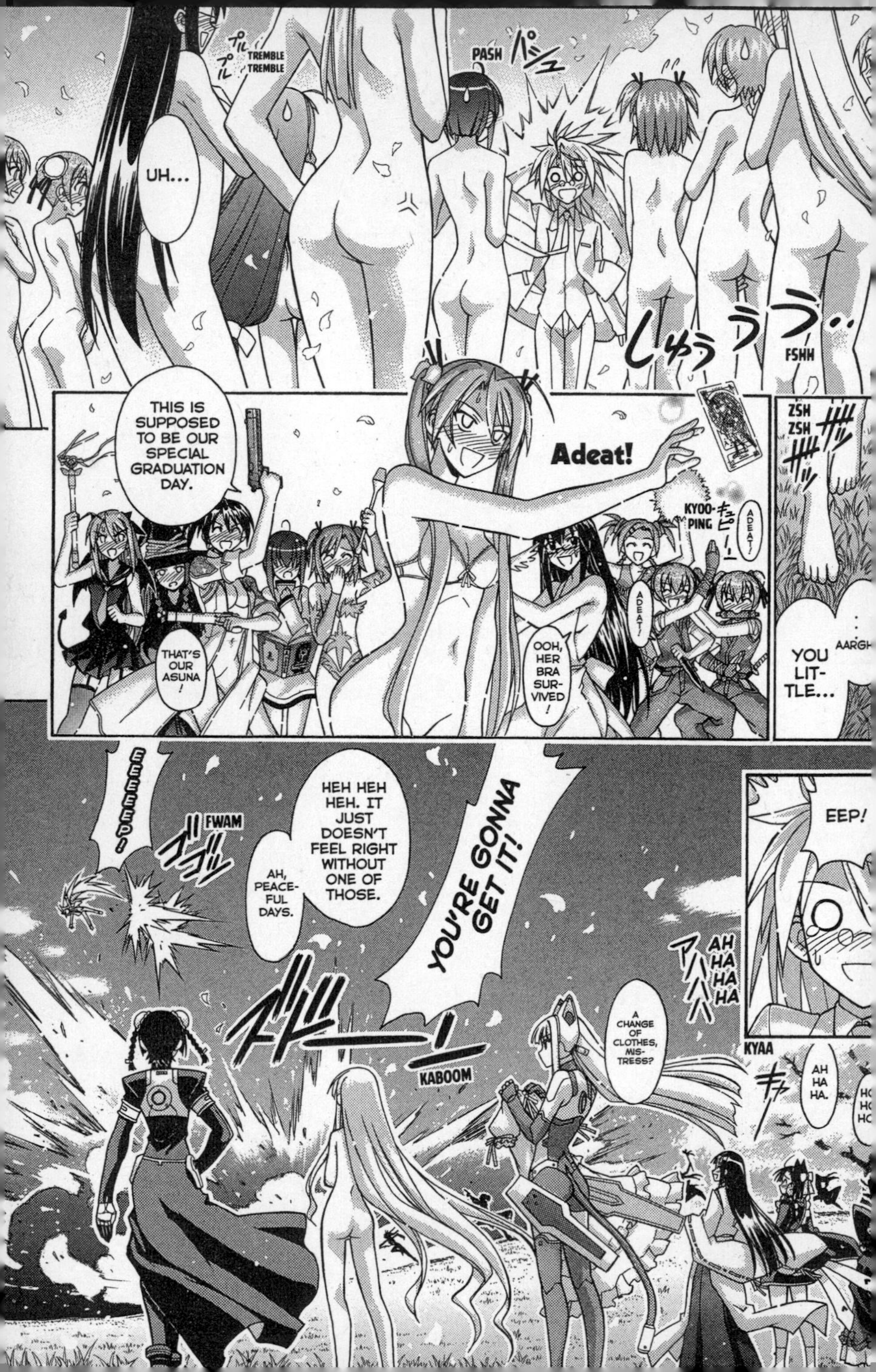
しゅううう..
FSHH
PASH パシュ
プルプル
TREMBLE TREMBLE
UH...
ZSH ZSH
YOU LIT-TLE...
AARGH
Adeat!
KYOO-PING
ADEAT!
ADEAT!
OOH, HER BRA SUR-VIVED!
THIS IS SUPPOSED TO BE OUR SPECIAL GRADUATION DAY.
THAT'S OUR ASUNA!
EEP!
AH HA HA HA HA
KYAA
AH HA HA.
A CHANGE OF CLOTHES, MIS-TRESS?
YOU'RE GONNA GET IT!
HEH HEH HEH. IT JUST DOESN'T FEEL RIGHT WITHOUT ONE OF THOSE.
AH, PEACE-FUL DAYS.
EEEEEP!
FWAM
KABOOM

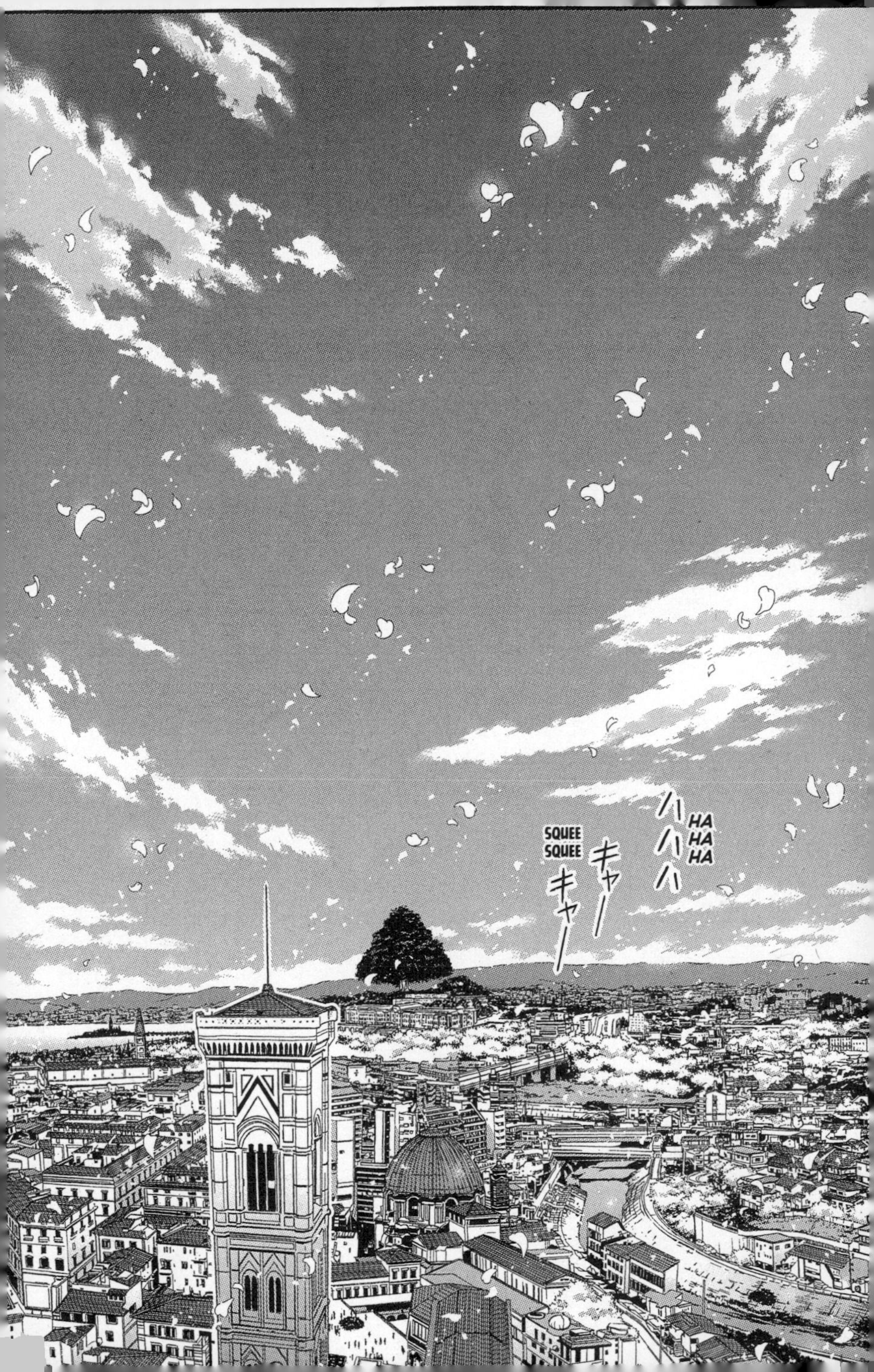
ハハハ
HA HA HA
キャーキャー
SQUEE SQUEE

-STAFF-

Ken Akamatsu
Takashi Takemoto
Kenichi Nakamura
Keiichi Yamashita
Tohru Mitsuhashi
Yuichi Yoshida
Susumu Kuwabara

Thanks to
Ran Ayanaga

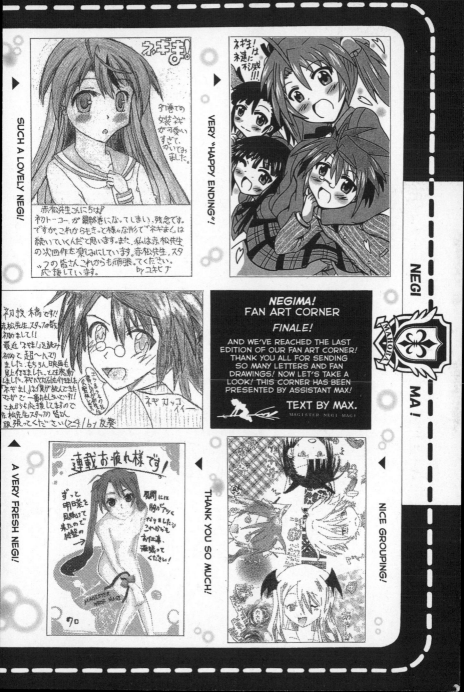

NEGI MA!

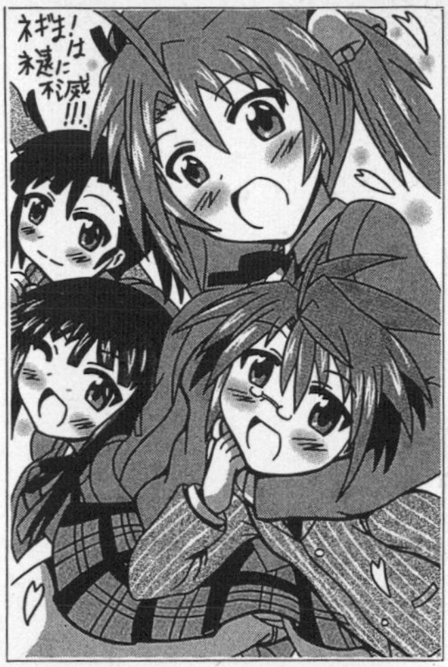

ネギま!は永遠に不滅!!!

VERY "HAPPY ENDING"!

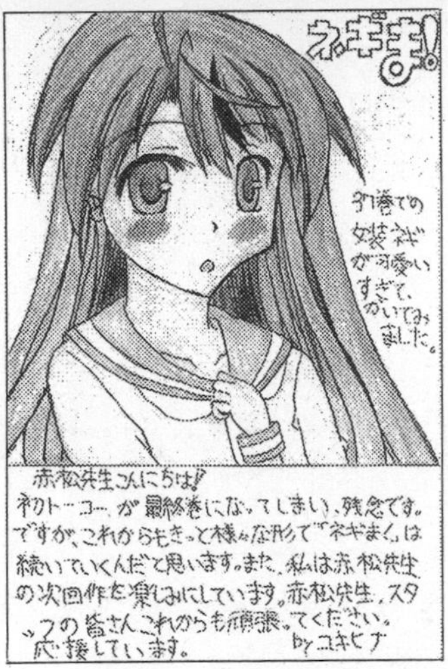

ネギま!
7巻での女装ネギが可愛いすぎて、かいてみました。
赤松先生こんにちは!
by ユキヒナ

SUCH A LOVELY NEGI!

NEGIMA! FAN ART CORNER

FINALE!

AND WE'VE REACHED THE LAST EDITION OF OUR FAN ART CORNER! THANK YOU ALL FOR SENDING SO MANY LETTERS AND FAN DRAWINGS! NOW LET'S TAKE A LOOK! THIS CORNER HAS BEEN PRESENTED BY ASSISTANT MAX!

TEXT BY MAX.

MAGISTER NEGI MAGI

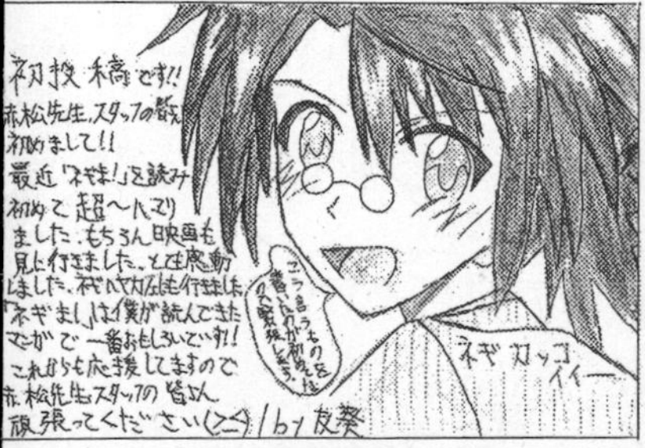

初投稿です!!
赤松先生、スタッフの皆さん初めまして!!

A VERY FRESH NEGI!

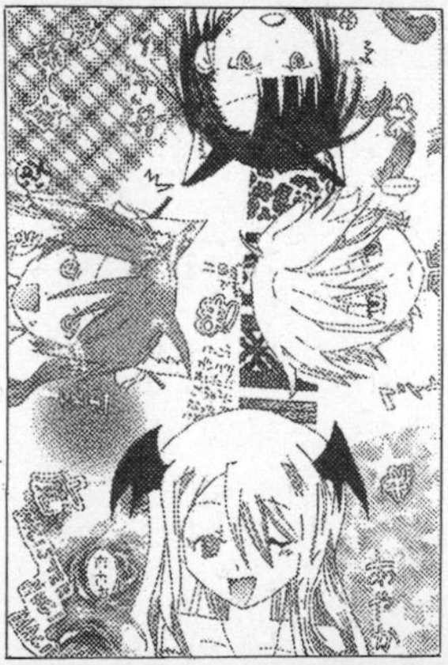

NICE GROUPING!

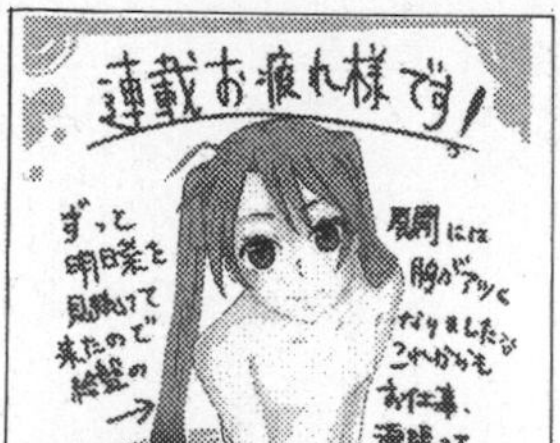

連載お疲れ様です!
MAGISTER NEGI MAGI

THANK YOU SO MUCH!

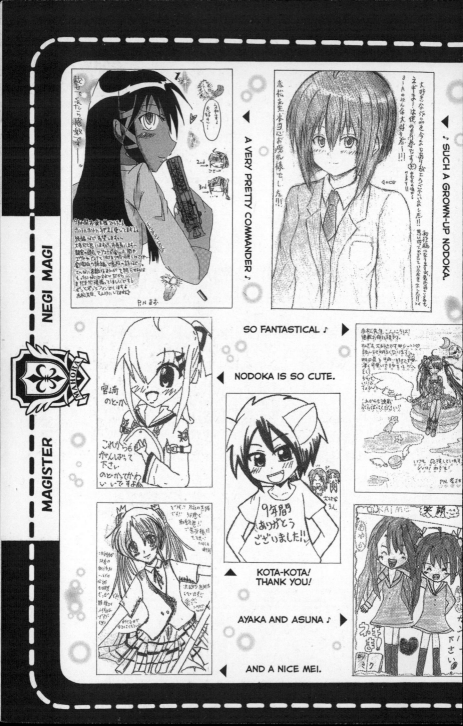

MAGISTER NEGI MAGI

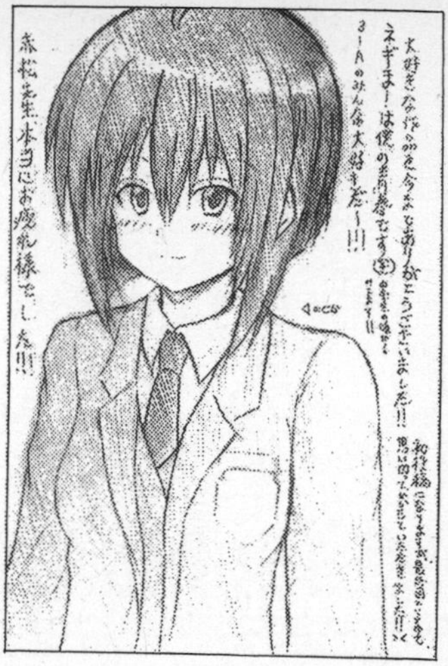
赤松先生本当にお疲れ様でした!!!

♪ SUCH A GROWN-UP NODOKA.

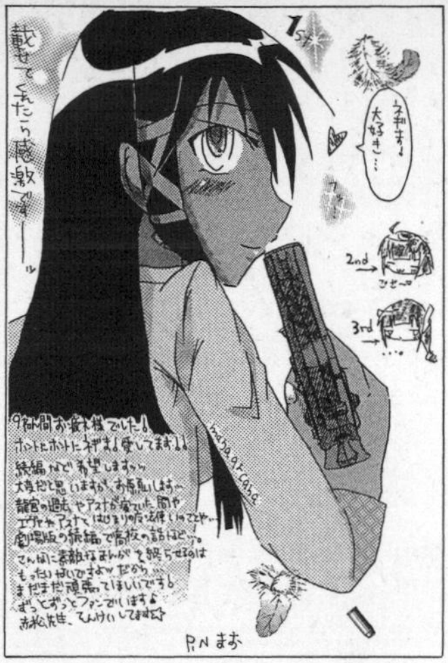
載せてくれたら感激です——ッ
P.N まお

A VERY PRETTY COMMANDER ♪

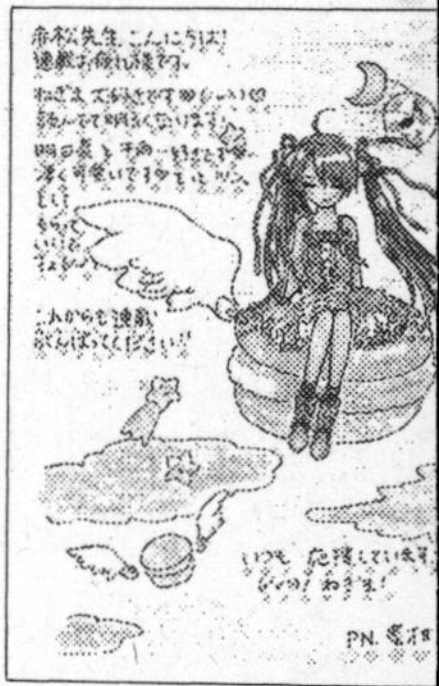

SO FANTASTICAL ♪

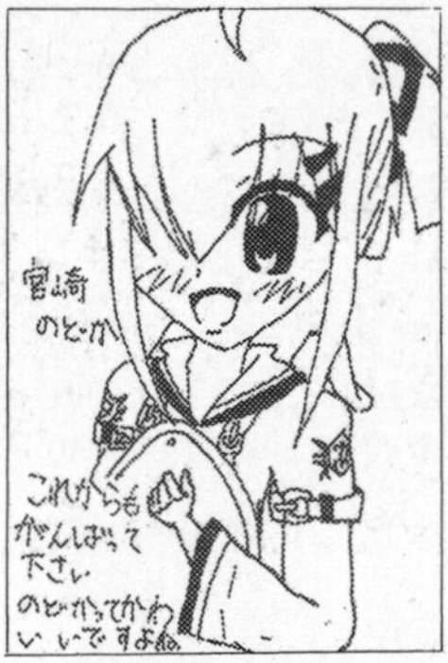
宮崎のどか
これからもがんばって下さい
のどかってかわいいですよね

NODOKA IS SO CUTE.

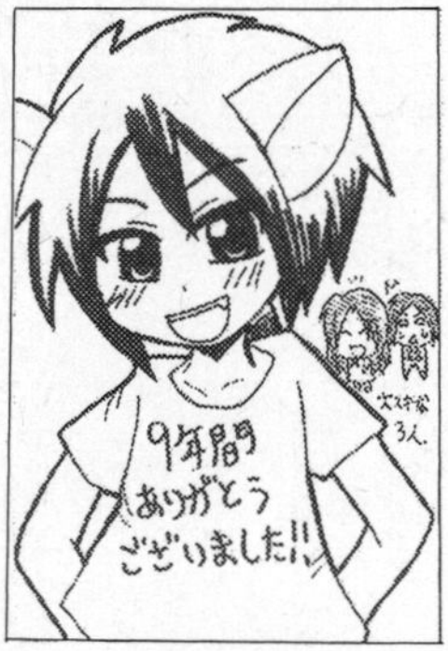
9年間ありがとうございました!!

KOTA-KOTA! THANK YOU!

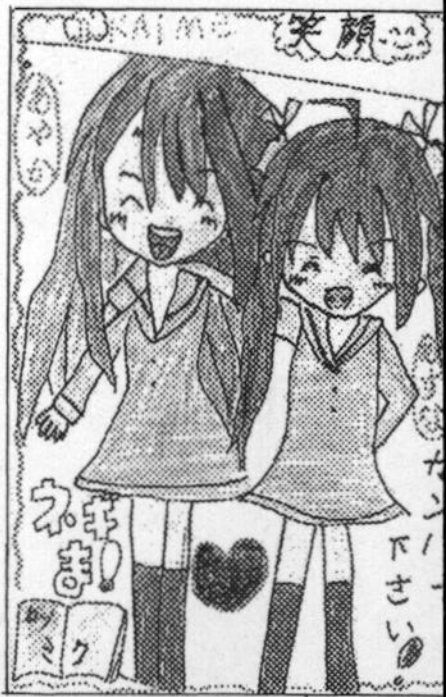
ネギま!

AYAKA AND ASUNA ♪

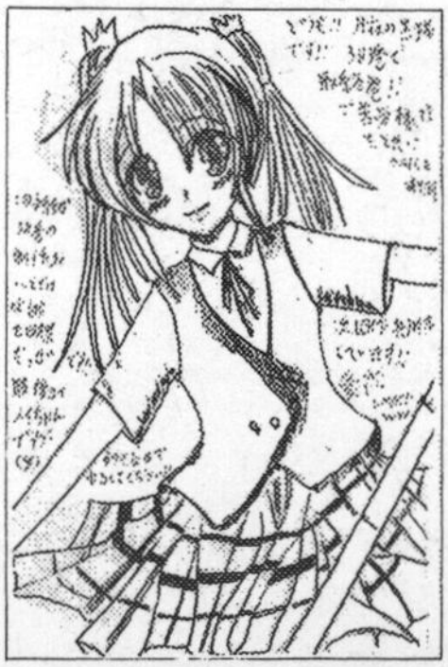

AND A NICE MEI.

GREAT ASUNA!

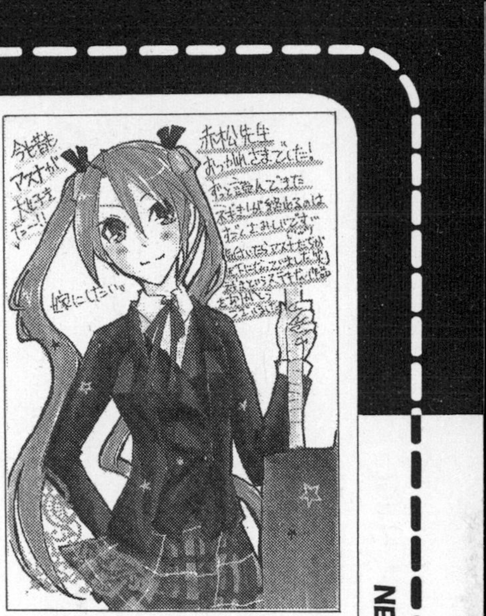
今でも アスナが 大好きだー!!
赤松先生 おつかれさまでした!!
嫁にしたい。

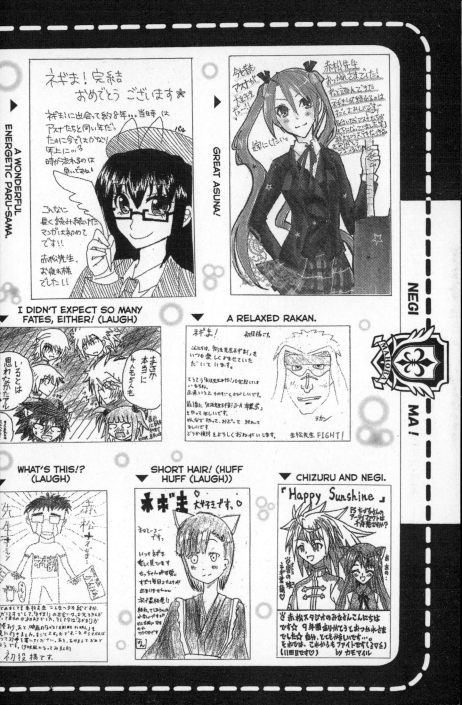

A WONDERFUL ENERGETIC PARU-SAMA.

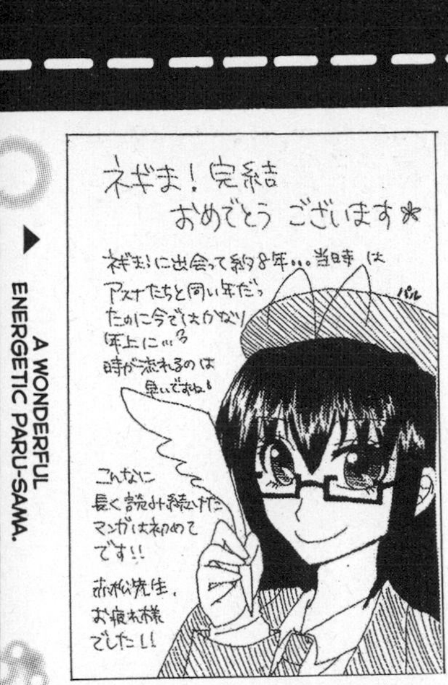
ネギま！完結
おめでとう ございます
ネギま!に出会って約8年…。当時はアスナたちと同い年だったのに今ではかなり年上に…。
時が流れるのは早いですね。
パル
こんなに長く読み続けたマンガは初めてです!!
赤松先生、お疲れ様でした!!

A RELAXED RAKAN.

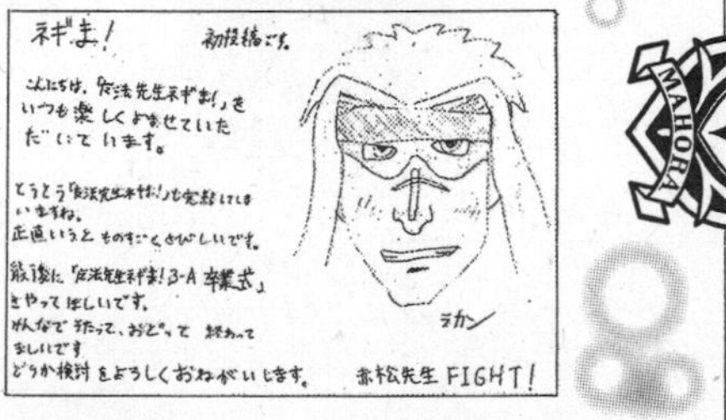
ネギま!
初投稿です。
こんにちは。「魔法先生ネギま!」をいつも楽しく読ませていただいています。
とうとう「魔法先生ネギま!」も完結してしまいますね。
正直いうとものすごくさびしいです。
最後に「魔法先生ネギま! 3-A 卒業式」をやってほしいです。
みんなで歌って、おどって、終わってほしいです
どうか検討をよろしくおねがいします。
ラカン
赤松先生 FIGHT!

I DIDN'T EXPECT SO MANY FATES, EITHER! (LAUGH)

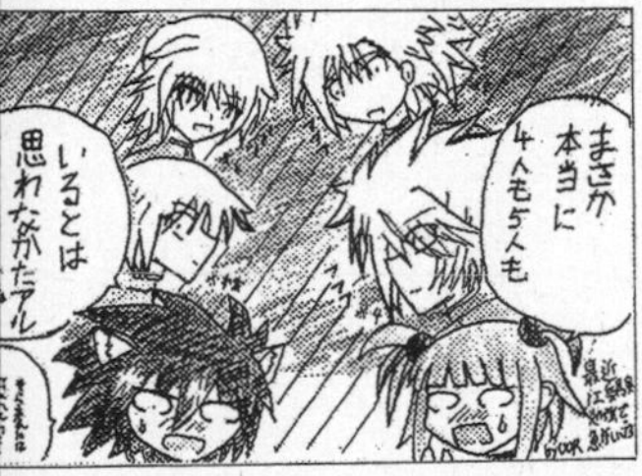
まさか本当に4人も5人も
いるとは思わなかったアル

CHIZURU AND NEGI.

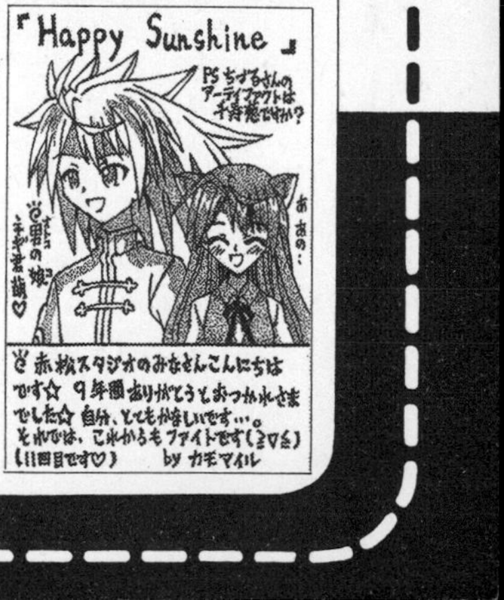
「Happy Sunshine」
PS ちづるさんのアーティファクトは千手観音ですか?
あ あの…
赤松スタジオのみなさんこんにちはです☆ 9年間ありがとうとおつかれさまでした☆ 自分、とてもかなしいです…。 それでは、これからもファイトです
by カモマイル

SHORT HAIR! (HUFF HUFF (LAUGH))

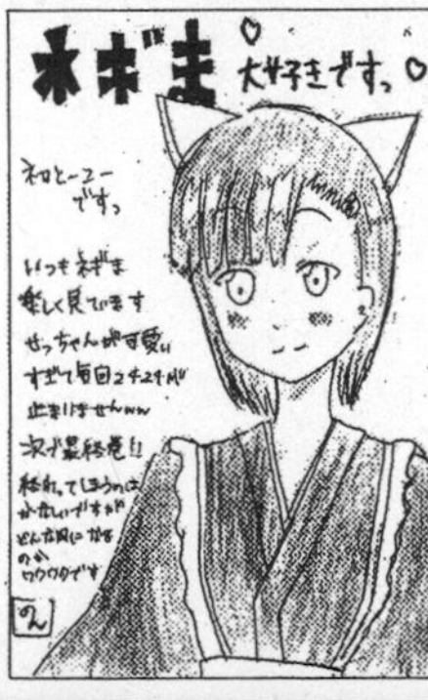
ネギま 大好きです。
次が最終巻!!

WHAT'S THIS!? (LAUGH)

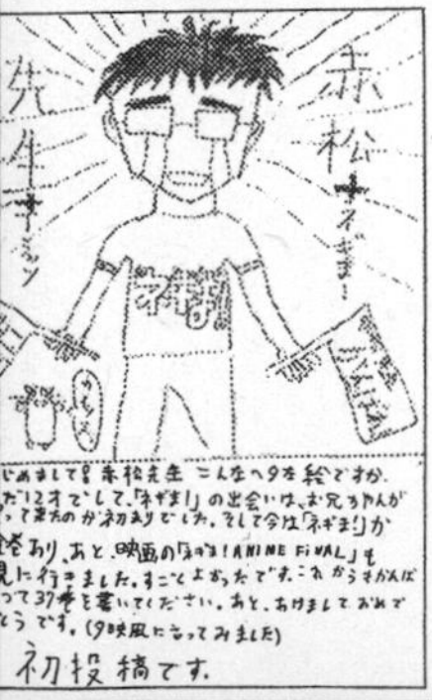
初投稿です。

NEGI MA!

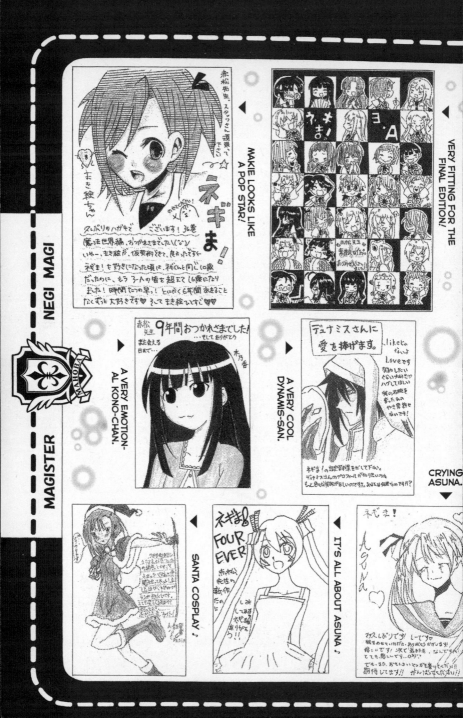

▼ VERY FITTING FOR THE FINAL EDITION!

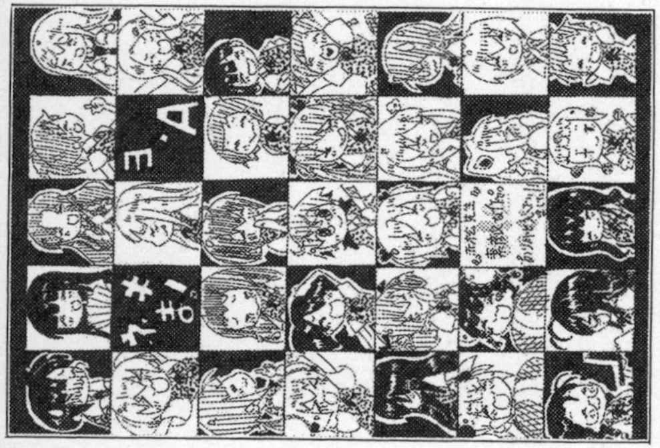
ネギま!

▼ MAKIE LOOKS LIKE A POP STAR!

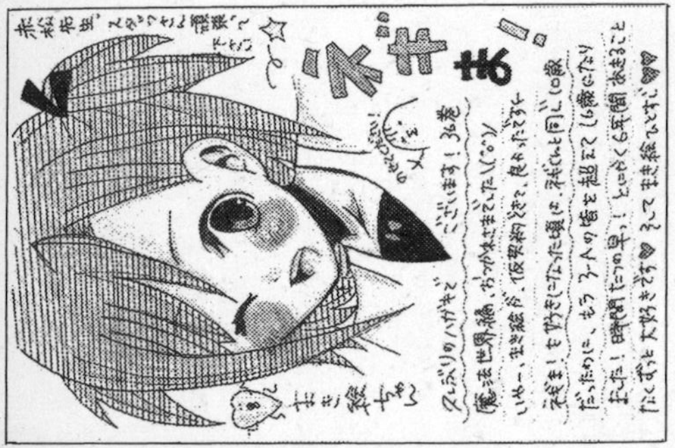
赤松先生、スタッフさん頑張って下さい☆
ネギま!
まき絵ちゃん
久しぶりのハガキでございます！36巻
魔法世界編、おつかれさまでした！
いやー、まき絵が仮契約できて良かったです～
ネギま！を好きになった頃は、ネギくんと同じ10歳
だったのに、もう3-Aの皆を超えて16歳になり
ました！時間たつの早っ！とにかく6年間あきること
なくずっと大好きです♥ そしてまき絵ひとすじ♥♥

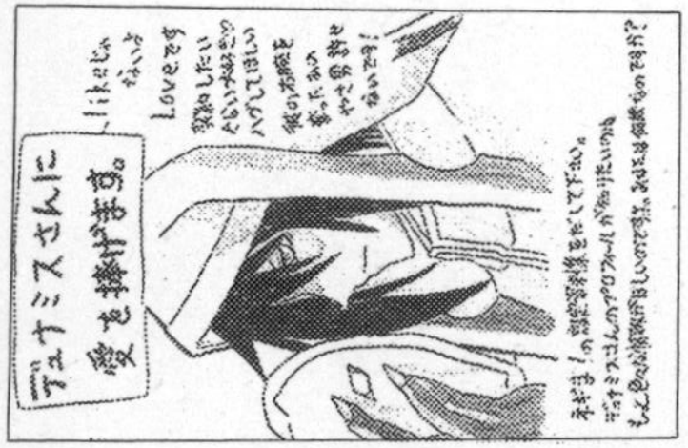
デュナミスさんに
愛を捧げます。
likeじゃないよ
Loveです

▲ A VERY COOL DYNAMIS-SAN.

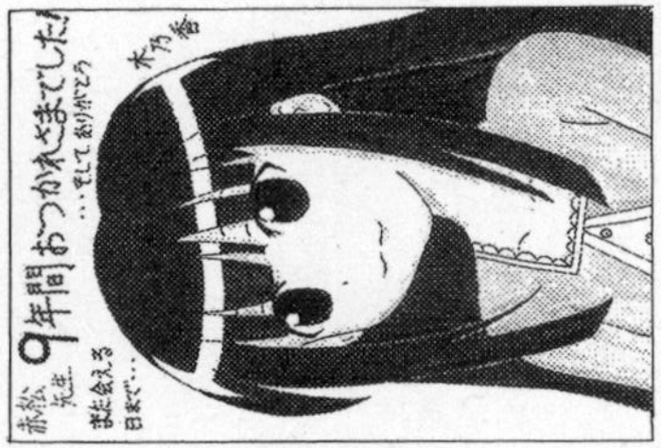
赤松先生 9年間おつかれさまでした！
…そして、ありがとう
また会える日まで…

▲ A VERY EMOTIONAL KONO-CHAN.

CRYING ASUNA. ▶

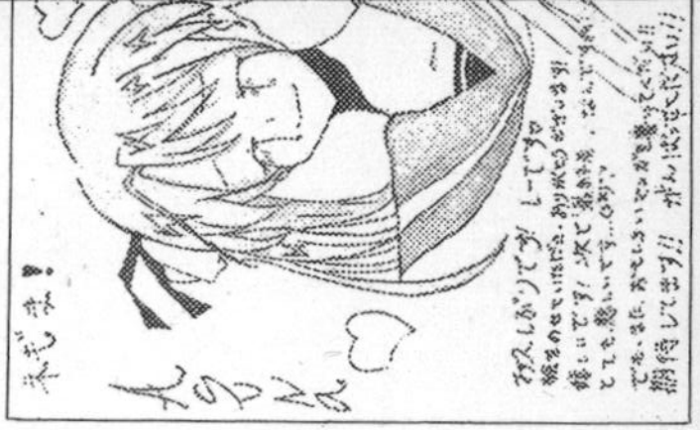
ネぎま!

▼ IT'S ALL ABOUT ASUNA ♪

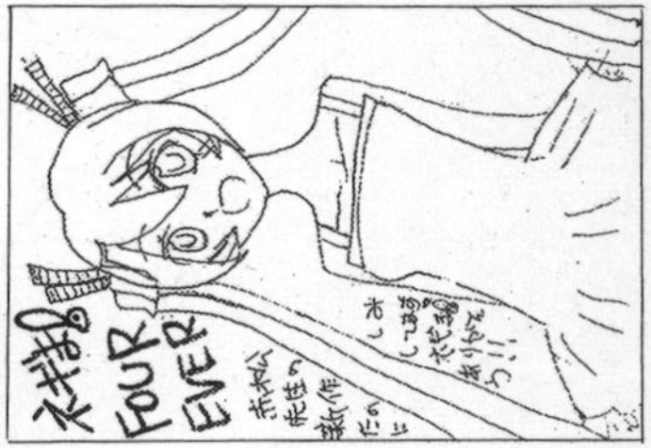
ネギま!
FOUR EVER

▼ SANTA COSPLAY ♪

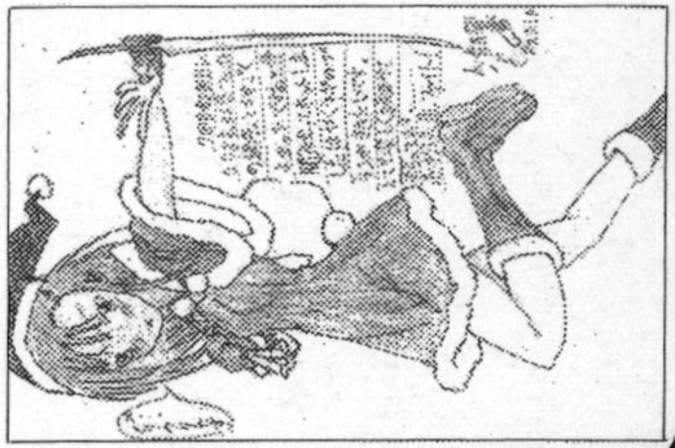

MAGISTER NEGI MAGI

And so we come

To one possible ending.

That world is most likely the happiest.

Magister Negi Magi –Happy End–

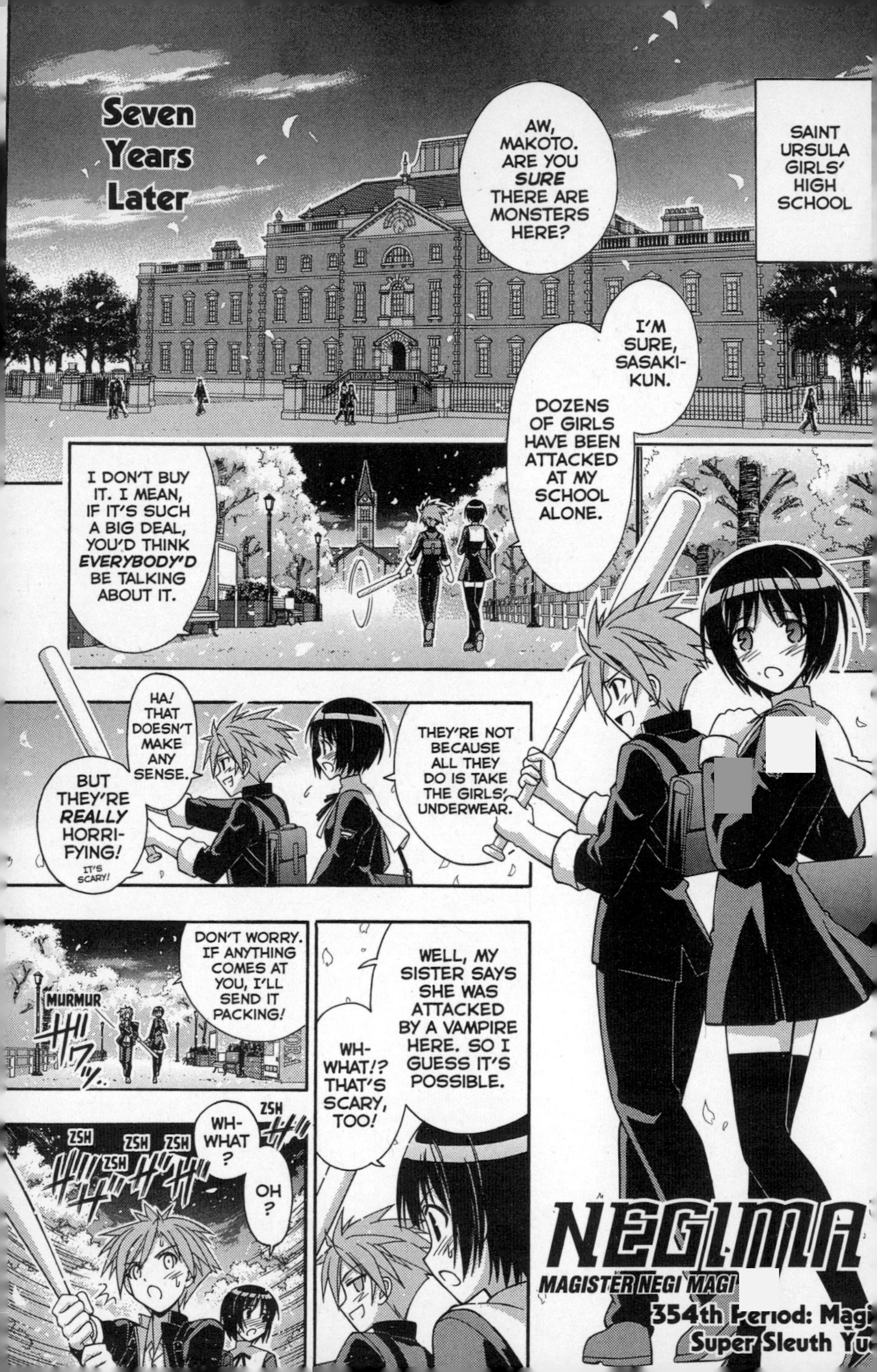
SAINT URSULA GIRLS' HIGH SCHOOL
AW, MAKOTO. ARE YOU SURE THERE ARE MONSTERS HERE?
Seven Years Later
I'M SURE, SASAKI-KUN.
DOZENS OF GIRLS HAVE BEEN ATTACKED AT MY SCHOOL ALONE.
I DON'T BUY IT. I MEAN, IF IT'S SUCH A BIG DEAL, YOU'D THINK EVERYBODY'D BE TALKING ABOUT IT.
THEY'RE NOT BECAUSE ALL THEY DO IS TAKE THE GIRLS' UNDERWEAR.
HA! THAT DOESN'T MAKE ANY SENSE.
BUT THEY'RE REALLY HORRIFYING!
IT'S SCARY!
WELL, MY SISTER SAYS SHE WAS ATTACKED BY A VAMPIRE HERE. SO I GUESS IT'S POSSIBLE.
WH-WHAT!? THAT'S SCARY, TOO!
DON'T WORRY. IF ANYTHING COMES AT YOU, I'LL SEND IT PACKING!
MURMUR
ZSH
WH-WHAT?
OH?
ZSH ZSH ZSH ZSH
NEGIMA
MAGISTER NEGI MAGI
354th Period: Magi
Super Sleuth Yu

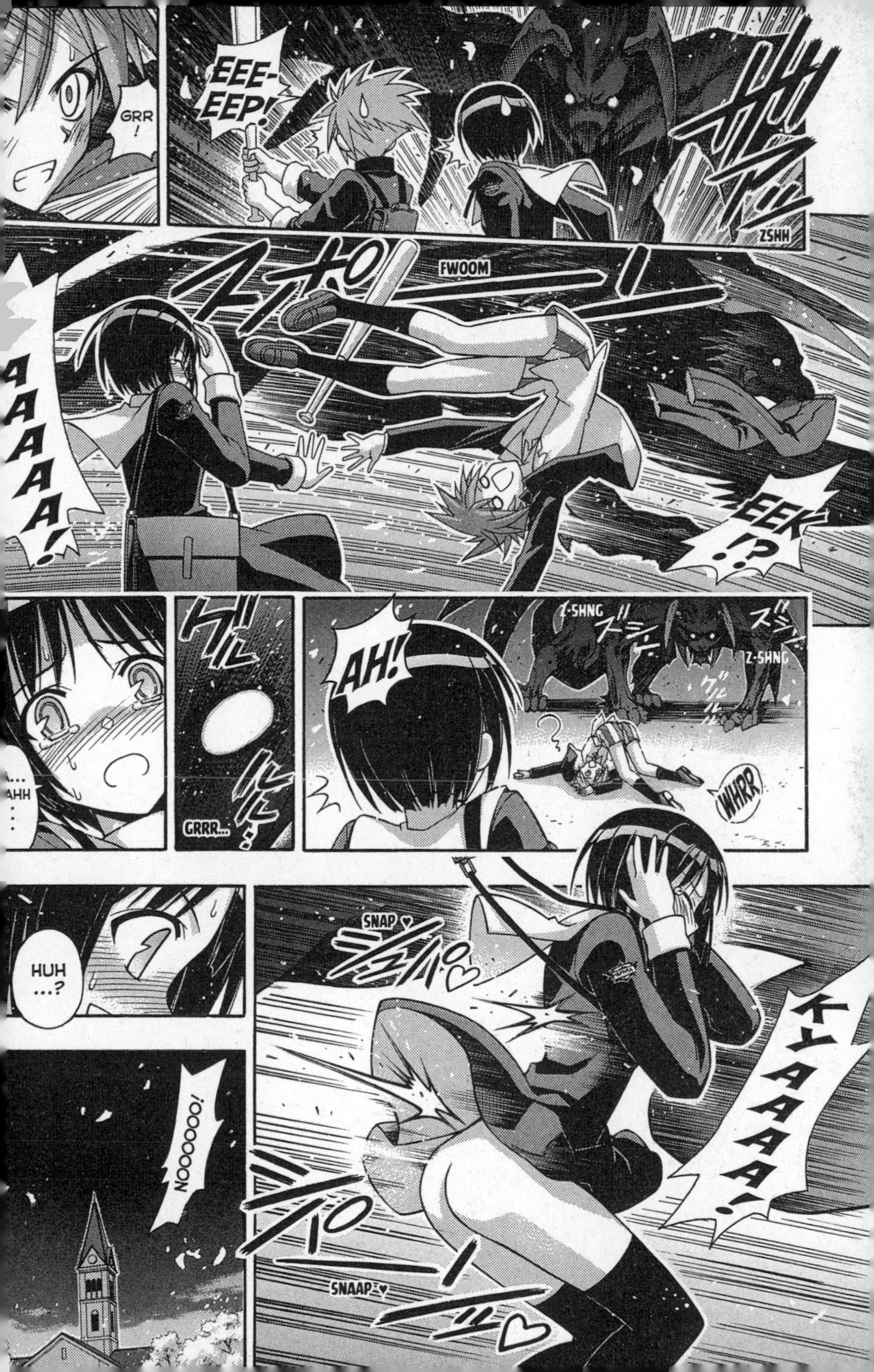
ZSHH
EEE-EEP!
GRR!
FWOOM
EEK!?
AAAAAA!
Z-SHNG
Z-SHNG
AH!
WHRR
GRRR...
A... AHH...
KYAAAAAA!
SNAP ♥
SNAAP ♥
HUH...?
NOOOOOO!

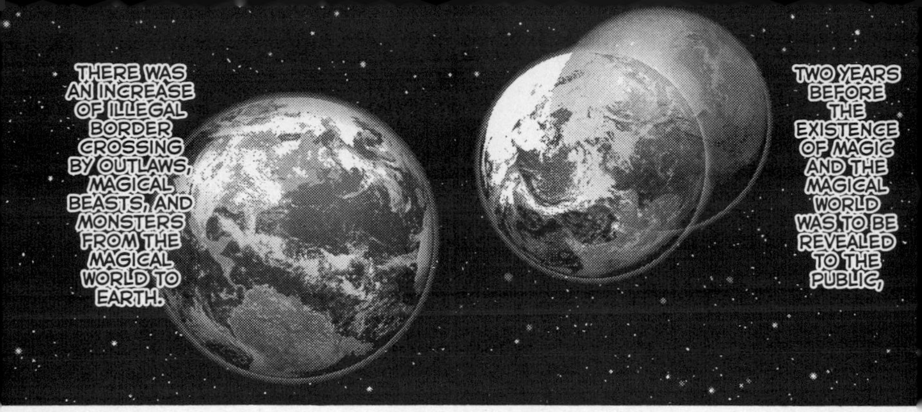
TWO YEARS BEFORE THE EXISTENCE OF MAGIC AND THE MAGICAL WORLD WAS TO BE REVEALED TO THE PUBLIC,
THERE WAS AN INCREASE OF ILLEGAL BORDER CROSSING BY OUTLAWS, MAGICAL BEASTS, AND MONSTERS FROM THE MAGICAL WORLD TO EARTH.

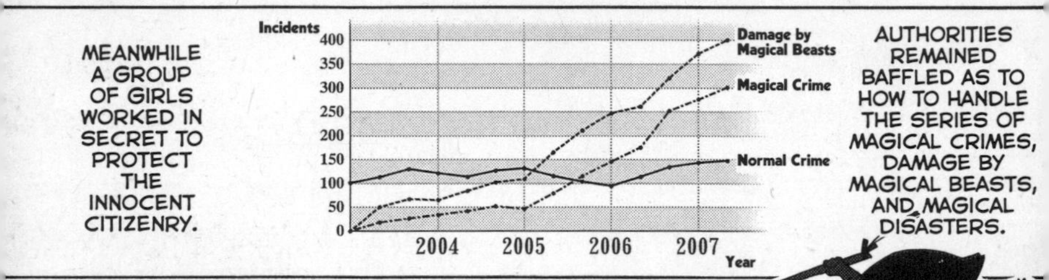
AUTHORITIES REMAINED BAFFLED AS TO HOW TO HANDLE THE SERIES OF MAGICAL CRIMES, DAMAGE BY MAGICAL BEASTS, AND MAGICAL DISASTERS.
Incidents
400
350
300
250
200
150
100
50
0
Damage by Magical Beasts
Magical Crime
Normal Crime
2004
2005
2006
2007
Year
MEANWHILE A GROUP OF GIRLS WORKED IN SECRET TO PROTECT THE INNOCENT CITIZENRY.

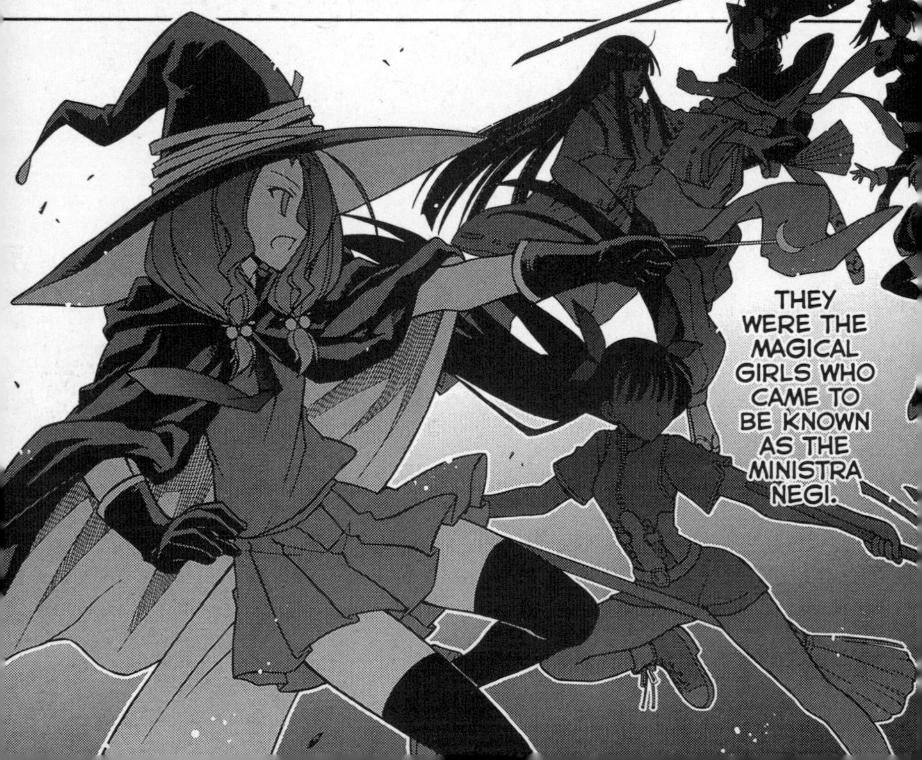
THEY WERE THE MAGICAL GIRLS WHO CAME TO BE KNOWN AS THE MINISTRA NEGI.

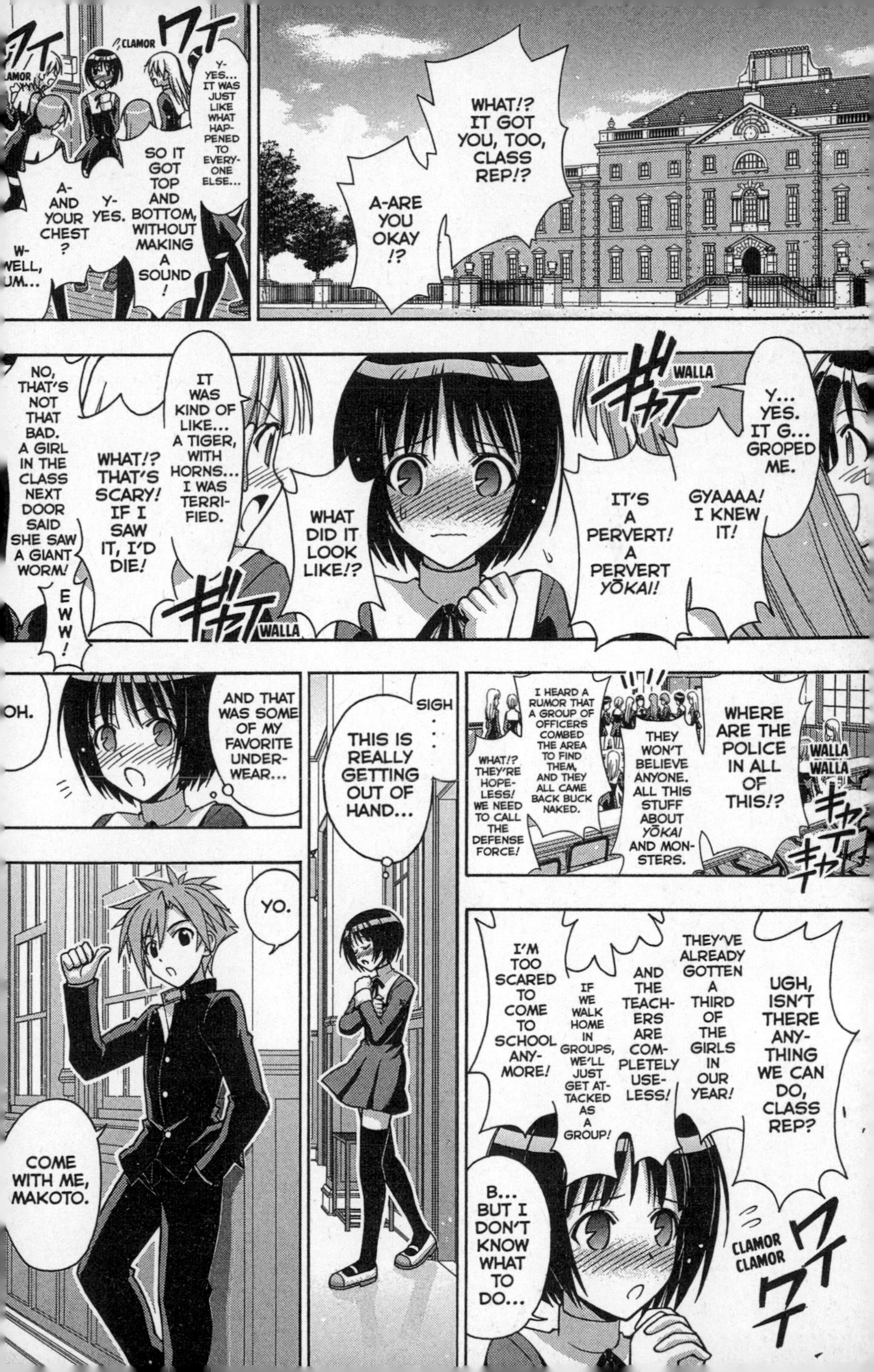
WHAT!? IT GOT YOU, TOO, CLASS REP!?
A-ARE YOU OKAY!?
CLAMOR
Y-YES... IT WAS JUST LIKE WHAT HAPPENED TO EVERYONE ELSE...
SO IT GOT TOP AND BOTTOM, WITHOUT MAKING A SOUND!
Y-YES.
A-AND YOUR CHEST?
W-WELL, UM...
CLAMOR
Y... YES. IT G... GROPED ME.
WALLA
GYAAAA! I KNEW IT!
IT'S A PERVERT! A PERVERT YŌKAI!
WHAT DID IT LOOK LIKE!?
IT WAS KIND OF LIKE... A TIGER, WITH HORNS... I WAS TERRIFIED.
WHAT!? THAT'S SCARY! IF I SAW IT, I'D DIE!
NO, THAT'S NOT THAT BAD. A GIRL IN THE CLASS NEXT DOOR SAID SHE SAW A GIANT WORM!
EWW!
WALLA
WHERE ARE THE POLICE IN ALL OF THIS!?
WALLA WALLA
THEY WON'T BELIEVE ANYONE. ALL THIS STUFF ABOUT YŌKAI AND MONSTERS.
I HEARD A RUMOR THAT A GROUP OF OFFICERS COMBED THE AREA TO FIND THEM, AND THEY ALL CAME BACK BUCK NAKED.
WHAT!? THEY'RE HOPELESS! WE NEED TO CALL THE DEFENSE FORCE!
SIGH...
THIS IS REALLY GETTING OUT OF HAND...
AND THAT WAS SOME OF MY FAVORITE UNDERWEAR...
OH.
UGH, ISN'T THERE ANYTHING WE CAN DO, CLASS REP?
THEY'VE ALREADY GOTTEN A THIRD OF THE GIRLS IN OUR YEAR!
AND THE TEACHERS ARE COMPLETELY USELESS!
IF WE WALK HOME IN GROUPS, WE'LL JUST GET ATTACKED AS A GROUP!
I'M TOO SCARED TO COME TO SCHOOL ANYMORE!
CLAMOR CLAMOR
B... BUT I DON'T KNOW WHAT TO DO...
YO.
COME WITH ME, MAKOTO.

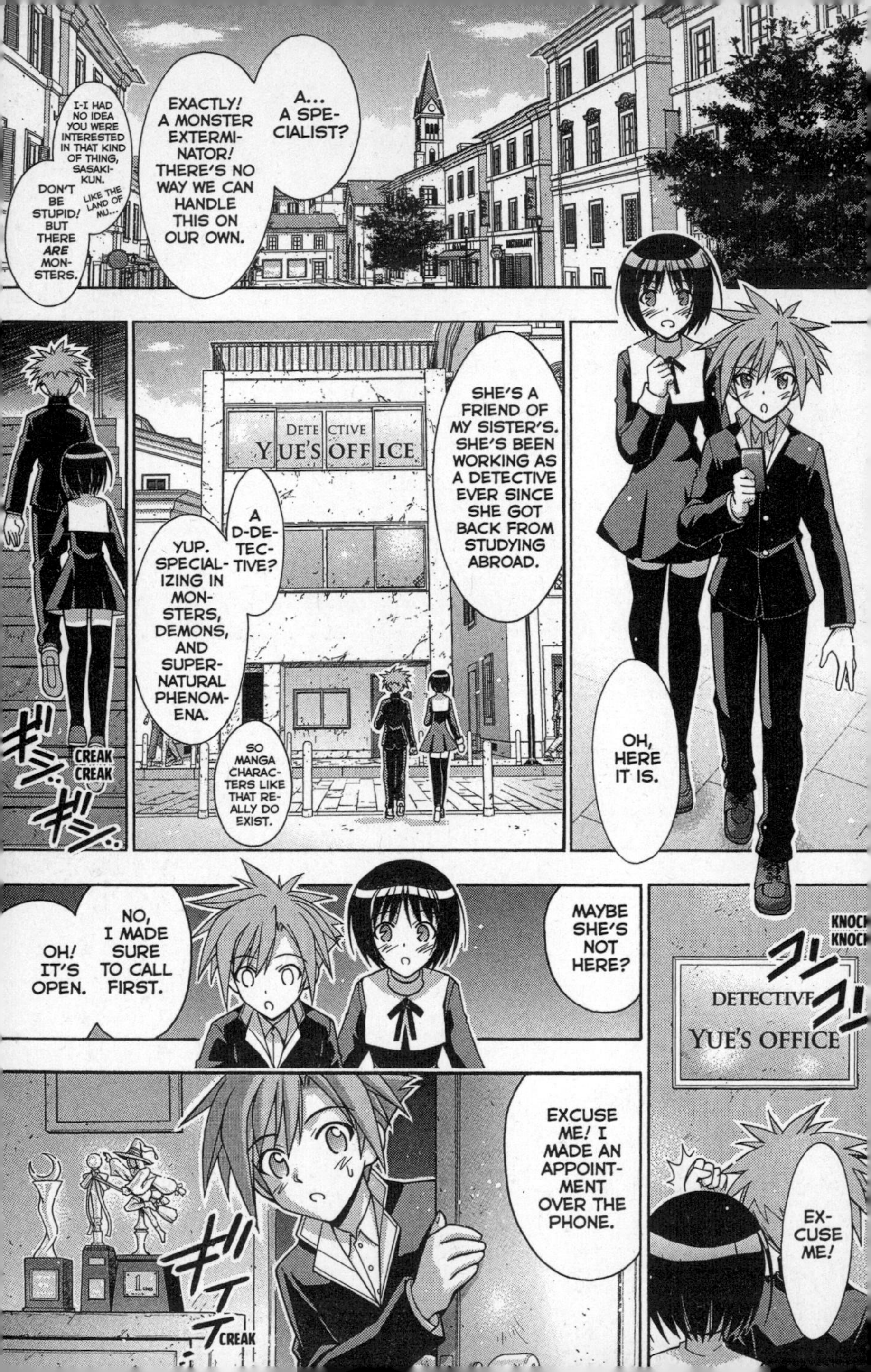
A... A SPECIALIST?
EXACTLY! A MONSTER EXTERMINATOR! THERE'S NO WAY WE CAN HANDLE THIS ON OUR OWN.
I-I HAD NO IDEA YOU WERE INTERESTED IN THAT KIND OF THING, SASAKI-KUN.
LIKE THE LAND OF MU...
DON'T BE STUPID! BUT THERE *ARE* MONSTERS.
SHE'S A FRIEND OF MY SISTER'S. SHE'S BEEN WORKING AS A DETECTIVE EVER SINCE SHE GOT BACK FROM STUDYING ABROAD.
OH, HERE IT IS.
DETECTIVE YUE'S OFFICE
A D-DETECTIVE?
YUP. SPECIALIZING IN MONSTERS, DEMONS, AND SUPERNATURAL PHENOMENA.
SO MANGA CHARACTERS LIKE THAT REALLY DO EXIST.
CREAK CREAK
KNOCK KNOCK
DETECTIVE YUE'S OFFICE
MAYBE SHE'S NOT HERE?
NO, I MADE SURE TO CALL FIRST.
OH! IT'S OPEN.
EXCUSE ME!
EXCUSE ME! I MADE AN APPOINTMENT OVER THE PHONE.
CREAK

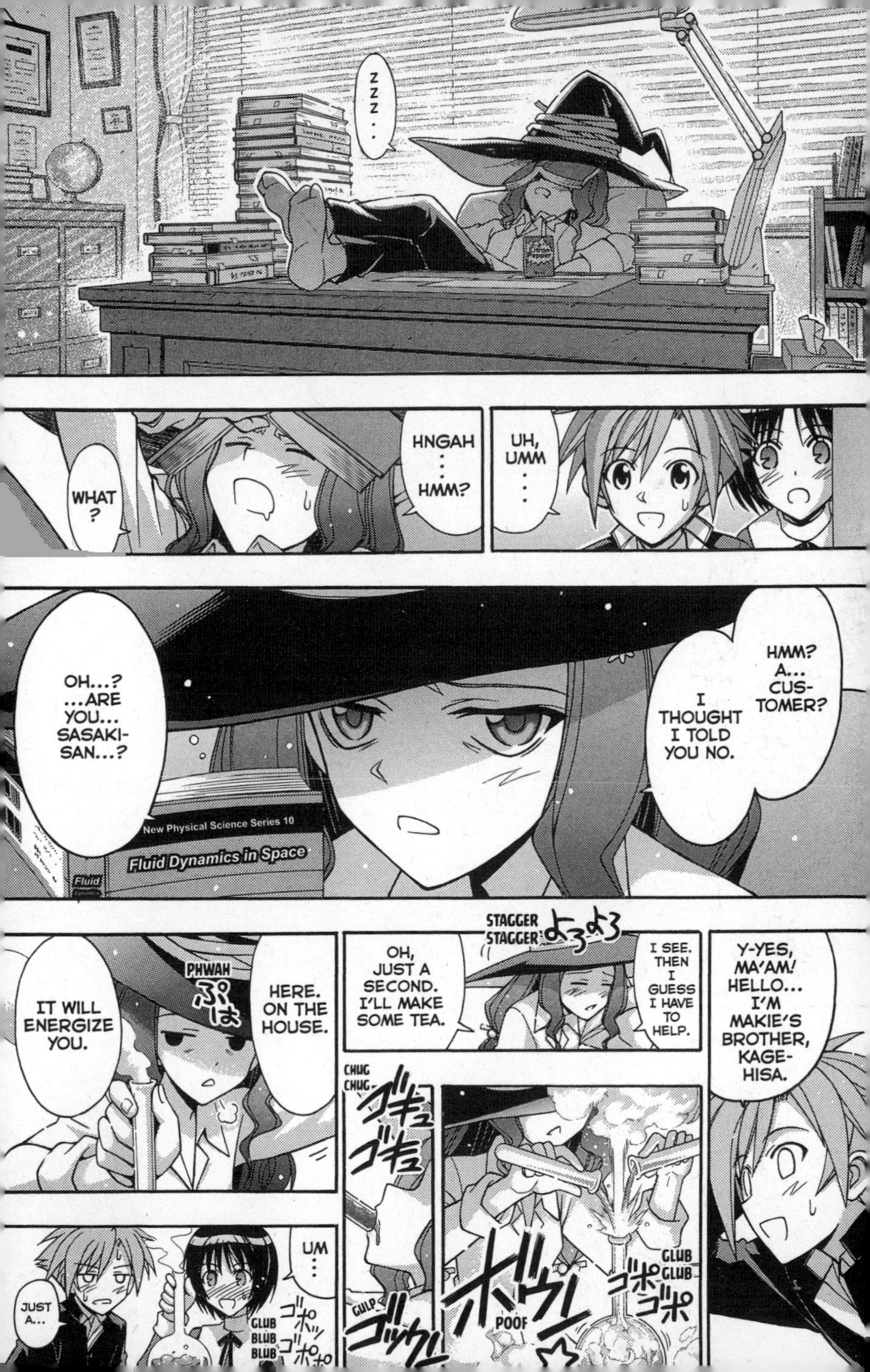
ZZZ...
UH, UMM...
HNGAH... HMM?
WHAT?
HMM? A... CUS-TOMER?
I THOUGHT I TOLD YOU NO.
OH...? ...ARE YOU... SASAKI-SAN...?
New Physical Science Series 10
Fluid Dynamics in Space
Fluid
Y-YES, MA'AM! HELLO... I'M MAKIE'S BROTHER, KAGE-HISA.
STAGGER STAGGER よろよろ
I SEE. THEN I GUESS I HAVE TO HELP.
OH, JUST A SECOND. I'LL MAKE SOME TEA.
CHUG CHUG ゴキュゴキュ
GLUB GLUB ゴポゴポ
POOF ボウン
GULP ゴック
PHWAH ぷは
HERE. ON THE HOUSE.
IT WILL ENERGIZE YOU.
UM...
JUST A...
GLUB BLUB BLUB ゴポッゴポポ

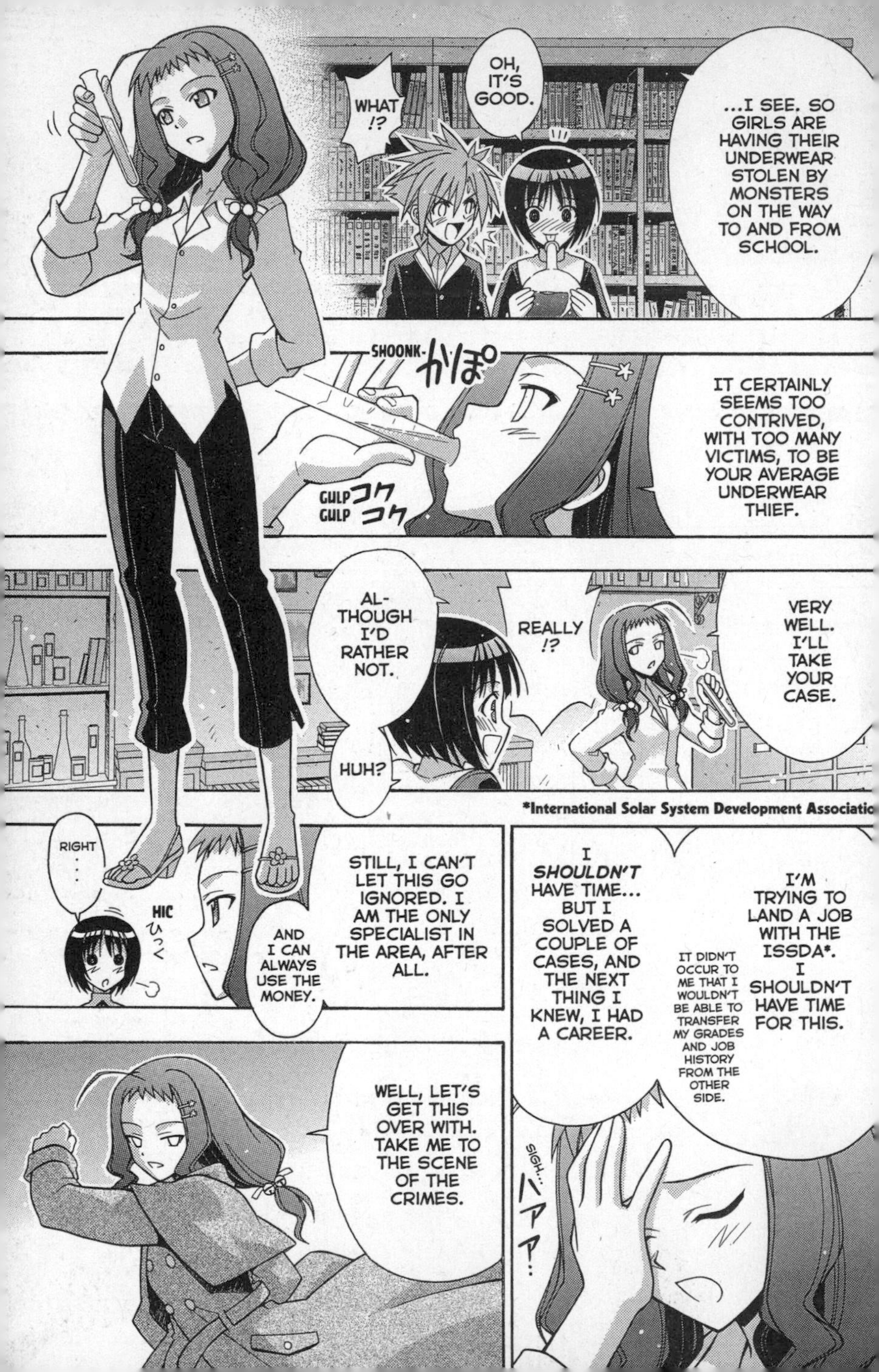
...I SEE. SO GIRLS ARE HAVING THEIR UNDERWEAR STOLEN BY MONSTERS ON THE WAY TO AND FROM SCHOOL.
OH, IT'S GOOD.
WHAT !?
IT CERTAINLY SEEMS TOO CONTRIVED, WITH TOO MANY VICTIMS, TO BE YOUR AVERAGE UNDERWEAR THIEF.
SHOONK かぽ
GULP GULP コクコク
VERY WELL. I'LL TAKE YOUR CASE.
REALLY !?
AL-THOUGH I'D RATHER NOT.
HUH?
*International Solar System Development Associatio
I'M TRYING TO LAND A JOB WITH THE ISSDA*. I SHOULDN'T HAVE TIME FOR THIS.
IT DIDN'T OCCUR TO ME THAT I WOULDN'T BE ABLE TO TRANSFER MY GRADES AND JOB HISTORY FROM THE OTHER SIDE.
I *SHOULDN'T* HAVE TIME... BUT I SOLVED A COUPLE OF CASES, AND THE NEXT THING I KNEW, I HAD A CAREER.
SIGH... ハァア...
STILL, I CAN'T LET THIS GO IGNORED. I AM THE ONLY SPECIALIST IN THE AREA, AFTER ALL.
AND I CAN ALWAYS USE THE MONEY.
RIGHT...
HIC ひっく
WELL, LET'S GET THIS OVER WITH. TAKE ME TO THE SCENE OF THE CRIMES.

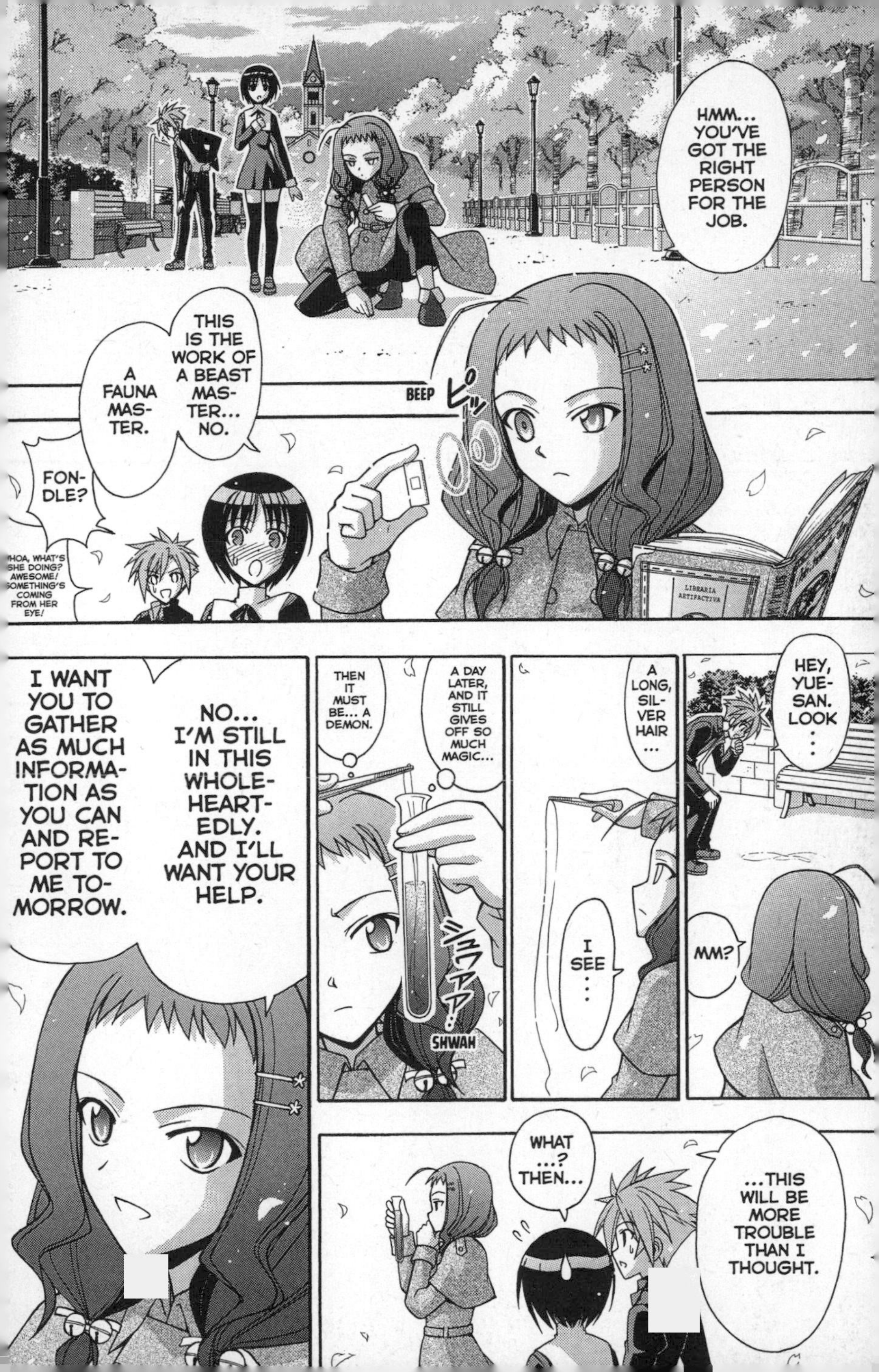
HMM... YOU'VE GOT THE RIGHT PERSON FOR THE JOB.
BEEP
THIS IS THE WORK OF A BEAST MASTER... NO.
A FAUNA MASTER.
FONDLE?
WHOA, WHAT'S SHE DOING? AWESOME! SOMETHING'S COMING FROM HER EYE!
LIBRARIA ARTIFACTIVA
HEY, YUE-SAN. LOOK...
MM?
A LONG, SILVER HAIR...
I SEE...
A DAY LATER, AND IT STILL GIVES OFF SO MUCH MAGIC...
THEN IT MUST BE... A DEMON.
SHWAH
...THIS WILL BE MORE TROUBLE THAN I THOUGHT.
WHAT...? THEN...
NO... I'M STILL IN THIS WHOLEHEARTEDLY. AND I'LL WANT YOUR HELP.
I WANT YOU TO GATHER AS MUCH INFORMATION AS YOU CAN AND REPORT TO ME TOMORROW.

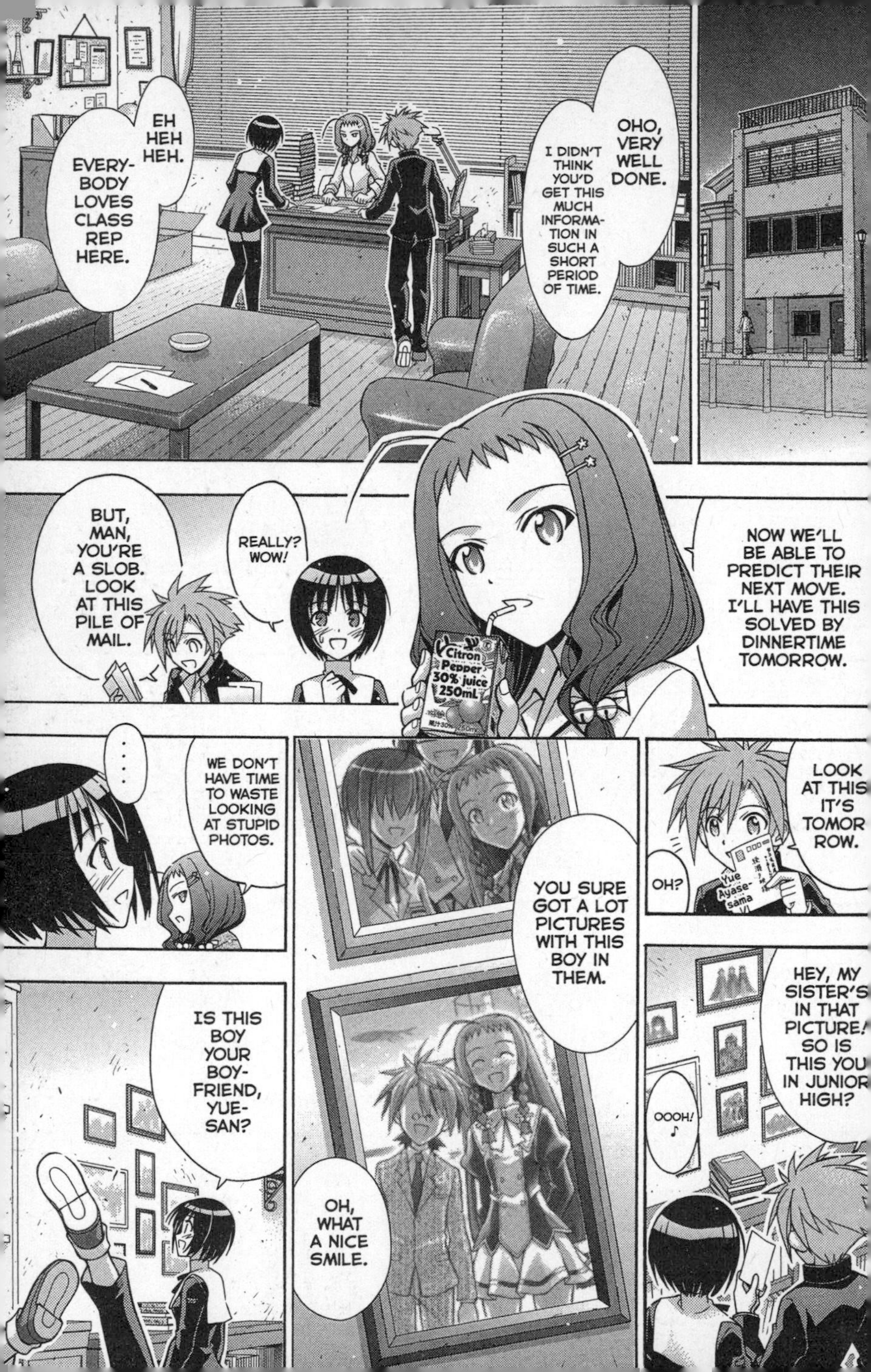
OHO, VERY WELL DONE.
I DIDN'T THINK YOU'D GET THIS MUCH INFORMATION IN SUCH A SHORT PERIOD OF TIME.
EH HEH HEH.
EVERYBODY LOVES CLASS REP HERE.
NOW WE'LL BE ABLE TO PREDICT THEIR NEXT MOVE. I'LL HAVE THIS SOLVED BY DINNERTIME TOMORROW.
Citron Pepper 30% juice 250mL
REALLY? WOW!
BUT, MAN, YOU'RE A SLOB. LOOK AT THIS PILE OF MAIL.
LOOK AT THIS IT'S TOMORROW.
OH?
Yue Ayase-sama
HEY, MY SISTER'S IN THAT PICTURE! SO IS THIS YOU IN JUNIOR HIGH?
OOOH! ♪
YOU SURE GOT A LOT PICTURES WITH THIS BOY IN THEM.
OH, WHAT A NICE SMILE.
......
WE DON'T HAVE TIME TO WASTE LOOKING AT STUPID PHOTOS.
IS THIS BOY YOUR BOYFRIEND, YUE-SAN?

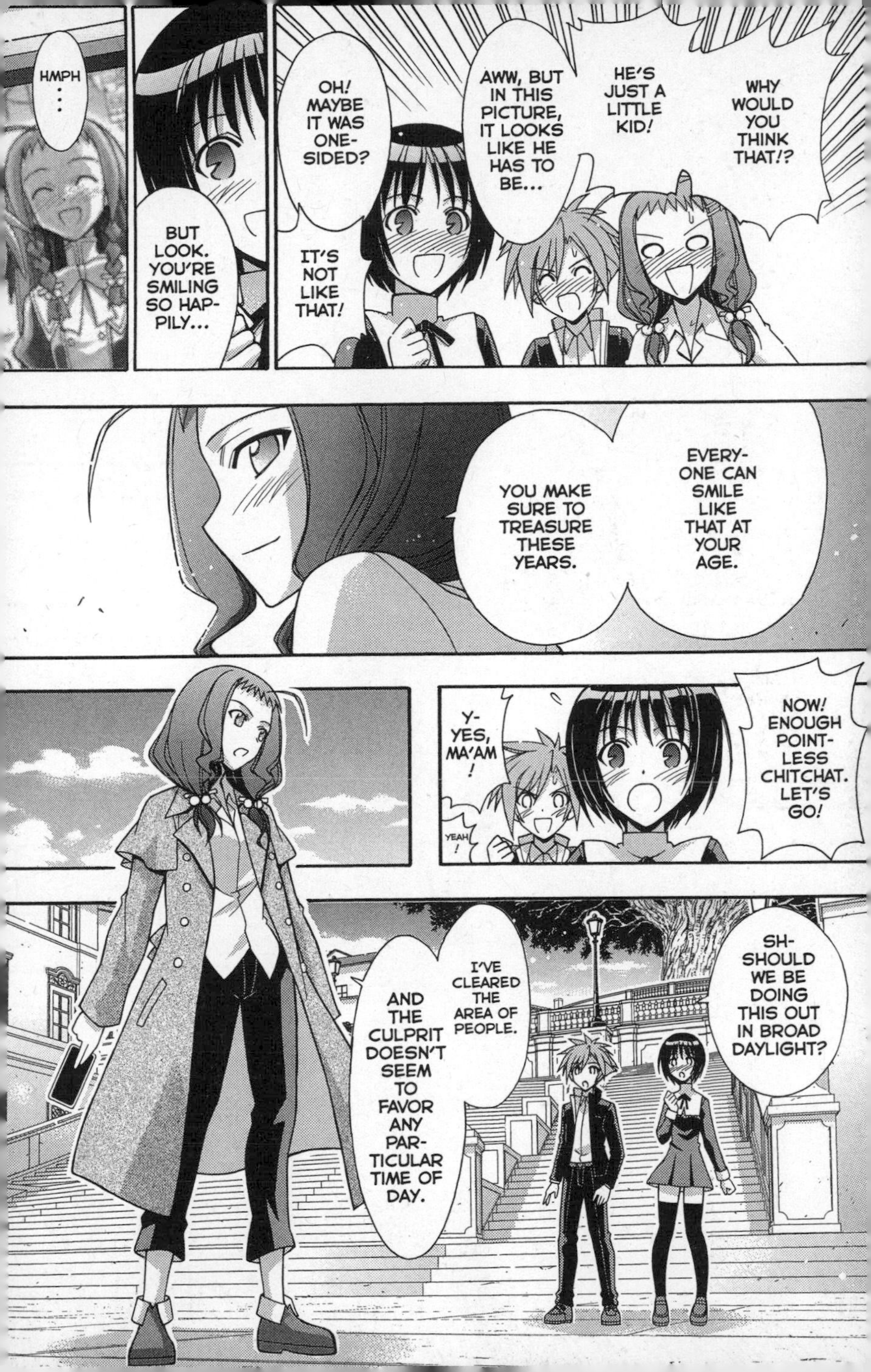
WHY WOULD YOU THINK THAT!?
HE'S JUST A LITTLE KID!
AWW, BUT IN THIS PICTURE, IT LOOKS LIKE HE HAS TO BE...
OH! MAYBE IT WAS ONE-SIDED?
IT'S NOT LIKE THAT!
BUT LOOK. YOU'RE SMILING SO HAP-PILY...
HMPH...
EVERY-ONE CAN SMILE LIKE THAT AT YOUR AGE.
YOU MAKE SURE TO TREASURE THESE YEARS.
NOW! ENOUGH POINT-LESS CHITCHAT. LET'S GO!
Y-YES, MA'AM!
YEAH!
SH-SHOULD WE BE DOING THIS OUT IN BROAD DAYLIGHT?
I'VE CLEARED THE AREA OF PEOPLE.
AND THE CULPRIT DOESN'T SEEM TO FAVOR ANY PAR-TICULAR TIME OF DAY.

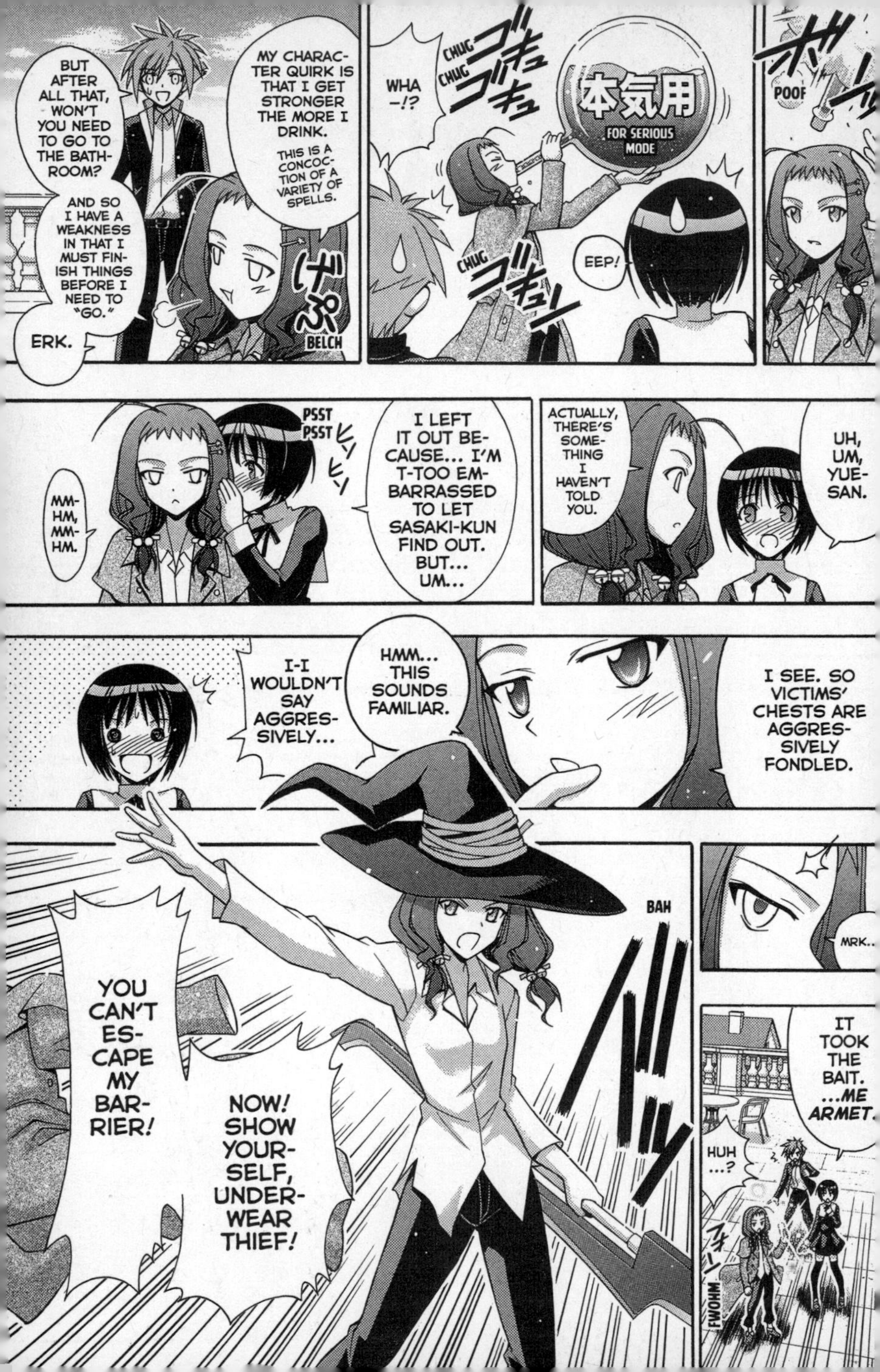
POOF
CHUG
CHUG
本気用
FOR SERIOUS MODE
WHA-!?
CHUG
EEP!
MY CHARACTER QUIRK IS THAT I GET STRONGER THE MORE I DRINK.
THIS IS A CONCOCTION OF A VARIETY OF SPELLS.
BUT AFTER ALL THAT, WON'T YOU NEED TO GO TO THE BATHROOM?
AND SO I HAVE A WEAKNESS IN THAT I MUST FINISH THINGS BEFORE I NEED TO "GO."
げぷ
BELCH
ERK.
UH, UM, YUE-SAN.
ACTUALLY, THERE'S SOMETHING I HAVEN'T TOLD YOU.
I LEFT IT OUT BECAUSE... I'M T-TOO EMBARRASSED TO LET SASAKI-KUN FIND OUT. BUT... UM...
PSST PSST
MM-HM, MM-HM.
I SEE. SO VICTIMS' CHESTS ARE AGGRESSIVELY FONDLED.
HMM... THIS SOUNDS FAMILIAR.
I-I WOULDN'T SAY AGGRESSIVELY...
MRK...
IT TOOK THE BAIT. ...ME ARMET.
HUH ...?
FWOHM
BAH
NOW! SHOW YOURSELF, UNDERWEAR THIEF!
YOU CAN'T ESCAPE MY BARRIER!

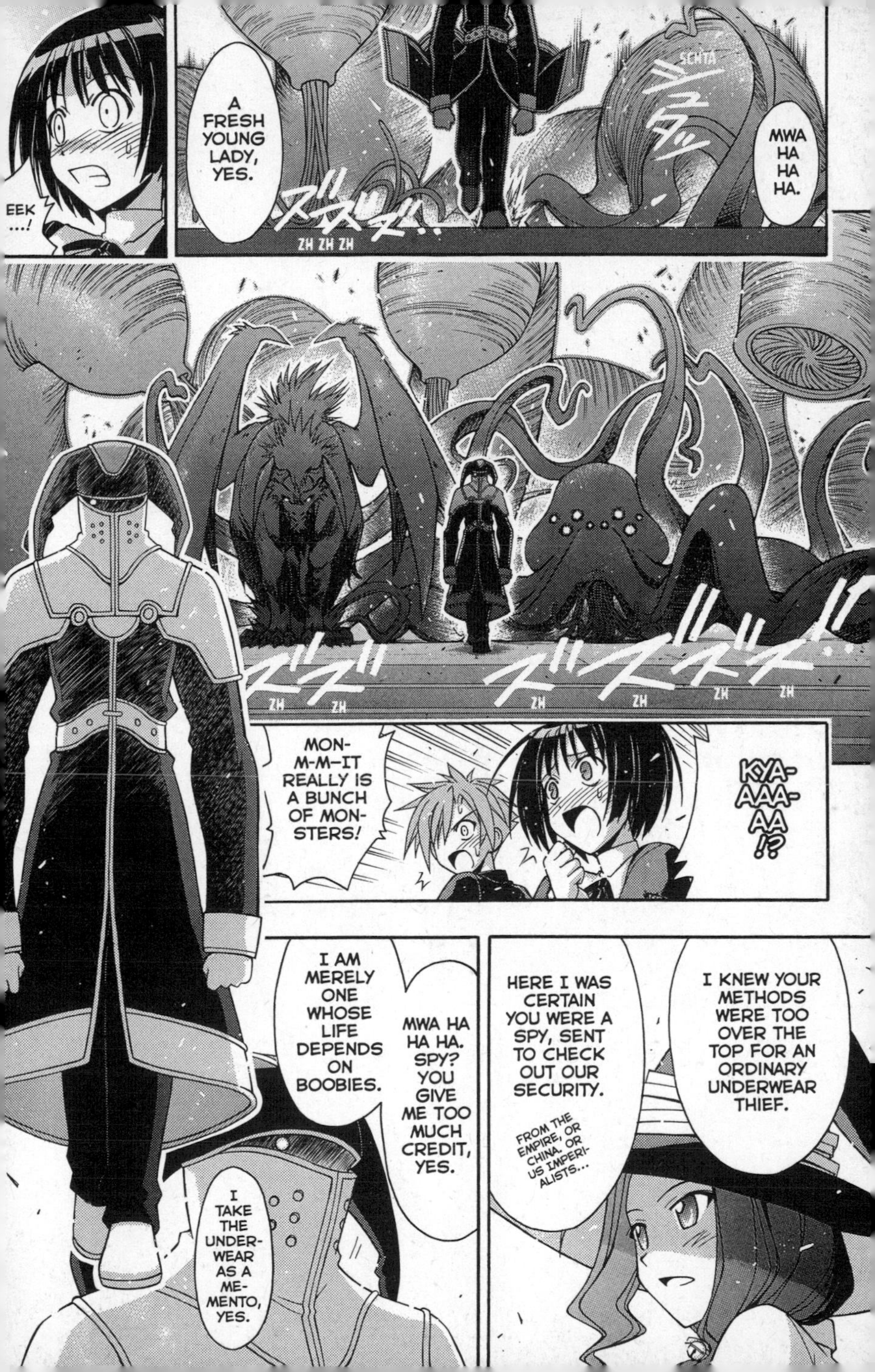
SCHTA
MWA HA HA HA.
A FRESH YOUNG LADY, YES.
ZH ZH ZH
EEK ...!
ZH ZH ZH ZH ZH ZH
KYA-AAA-AA!?
MON-M-M—IT REALLY IS A BUNCH OF MON-STERS!
I KNEW YOUR METHODS WERE TOO OVER THE TOP FOR AN ORDINARY UNDERWEAR THIEF.
HERE I WAS CERTAIN YOU WERE A SPY, SENT TO CHECK OUT OUR SECURITY.
FROM THE EMPIRE, OR CHINA, OR US IMPERI-ALISTS...
MWA HA HA HA. SPY? YOU GIVE ME TOO MUCH CREDIT, YES.
I AM MERELY ONE WHOSE LIFE DEPENDS ON BOOBIES.
I TAKE THE UNDER-WEAR AS A ME-MENTO, YES.

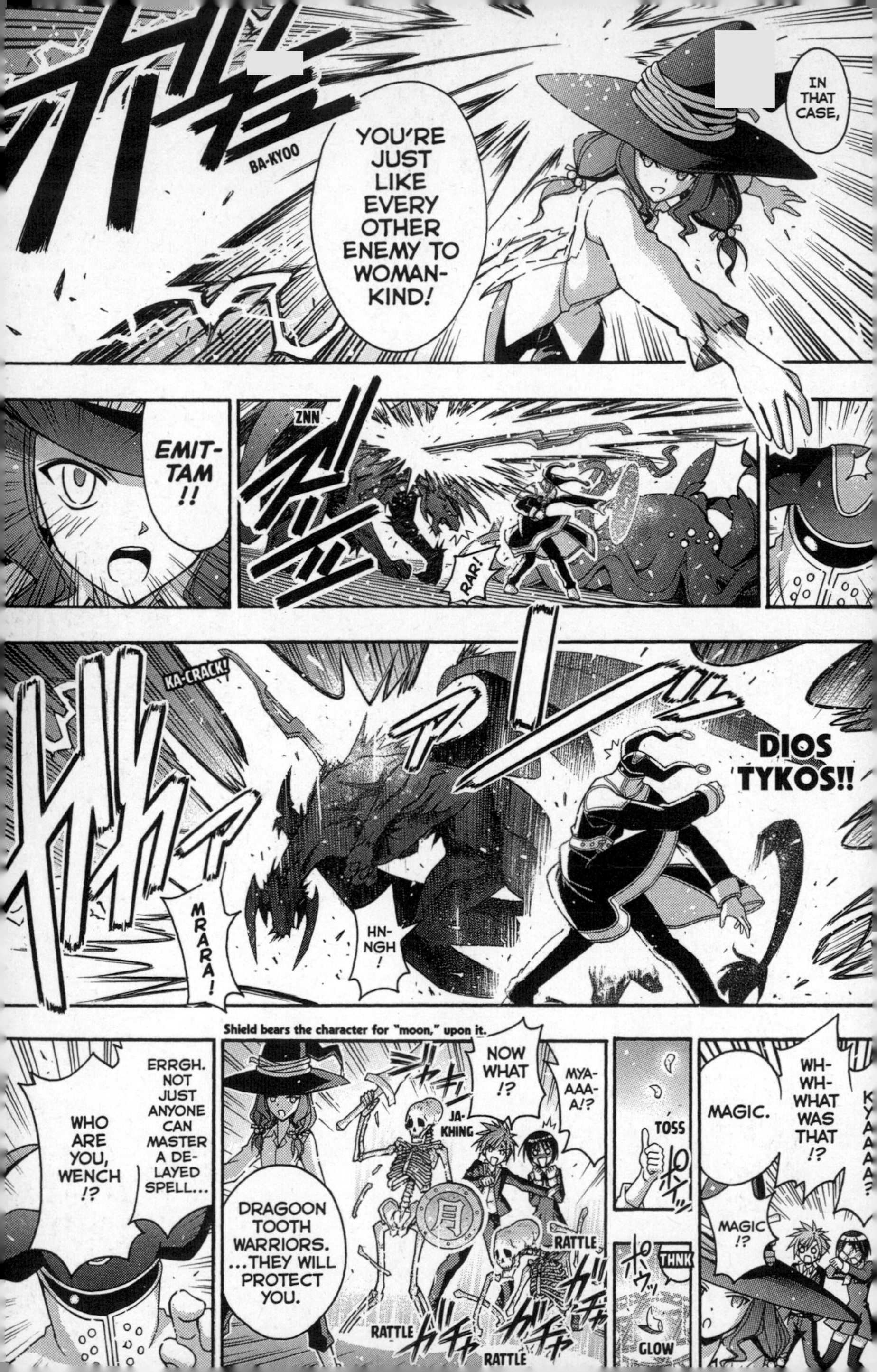

IN THAT CASE,
YOU'RE JUST LIKE EVERY OTHER ENEMY TO WOMAN-KIND!
BA-KYOO
ZNN
RAR!
EMIT-TAM!!
DIOS TYKOS!!
KA-CRACK!
HN-NGH!
MRARA!
KYAAAAA!?
WH-WH-WHAT WAS THAT!?
MAGIC.
MAGIC!?
TOSS
THNK
GLOW
Shield bears the character for "moon," upon it.
MYA-AAAA!?
NOW WHAT!?
JA-KHING
RATTLE
DRAGOON TOOTH WARRIORS. ...THEY WILL PROTECT YOU.
RATTLE
RATTLE
ERRGH. NOT JUST ANYONE CAN MASTER A DE-LAYED SPELL...
WHO ARE YOU, WENCH!?

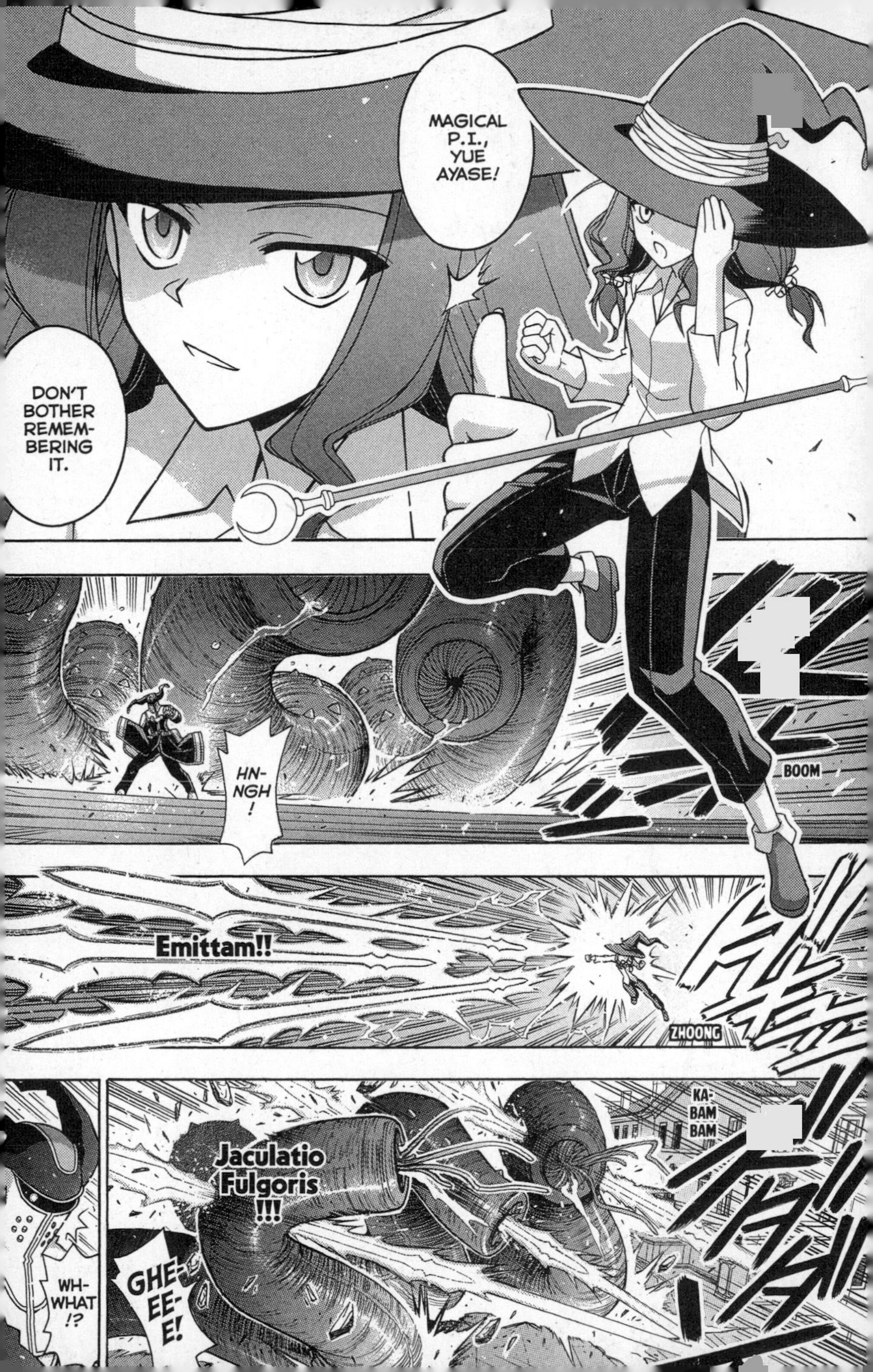
MAGICAL P.I., YUE AYASE!
DON'T BOTHER REMEM-BERING IT.
BOOM
HN-NGH!
ZHOONG
Emittam!!
KA-BAM BAM
Jaculatio Fulgoris!!!
GHEE-EE-E!
WH-WHAT!?

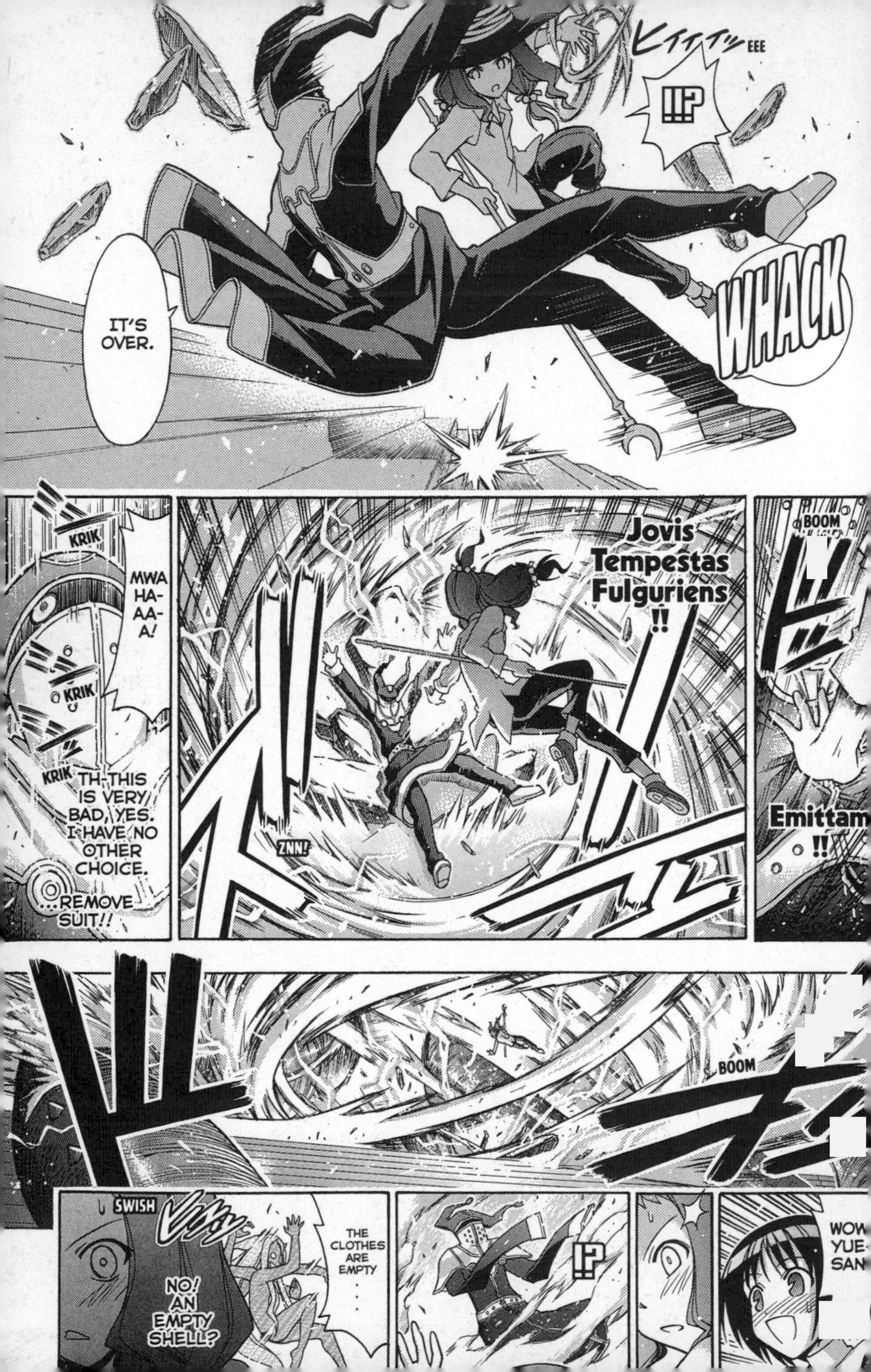
EEE
!!?
WHACK
IT'S OVER.
BOOM
Emittam !!
Jovis Tempestas Fulguriens !!
ZNN!
KRIK
MWA HA-AA-A!
KRIK
KRIK
TH-THIS IS VERY BAD, YES. I HAVE NO OTHER CHOICE.
...REMOVE SUIT!!
BOOM
WOW YUE-SAN
!?
THE CLOTHES ARE EMPTY . . .
SWISH
NO! AN EMPTY SHELL?

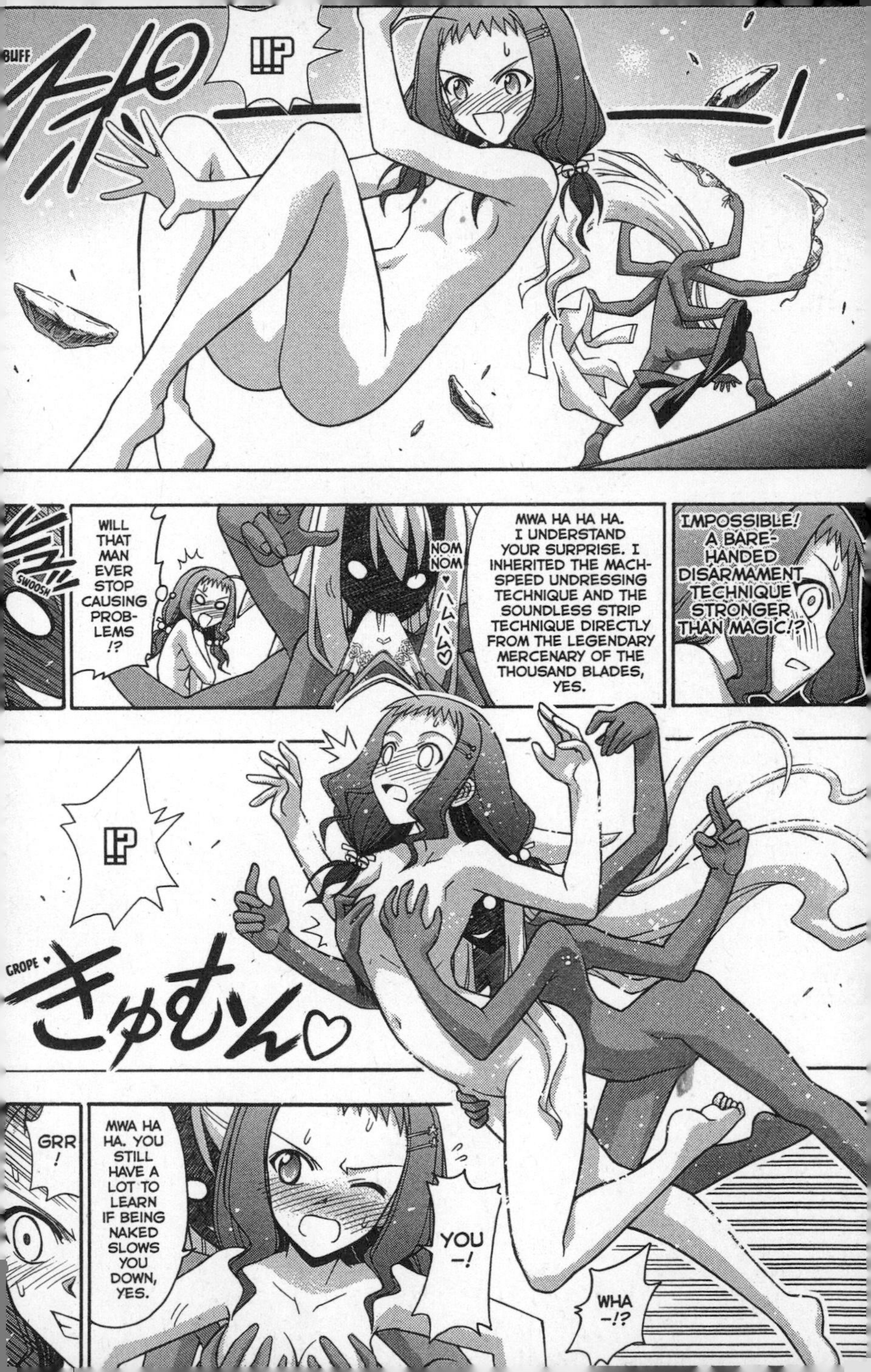
BUFF
!?
IMPOSSIBLE! A BARE-HANDED DISARMAMENT TECHNIQUE STRONGER THAN MAGIC!?
MWA HA HA HA. I UNDERSTAND YOUR SURPRISE. I INHERITED THE MACH-SPEED UNDRESSING TECHNIQUE AND THE SOUNDLESS STRIP TECHNIQUE DIRECTLY FROM THE LEGENDARY MERCENARY OF THE THOUSAND BLADES, YES.
NOM NOM ♥
ハムハム♡
WILL THAT MAN EVER STOP CAUSING PROBLEMS!?
SWOOSH
!?
GROPE ♥
きゅむん♡
WHA-!?
YOU-!
MWA HA HA. YOU STILL HAVE A LOT TO LEARN IF BEING NAKED SLOWS YOU DOWN, YES.
GRR!

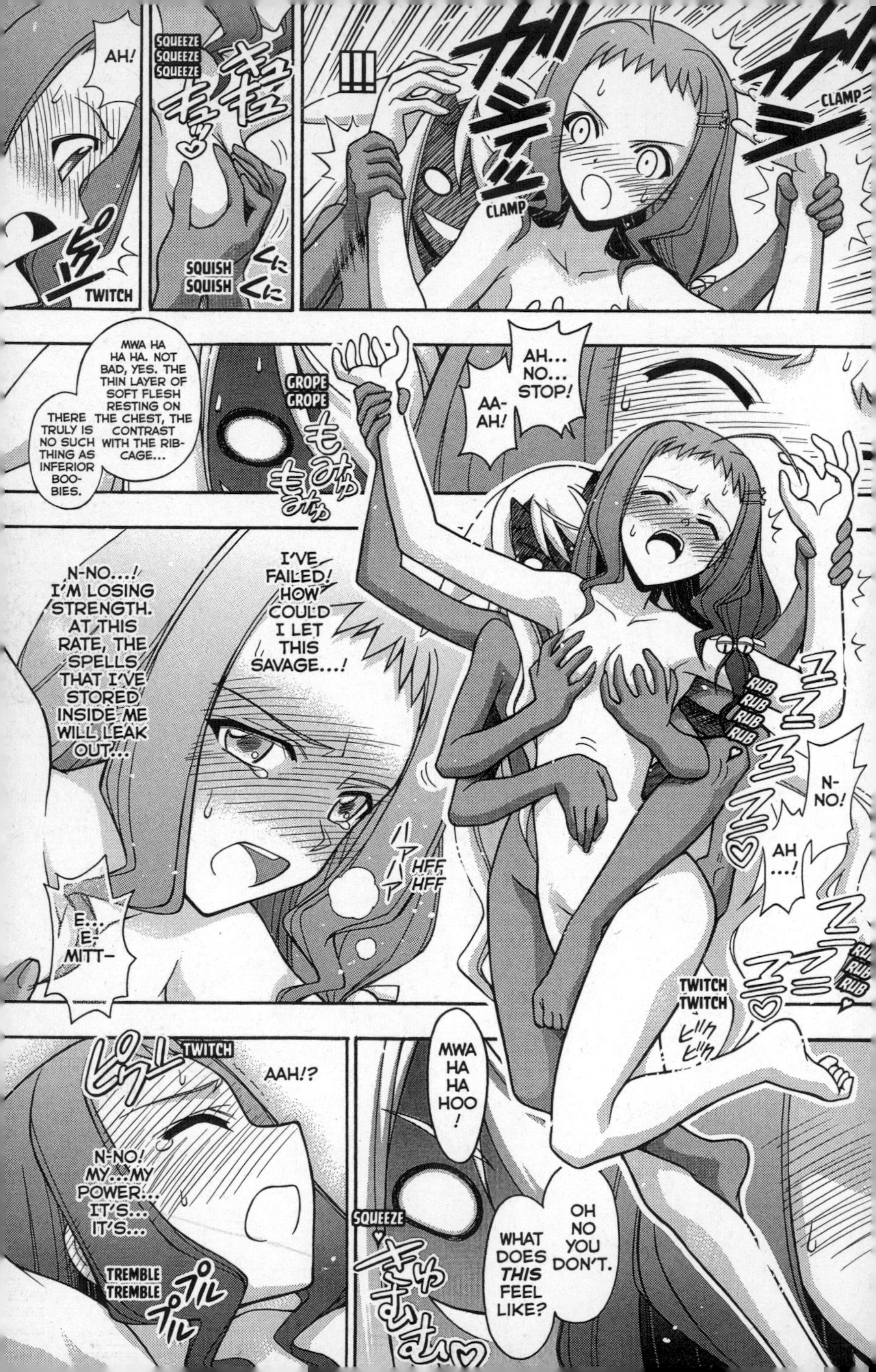
!!!
CLAMP
CLAMP
SQUEEZE SQUEEZE SQUEEZE
SQUISH SQUISH
AH!
TWITCH
AH... NO... STOP!
AA-AH!
N-NO!
AH...!
RUB RUB RUB RUB
RUB RUB RUB
TWITCH TWITCH
MWA HA HA. NOT BAD, YES. THE THIN LAYER OF SOFT FLESH RESTING ON THE CHEST, THE CONTRAST WITH THE RIBCAGE...
THERE TRULY IS NO SUCH THING AS INFERIOR BOOBIES.
GROPE GROPE
I'VE FAILED! HOW COULD I LET THIS SAVAGE...!
N-NO...! I'M LOSING STRENGTH. AT THIS RATE, THE SPELLS THAT I'VE STORED INSIDE ME WILL LEAK OUT...
HFF HFF
E... E-MITT-
MWA HA HA HOO!
OH NO YOU DON'T.
WHAT DOES THIS FEEL LIKE?
SQUEEZE
TWITCH
AAH!?
N-NO! MY... MY POWER... IT'S... IT'S...
TREMBLE TREMBLE

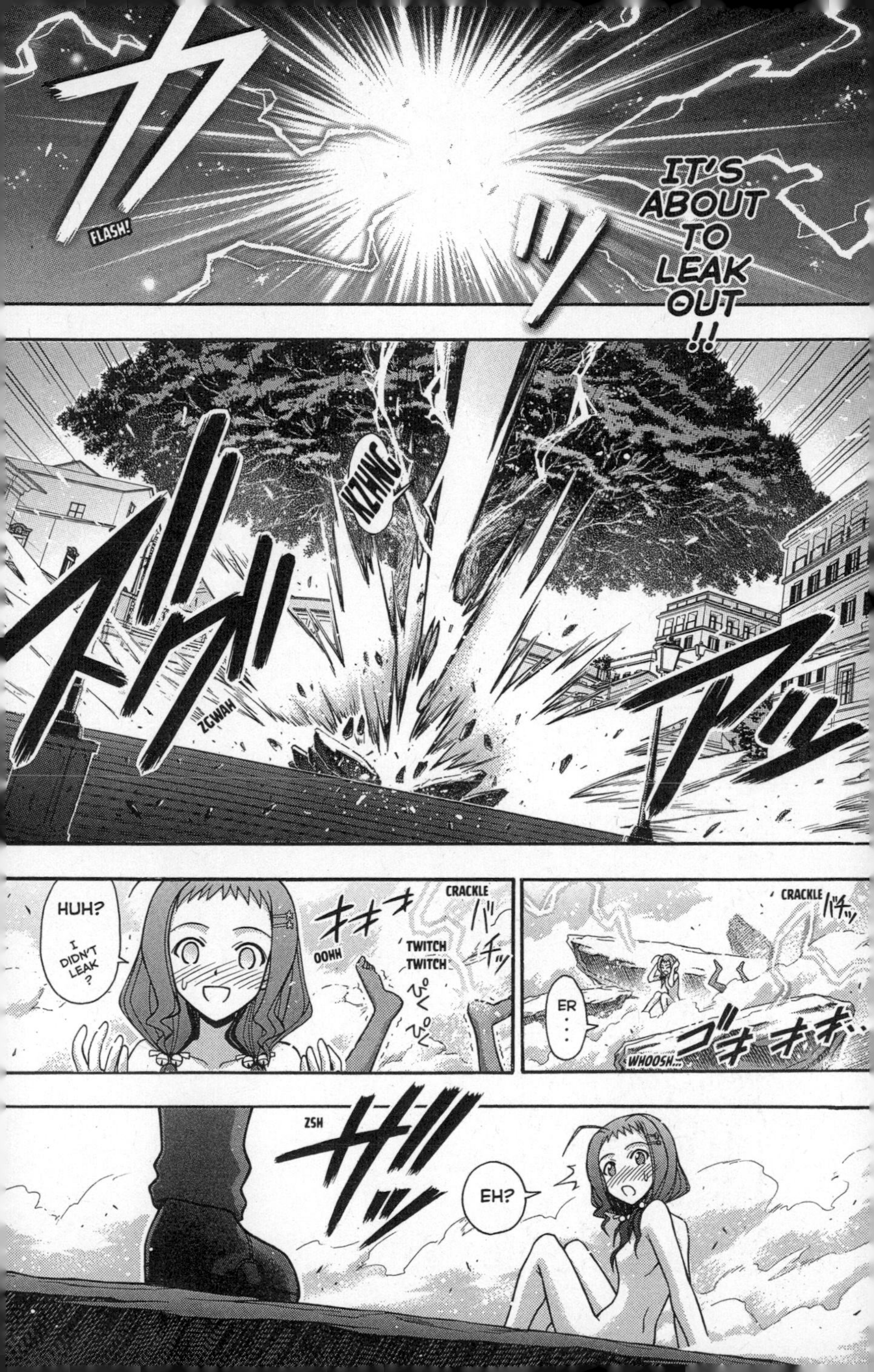

IT'S ABOUT TO LEAK OUT!!
FLASH!
KZHNG
ZGWAH
CRACKLE
バチッ
ER...
WHOOSH...
CRACKLE
バチッ
TWITCH TWITCH
ぴくぴく
OOHH
HUH?
I DIDN'T LEAK?
ZSH
EH?

55th Period: 3-A Forever

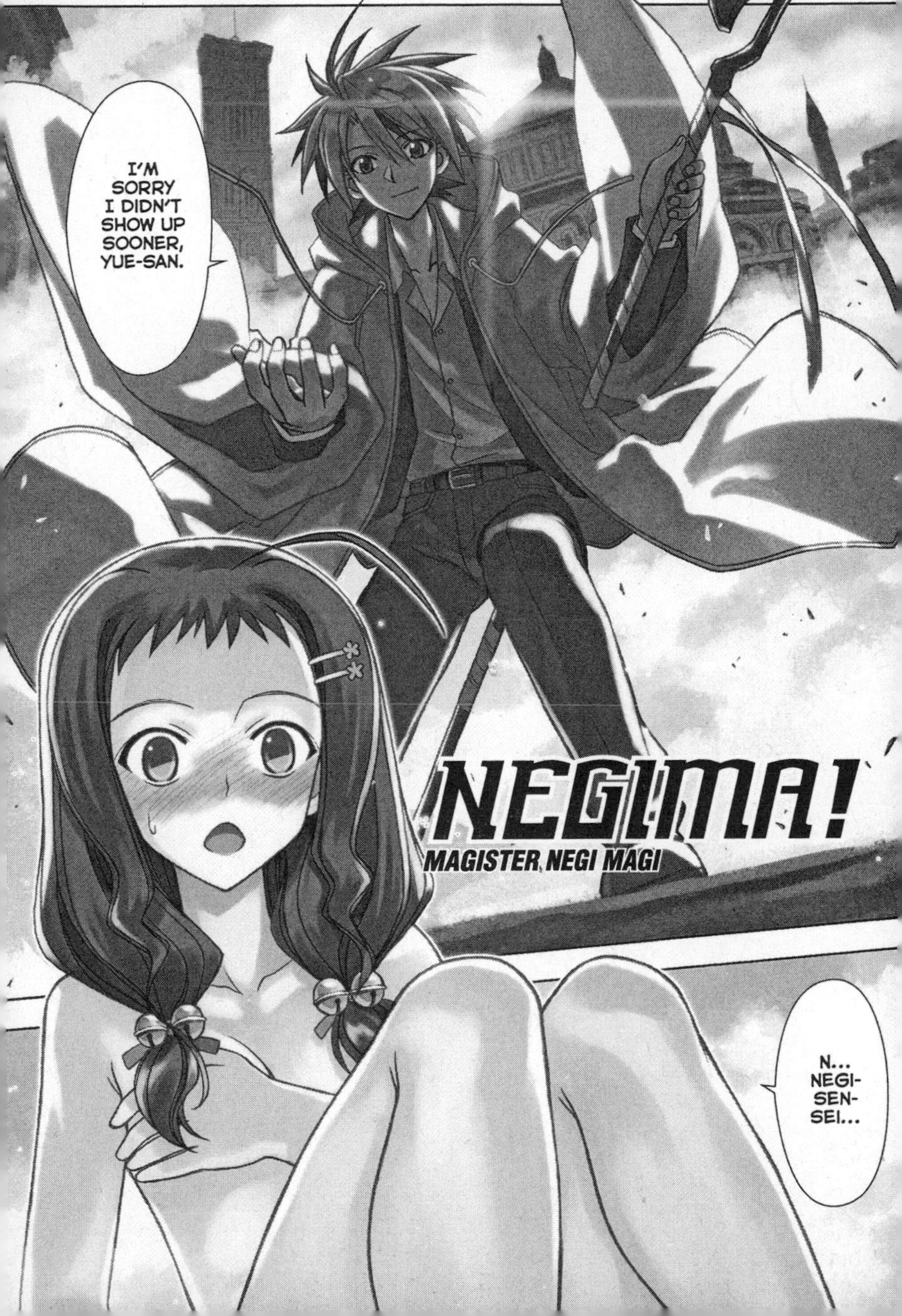
I'M SORRY I DIDN'T SHOW UP SOONER, YUE-SAN.
NEGIMA!
MAGISTER NEGI MAGI
N... NEGI-SEN-SEI...

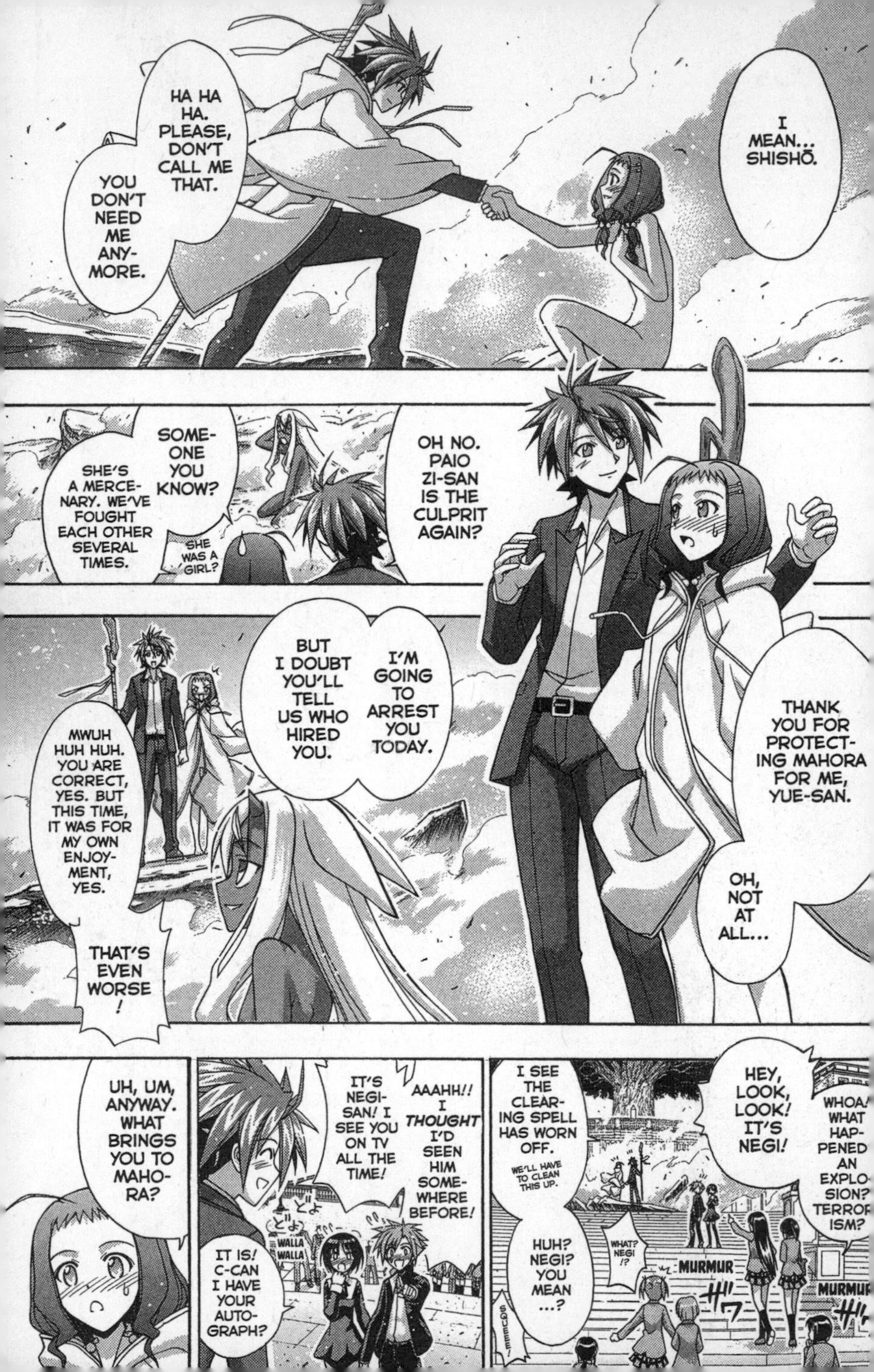
I MEAN... SHISHŌ.
HA HA HA. PLEASE, DON'T CALL ME THAT.
YOU DON'T NEED ME ANY-MORE.
THANK YOU FOR PROTECT-ING MAHORA FOR ME, YUE-SAN.
OH, NOT AT ALL...
OH NO. PAIO ZI-SAN IS THE CULPRIT AGAIN?
SOME-ONE YOU KNOW?
SHE'S A MERCE-NARY. WE'VE FOUGHT EACH OTHER SEVERAL TIMES.
SHE WAS A GIRL?
I'M GOING TO ARREST YOU TODAY.
BUT I DOUBT YOU'LL TELL US WHO HIRED YOU.
MWUH HUH HUH. YOU ARE CORRECT, YES. BUT THIS TIME, IT WAS FOR MY OWN ENJOY-MENT, YES.
THAT'S EVEN WORSE!
HEY, LOOK, LOOK! IT'S NEGI!
WHOA! WHAT HAP-PENED AN EXPLO-SION? TERROR ISM?
I SEE THE CLEAR-ING SPELL HAS WORN OFF.
WE'LL HAVE TO CLEAN THIS UP.
HUH? NEGI? YOU MEAN ...?
WHAT? NEGI!?
MURMUR
MURMUR
SQUEEE!
AAAHH!! I *THOUGHT* I'D SEEN HIM SOME-WHERE BEFORE!
IT'S NEGI-SAN! I SEE YOU ON TV ALL THE TIME!
WALLA WALLA
IT IS! C-CAN I HAVE YOUR AUTO-GRAPH?
UH, UM, ANYWAY. WHAT BRINGS YOU TO MAHO-RA?

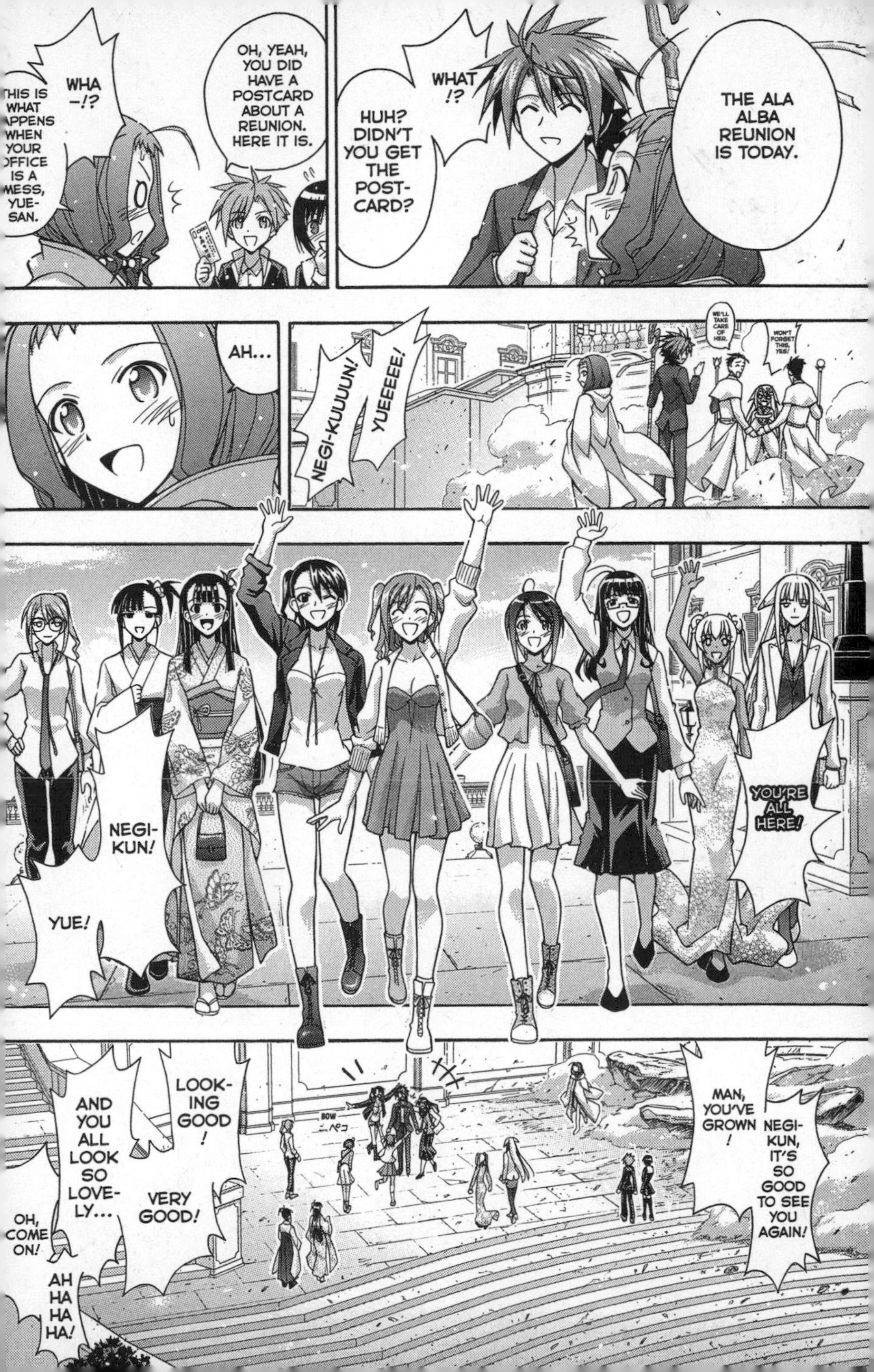
THE ALA ALBA REUNION IS TODAY.
WHAT !?
HUH? DIDN'T YOU GET THE POST-CARD?
OH, YEAH, YOU DID HAVE A POSTCARD ABOUT A REUNION. HERE IT IS.
WHA-!?
THIS IS WHAT APPENS WHEN YOUR OFFICE IS A MESS, YUE-SAN.
WE'LL TAKE CARE OF HER.
WON'T FORGET THIS, YES!
YUEEEEE!
NEGI-KUUUUN!
AH...
YOU'RE ALL HERE!
NEGI-KUN!
YUE!
MAN, YOU'VE GROWN!
NEGI-KUN, IT'S SO GOOD TO SEE YOU AGAIN!
BOW
LOOKING GOOD!
VERY GOOD!
AND YOU ALL LOOK SO LOVELY...
OH, COME ON!
AH HA HA HA!

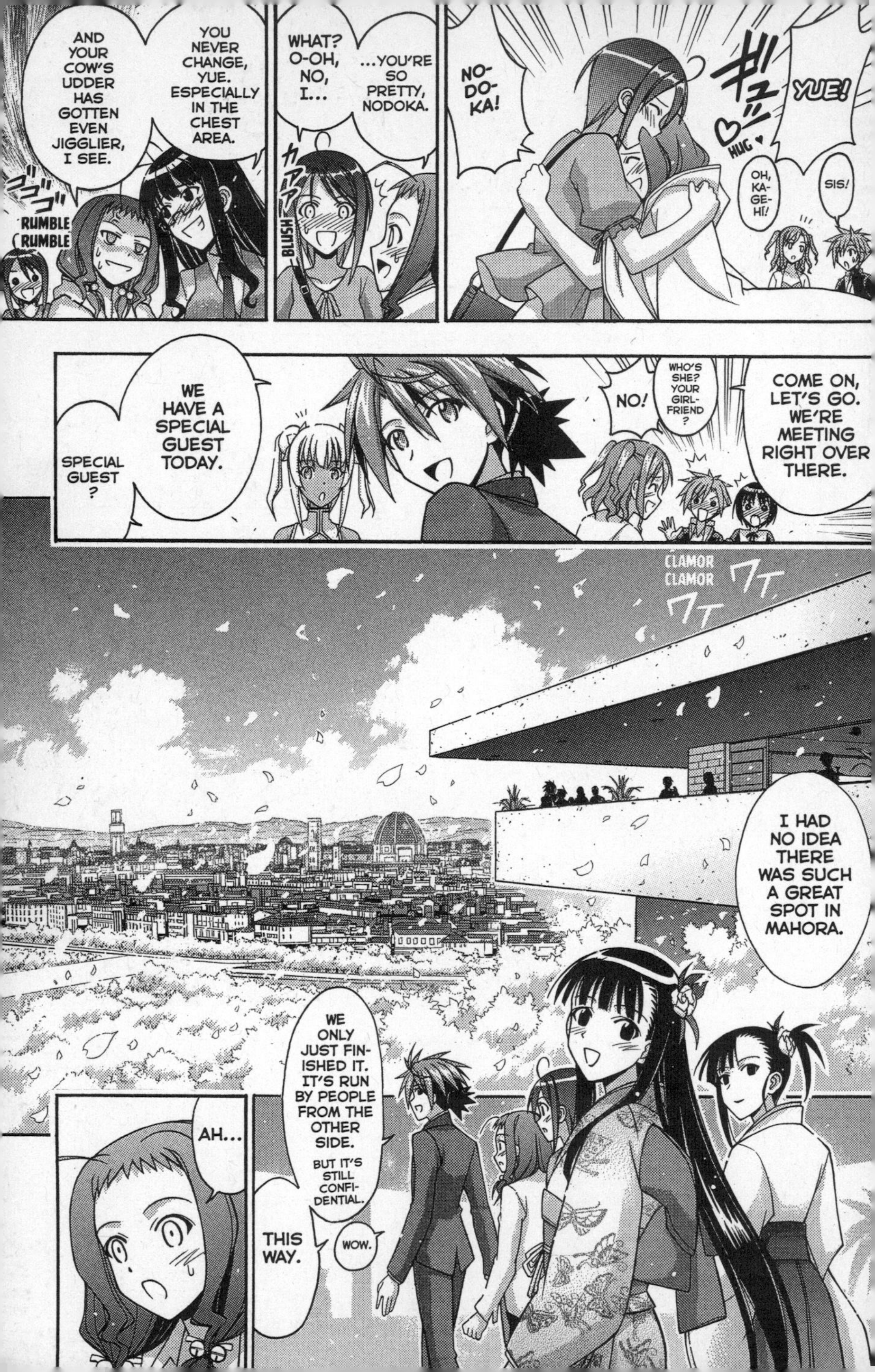
YUE!
HUG
NO-DO-KA!
SIS!
OH, KA-GE-HI!
...YOU'RE SO PRETTY, NODOKA.
WHAT? O-OH, NO, I...
BLUSH
YOU NEVER CHANGE, YUE. ESPECIALLY IN THE CHEST AREA.
AND YOUR COW'S UDDER HAS GOTTEN EVEN JIGGLIER, I SEE.
RUMBLE RUMBLE
COME ON, LET'S GO. WE'RE MEETING RIGHT OVER THERE.
WHO'S SHE? YOUR GIRL-FRIEND?
NO!
WE HAVE A SPECIAL GUEST TODAY.
SPECIAL GUEST?
CLAMOR CLAMOR
I HAD NO IDEA THERE WAS SUCH A GREAT SPOT IN MAHORA.
WE ONLY JUST FIN-ISHED IT. IT'S RUN BY PEOPLE FROM THE OTHER SIDE.
BUT IT'S STILL CONFI-DENTIAL.
WOW.
THIS WAY.
AH...

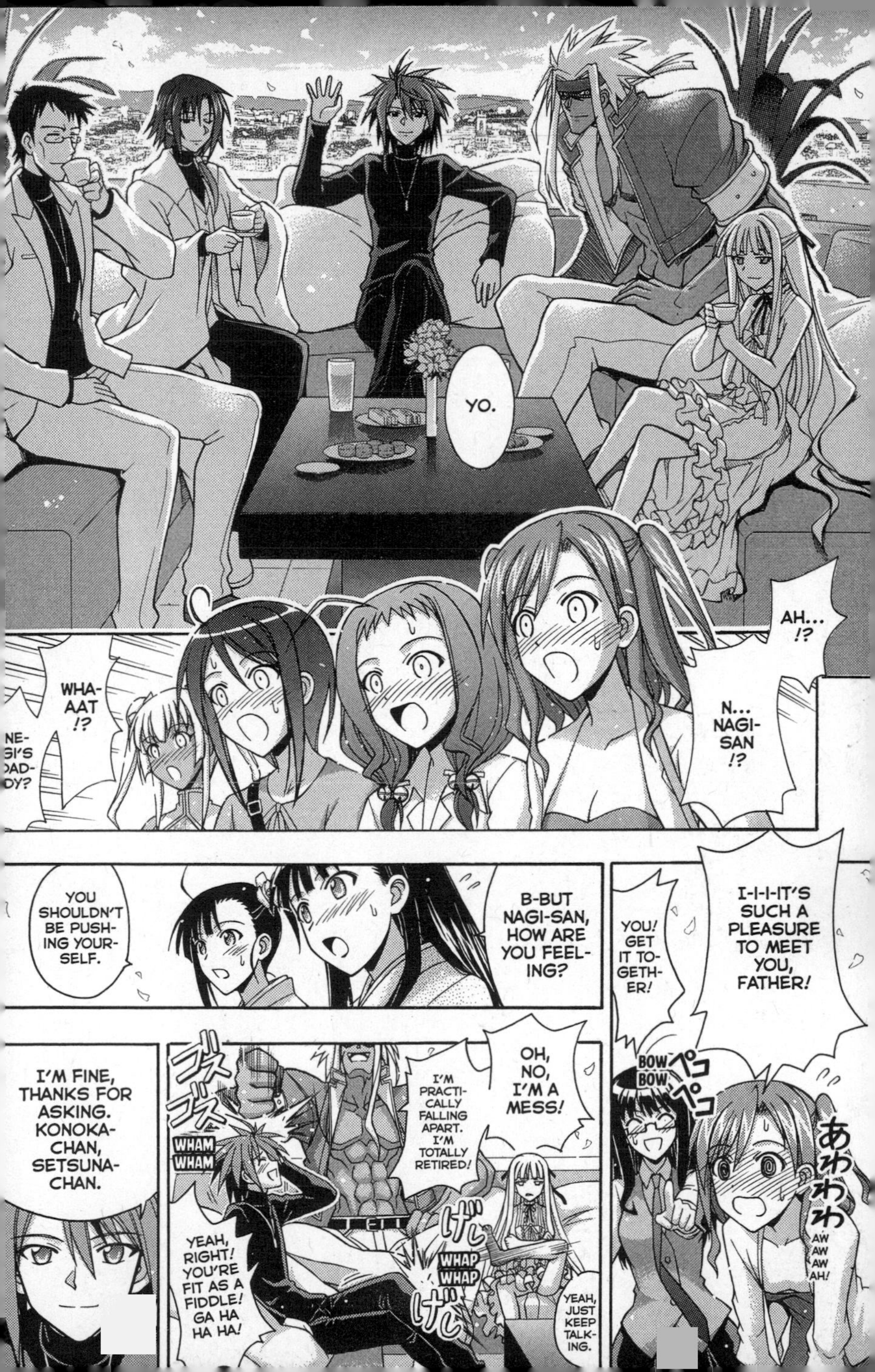
YO.
AH... !?
N... NAGI-SAN !?
WHA-AAT !?
NE-GI'S DAD-DY?
I-I-I-IT'S SUCH A PLEASURE TO MEET YOU, FATHER!
YOU! GET IT TO-GETH-ER!
B-BUT NAGI-SAN, HOW ARE YOU FEEL-ING?
YOU SHOULDN'T BE PUSH-ING YOUR-SELF.
ペコペコ
BOW BOW
あわわわ
AW AW AW AH!
OH, NO, I'M A MESS!
I'M PRACTI-CALLY FALLING APART. I'M TOTALLY RETIRED!
ゴスゴス
WHAM WHAM
YEAH, RIGHT! YOU'RE FIT AS A FIDDLE! GA HA HA HA!
げしげし
WHAP WHAP
YEAH, JUST KEEP TALK-ING.
I'M FINE, THANKS FOR ASKING. KONOKA-CHAN, SETSUNA-CHAN.

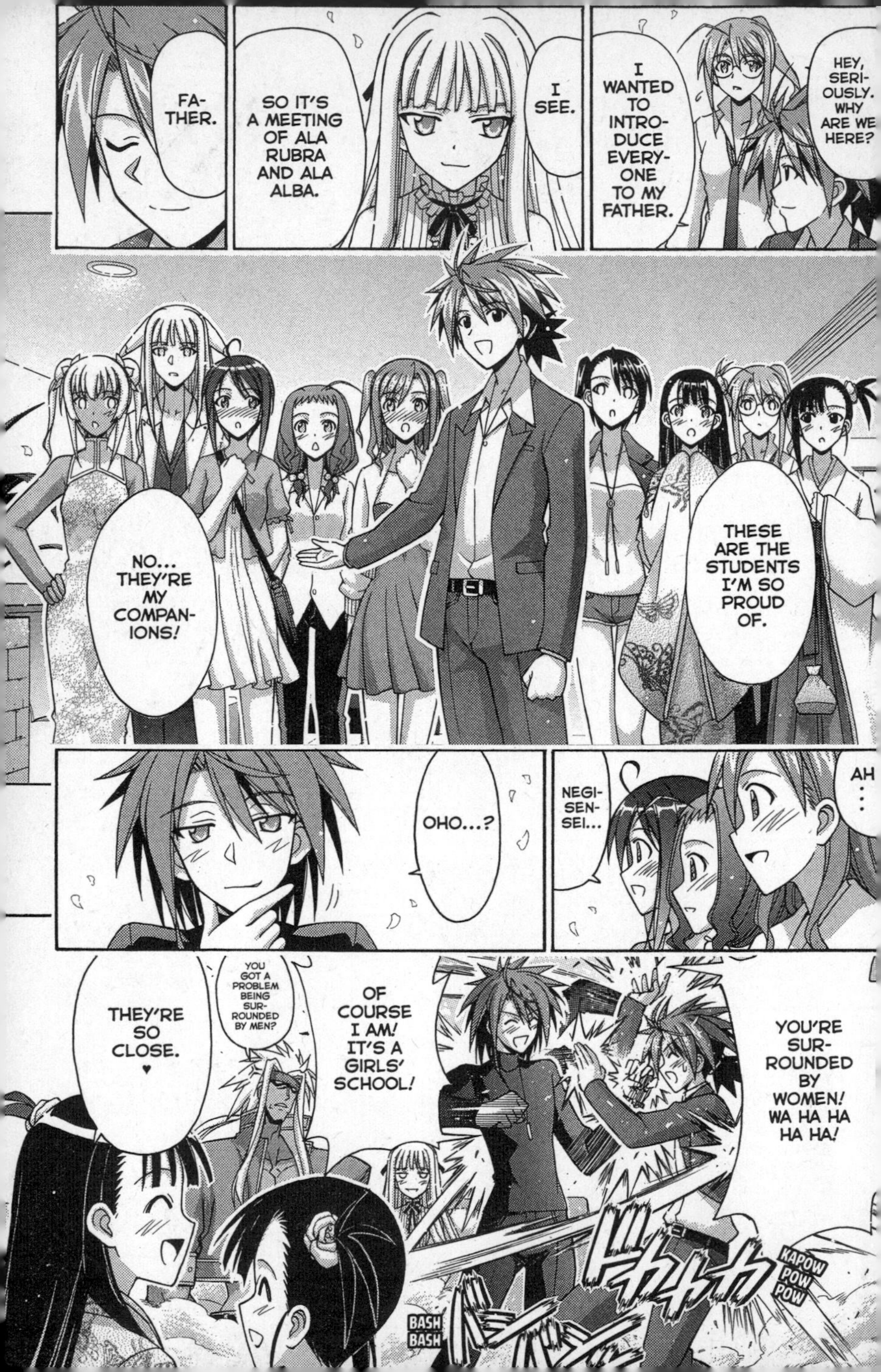
HEY, SERIOUSLY. WHY ARE WE HERE?
I WANTED TO INTRODUCE EVERYONE TO MY FATHER.
I SEE.
SO IT'S A MEETING OF ALA RUBRA AND ALA ALBA.
FATHER.
THESE ARE THE STUDENTS I'M SO PROUD OF.
NO... THEY'RE MY COMPANIONS!
AH...
NEGI-SENSEI...
OHO...?
YOU'RE SURROUNDED BY WOMEN! WA HA HA HA HA!
KAPOW POW POW
OF COURSE I AM! IT'S A GIRLS' SCHOOL!
YOU GOT A PROBLEM BEING SURROUNDED BY MEN?
THEY'RE SO CLOSE. ♥
BASH BASH

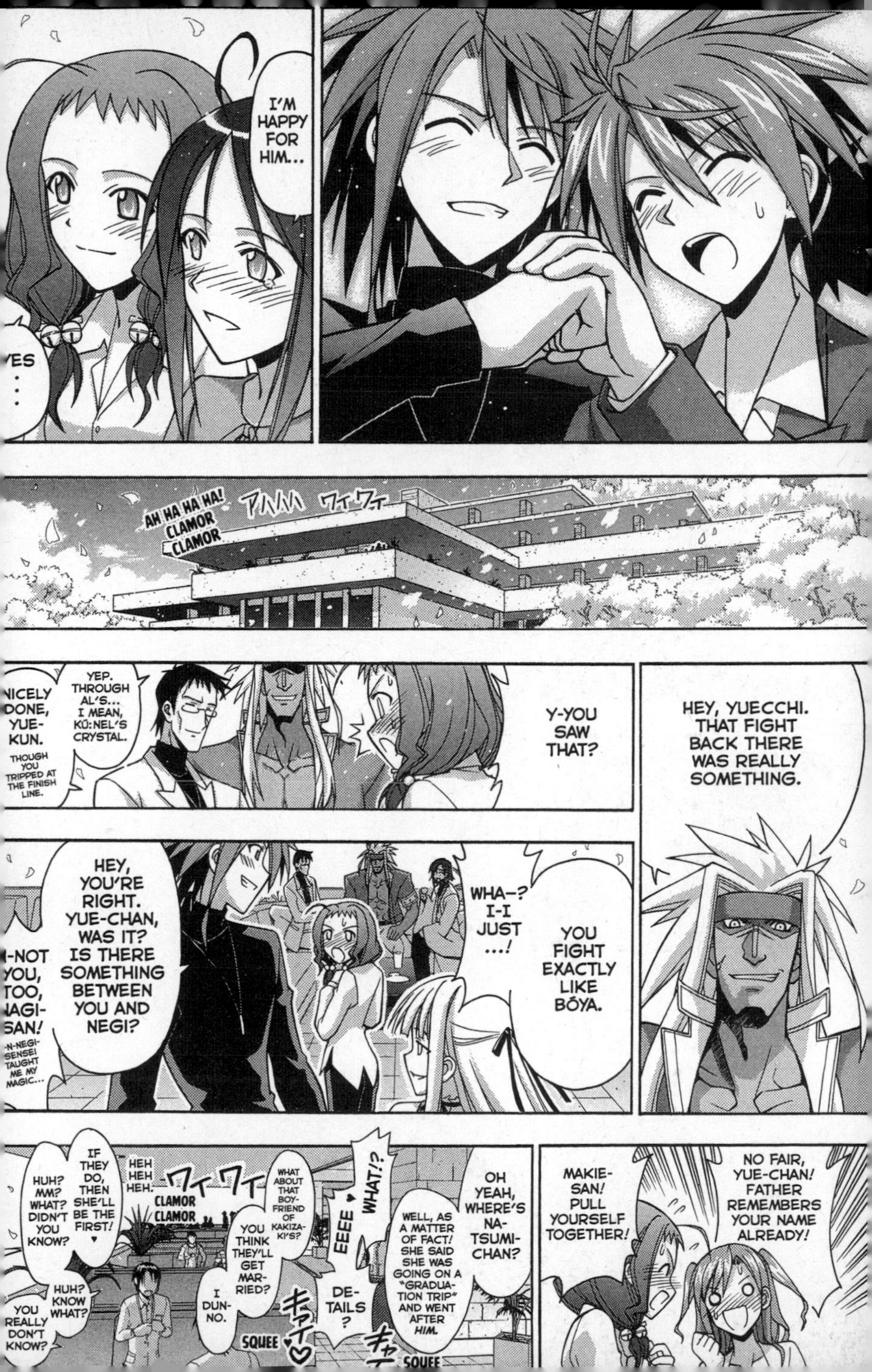
I'M HAPPY FOR HIM...
YES ...
AH HA HA HA!
CLAMOR
CLAMOR
HEY, YUECCHI. THAT FIGHT BACK THERE WAS REALLY SOMETHING.
Y-YOU SAW THAT?
YEP. THROUGH AL'S... I MEAN, KŪ:NEL'S CRYSTAL.
NICELY DONE, YUE-KUN.
THOUGH YOU TRIPPED AT THE FINISH LINE.
YOU FIGHT EXACTLY LIKE BŌYA.
WHA-? I-I JUST ...!
HEY, YOU'RE RIGHT. YUE-CHAN, WAS IT? IS THERE SOMETHING BETWEEN YOU AND NEGI?
N-NOT YOU, TOO, NAGI-SAN!
N-NEGI-SENSEI TAUGHT ME MY MAGIC...
NO FAIR, YUE-CHAN! FATHER REMEMBERS YOUR NAME ALREADY!
MAKIE-SAN! PULL YOURSELF TOGETHER!
OH YEAH, WHERE'S NATSUMI-CHAN?
WELL, AS A MATTER OF FACT! SHE SAID SHE WAS GOING ON A "GRADUATION TRIP" AND WENT AFTER HIM.
WHAT!?
EEEE ♥
DETAILS?
SQUEE
SQUEE
WHAT ABOUT THAT BOYFRIEND OF KAKIZAKI'S?
YOU THINK THEY'LL GET MARRIED?
I DUNNO.
HEH HEH HEH.
CLAMOR
CLAMOR
IF THEY DO, THEN SHE'LL BE THE FIRST! ♥
HUH? MM? WHAT? DIDN'T YOU KNOW?
HUH? KNOW WHAT?
YOU REALLY DON'T KNOW?

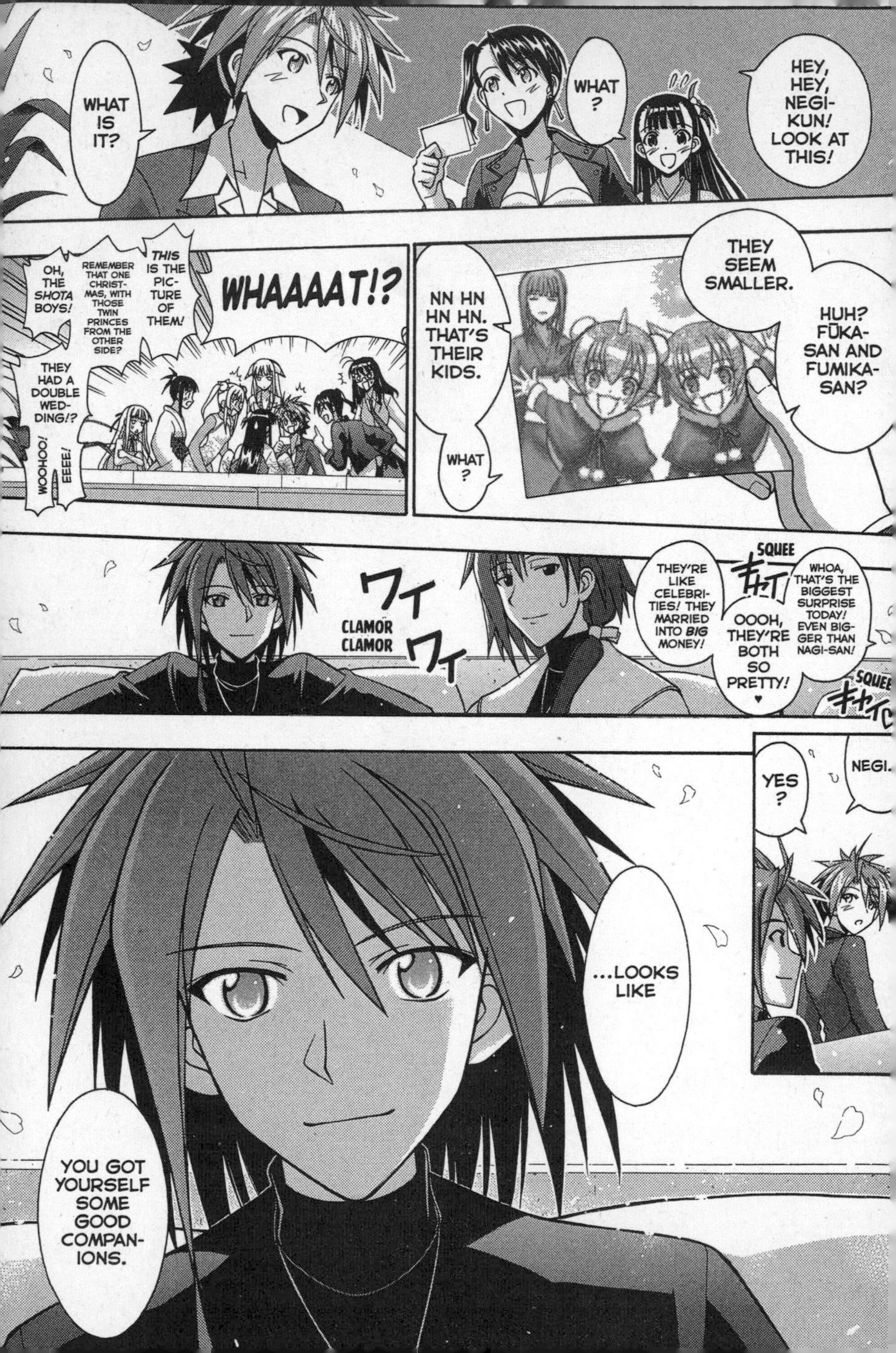

HEY, HEY, NEGI-KUN! LOOK AT THIS!
WHAT?
WHAT IS IT?
THEY SEEM SMALLER.
HUH? FŪKA-SAN AND FUMIKA-SAN?
NN HN HN HN. THAT'S THEIR KIDS.
WHAT?
WHAAAAT!?
THIS IS THE PICTURE OF THEM!
REMEMBER THAT ONE CHRISTMAS, WITH THOSE TWIN PRINCES FROM THE OTHER SIDE?
OH, THE *SHOTA* BOYS!
THEY HAD A DOUBLE WEDDING!?
EEEE!
WOOHOO!
SQUEE
WHOA, THAT'S THE BIGGEST SURPRISE TODAY! EVEN BIGGER THAN NAGI-SAN!
OOOH, THEY'RE BOTH SO PRETTY! ♥
SQUEE
THEY'RE LIKE CELEBRITIES! THEY MARRIED INTO *BIG* MONEY!
CLAMOR CLAMOR
NEGI.
YES?
...LOOKS LIKE
YOU GOT YOURSELF SOME GOOD COMPANIONS.

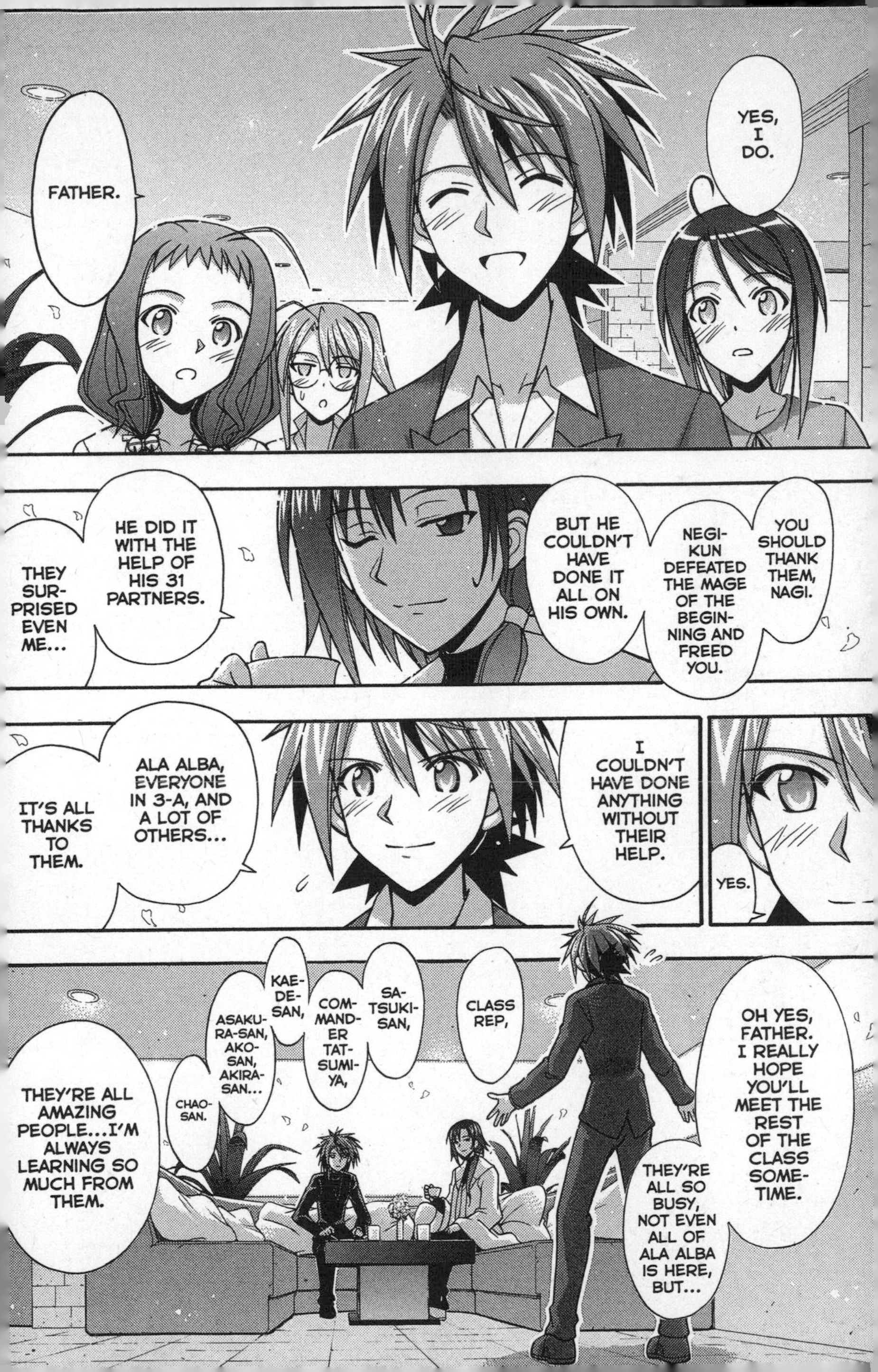
YES, I DO.
FATHER.
YOU SHOULD THANK THEM, NAGI.
NEGI-KUN DEFEATED THE MAGE OF THE BEGIN-NING AND FREED YOU.
BUT HE COULDN'T HAVE DONE IT ALL ON HIS OWN.
HE DID IT WITH THE HELP OF HIS 31 PARTNERS.
THEY SUR-PRISED EVEN ME...
YES.
I COULDN'T HAVE DONE ANYTHING WITHOUT THEIR HELP.
ALA ALBA, EVERYONE IN 3-A, AND A LOT OF OTHERS...
IT'S ALL THANKS TO THEM.
OH YES, FATHER. I REALLY HOPE YOU'LL MEET THE REST OF THE CLASS SOME-TIME.
THEY'RE ALL SO BUSY, NOT EVEN ALL OF ALA ALBA IS HERE, BUT...
CLASS REP,
SA-TSUKI-SAN,
COM-MAND-ER TAT-SUMI-YA,
KAE-DE-SAN,
ASAKU-RA-SAN, AKO-SAN, AKIRA-SAN...
CHAO-SAN.
THEY'RE ALL AMAZING PEOPLE...I'M ALWAYS LEARNING SO MUCH FROM THEM.

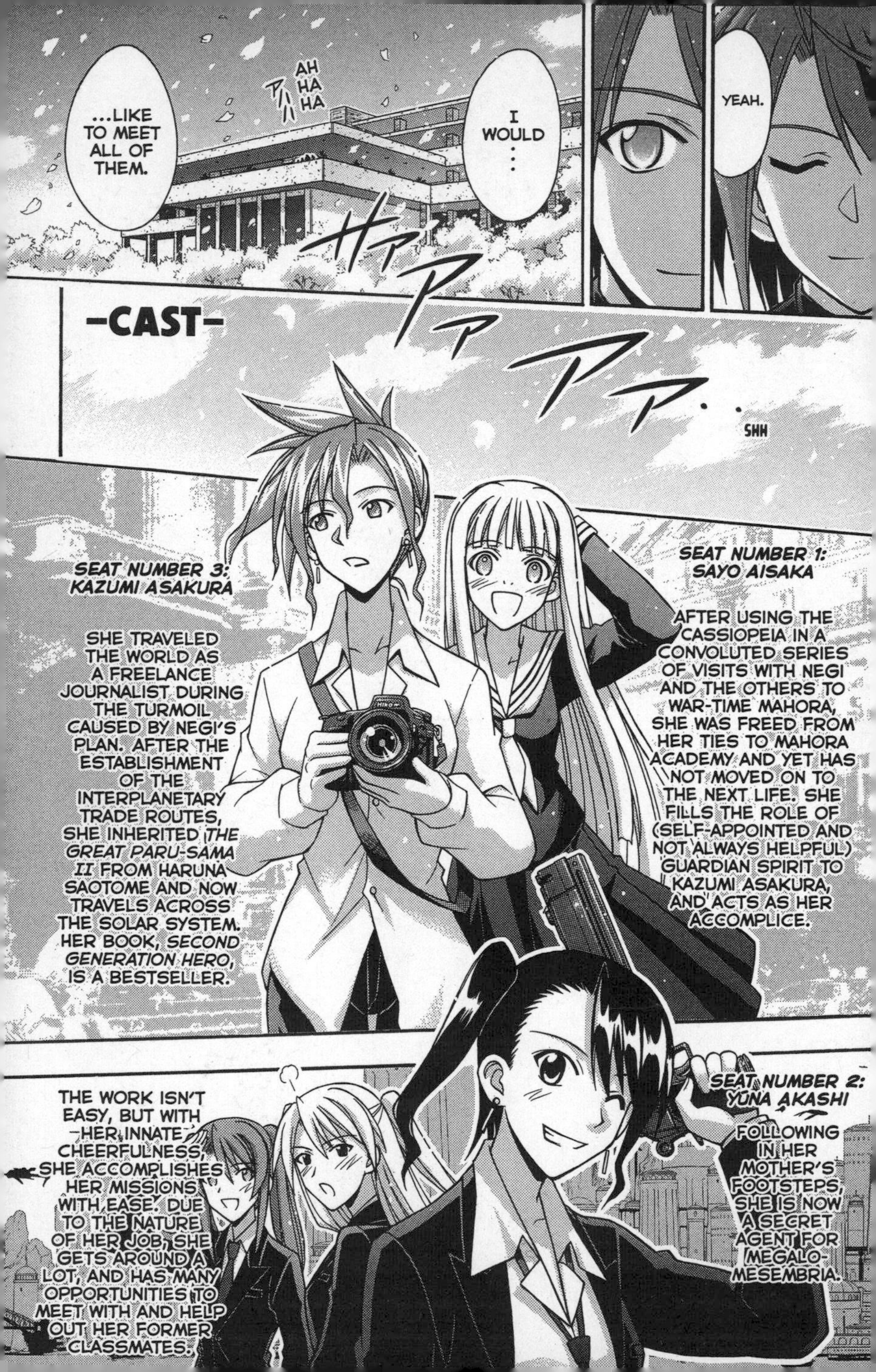
YEAH.
I WOULD ...
AH HA HA
...LIKE TO MEET ALL OF THEM.
SHH
-CAST-
SEAT NUMBER 1: SAYO AISAKA
AFTER USING THE CASSIOPEIA IN A CONVOLUTED SERIES OF VISITS WITH NEGI AND THE OTHERS TO WAR-TIME MAHORA, SHE WAS FREED FROM HER TIES TO MAHORA ACADEMY AND YET HAS NOT MOVED ON TO THE NEXT LIFE. SHE FILLS THE ROLE OF (SELF-APPOINTED AND NOT ALWAYS HELPFUL) GUARDIAN SPIRIT TO KAZUMI ASAKURA, AND ACTS AS HER ACCOMPLICE.
SEAT NUMBER 3: KAZUMI ASAKURA
SHE TRAVELED THE WORLD AS A FREELANCE JOURNALIST DURING THE TURMOIL CAUSED BY NEGI'S PLAN. AFTER THE ESTABLISHMENT OF THE INTERPLANETARY TRADE ROUTES, SHE INHERITED *THE GREAT PARU-SAMA II* FROM HARUNA SAOTOME AND NOW TRAVELS ACROSS THE SOLAR SYSTEM. HER BOOK, *SECOND GENERATION HERO*, IS A BESTSELLER.
SEAT NUMBER 2: YUNA AKASHI
FOLLOWING IN HER MOTHER'S FOOTSTEPS, SHE IS NOW A SECRET AGENT FOR MEGALO-MESEMBRIA.
THE WORK ISN'T EASY, BUT WITH HER INNATE CHEERFULNESS, SHE ACCOMPLISHES HER MISSIONS WITH EASE. DUE TO THE NATURE OF HER JOB, SHE GETS AROUND A LOT, AND HAS MANY OPPORTUNITIES TO MEET WITH AND HELP OUT HER FORMER CLASSMATES.

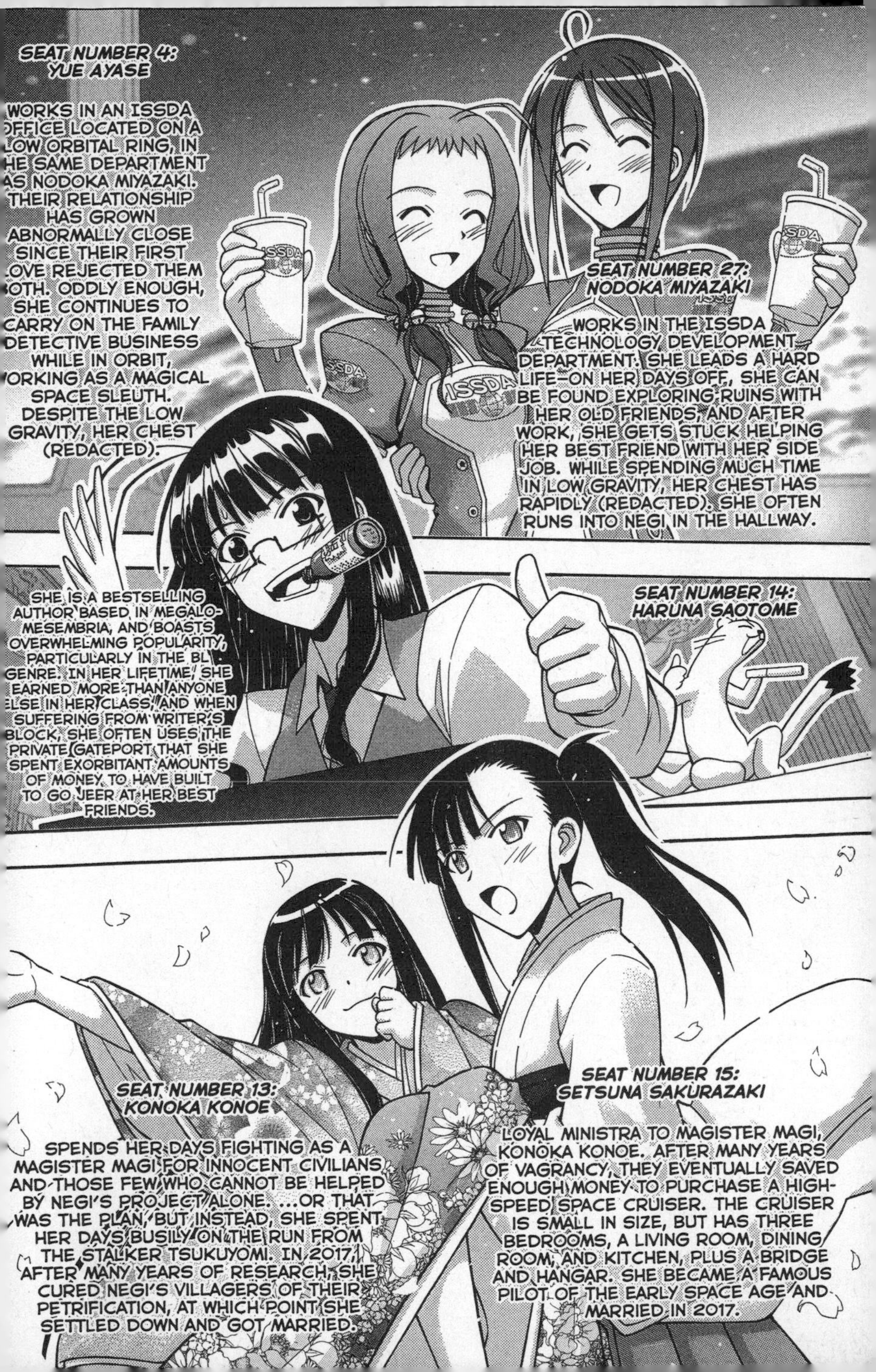
SEAT NUMBER 4:
YUE AYASE
WORKS IN AN ISSDA FFICE LOCATED ON A LOW ORBITAL RING, IN HE SAME DEPARTMENT AS NODOKA MIYAZAKI. THEIR RELATIONSHIP HAS GROWN ABNORMALLY CLOSE SINCE THEIR FIRST OVE REJECTED THEM OTH. ODDLY ENOUGH, SHE CONTINUES TO CARRY ON THE FAMILY DETECTIVE BUSINESS WHILE IN ORBIT, ORKING AS A MAGICAL SPACE SLEUTH. DESPITE THE LOW GRAVITY, HER CHEST (REDACTED).
SEAT NUMBER 27:
NODOKA MIYAZAKI
WORKS IN THE ISSDA TECHNOLOGY DEVELOPMENT DEPARTMENT. SHE LEADS A HARD LIFE—ON HER DAYS OFF, SHE CAN BE FOUND EXPLORING RUINS WITH HER OLD FRIENDS, AND AFTER WORK, SHE GETS STUCK HELPING HER BEST FRIEND WITH HER SIDE JOB. WHILE SPENDING MUCH TIME IN LOW GRAVITY, HER CHEST HAS RAPIDLY (REDACTED). SHE OFTEN RUNS INTO NEGI IN THE HALLWAY.
ISSDA
SEAT NUMBER 14:
HARUNA SAOTOME
SHE IS A BESTSELLING AUTHOR BASED IN MEGALO-MESEMBRIA, AND BOASTS OVERWHELMING POPULARITY, PARTICULARLY IN THE BL GENRE. IN HER LIFETIME, SHE EARNED MORE THAN ANYONE LSE IN HER CLASS, AND WHEN SUFFERING FROM WRITER'S BLOCK, SHE OFTEN USES THE PRIVATE GATEPORT THAT SHE SPENT EXORBITANT AMOUNTS OF MONEY TO HAVE BUILT TO GO JEER AT HER BEST FRIENDS.
SEAT NUMBER 15:
SETSUNA SAKURAZAKI
LOYAL MINISTRA TO MAGISTER MAGI, KONOKA KONOE. AFTER MANY YEARS OF VAGRANCY, THEY EVENTUALLY SAVED ENOUGH MONEY TO PURCHASE A HIGH-SPEED SPACE CRUISER. THE CRUISER IS SMALL IN SIZE, BUT HAS THREE BEDROOMS, A LIVING ROOM, DINING ROOM, AND KITCHEN, PLUS A BRIDGE AND HANGAR. SHE BECAME A FAMOUS PILOT OF THE EARLY SPACE AGE AND MARRIED IN 2017.
SEAT NUMBER 13:
KONOKA KONOE
SPENDS HER DAYS FIGHTING AS A MAGISTER MAGI FOR INNOCENT CIVILIANS AND THOSE FEW WHO CANNOT BE HELPED BY NEGI'S PROJECT ALONE. ...OR THAT WAS THE PLAN, BUT INSTEAD, SHE SPENT HER DAYS BUSILY ON THE RUN FROM THE STALKER TSUKUYOMI. IN 2017, AFTER MANY YEARS OF RESEARCH, SHE CURED NEGI'S VILLAGERS OF THEIR PETRIFICATION, AT WHICH POINT SHE SETTLED DOWN AND GOT MARRIED.

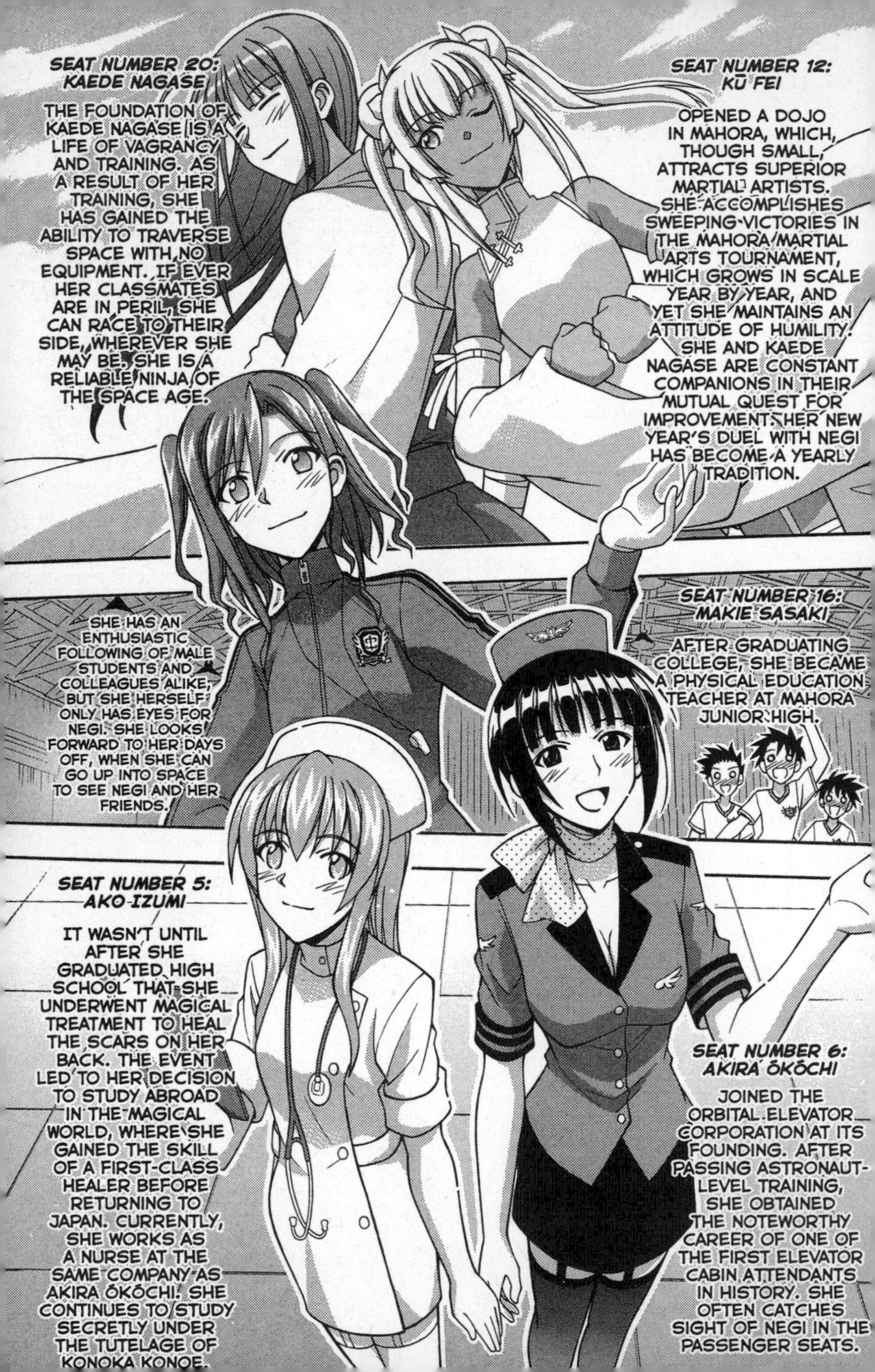
SEAT NUMBER 12: KŪ FEI
OPENED A DOJO IN MAHORA, WHICH, THOUGH SMALL, ATTRACTS SUPERIOR MARTIAL ARTISTS. SHE ACCOMPLISHES SWEEPING VICTORIES IN THE MAHORA MARTIAL ARTS TOURNAMENT, WHICH GROWS IN SCALE YEAR BY YEAR, AND YET SHE MAINTAINS AN ATTITUDE OF HUMILITY. SHE AND KAEDE NAGASE ARE CONSTANT COMPANIONS IN THEIR MUTUAL QUEST FOR IMPROVEMENT. HER NEW YEAR'S DUEL WITH NEGI HAS BECOME A YEARLY TRADITION.
SEAT NUMBER 20: KAEDE NAGASE
THE FOUNDATION OF KAEDE NAGASE IS A LIFE OF VAGRANCY AND TRAINING. AS A RESULT OF HER TRAINING, SHE HAS GAINED THE ABILITY TO TRAVERSE SPACE WITH NO EQUIPMENT. IF EVER HER CLASSMATES ARE IN PERIL, SHE CAN RACE TO THEIR SIDE, WHEREVER SHE MAY BE. SHE IS A RELIABLE NINJA OF THE SPACE AGE.
SEAT NUMBER 16: MAKIE SASAKI
AFTER GRADUATING COLLEGE, SHE BECAME A PHYSICAL EDUCATION TEACHER AT MAHORA JUNIOR HIGH.
SHE HAS AN ENTHUSIASTIC FOLLOWING OF MALE STUDENTS AND COLLEAGUES ALIKE, BUT SHE HERSELF ONLY HAS EYES FOR NEGI. SHE LOOKS FORWARD TO HER DAYS OFF, WHEN SHE CAN GO UP INTO SPACE TO SEE NEGI AND HER FRIENDS.
SEAT NUMBER 6: AKIRA ŌKŌCHI
JOINED THE ORBITAL ELEVATOR CORPORATION AT ITS FOUNDING. AFTER PASSING ASTRONAUT-LEVEL TRAINING, SHE OBTAINED THE NOTEWORTHY CAREER OF ONE OF THE FIRST ELEVATOR CABIN ATTENDANTS IN HISTORY. SHE OFTEN CATCHES SIGHT OF NEGI IN THE PASSENGER SEATS.
SEAT NUMBER 5: AKO IZUMI
IT WASN'T UNTIL AFTER SHE GRADUATED HIGH SCHOOL THAT SHE UNDERWENT MAGICAL TREATMENT TO HEAL THE SCARS ON HER BACK. THE EVENT LED TO HER DECISION TO STUDY ABROAD IN THE MAGICAL WORLD, WHERE SHE GAINED THE SKILL OF A FIRST-CLASS HEALER BEFORE RETURNING TO JAPAN. CURRENTLY, SHE WORKS AS A NURSE AT THE SAME COMPANY AS AKIRA ŌKŌCHI. SHE CONTINUES TO STUDY SECRETLY UNDER THE TUTELAGE OF KONOKA KONOE.

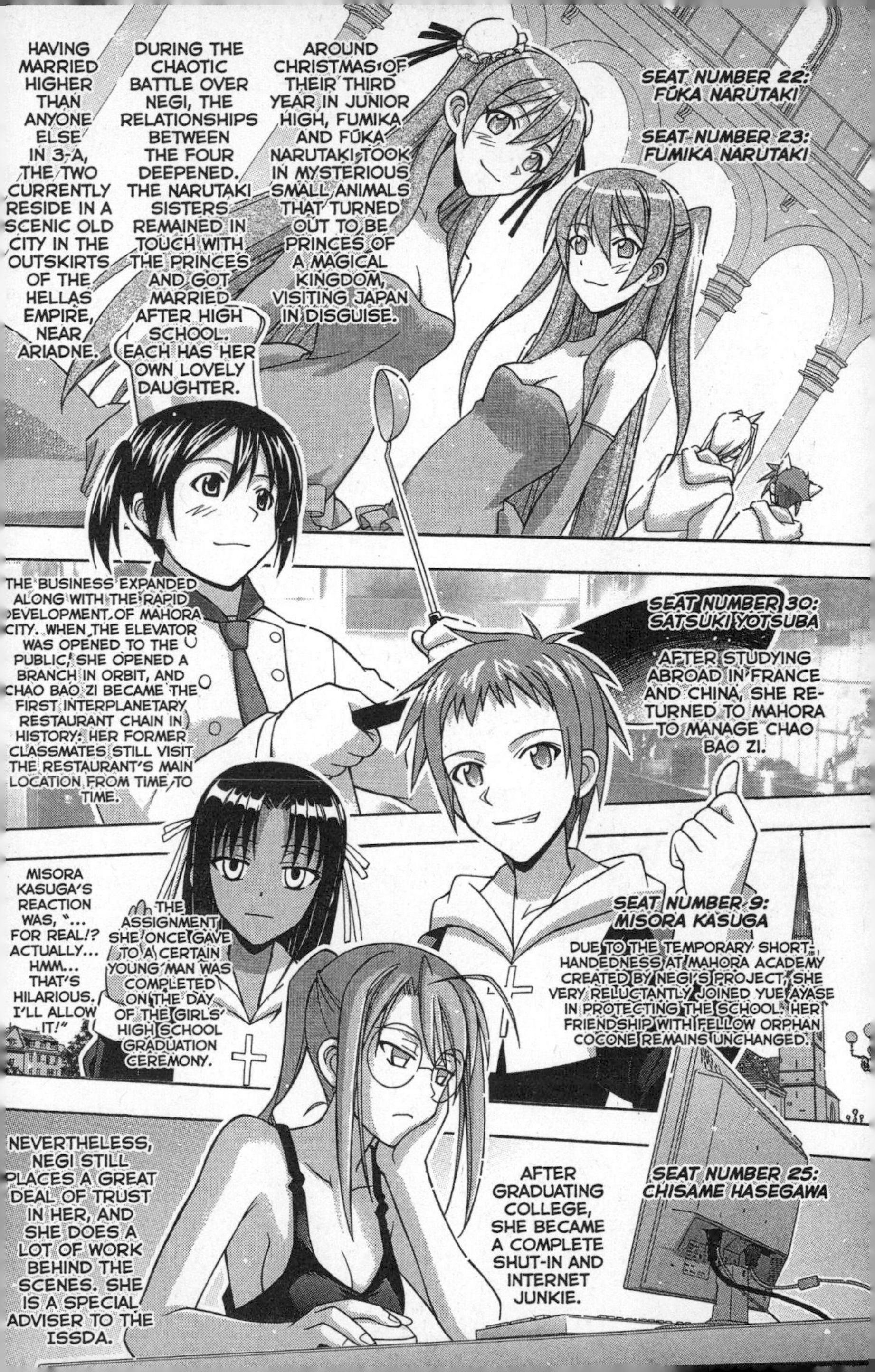
SEAT NUMBER 22: FŪKA NARUTAKI
SEAT NUMBER 23: FUMIKA NARUTAKI
AROUND CHRISTMAS OF THEIR THIRD YEAR IN JUNIOR HIGH, FUMIKA AND FŪKA NARUTAKI TOOK IN MYSTERIOUS SMALL ANIMALS THAT TURNED OUT TO BE PRINCES OF A MAGICAL KINGDOM, VISITING JAPAN IN DISGUISE.
DURING THE CHAOTIC BATTLE OVER NEGI, THE RELATIONSHIPS BETWEEN THE FOUR DEEPENED. THE NARUTAKI SISTERS REMAINED IN TOUCH WITH THE PRINCES AND GOT MARRIED AFTER HIGH SCHOOL. EACH HAS HER OWN LOVELY DAUGHTER.
HAVING MARRIED HIGHER THAN ANYONE ELSE IN 3-A, THE TWO CURRENTLY RESIDE IN A SCENIC OLD CITY IN THE OUTSKIRTS OF THE HELLAS EMPIRE, NEAR ARIADNE.
SEAT NUMBER 30: SATSUKI YOTSUBA
AFTER STUDYING ABROAD IN FRANCE AND CHINA, SHE RETURNED TO MAHORA TO MANAGE CHAO BAO ZI.
THE BUSINESS EXPANDED ALONG WITH THE RAPID DEVELOPMENT OF MAHORA CITY. WHEN THE ELEVATOR WAS OPENED TO THE PUBLIC, SHE OPENED A BRANCH IN ORBIT, AND CHAO BAO ZI BECAME THE FIRST INTERPLANETARY RESTAURANT CHAIN IN HISTORY. HER FORMER CLASSMATES STILL VISIT THE RESTAURANT'S MAIN LOCATION FROM TIME TO TIME.
SEAT NUMBER 9: MISORA KASUGA
DUE TO THE TEMPORARY SHORT-HANDEDNESS AT MAHORA ACADEMY CREATED BY NEGI'S PROJECT, SHE VERY RELUCTANTLY JOINED YUE AYASE IN PROTECTING THE SCHOOL. HER FRIENDSHIP WITH FELLOW ORPHAN COCONE REMAINS UNCHANGED.
THE ASSIGNMENT SHE ONCE GAVE TO A CERTAIN YOUNG MAN WAS COMPLETED ON THE DAY OF THE GIRLS' HIGH SCHOOL GRADUATION CEREMONY.
MISORA KASUGA'S REACTION WAS, "...FOR REAL!? ACTUALLY... HMM... THAT'S HILARIOUS. I'LL ALLOW IT!"
SEAT NUMBER 25: CHISAME HASEGAWA
AFTER GRADUATING COLLEGE, SHE BECAME A COMPLETE SHUT-IN AND INTERNET JUNKIE.
NEVERTHELESS, NEGI STILL PLACES A GREAT DEAL OF TRUST IN HER, AND SHE DOES A LOT OF WORK BEHIND THE SCENES. SHE IS A SPECIAL ADVISER TO THE ISSDA.

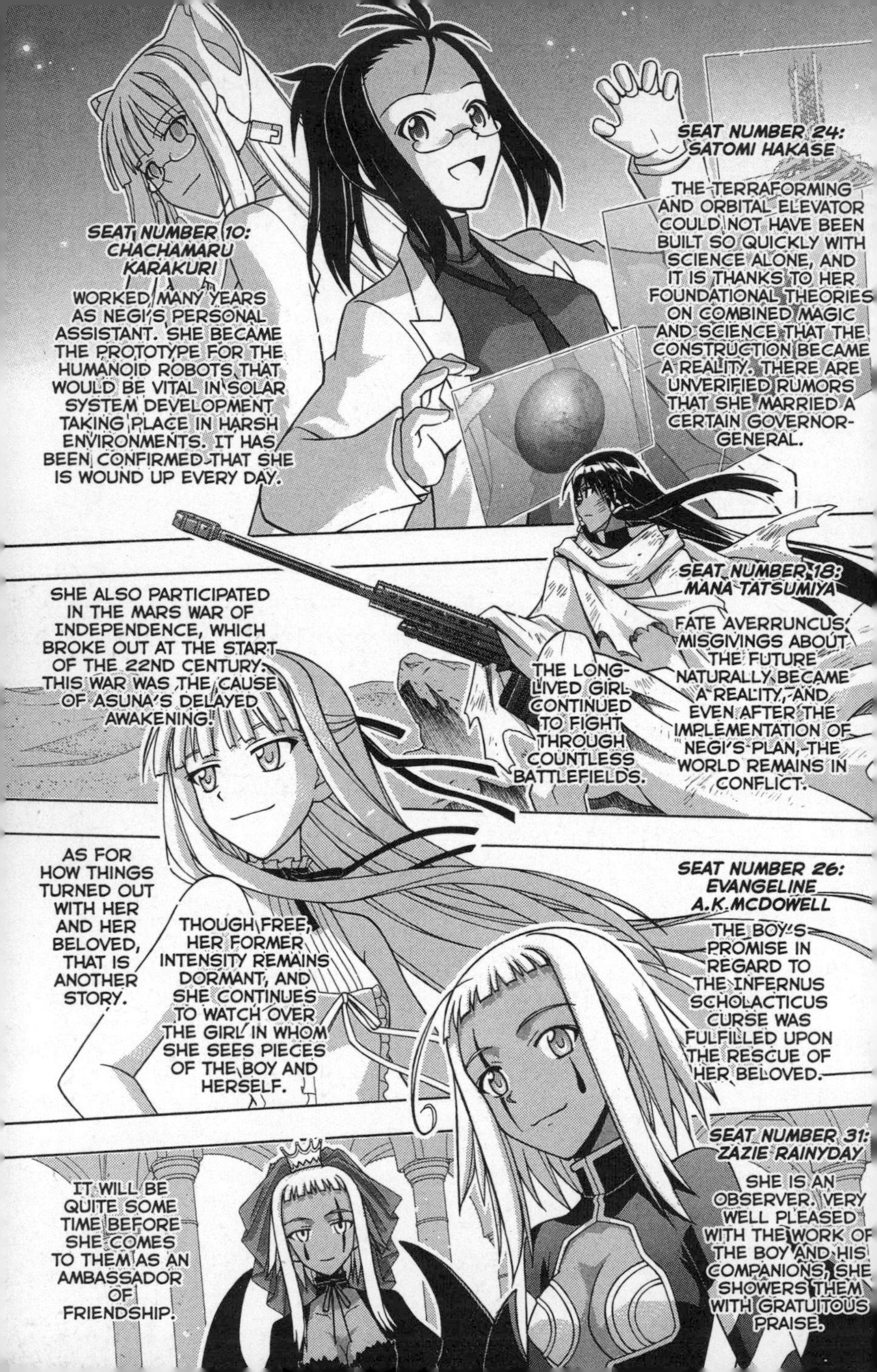
SEAT NUMBER 24: SATOMI HAKASE
THE TERRAFORMING AND ORBITAL ELEVATOR COULD NOT HAVE BEEN BUILT SO QUICKLY WITH SCIENCE ALONE, AND IT IS THANKS TO HER FOUNDATIONAL THEORIES ON COMBINED MAGIC AND SCIENCE THAT THE CONSTRUCTION BECAME A REALITY. THERE ARE UNVERIFIED RUMORS THAT SHE MARRIED A CERTAIN GOVERNOR-GENERAL.
SEAT NUMBER 10: CHACHAMARU KARAKURI
WORKED MANY YEARS AS NEGI'S PERSONAL ASSISTANT. SHE BECAME THE PROTOTYPE FOR THE HUMANOID ROBOTS THAT WOULD BE VITAL IN SOLAR SYSTEM DEVELOPMENT TAKING PLACE IN HARSH ENVIRONMENTS. IT HAS BEEN CONFIRMED THAT SHE IS WOUND UP EVERY DAY.
SEAT NUMBER 18: MANA TATSUMIYA
FATE AVERRUNCUS' MISGIVINGS ABOUT THE FUTURE NATURALLY BECAME A REALITY, AND EVEN AFTER THE IMPLEMENTATION OF NEGI'S PLAN, THE WORLD REMAINS IN CONFLICT.
THE LONG-LIVED GIRL CONTINUED TO FIGHT THROUGH COUNTLESS BATTLEFIELDS.
SHE ALSO PARTICIPATED IN THE MARS WAR OF INDEPENDENCE, WHICH BROKE OUT AT THE START OF THE 22ND CENTURY. THIS WAR WAS THE CAUSE OF ASUNA'S DELAYED AWAKENING.
SEAT NUMBER 26: EVANGELINE A.K.MCDOWELL
THE BOY'S PROMISE IN REGARD TO THE INFERNUS SCHOLACTICUS CURSE WAS FULFILLED UPON THE RESCUE OF HER BELOVED.
THOUGH FREE, HER FORMER INTENSITY REMAINS DORMANT, AND SHE CONTINUES TO WATCH OVER THE GIRL IN WHOM SHE SEES PIECES OF THE BOY AND HERSELF.
AS FOR HOW THINGS TURNED OUT WITH HER AND HER BELOVED, THAT IS ANOTHER STORY.
SEAT NUMBER 31: ZAZIE RAINYDAY
SHE IS AN OBSERVER. VERY WELL PLEASED WITH THE WORK OF THE BOY AND HIS COMPANIONS, SHE SHOWERS THEM WITH GRATUITOUS PRAISE.
IT WILL BE QUITE SOME TIME BEFORE SHE COMES TO THEM AS AN AMBASSADOR OF FRIENDSHIP.

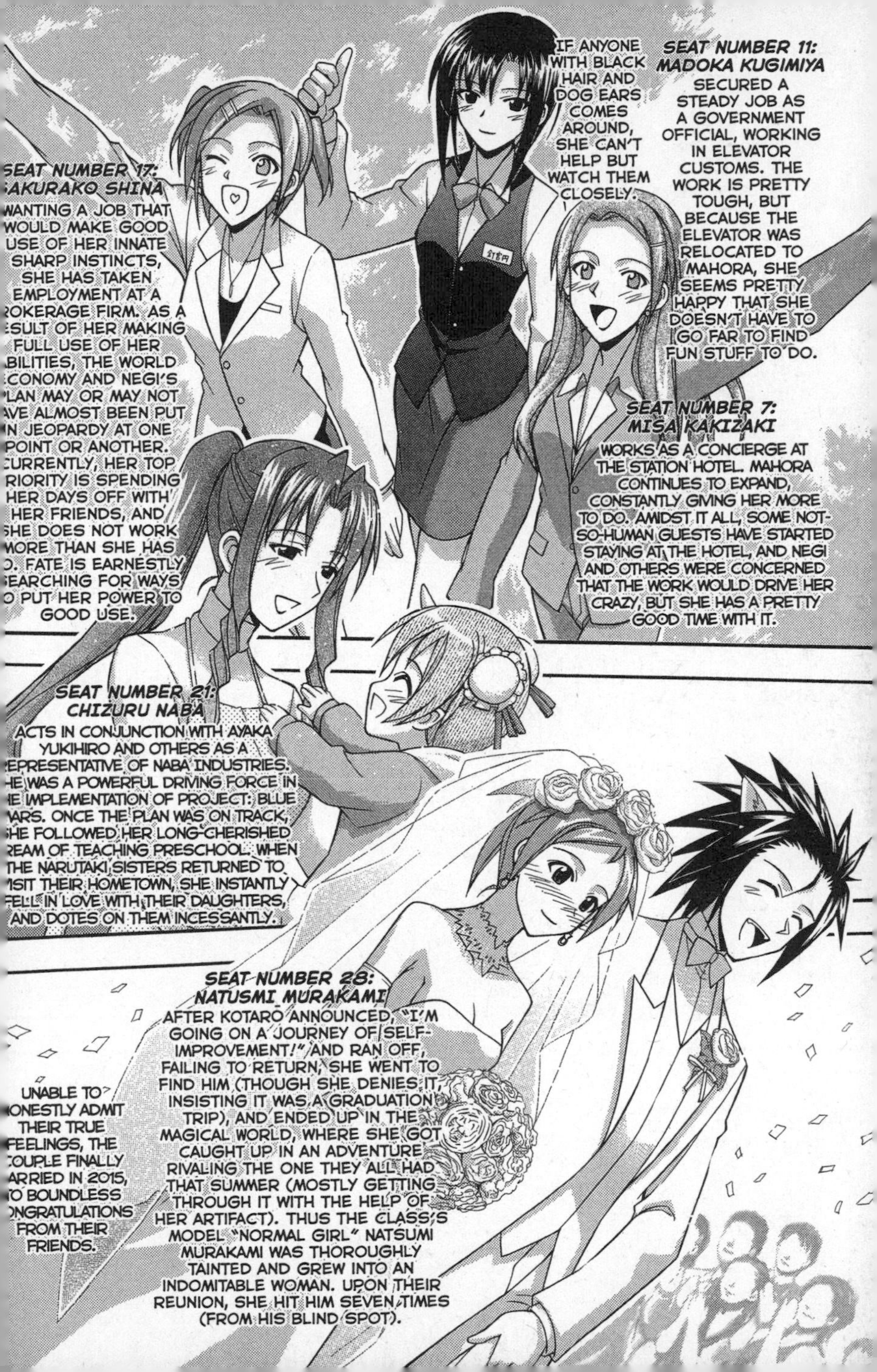
SEAT NUMBER 11: MADOKA KUGIMIYA
SECURED A STEADY JOB AS A GOVERNMENT OFFICIAL, WORKING IN ELEVATOR CUSTOMS. THE WORK IS PRETTY TOUGH, BUT BECAUSE THE ELEVATOR WAS RELOCATED TO MAHORA, SHE SEEMS PRETTY HAPPY THAT SHE DOESN'T HAVE TO GO FAR TO FIND FUN STUFF TO DO.
IF ANYONE WITH BLACK HAIR AND DOG EARS COMES AROUND, SHE CAN'T HELP BUT WATCH THEM CLOSELY.
SEAT NUMBER 7: MISA KAKIZAKI
WORKS AS A CONCIERGE AT THE STATION HOTEL. MAHORA CONTINUES TO EXPAND, CONSTANTLY GIVING HER MORE TO DO. AMIDST IT ALL, SOME NOT-SO-HUMAN GUESTS HAVE STARTED STAYING AT THE HOTEL, AND NEGI AND OTHERS WERE CONCERNED THAT THE WORK WOULD DRIVE HER CRAZY, BUT SHE HAS A PRETTY GOOD TIME WITH IT.
SEAT NUMBER 17: AKURAKO SHINA
WANTING A JOB THAT WOULD MAKE GOOD USE OF HER INNATE SHARP INSTINCTS, SHE HAS TAKEN EMPLOYMENT AT A ROKERAGE FIRM. AS A ESULT OF HER MAKING FULL USE OF HER ABILITIES, THE WORLD ECONOMY AND NEGI'S PLAN MAY OR MAY NOT AVE ALMOST BEEN PUT N JEOPARDY AT ONE POINT OR ANOTHER. CURRENTLY, HER TOP RIORITY IS SPENDING HER DAYS OFF WITH HER FRIENDS, AND HE DOES NOT WORK MORE THAN SHE HAS O. FATE IS EARNESTLY EARCHING FOR WAYS O PUT HER POWER TO GOOD USE.
SEAT NUMBER 21: CHIZURU NABA
ACTS IN CONJUNCTION WITH AYAKA YUKIHIRO AND OTHERS AS A REPRESENTATIVE OF NABA INDUSTRIES. HE WAS A POWERFUL DRIVING FORCE IN E IMPLEMENTATION OF PROJECT: BLUE ARS. ONCE THE PLAN WAS ON TRACK, HE FOLLOWED HER LONG-CHERISHED REAM OF TEACHING PRESCHOOL. WHEN THE NARUTAKI SISTERS RETURNED TO VISIT THEIR HOMETOWN, SHE INSTANTLY FELL IN LOVE WITH THEIR DAUGHTERS, AND DOTES ON THEM INCESSANTLY.
SEAT NUMBER 28: NATUSMI MURAKAMI
AFTER KOTARO ANNOUNCED, "I'M GOING ON A JOURNEY OF SELF-IMPROVEMENT!" AND RAN OFF, FAILING TO RETURN, SHE WENT TO FIND HIM (THOUGH SHE DENIES IT, INSISTING IT WAS A GRADUATION TRIP), AND ENDED UP IN THE MAGICAL WORLD, WHERE SHE GOT CAUGHT UP IN AN ADVENTURE RIVALING THE ONE THEY ALL HAD THAT SUMMER (MOSTLY GETTING THROUGH IT WITH THE HELP OF HER ARTIFACT). THUS THE CLASS'S MODEL "NORMAL GIRL" NATSUMI MURAKAMI WAS THOROUGHLY TAINTED AND GREW INTO AN INDOMITABLE WOMAN. UPON THEIR REUNION, SHE HIT HIM SEVEN TIMES (FROM HIS BLIND SPOT).
UNABLE TO ONESTLY ADMIT THEIR TRUE FEELINGS, THE COUPLE FINALLY ARRIED IN 2015, TO BOUNDLESS ONGRATULATIONS FROM THEIR FRIENDS.

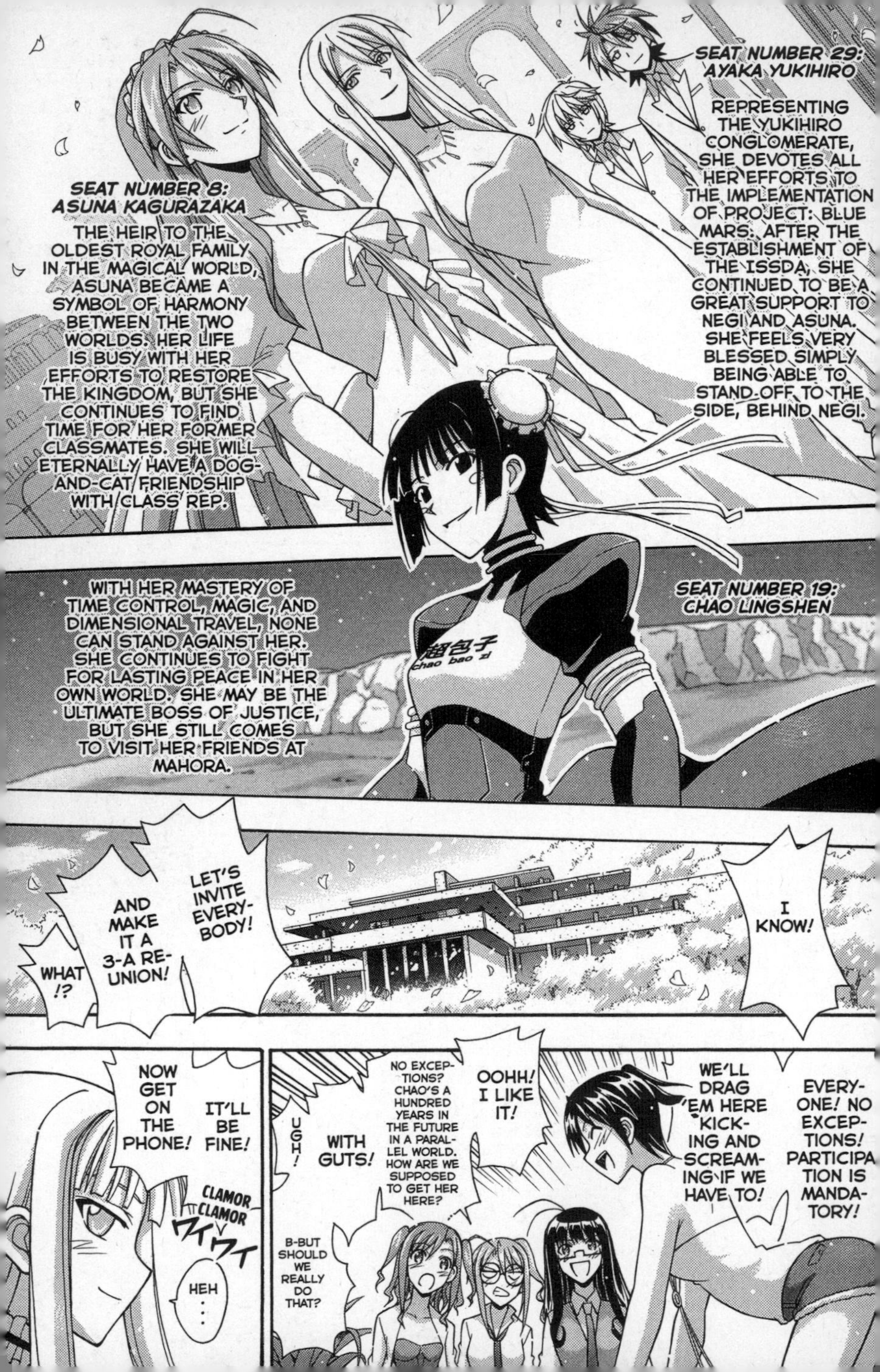
SEAT NUMBER 29: AYAKA YUKIHIRO
REPRESENTING THE YUKIHIRO CONGLOMERATE, SHE DEVOTES ALL HER EFFORTS TO THE IMPLEMENTATION OF PROJECT: BLUE MARS. AFTER THE ESTABLISHMENT OF THE ISSDA, SHE CONTINUED TO BE A GREAT SUPPORT TO NEGI AND ASUNA. SHE FEELS VERY BLESSED SIMPLY BEING ABLE TO STAND OFF TO THE SIDE, BEHIND NEGI.
SEAT NUMBER 8: ASUNA KAGURAZAKA
THE HEIR TO THE OLDEST ROYAL FAMILY IN THE MAGICAL WORLD, ASUNA BECAME A SYMBOL OF HARMONY BETWEEN THE TWO WORLDS. HER LIFE IS BUSY WITH HER EFFORTS TO RESTORE THE KINGDOM, BUT SHE CONTINUES TO FIND TIME FOR HER FORMER CLASSMATES. SHE WILL ETERNALLY HAVE A DOG-AND-CAT FRIENDSHIP WITH CLASS REP.
SEAT NUMBER 19: CHAO LINGSHEN
超包子
chao bao zi
WITH HER MASTERY OF TIME CONTROL, MAGIC, AND DIMENSIONAL TRAVEL, NONE CAN STAND AGAINST HER. SHE CONTINUES TO FIGHT FOR LASTING PEACE IN HER OWN WORLD. SHE MAY BE THE ULTIMATE BOSS OF JUSTICE, BUT SHE STILL COMES TO VISIT HER FRIENDS AT MAHORA.
I KNOW!
LET'S INVITE EVERYBODY!
AND MAKE IT A 3-A REUNION!
WHAT!?
EVERYONE! NO EXCEPTIONS! PARTICIPATION IS MANDATORY!
WE'LL DRAG 'EM HERE KICKING AND SCREAMING IF WE HAVE TO!
OOHH! I LIKE IT!
NO EXCEPTIONS? CHAO'S A HUNDRED YEARS IN THE FUTURE IN A PARALLEL WORLD. HOW ARE WE SUPPOSED TO GET HER HERE?
WITH GUTS!
UGH!
B-BUT SHOULD WE REALLY DO THAT?
NOW GET ON THE PHONE!
IT'LL BE FINE!
CLAMOR CLAMOR
ワイワイ
HEH...

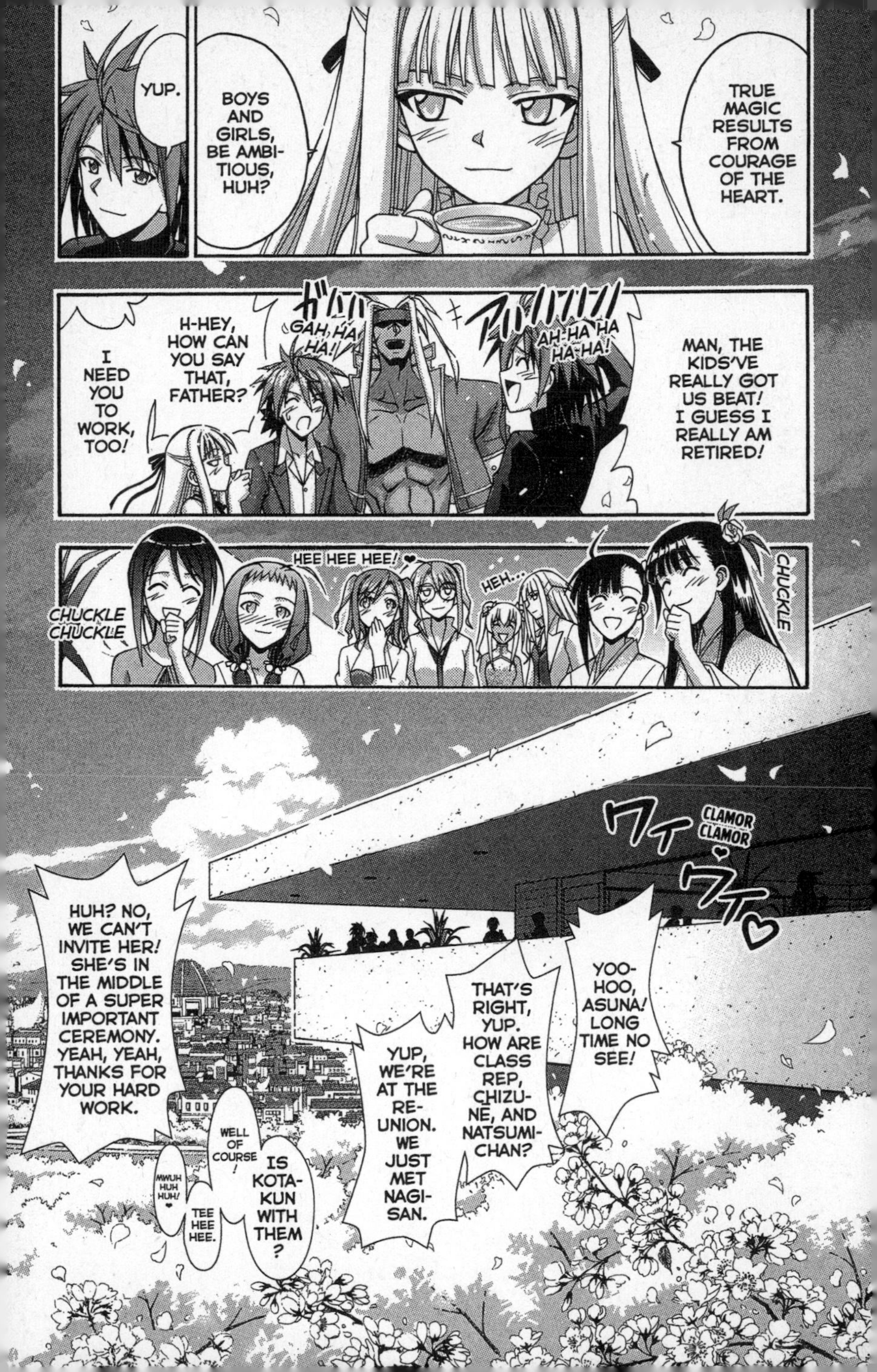
TRUE MAGIC RESULTS FROM COURAGE OF THE HEART.
BOYS AND GIRLS, BE AMBITIOUS, HUH?
YUP.
MAN, THE KIDS'VE REALLY GOT US BEAT! I GUESS I REALLY AM RETIRED!
AH-HA HA HA-HA!
GAH, HA HA!
H-HEY, HOW CAN YOU SAY THAT, FATHER?
I NEED YOU TO WORK, TOO!
CHUCKLE
HEH...
HEE HEE HEE! ♥
CHUCKLE CHUCKLE
CLAMOR CLAMOR ♥
YOO-HOO, ASUNA! LONG TIME NO SEE!
THAT'S RIGHT, YUP. HOW ARE CLASS REP, CHIZU-NE, AND NATSUMI-CHAN?
YUP, WE'RE AT THE RE-UNION. WE JUST MET NAGI-SAN.
IS KOTA-KUN WITH THEM?
WELL OF COURSE!
TEE HEE HEE.
MWUH HUH HUH! ♥
HUH? NO, WE CAN'T INVITE HER! SHE'S IN THE MIDDLE OF A SUPER IMPORTANT CEREMONY. YEAH, YEAH, THANKS FOR YOUR HARD WORK.

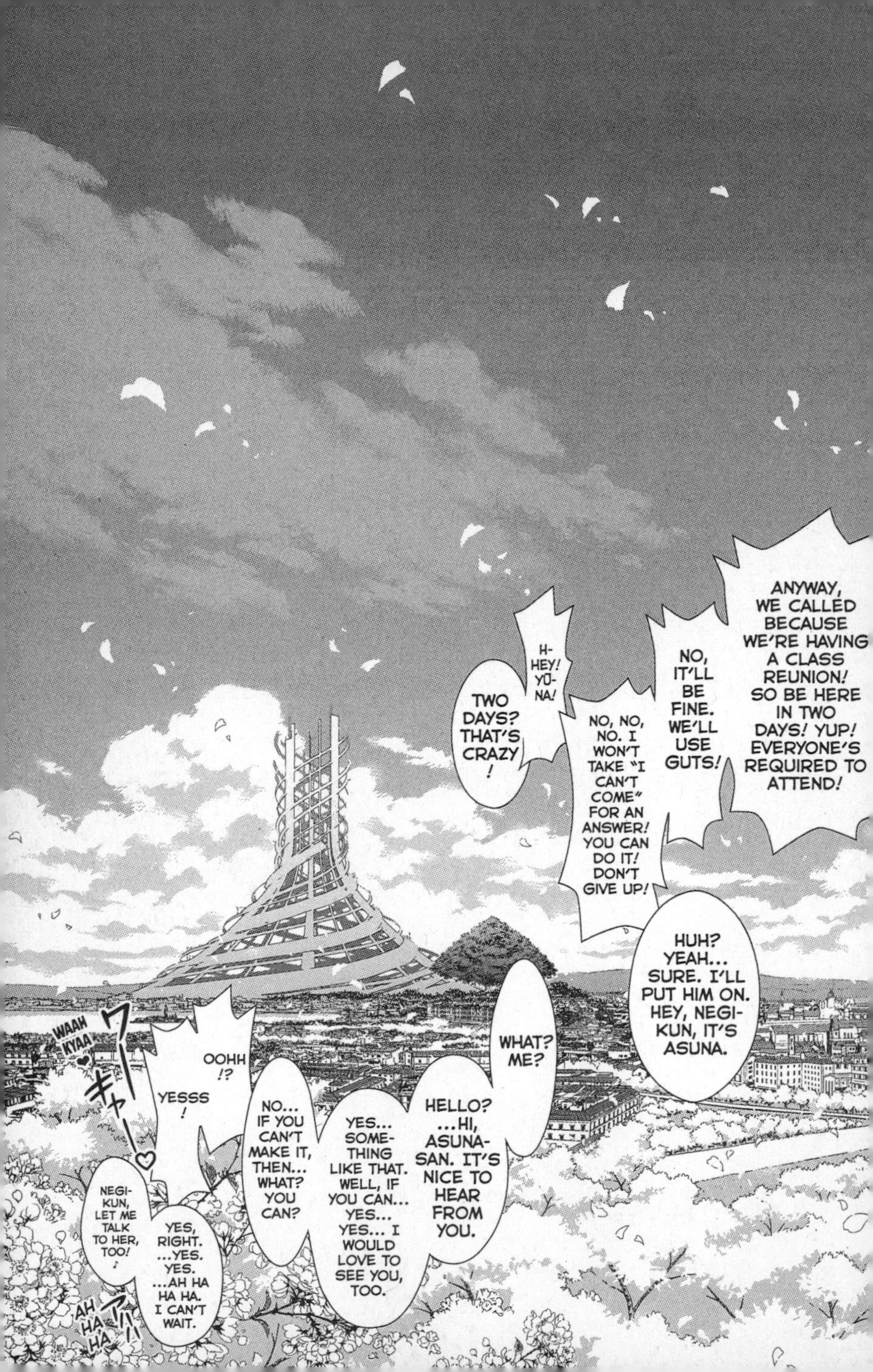
ANYWAY, WE CALLED BECAUSE WE'RE HAVING A CLASS REUNION! SO BE HERE IN TWO DAYS! YUP! EVERYONE'S REQUIRED TO ATTEND!
NO, IT'LL BE FINE. WE'LL USE GUTS!
H-HEY! YŪ-NA!
TWO DAYS? THAT'S CRAZY!
NO, NO, NO. I WON'T TAKE "I CAN'T COME" FOR AN ANSWER! YOU CAN DO IT! DON'T GIVE UP!
HUH? YEAH... SURE. I'LL PUT HIM ON. HEY, NEGI-KUN, IT'S ASUNA.
WHAT? ME?
HELLO? ...HI, ASUNA-SAN. IT'S NICE TO HEAR FROM YOU.
YES... SOMETHING LIKE THAT. WELL, IF YOU CAN... YES... YES... I WOULD LOVE TO SEE YOU, TOO.
NO... IF YOU CAN'T MAKE IT, THEN... WHAT? YOU CAN?
OOHH!?
YESSS!
ワーキャー
WAAH KYAA
NEGI-KUN, LET ME TALK TO HER, TOO!
YES, RIGHT. ...YES. YES. ...AH HA HA HA. I CAN'T WAIT.
アハハ
AH HA HA

True magic results from courage of the heart.
Boys and girls be ambitious.
One step can change the world.

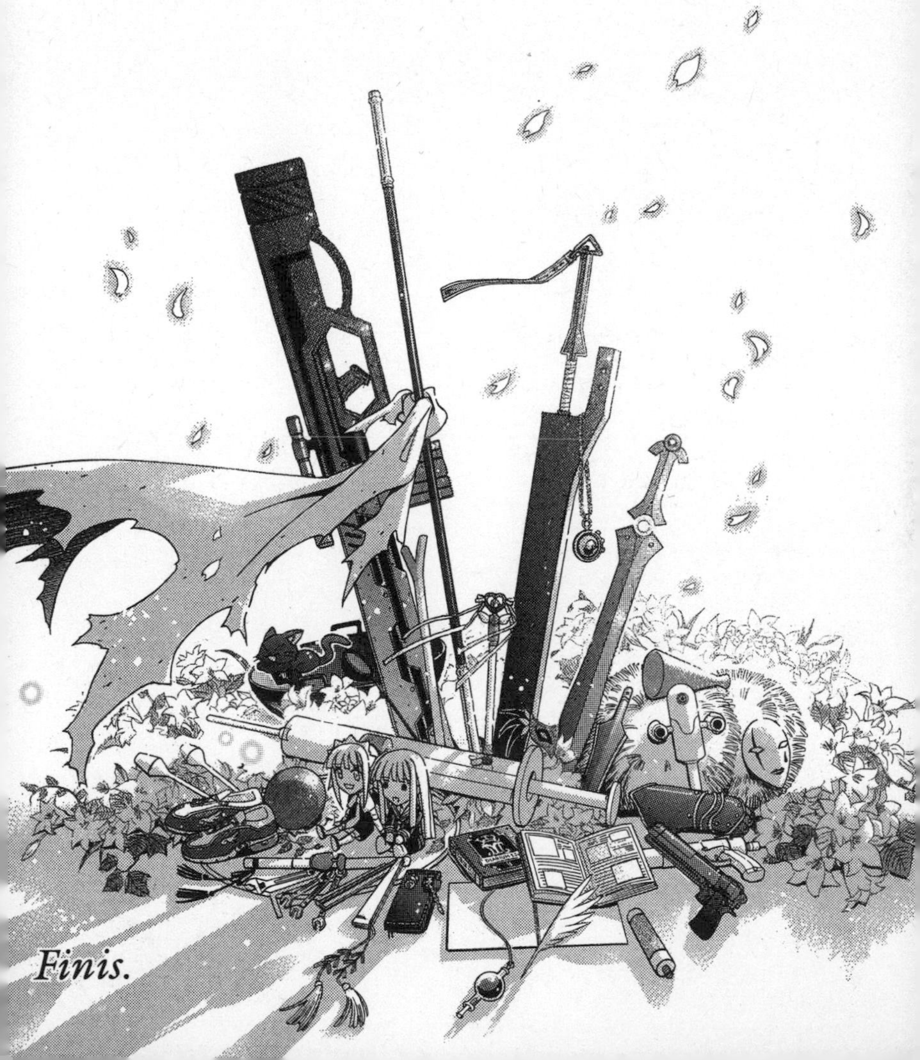

Finis.

A Word of Thanks

I'm Ken Akamatsu, the author of this manga.

During the run of *Negima!*, we had a lot of excitement, with all kinds of media—there were anime series, video games, a live action drama, a movie, CDs, merchandise, and voice actress events. I would like to express my gratitude once again to all who were involved.

First, to all the voice cast of the anime. You gave the characters more depth, and that really helped me out. Thank you so much. About midway through the series, I feel the characters were pulled along by "the people inside them" (laugh). And thanks for your hard work recording all those CDs and performing at all those concerts.

To the staff of the anime. Thank you for keeping up with this anime and its many characters through the harsh schedules of the TV version and all the OADs. They all sold really well.

To the cast of the drama. I was very happy to spend so much time with so many beautiful and adorable young girls (laugh). I think fondly on the dodgeball game we played when we were introduced.

To the staff of the drama. I was in a film club, so it was fascinating to experience a professional filming studio. There really is industry lingo!

To the video game developers. Thank you for proving to me the theory that a video game would be the easiest adaptation of *Negima!* to make. I was surprised at how well it turned out.

To everyone who worked to produce the CDs and music. Thank you for creating melodies, starting with "Happy Material," that will go down in anime music history. There are so many good songs, they're still in heavy rotation.

To all my editors at Shonen Magazine. I had a lot of different ones over these nine years, and I thank you all. I never imagined that I could have man vs man battles go on for so long and it would be okay.

To all my assistants. Thank you for supporting *Negima!* for so long. I'm sorry you had to spend so much time confined to my studio. Please take a nice, long break.

And to all my readers. Thank you so much for supporting *Negima!* all this time.

...By now you are all citizens of Mahora.

With a little courage, maybe you...can use some magic.

NEGIMA!

MAGISTER NEGI MAGI

SHONEN MAGAZINE COMICS

KEN AKAMATSU

38

• The What and Why of Negima!?

Q. Wasn't Negi born in 1994? (according to vol.2)

A. This volume has the correct character data, so please assume that the other one was a misprint.

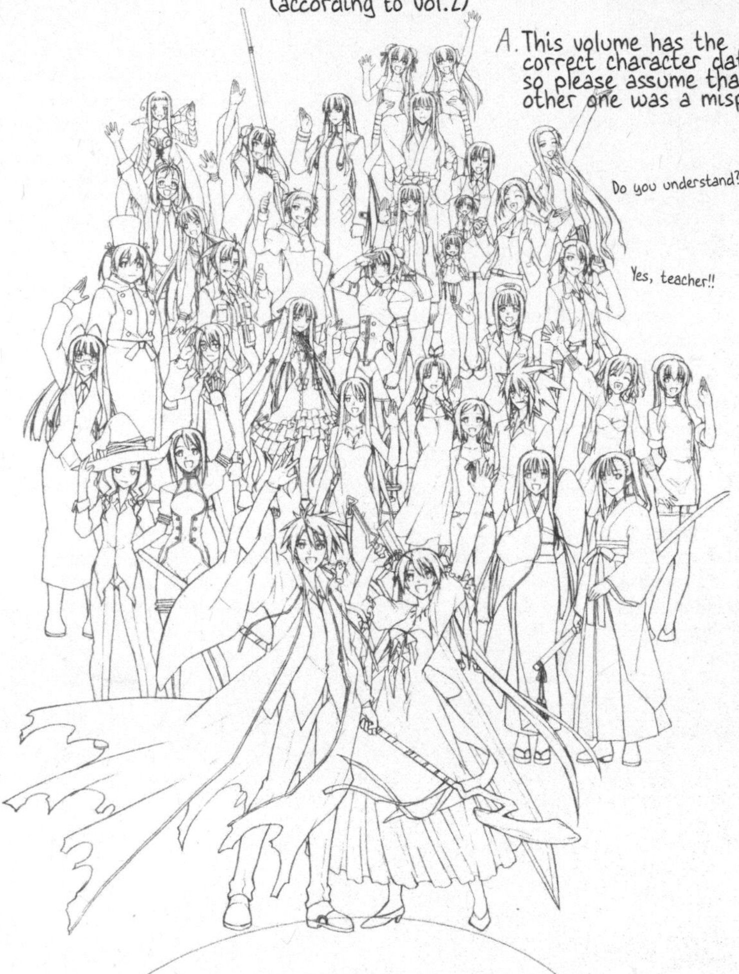

Do you understand?
Yes, teacher!!

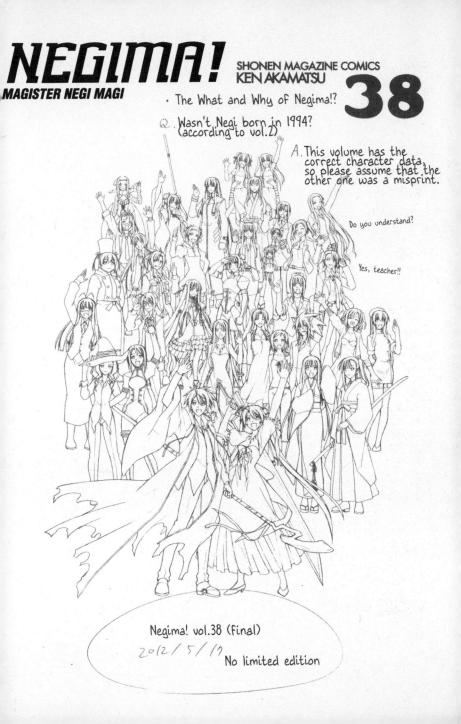

Negima! vol.38 (final)

2012/5/17 No limited edition

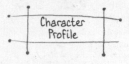

Character
Profile

• Arika Anarchia Entheofushia

Negi's mother, and the last queen
of the Vespertatia Kingdom. Public
record states she was executed, but
in reality, she married Nagi, and
they spent a long time being deeply
in love.

What happened to her
after she gave birth to
Negi was never revealed
in the story. (Maybe
at the end of the
anime...?)

JUST
A-!

She has no black
shadow under her chin.
I wanted to somehow
give a sense of
brightness.

← Insignificant
physical
feature
(laugh).

In the drama CD, she is voiced by
Megumi Hayashibara-sama. It was
just too perfect! I have nothing
else to say! Man, it was sooo
good!! (laugh)

I hope we meet again.

Ken Akamatsu
2012/5/17

Translation Notes

Japanese is a tricky language for most Westerners, and translation is often more art than science. For your edification and reading pleasure, here are notes on some of the places where we could have gone in a different direction with our translation of the work, or where a Japanese cultural reference is used.

Red rice, page 13

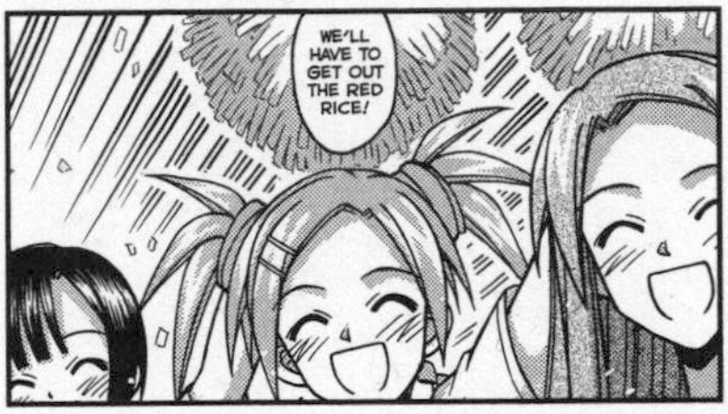
WE'LL HAVE TO GET OUT THE RED RICE!

More specifically, Sakurako is referring to the dish known as sekihan. Sekihan is rice that is steamed with azuki red beans (making it red), and is eaten to celebrate special occasions. Here, they are celebrating that fact that Negi has acknowledged that he has potential romantic feelings.

The Love Won't Stop, page 20

This chapter title might sound a little familiar to long-time hardcore Ken Akamatsu fans, as it bears a striking similarity to the title of his pre-*Love Hina* series, *AI ga Tomaranai*, which was published in English as *A.I. Love You*, but literally means "the love (or the AI) won't stop." We don't know if the similarity was intentional, but Chachamaru is an AI, so it's possible. In this case, the title is Daisuki ga Tomaranai, but it means roughly the same thing (minus the AI pun, of course).

It's gonna rain spears, page 87

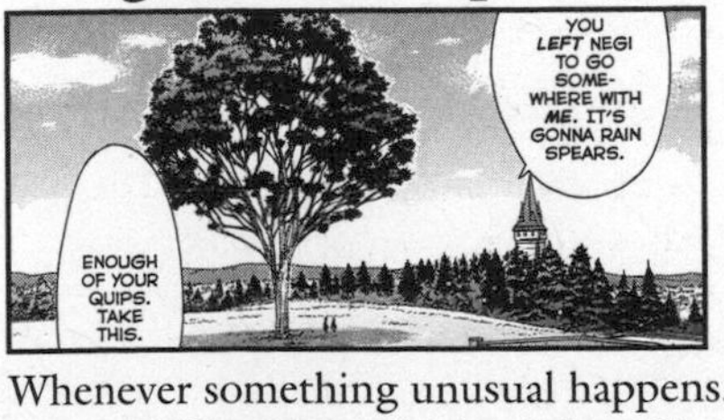
YOU *LEFT* NEGI TO GO SOMEWHERE WITH *ME*. IT'S GONNA RAIN SPEARS.
ENOUGH OF YOUR QUIPS. TAKE THIS.

Whenever something unusual happens, people joke about it being a portent of imminent bad weather. The more unusual the occurrence, the more disastrous the coming storm.

Chūnin, page 97

As anyone familiar with a certain popular manga series about ninja will know, ninja are divided into ranks. Chūnin literally means "middle ninja," and so would normally refer to a ninja who is not the lowest class, but not the highest class, either. However, Kaede is from the Koga ninja clan, and in the Koga, chūnin is the highest rank. Possibly, she was promoted to chūnin during the alleged "family incident."

Fauna master, page 160

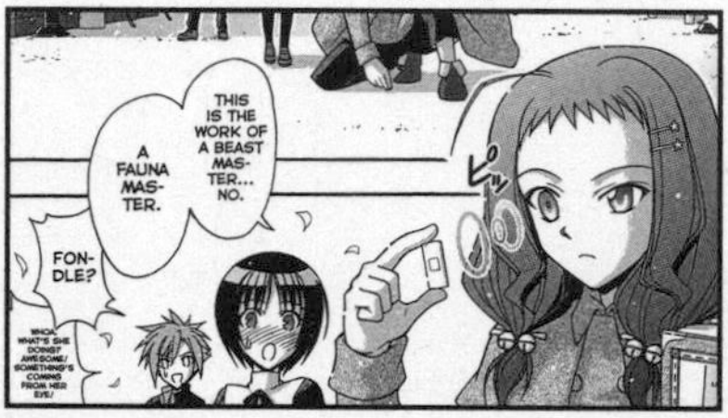
THIS IS THE WORK OF A BEAST MAS-TER... NO.
A FAUNA MAS-TER.
FON-DLE?
WHOA, WHAT'S SHE DOING? AWESOME! SOMETHING'S COMING FROM HER EYE!

In the Japanese text, Yue surmises that the culprit in this case must be a mushi-tsukai, or master (or controller) of mushi. The word mushi means "insect" or "bug," which is probably what caused Makoto's alarm, but the Chinese character that Yue uses is an older version of mushi (generally pronounced chū), which actually refers to all animal life.

The shota boys, page 179

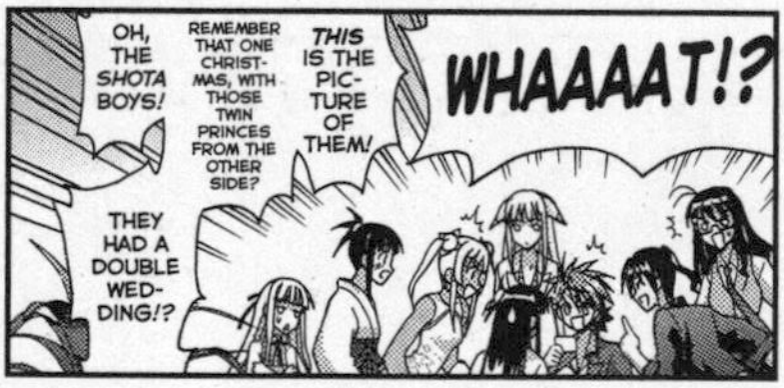
WHAAAAT!?
THIS IS THE PIC-TURE OF THEM!
REMEMBER THAT ONE CHRIST-MAS, WITH THOSE TWIN PRINCES FROM THE OTHER SIDE?
OH, THE SHOTA BOYS!
THEY HAD A DOUBLE WED-DING!?

The term shota comes from shotacon, short for shōtarō complex, which refers to an older person who is abnormally attracted to young boys. The object of affection for someone with a shōtarō complex would be a shōtarō, or shota, and so the term can also refer to a young (or young-looking) boy. The girls are most likely using this term to indicate that, like Fūka and Fumika, the twin princes looked much younger than they actually were, and possibly to indicate that they used their youthful appearances to charm the girls of Mahora.

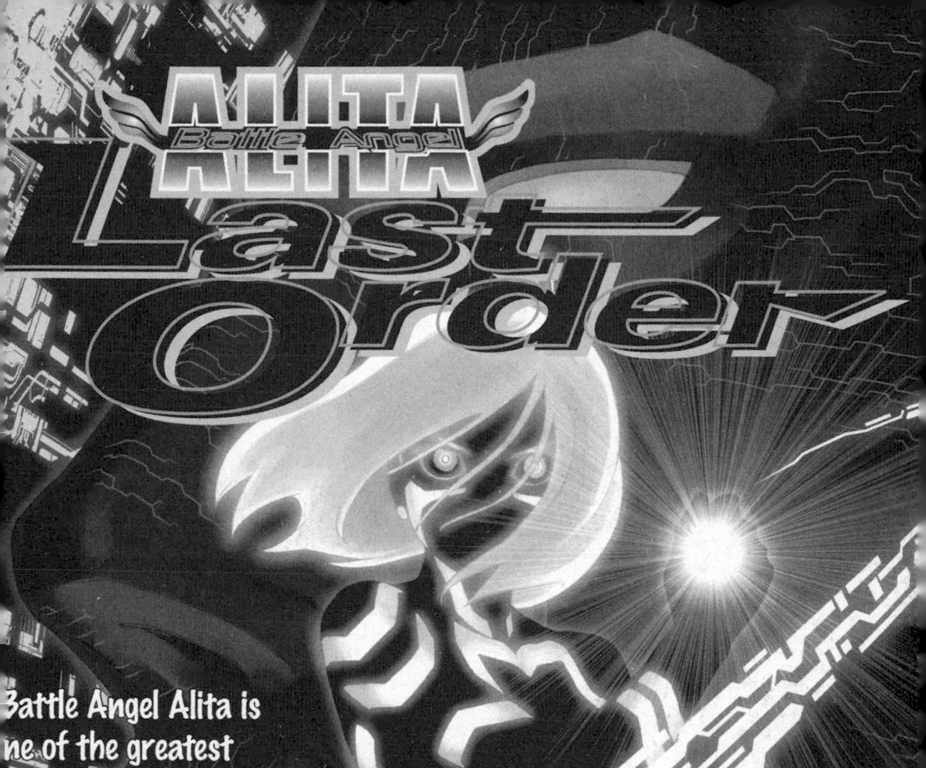

ALITA
Battle Angel
ALITA
Last Order

"Battle Angel Alita is one of the greatest (and possibly *the* greatest) of all sci-fi action manga series."

Anime News Network

The Cyberpunk Legend is Back!

n deluxe omnibus editions of 600+ pages,
ncluding ALL-NEW original stories by
Alita creator Yukito Kishiro!
ol. 1 Coming March 2013

KC
KODANSHA
COMICS

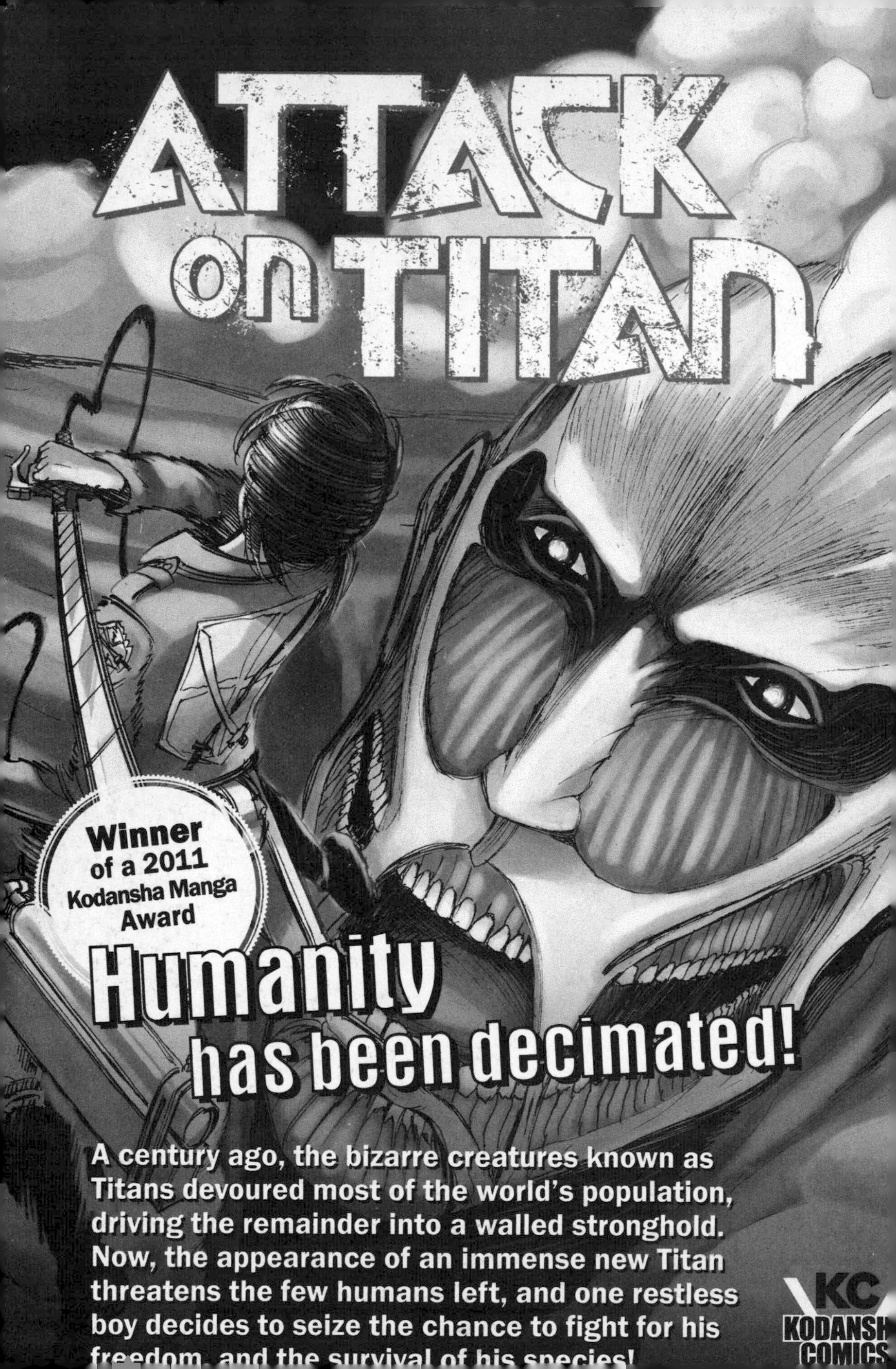

ATTACK ON TITAN

Humanity has been decimated!

A century ago, the bizarre creatures known as Titans devoured most of the world's population, driving the remainder into a walled stronghold. Now, the appearance of an immense new Titan threatens the few humans left, and one restless boy decides to seize the chance to fight for his freedom, and the survival of his species!

KC
KODANSHA COMICS

MARDOCK
マルドゥック・スクランブル
SCRAMBLE

Created by
Tow Ubukata

Manga by
Yoshitoki Oima

"I'd rather be dead."

Rune Balot was a lost girl with nothing to live for. A man named Shell took her in and cared for her...until he tried to murder her. Standing at the precipice of death Rune is saved by Dr. Easter, a private investigator, who uses an experimental procedure known as "Mardock Scramble 09." The procedure grants Balot extraordinary abilities. Now, Rune must decide whether to use her new powers to help Dr. Easter bring Shell to justice, or if she even has the will to keep living a life that's been broken so badly.

Ages: 16+

ANIMAL LAND

BY MAKOTO RAIKU

In a world of animals, where the strong eat the weak, Monoko the tanuki stumbles across a strange creature the likes of which has never been seen before–a human baby! While the newborn has no claws or teeth to protect itself, it does have the special ability to speak to and understand all different animals. Can the gift of speech between species change the balance of power in a land where the weak must always fear the strong?

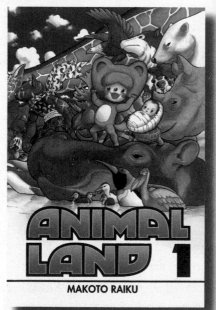

ANIMAL LAND 1

MAKOTO RAIKU

Ages 13+

VISIT KODANSHACOMICS.COM TO:
• View release date calendars for upcoming volumes
• Find out the latest about upcoming Kodansha Comics series

Negima! volume 38 is a work of fiction. Names, characters, places, and incidents are the products of the author's imagination or are used fictitiously. Any resemblance to actual events, locales, or persons, living or dead, is entirely coincidental.

A Kodansha Comics Trade Paperback Original

Published in the United States by Kodansha Comics, an imprint of Kodansha USA Publishing, LLC, New York.

Publication rights arranged through Kodansha Ltd., Tokyo.

First published in Japan in 2012 by Kodansha Ltd., Tokyo, as *Maho sensei Negima!*, volume 38.

ISBN 978-1-61262-243-9

Printed in the United States of America

www.kodanshacomics.com

9 8 7 6 5 4 3 2 1

Translator/Adapter: Alethea Nibley and Athena Nibley
Lettering: Scott O. Brown

TOMARE!

[STOP!]

You're going the wrong way!

Manga is a completely different type of reading experience.

To start at the *beginning*, go to the *end*!

That's right! Authentic manga is read the traditional Japanese way—from right to left. Exactly the *opposite* of how American books are read. It's easy to follow: Just go to the other end of the book, and read each page—and each panel—from the right side to the left side, starting at the top right. Now you're experiencing manga as it was meant to be!